# Miscellaneous Writings

D0165729

# Miscellaneous Writings
# 1883–1896

by

Mary Baker Eddy

Discoverer and Founder of Christian Science
and Author of Science and Health with
Key to the Scriptures

ISBN 0-930227-18-2

Published by
The Bookmark
Post Office Box 801143
Santa Clarita, California 91380

TO

# LOYAL CHRISTIAN SCIENTISTS

IN THIS AND EVERY LAND

I LOVINGLY DEDICATE THESE PRACTICAL TEACHINGS
INDISPENSABLE TO THE CULTURE AND ACHIEVEMENTS WHICH
CONSTITUTE THE SUCCESS OF A STUDENT
AND DEMONSTRATE THE ETHICS
OF CHRISTIAN SCIENCE

MARY BAKER EDDY

PRAY thee, take care, that tak'st my book in hand,
To read it well; that is, to understand.
BEN JONSON: *Epigram* 1

WHEN I would know thee . . . my thought looks
Upon thy well made choice of friends and books;
Then do I love thee, and behold thy ends
In making thy friends books, and thy books friends.
BEN JONSON: *Epigram* 86

———

IF worlds were formed by matter,
And mankind from the dust;
Till time shall end more timely,
There's nothing here to trust.

Thenceforth to evolution's
Geology, we say, —
Nothing have we gained therefrom,
And nothing have to pray:

My world has sprung from Spirit,
In everlasting day;
Whereof, I've more to glory,
Wherefor, have much to pay.
MARY BAKER EDDY

# Preface

A CERTAIN apothegm of a Talmudical philosopher 1
suits my sense of doing good. It reads thus: "The
noblest charity is to prevent a man from accepting 3
charity; and the best alms are to show and to enable a
man to dispense with alms."

In the early history of Christian Science, among my 6
thousands of students few were wealthy. Now, Christian
Scientists are not indigent; and their comfortable fortunes
are acquired by healing mankind morally, physically, 9
spiritually. The easel of time presents pictures — once
fragmentary and faint — now rejuvenated by the touch
of God's right hand. Where joy, sorrow, hope, disap- 12
pointment, sigh, and smile commingled, now hope sits
dove-like.

To preserve a long course of years still and uniform, 15
amid the uniform darkness of storm and cloud and
tempest, requires strength from above, — deep draughts
from the fount of divine Love. Truly may it be said: 18
There is an old age of the heart, and a youth that never
grows old; a Love that is a boy, and a Psyche who is
ever a girl. The fleeting freshness of youth, however, 21
is not the evergreen of Soul; the coloring glory of

perpetual bloom; the spiritual glow and grandeur of a consecrated life wherein dwelleth peace, sacred and sincere in trial or in triumph.

The opportunity has at length offered itself for me to comply with an oft-repeated request; namely, to collect my miscellaneous writings published in *The Christian Science Journal,* since April, 1883, and republish them in book form, — accessible as reference, and reliable as old landmarks. Owing to the manifold demands on my time in the early pioneer days, most of these articles were originally written in haste, without due preparation. To those heretofore in print, a few articles are herein appended. To some articles are affixed data, where these are most requisite, to serve as mile-stones measuring the distance, — or the difference between then and now, — in the opinions of men and the progress of our Cause.

My signature has been slightly changed from my Christian name, Mary Morse Baker. Timidity in early years caused me, as an author, to assume various *noms de plume.* After my first marriage, to Colonel Glover of Charleston, South Carolina, I dropped the name of Morse to retain my maiden name, — thinking that otherwise the name would be too long.

In 1894, I received from the Daughters of the American Revolution a certificate of membership made out to Mary Baker Eddy, and thereafter adopted that form of signature, except in connection with my published works.

The first edition of Science and Health having been 1
copyrighted at the date of its issue, 1875, in my name
of Glover, caused me to retain the initial "G" on my 3
subsequent books.

These pages, although a reproduction of what has
been written, are still in advance of their time; and are 6
richly rewarded by what they have hitherto achieved for
the race. While no offering can liquidate one's debt of
gratitude to God, the fervent heart and willing hand are 9
not unknown to nor unrewarded by Him.

May this volume be to the reader a graphic guide-
book, pointing the path, dating the unseen, and enabling 12
him to walk the untrodden in the hitherto unexplored
fields of Science. At each recurring holiday the Christian
Scientist will find herein a "canny" crumb; and thus 15
may time's pastimes become footsteps to joys eternal.

Realism will at length be found to surpass imagination,
and to suit and savor all literature. The shuttlecock of 18
religious intolerance will fall to the ground, if there be
no battledores to fling it back and forth. It is reason for
rejoicing that the *vox populi* is inclined to grant us peace, 21
together with pardon for the preliminary battles that
purchased it.

With tender tread, thought sometimes walks in memory, 24
through the dim corridors of years, on to old battle-
grounds, there sadly to survey the fields of the slain and
the enemy's losses. In compiling this work, I have tried 27

1 to remove the pioneer signs and ensigns of war, and to
retain at this date the privileged armaments of peace.

3   With armor on, I continue the march, command and
countermand; meantime interluding with loving thought
this afterpiece of battle.   Supported, cheered, I take my
6 pen and pruning-hook, to "learn war no more," and with
strong wing to lift my readers above the smoke of conflict
into light and liberty.

MARY BAKER EDDY

CONCORD, N. H.
January, 1897

# Contents

## CHAPTER I

### INTRODUCTORY

## CHAPTER II

## CHAPTER III

## CHAPTER IV

### ADDRESSES

# Contents

## CHAPTER V

### LETTERS

## CHAPTER VI

### SERMONS

# Contents

## CHAPTER VII

## CHAPTER VIII

### PRECEPT UPON PRECEPT

# Contents

## CHAPTER IX

### THE FRUIT OF SPIRIT

# Contents xvii

## CHAPTER X

## CHAPTER XI

### POEMS

## CHAPTER XII

# Miscellaneous Writings

## CHAPTER I

### INTRODUCTORY

#### PROSPECTUS

THE ancient Greek looked longingly for the Olympiad. The Chaldee watched the appearing of a 3 star; to him, no higher destiny dawned on the dome of being than that foreshadowed by signs in the heavens. The meek Nazarene, the scoffed of all scoffers, 6 said, "Ye can discern the face of the sky; but can ye not discern the signs of the times?" — for he forefelt and foresaw the ordeal of a perfect Christianity, hated 9 by sinners.

To kindle all minds with a gleam of gratitude, the new idea that comes welling up from infinite Truth needs 12 to be understood. The seer of this age should be a sage.

Humility is the stepping-stone to a higher recognition 15 of Deity. The mounting sense gathers fresh forms and strange fire from the ashes of dissolving self, and drops the world. Meekness heightens immortal attributes 18 only by removing the dust that dims them. Goodness reveals another scene and another self seemingly rolled up in shades, but brought to light by the evolutions of 21

1 advancing thought, whereby we discern the power of Truth and Love to heal the sick.

3 Pride is ignorance; those assume most who have the least wisdom or experience; and they steal from their neighbor, because they have so little of their own.

6 The signs of these times portend a long and strong determination of mankind to cleave to the world, the flesh, and evil, causing great obscuration of Spirit. 9 When we remember that God is just, and admit the total depravity of mortals, *alias* mortal mind, — and that this Adam legacy must first be seen, and then must be 12 subdued and recompensed by justice, the eternal attribute of Truth, — the outlook demands labor, and the laborers seem few. To-day we behold but the first 15 faint view of a more spiritual Christianity, that embraces a deeper and broader philosophy and a more rational and divine healing. The time approaches when divine Life, 18 Truth, and Love will be found alone the remedy for sin, sickness, and death; when God, man's saving Principle, and Christ, the spiritual idea of God, will be revealed.

21 Man's probation after death is the necessity of his immortality; for good dies not and evil is self-destructive, therefore evil must be mortal and self-destroyed. 24 If man should not progress after death, but should remain in error, he would be inevitably self-annihilated. Those upon whom "the second death hath no power" 27 are those who progress here and hereafter out of evil, their mortal element, and into good that is immortal; thus laying off the material beliefs that war against 30 Spirit, and putting on the spiritual elements in divine Science.

While we entertain decided views as to the best method

for elevating the race physically, morally, and spiritu- 1
ally, and shall express these views as duty demands, we
shall claim no especial gift from our divine origin, no 3
supernatural power.   If we regard good as more natural
than evil, and spiritual understanding — the true knowledge of God — as imparting the only power to heal the 6
sick and the sinner, we shall demonstrate in our lives the
power of Truth and Love.

The lessons we learn in divine Science are applica- 9
ble to all the needs of man.   Jesus taught them for this
very purpose;  and his demonstration hath taught us
that "through his stripes" — his life-experience — and 12
divine Science, brought to the understanding through
Christ, the Spirit-revelator, is man healed and saved.
No opinions of mortals nor human hypotheses enter this 15
line of thought or action.   Drugs, inert matter, never are
needed to aid spiritual power.   Hygiene, manipulation,
and mesmerism are not Mind's medicine.   The Prin- 18
ciple of all cure is God, unerring and immortal Mind.
We have learned that the erring or mortal thought holds
in itself all sin, sickness, and death, and imparts these 21
states to the body;  while the supreme and perfect Mind,
as seen in the truth of being, antidotes and destroys these
material elements of sin and death.                                24

Because God is supreme and omnipotent, *materia
medica*, hygiene, and animal magnetism are impotent;
and their only supposed efficacy is in apparently delud- 27
ing reason, denying revelation, and dethroning Deity.
The tendency of mental healing is to uplift mankind;  but
this method perverted, is "Satan let loose."   Hence the 30
deep demand for the Science of psychology to meet sin,
and uncover it;  thus to annihilate hallucination.

1 Thought imbued with purity, Truth, and Love, instructed in the Science of metaphysical healing, is the
3 most potent and desirable remedial agent on the earth.
At this period there is a marked tendency of mortal
mind to plant mental healing on the basis of hypnotism,
6 calling this method "mental science." All *Science* is
*Christian* Science; the Science of the Mind that is God,
and of the universe as His idea, and their relation to each
9 other. Its only power to heal is its power to do good,
not evil.

## A TIMELY ISSUE

12 At this date, 1883, a newspaper edited and published
by the Christian Scientists has become a necessity. Many
questions important to be disposed of come to the Col-
15 lege and to the practising students, yet but little time
has been devoted to their answer. Further enlightenment is necessary for the age, and a periodical de-
18 voted to this work seems alone adequate to meet the
requirement. Much interest is awakened and expressed
on the subject of metaphysical healing, but in many
21 minds it is confounded with isms, and even infidelity, so
that its religious specialty and the vastness of its worth
are not understood.

24 It is often said, "You must have a very strong will-
power to heal," or, "It must require a great deal of faith
to make your demonstrations." When it is answered
27 that there is no will-power required, and that something
more than faith is necessary, we meet with an expression
of incredulity. It is not alone the mission of Christian
30 Science to heal the sick, but to destroy sin in mortal

thought. This work well done will elevate and purify 1
the race. It cannot fail to do this if we devote our best
energies to the work. 3

Science reveals man as spiritual, harmonious, and eternal. This should be understood. Our College should
be crowded with students who are willing to consecrate 6
themselves to this Christian work. Mothers should be
able to produce perfect health and perfect morals in their
children — and ministers, to heal the sick — by study- 9
ing this scientific method of practising Christianity.
Many say, "I should like to study, but have not sufficient faith that I have the power to heal." The healing 12
power is Truth and Love, and these do not fail in the
greatest emergencies.

*Materia medica* says, "I can do no more. I have 15
done all that can be done. There is nothing to build
upon. There is no longer any reason for hope." Then
metaphysics comes in, armed with the power of Spirit, 18
not matter, takes up the case hopefully and builds on
the stone that the builders have rejected, and is successful. 21

Metaphysical therapeutics can seem a miracle and a
mystery to those only who do not understand the grand
reality that Mind controls the body. They acknowledge 24
an erring or mortal mind, but believe it to be brain matter. That man is the idea of infinite Mind, always perfect
in God, in Truth, Life, and Love, is something not easily 27
accepted, weighed down as is mortal thought with material beliefs. That which never existed, can seem solid
substance to this thought. It is much easier for people 30
to believe that the body affects the mind, than that the
mind affects the body.

1  We hear from the pulpits that sickness is sent as a discipline to bring man nearer to God, — even though
3 sickness often leaves mortals but little time free from complaints and fretfulness, and Jesus cast out disease as evil.

6  The most of our Christian Science practitioners have plenty to do, and many more are needed for the advancement of the age.  At present the majority of the
9 acute cases are given to the M. D.'s, and only those cases that are pronounced incurable are passed over to the Scientist.  The healing of such cases should cer-
12 tainly prove to all minds the power of metaphysics over physics;  and it surely does, to many thinkers, as the rapid growth of the work shows.  At no distant day,
15 Christian healing will rank far in advance of allopathy and homœopathy;  for Truth must ultimately succeed where error fails.

18  Mind governs all.  That we exist in God, perfect, there is no doubt, for the conceptions of Life, Truth, and Love must be perfect;  and with that basic truth we con-
21 quer sickness, sin, and death.  Frequently it requires time to overcome the patient's faith in drugs and material hygiene;  but when once convinced of the uselessness
24 of such material methods, the gain is rapid.

It is a noticeable fact, that in families where laws of health are strictly enforced, great caution is observed
27 in regard to diet, and the conversation chiefly confined to the ailments of the body, there is the most sickness. Take a large family of children where the mother has
30 all that she can attend to in keeping them clothed and fed, and health is generally the rule;  whereas, in small families of one or two children, sickness is by no means

the exception. These children must not be allowed to 1
eat certain food, nor to breathe the cold air, because
there is danger in it; when they perspire, they must be 3
loaded down with coverings until their bodies become
dry, — and the mother of one child is often busier than
the mother of eight. 6

Great charity and humility is necessary in this work
of healing. The loving patience of Jesus, we must
strive to emulate. "Thou shalt love thy neighbor as 9
thyself" has daily to be exemplified; and, although
skepticism and incredulity prevail in places where
one would least expect it, it harms not; for if serving 12
Christ, Truth, of what can mortal opinion avail? Cast
not your pearls before swine; but if you cannot bring
peace to all, you can to many, if faithful laborers in His 15
vineyard.

Looking over the newspapers of the day, one naturally
reflects that it is dangerous to live, so loaded with disease 18
seems the very air. These descriptions carry fears to
many minds, to be depicted in some future time upon
the body. A periodical of our own will counteract to 21
some extent this public nuisance; for through our paper,
at the price at which we shall issue it, we shall be able
to reach many homes with healing, purifying thought. 24
A great work already has been done, and a greater work
yet remains to be done. Oftentimes we are denied the
results of our labors because people do not understand 27
the nature and power of metaphysics, and they think
that health and strength would have returned naturally without any assistance. This is not so much from 30
a lack of justice, as it is that the *mens populi* is not sufficiently enlightened on this great subject. More thought

2

1 is given to material illusions than to spiritual facts.   If
we can aid in abating suffering and diminishing sin,
3 we shall have accomplished much;  but if we can bring
to the general thought this great fact that drugs do not,
cannot, produce health and harmony, since "in Him
6 [Mind] we live, and move, and have our being," we shall
have done more.

### LOVE YOUR ENEMIES

9    Who is thine enemy that thou shouldst love him?  Is
it a creature or a thing outside thine own creation?
Can you see an enemy, except you first formulate this
12 enemy and then look upon the object of your own conception?  What is it that harms you?  Can height, or
depth, or any other creature separate you from the
15 Love that is omnipresent good, — that blesses infinitely
one and all?
Simply count your enemy to be that which defiles,
18 defaces, and dethrones the Christ-image that you should
reflect.   Whatever purifies, sanctifies, and consecrates
human life, is not an enemy, however much we suffer in
21 the process.   Shakespeare writes: "Sweet are the uses
of adversity."   Jesus said: "Blessed are ye, when men
shall revile you, and persecute you, and shall say all
24 manner of evil against you *falsely,* for my sake; . . .
for so persecuted they the prophets which were before
you."
27    The Hebrew law with its "Thou shalt not," its demand and sentence, can only be fulfilled through the
gospel's benediction.   Then, "Blessed are ye," inso-

much as the consciousness of good, grace, and peace, 1
comes through affliction rightly understood, as sanctified
by the purification it brings to the flesh, — to pride, self- 3
ignorance, self-will, self-love, self-justification. Sweet,
indeed, are these uses of His rod! Well is it that the
Shepherd of Israel passes all His flock under His rod 6
into His fold; thereby numbering them, and giving them
refuge at last from the elements of earth.

"Love thine enemies" is identical with "Thou hast 9
no enemies." Wherein is this conclusion relative to
those who have hated thee without a cause? Simply, in
that those unfortunate individuals are virtually thy best 12
friends. Primarily and ultimately, they are doing thee
good far beyond the present sense which thou canst entertain of good. 15

Whom we call friends seem to sweeten life's cup and
to fill it with the nectar of the gods. We lift this cup
to our lips; but it slips from our grasp, to fall in frag- 18
ments before our eyes. Perchance, having tasted its
tempting wine, we become intoxicated; become lethar-
gic, dreamy objects of self-satisfaction; else, the con- 21
tents of this cup of selfish human enjoyment having lost
its flavor, we voluntarily set it aside as tasteless and
unworthy of human aims. 24

And wherefore our failure longer to relish this fleeting sense, with its delicious forms of friendship,
wherewith mortals become educated to gratification in 27
personal pleasure and trained in treacherous peace?
Because it is the great and only danger in the path
that winds upward. A false sense of what consti- 30
tutes happiness is more disastrous to human progress
than all that an enemy or enmity can obtrude upon

1 the mind or engraft upon its purposes and achievements
wherewith to obstruct life's joys and enhance its sor-
3 rows.

We have no enemies.  Whatever envy, hatred, revenge
— the most remorseless motives that govern mortal mind
6 — whatever these try to do, shall "work together for good
to them that love God."

Why?

9 Because He has called His own, armed them, equipped
them, and furnished them defenses impregnable.  Their
God will not let them be lost;  and if they fall they shall
12 rise again, stronger than before the stumble.  The good
cannot lose their God, their help in times of trouble.
If they mistake the divine command, they will recover
15 it, countermand their order, retrace their steps, and
reinstate His orders, more assured to press on safely.
The best lesson of their lives is gained by crossing
18 swords with temptation, with fear and the besetments
of evil;  insomuch as they thereby have tried their
strength and proven it;  insomuch as they have found
21 their strength made perfect in weakness, and their fear
is self-immolated.

This destruction is a moral chemicalization, wherein
24 old things pass away and all things become new.  The
worldly or material tendencies of human affections and
pursuits are thus annihilated;  and this is the advent of
27 spiritualization.  Heaven comes down to earth, and
mortals learn at last the lesson, "I have no enemies."

Even in belief you have but one (that, not in reality),
30 and this one enemy is yourself — your erroneous belief
that you have enemies;  that evil is real;  that aught but
good exists in Science.  Soon or late, your enemy will

wake from his delusion to suffer for his evil intent; to 1
find that, though thwarted, its punishment is tenfold.

Love is the fulfilling of the law: it is grace, mercy, 3
and justice. I used to think it sufficiently just to abide
by our State statutes; that if a man should aim a ball at
my heart, and I by firing first could kill him and save 6
my own life, that this was right. I thought, also, that
if I taught indigent students gratuitously, afterwards
assisting them pecuniarily, and did not cease teach- 9
ing the wayward ones at close of the class term, but
followed them with precept upon precept; that if my
instructions had healed them and shown them the sure way 12
of salvation, — I had done my whole duty to students.

Love metes not out human justice, but divine mercy.
If one's life were attacked, and one could save it only 15
in accordance with common law, by taking another's,
would one sooner give up his own? We must love our
enemies in all the manifestations wherein and whereby 18
we love our friends; must even try not to expose their
faults, but to do them good whenever opportunity
occurs. To mete out human justice to those who per- 21
secute and despitefully use one, is not leaving all retribu-
tion to God and returning blessing for cursing. If special
opportunity for doing good to one's enemies occur not, 24
one can include them in his general effort to benefit the
race. Because I can do much general good to such as
hate me, I do it with earnest, special care — since they 27
permit me no other way, though with tears have I striven
for it. When smitten on one cheek, I have turned the
other: I have but two to present.                    30

I would enjoy taking by the hand all who love me not,
and saying to them, "*I* love *you,* and would not know-

1 ingly harm you." *Because* I thus feel, I say to others:
Hate no one; for hatred is a plague-spot that spreads
3 its virus and kills at last. If indulged, it masters us;
brings suffering upon suffering to its possessor, throughout time and beyond the grave. If you have been badly
6 wronged, forgive and forget: God will recompense this
wrong, and punish, more severely than you could, him
who has striven to injure you. Never return evil for evil;
9 and, above all, do not fancy that you have been wronged
when you have not been.

The present is ours; the future, big with events.
12 Every man and woman should be to-day a law to himself, herself, — a law of loyalty to Jesus' Sermon on the
Mount. The means for sinning unseen and unpunished
15 have so increased that, unless one be watchful and steadfast in Love, one's temptations to sin are increased a
hundredfold. Mortal mind at this period mutely works
18 in the interest of both good and evil in a manner least
understood; hence the need of watching, and the danger
of yielding to temptation from causes that at former
21 periods in human history were not existent. The action
and effects of this so-called human mind in its silent arguments, are yet to be uncovered and summarily dealt with
24 by divine justice.

In Christian Science, the law of Love rejoices the heart;
and Love is Life and Truth. Whatever manifests aught
27 else in its effects upon mankind, demonstrably is not Love.
We should measure our love for God by our love for man;
and our sense of Science will be measured by our obedience
30 to God, — fulfilling the law of Love, doing good to all;
imparting, so far as we reflect them, Truth, Life, and Love
to all within the radius of our atmosphere of thought.

The only justice of which I feel at present capable, 1
is mercy and charity toward every one, — just so far as
one and all permit me to exercise these sentiments toward 3
them, — taking special care to mind my own business.

The falsehood, ingratitude, misjudgment, and sharp
return of evil for good — yea, the real wrongs (if wrong 6
can be real) which I have long endured at the hands of
others — have most happily wrought out for me the law
of loving mine enemies. This law I now urge upon the 9
solemn consideration of all Christian Scientists. Jesus
said, "If ye love them which love you, what thank have
ye? for sinners also love those that love them." 12

## CHRISTIAN THEISM

Scholastic theology elaborates the proposition that
evil is a factor of good, and that to believe in the reality 15
of evil is essential to a rounded sense of the existence of
good.

This frail hypothesis is founded upon the basis of mate- 18
rial and mortal evidence — only upon what the shifting
mortal senses confirm and frail human reason accepts.
The Science of Soul reverses this proposition, overturns 21
the testimony of the five erring senses, and reveals in
clearer divinity the existence of good only; that is, of
God and His idea. 24

This postulate of divine Science only needs to be conceded, to afford opportunity for proof of its correctness
and the clearer discernment of good. 27

Seek the Anglo-Saxon term for God, and you will
find it to be good; then define good as God, and you
will find that good is omnipotence, has all power; it fills 30

1 all space, being omnipresent; hence, there is neither place
nor power left for evil. Divest your thought, then, of
3 the mortal and material view which contradicts the ever-
presence and all-power of good; take in only the immortal facts which include these, and where will you see or
6 feel evil, or find its existence necessary either to the origin
or ultimate of good?

It is urged that, from his original state of perfec-
9 tion, man has fallen into the imperfection that requires
evil through which to develop good. Were we to
admit this vague proposition, the Science of man could
12 never be learned; for in order to learn Science, we
begin with the correct statement, with harmony and
its Principle; and if man has lost his Principle and
15 its harmony, from evidences before him he is incapable of knowing the facts of existence and its con-
comitants: therefore to him evil is as real and eternal
18 as good, God! This awful deception is evil's umpire
and empire, that good, God, understood, forcibly
destroys.
21     What appears to mortals from their standpoint to be
the necessity for evil, is proven by the law of opposites
to be without necessity. Good is the primitive Princi-
24 ple of man; and evil, good's opposite, has no Principle,
and is not, and cannot be, the derivative of good.
Thus evil is neither a primitive nor a derivative, but
27 is suppositional; in other words, a lie that is incapable
of proof — therefore, wholly problematical.

The Science of Truth annihilates error, deprives evil
30 of all power, and thereby destroys all error, sin, sickness,
disease, and death. But the sinner is not sheltered from
suffering from sin: he makes a great reality of evil, iden-

tifies himself with it, fancies he finds pleasure in it, and 1
will reap what he sows; hence the sinner must endure
the effects of his delusion until he awakes from it. 3

## THE NEW BIRTH

St. Paul speaks of the new birth as "waiting for the
adoption, to wit, the redemption of our body." The 6
great Nazarene Prophet said, "Blessed are the pure in
heart: for they shall see God." Nothing aside from the
spiritualization — yea, the highest Christianization — of 9
thought and desire, can give the true perception of God
and divine Science, that results in health, happiness, and
holiness. 12

The new birth is not the work of a moment. It begins
with moments, and goes on with years; moments of surrender to God, of childlike trust and joyful adoption 15
of good; moments of self-abnegation, self-consecration,
heaven-born hope, and spiritual love.

Time may commence, but it cannot complete, the 18
new birth: eternity does this; for progress is the law
of infinity. Only through the sore travail of mortal mind
shall soul as sense be satisfied, and man awake in His 21
likeness. What a faith-lighted thought is this! that
mortals can lay off the "old man," until man is found
to be the image of the infinite good that we name God, 24
and the fulness of the stature of man in Christ appears.

In mortal and material man, goodness seems in em-
bryo. By suffering for sin, and the gradual fading out 27
of the mortal and material sense of man, thought is developed into an infant Christianity; and, feeding at first
on the milk of the Word, it drinks in the sweet revealings 30

1 of a new and more spiritual Life and Love. These nourish
the hungry hope, satisfy more the cravings for immor-
3 tality, and so comfort, cheer, and bless one, that he saith:
In mine infancy, this is enough of heaven to come down
to earth.

6    But, as one grows into the manhood or womanhood
of Christianity, one finds so much lacking, and so very
much requisite to become wholly Christlike, that one
9 saith: The Principle of Christianity is infinite: it is
indeed God; and this infinite Principle hath infinite
claims on man, and these claims are divine, not human;
12 and man's ability to meet them is from God; for, being
His likeness and image, man must reflect the full
dominion of Spirit — even its supremacy over sin, sick-
15 ness, and death.

Here, then, is the awakening from the dream of life
in matter, to the great fact that *God is the only Life;*
18 that, therefore, we must entertain a higher sense of both
God and man. We must learn that God is infinitely
more than a person, or finite form, can contain; that
21 God is a divine *Whole,* and *All,* an all-pervading intelligence and Love, a divine, infinite Principle; and
that Christianity is a divine Science. This newly
24 awakened consciousness is wholly spiritual; it emanates
from Soul instead of body, and is the new birth begun
in Christian Science.

27    Now, dear reader, pause for a moment with me, earnestly to contemplate this new-born spiritual altitude; for
this statement demands demonstration.

30    Here you stand face to face with the laws of infinite
Spirit, and behold for the first time the irresistible conflict between the flesh and Spirit. You stand before the

awful detonations of Sinai.  You hear and record the
thunderings of the spiritual law of Life, as opposed to
the material law of death;  the spiritual law of Love, as
opposed to the material sense of love;  the law of omnipotent harmony and good, as opposed to any supposititious law of sin, sickness, or death.  And, before the
flames have died away on this mount of revelation, like
the patriarch of old, you take off your shoes — lay aside
your material appendages, human opinions and doctrines, give up your more material religion with its rites
and ceremonies, put off your *materia medica* and hygiene
as worse than useless — to sit at the feet of Jesus.  Then,
you meekly bow before the Christ, the spiritual idea
that our great Master gave of the power of God to heal
and to save.  Then it is that you behold for the first
time the divine Principle that redeems man from under
the curse of materialism, — sin, disease, and death.
This spiritual birth opens to the enraptured understanding a much higher and holier conception of the supremacy
of Spirit, and of man as His likeness, whereby man reflects
the divine power to heal the sick.

A material or human birth is the appearing of a mortal, not the immortal man.  This birth is more or less
prolonged and painful, according to the timely or un-
timely circumstances, the normal or abnormal material
conditions attending it.

With the spiritual birth, man's primitive, sinless,
spiritual existence dawns on human thought, — through
the travail of mortal mind, hope deferred, the perishing
pleasure and accumulating pains of sense, — by which
one loses himself as matter, and gains a truer sense of
Spirit and spiritual man.

1   The purification or baptismals that come from Spirit,
develop, step by step, the original likeness of perfect man,
3 and efface the mark of the beast. "Whom the Lord
loveth He chasteneth, and scourgeth every son whom
He receiveth;" therefore rejoice in tribulation, and wel-
6 come these spiritual signs of the new birth under the law
and gospel of Christ, Truth.

The prominent laws which forward birth in the divine
9 order of Science, are these: "Thou shalt have no other
gods before me;" "Love thy neighbor as thyself."
These commands of infinite wisdom, translated into
12 the new tongue, their spiritual meaning, signify: Thou
shalt love Spirit only, not its opposite, in every God-
quality, even in substance; thou shalt recognize thy-
15 self as God's spiritual child only, and the true man
and true woman, the all-harmonious "male and female,"
as of spiritual origin, God's reflection, — thus as chil-
18 dren of one common Parent, — wherein and whereby
Father, Mother, and child are the divine Principle and
divine idea, even the divine "Us" — one in good, and
21 good in One.

With this recognition man could never separate himself from good, God; and he would necessarily entertain
24 habitual love for his fellow-man. Only by admitting
evil as a reality, and entering into a state of evil
thoughts, can we in belief separate one man's interests
27 from those of the whole human family, or thus attempt
to separate Life from God. This is the mistake that
causes much that must be repented of and overcome.
30 Not to know what is blessing you, but to believe that
aught that God sends is unjust, — or that those whom
He commissions bring to you at His demand that which

is unjust, — is wrong and cruel.  Envy, evil thinking, 1
evil speaking, covetousness, lust, hatred, malice, are
always wrong, and will break the rule of Christian 3
Science and prevent its demonstration;  but the rod of
God, and the obedience demanded of His servants in
carrying out what He teaches them, — these are never 6
unmerciful, never unwise.

The task of healing the sick is far lighter than that
of so teaching the divine Principle and rules of Chris- 9
tian Science as to lift the affections and motives of men
to adopt them and bring them out in human lives.  He
who has named the name of Christ, who has virtually 12
accepted the divine claims of Truth and Love in divine
Science, is daily departing from evil;  and all the wicked
endeavors of suppositional demons can never change the 15
current of that life from steadfastly flowing on to God,
its divine source.

But, taking the livery of heaven wherewith to cover 18
iniquity, is the most fearful sin that mortals can commit.
I should have more faith in an honest drugging-doctor,
one who abides by his statements and works upon as 21
high a basis as he understands, healing me, than I could
or would have in a smooth-tongued hypocrite or mental
malpractitioner.                                                24

Between the centripetal and centrifugal mental forces
of material and spiritual gravitations, we go into or we
go out of materialism or sin, and choose our course and 27
its results.  Which, then, shall be our choice, — the sinful, material, and perishable, or the spiritual, joy-giving,
and eternal?                                                    30

The spiritual sense of Life and its grand pursuits is
of itself a bliss, health-giving and joy-inspiring.  This

1 sense of Life illumes our pathway with the radiance of
divine Love;  heals man spontaneously, morally and
3 physically, — exhaling the aroma of Jesus' own words,
"Come unto me, all ye that labor and are heavy laden,
and I will give you rest."

# CHAPTER II

## ONE CAUSE AND EFFECT

CHRISTIAN SCIENCE begins with the First Com- 1
mandment of the Hebrew Decalogue, "Thou
shalt have no other gods before me." It goes on in 3
perfect unity with Christ's Sermon on the Mount, and
in that age culminates in the Revelation of St. John,
who, while on earth and in the flesh, like ourselves, 6
beheld "a new heaven and a new earth," — the spiritual
universe, whereof Christian Science now bears testimony.

Our Master said, "The works that I do shall ye do 9
also;" and, "The kingdom of God is within you." This
makes practical all his words and works. As the ages
advance in spirituality, Christian Science will be seen 12
to depart from the trend of other Christian denomina-
tions in no wise except by increase of spirituality.

My first plank in the platform of Christian Science 15
is as follows: "There is no life, truth, intelligence, nor
substance in matter. All is infinite Mind and its infinite
manifestation, for God is All-in-all. Spirit is immortal 18
Truth; matter is mortal error. Spirit is the real and
eternal; matter is the unreal and temporal. Spirit is
God, and man is His image and likeness. Therefore man 21
is not material; he is spiritual." [1]

[1] The order of this sentence has been conformed to the text of
the 1908 edition of Science and Health.                    24

[ 21 ]

1  I am strictly a theist — believe in one God, one Christ
or Messiah.

3  Science is neither a law of matter nor of man. It is
the unerring manifesto of Mind, the law of God, its
divine Principle. Who dare say that matter or
6 mortals can evolve Science? Whence, then, is it, if not
from the divine source, and what, but the contemporary of Christianity, so far in advance of human knowl-
9 edge that mortals must work for the discovery of even a
portion of it? Christian Science translates Mind, God,
to mortals. It is the infinite calculus defining the line,
12 plane, space, and fourth dimension of Spirit. It absolutely refutes the amalgamation, transmigration, absorption, or annihilation of individuality. It shows the
15 impossibility of transmitting human ills, or evil, from one
individual to another; that all true thoughts revolve
in God's orbits: they come from God and return to
18 Him, — and untruths belong not to His creation, therefore these are null and void. It hath no peer, no com-
petitor, for it dwelleth in Him besides whom "there is
21 none other."

That Christian Science is Christian, those who have
demonstrated it, according to the rules of its divine
24 Principle, — together with the sick, the lame, the deaf, and
the blind, healed by it, — have proven to a waiting world.
He who has not tested it, is incompetent to condemn it;
27 and he who is a willing sinner, cannot demonstrate it.

A falling apple suggested to Newton more than the
simple fact cognized by the senses, to which it seemed
30 to fall by reason of its own ponderosity; but the primal
cause, or Mind-force, invisible to material sense, lay
concealed in the treasure-troves of Science. True,

Newton named it gravitation, having learned so much; 1
but Science, demanding more, pushes the question:
Whence or what is the power back of gravitation, — the 3
intelligence that manifests power?   Is pantheism true?
Does mind "sleep in the mineral, or dream in the
animal, and wake in man"?   Christianity answers this 6
question.  The prophets, Jesus, and the apostles, demonstrated a divine intelligence that subordinates so-called
material laws;  and disease, death, winds, and waves, 9
obey this intelligence.  Was it Mind or matter that spake
in creation, "and it was done"?   The answer is self-
evident, and the command remains, "Thou shalt have 12
no other gods before me."

It is plain that the Me spoken of in the First Commandment, must be Mind;  for matter is not the Chris- 15
tian's God, and is not intelligent.  Matter cannot even
talk;  and the serpent, Satan, the first talker in its behalf,
lied.  Reason and revelation declare that God is both 18
noumenon and phenomena, — the first and only cause.
The universe, including man, is not a result of atomic
action, material force or energy;  it is not organized dust. 21
God, Spirit, Mind, are terms synonymous for the one
God, whose reflection is creation, and man is His image
and likeness.  Few there are who comprehend what Chris- 24
tian Science means by the word *reflection*.  God is seen
only in that which reflects good, Life, Truth, Love —
yea, which manifests all His attributes and power, even 27
as the human likeness thrown upon the mirror repeats
precisely the looks and actions of the object in front of it.
All must be Mind and Mind's ideas;  since, according to 30
natural science, God, Spirit, could not change its species
and evolve matter.

1 These facts enjoin the First Commandment; and knowledge of them makes man spiritually minded. St.
3 Paul writes: "For to be carnally minded is death; but to be spiritually minded is life and peace." This knowledge came to me in an hour of great need; and I give it
6 to you as death-bed testimony to the daystar that dawned on the night of material sense. This knowledge is practical, for it wrought my immediate recovery from
9 an injury caused by an accident, and pronounced fatal by the physicians. On the third day thereafter, I called for my Bible, and opened it at Matthew ix. 2. As I
12 read, the healing Truth dawned upon my sense; and the result was that I rose, dressed myself, and ever after was in better health than I had before enjoyed. That
15 short experience included a glimpse of the great fact that I have since tried to make plain to others, namely, Life in and of Spirit; this Life being the sole reality of
18 existence. I learned that mortal thought evolves a subjective state which it names matter, thereby shutting out the true sense of Spirit. *Per contra,* Mind and man
21 are immortal; and knowledge gained from mortal sense is illusion, error, the opposite of Truth; therefore it cannot be true. A knowledge of both good and evil
24 (when good is God, and God is All) is impossible. Speaking of the origin of evil, the Master said: "When he speaketh a lie, he speaketh of his own: for he is a liar,
27 and the father of it." God warned man not to believe the talking serpent, or rather the allegory describing it. The Nazarene Prophet declared that his followers
30 should handle serpents; that is, put down all subtle falsities or illusions, and thus destroy any supposed effect arising from false claims exercising their supposed power

on the mind and body of man, against his holiness and ₁
health.

That there is but one God or Life, one cause and ₃
one effect, is the *multum in parvo* of Christian Science;
and to my understanding it is the heart of Christianity,
the religion that Jesus taught and demonstrated. In ₆
divine Science it is found that matter is a phase of
error, and that neither one really exists, since God is
Truth, and All-in-all. Christ's Sermon on the Mount, ₉
in its direct application to human needs, confirms this
conclusion.

Science, understood, translates matter into Mind, ₁₂
rejects all other theories of causation, restores the spiritual and original meaning of the Scriptures, and explains the teachings and life of our Lord. It is religion's ₁₅
"new tongue," with "signs following," spoken of by
St. Mark. It gives God's infinite meaning to mankind,
healing the sick, casting out evil, and raising the spirit- ₁₈
ually dead. Christianity is Christlike only as it re-
iterates the word, repeats the works, and manifests the
spirit of Christ. ₂₁

Jesus' only medicine was omnipotent and omniscient
Mind. As *omni* is from the Latin word meaning *all*,
this medicine is all-power; and omniscience means as ₂₄
well, all-science. The sick are more deplorably situated
than the sinful, if the sick cannot trust God for help and
the sinful can. If God created drugs good, they cannot be ₂₇
harmful; if He could create them otherwise, then they
are bad and unfit for man; and if He created drugs for
healing the sick, why did not Jesus employ them and ₃₀
recommend them for that purpose?

No human hypotheses, whether in philosophy, medi-

1 cine, or religion, can survive the wreck of time; but
whatever is of God, hath life abiding in it, and ulti-
3 mately will be known as self-evident truth, as demonstrable as mathematics.  Each successive period of progress
is a period more humane and spiritual.  The only logical
6 conclusion is that all is Mind and its manifestation, from
the rolling of worlds, in the most subtle ether, to a potato-
patch.
9   The agriculturist ponders the history of a seed, and
believes that his crops come from the seedling and the
loam; even while the Scripture declares He made "every
12 plant of the field before it was in the earth."  The Scientist asks, Whence came the first seed, and what made
the soil?  Was it molecules, or material atoms?  Whence
15 came the infinitesimals, — from infinite Mind, or from
matter?  If from matter, how did matter originate?  Was
it self-existent?  Matter is not intelligent, and thus able
18 to evolve or create itself:  it is the very opposite of Spirit,
intelligent, self-creative, and infinite Mind.  The belief
of mind in matter is pantheism.  Natural history shows
21 that neither a genus nor a species produces its opposite.
God is All, in all.  What can be more than All?  Nothing: and this is just what I call matter, *nothing*.  Spirit,
24 God, has no antecedent; and God's consequent is the
spiritual cosmos.  The phrase, "express image," in the
common version of Hebrews i. 3, is, in the Greek Tes-
27 tament, *character*.
The Scriptures name God as good, and the Saxon
term for God is also good.  From this premise comes
30 the logical conclusion that God is naturally and divinely
infinite good.  How, then, can this conclusion change,
or be changed, to mean that good is evil, or the creator

of evil? What can there be besides infinity? Nothing! 1
Therefore the Science of good calls evil *nothing*. In
divine Science the terms God and good, as Spirit, are 3
synonymous. That God, good, creates evil, or aught
that can result in evil, — or that Spirit creates its opposite, named matter, — are conclusions that destroy their 6
premise and prove themselves invalid. Here is where
Christian Science sticks to its text, and other systems
of religion abandon their own logic. Here also is found 9
the pith of the basal statement, the cardinal point in
Christian Science, that matter and evil (including all
inharmony, sin, disease, death) are *unreal*. Mortals 12
accept natural science, wherein no species ever produces its opposite. Then why not accept divine Science on this ground? since the Scriptures maintain 15
this fact by parable and proof, asking, "Do men
gather grapes of thorns, or figs of thistles?" "Doth a
fountain send forth at the same place sweet water and 18
bitter?"

According to reason and revelation, evil and matter
are negation: for evil signifies the absence of good, God, 21
though God is ever present; and matter claims something besides God, when God is really *All*. Creation,
evolution, or manifestation, — being in and of Spirit, 24
Mind, and all that really is, — must be spiritual and
mental. This is Science, and is susceptible of proof.

But, say you, is a stone spiritual? 27

To erring material sense, No! but to unerring spiritual
sense, it is a small manifestation of Mind, a type of spiritual substance, "the substance of things hoped for." 30
Mortals can know a stone as substance, only by first admitting that it is substantial. Take away the mortal sense

1 of substance, and the stone itself would disappear, only
to reappear in the spiritual sense thereof.  Matter can
3 neither see, hear, feel, taste, nor smell; having no sensation of its own.  Perception by the five personal senses
is mental, and dependent on the beliefs that mortals
6 entertain.  Destroy the belief that you can walk, and
volition ceases; for muscles cannot move without mind.
Matter takes no cognizance of matter.  In dreams, things
9 are only what mortal mind makes them; and the phenomena of mortal life are as dreams; and this so-called
life is a dream soon told.  In proportion as mortals turn
12 from this mortal and material dream, to the true sense
of reality, everlasting Life will be found to be the only
Life.  That death does not destroy the beliefs of the flesh,
15 our Master proved to his doubting disciple, Thomas.  Also,
he demonstrated that divine Science alone can overbear
materiality and mortality; and this great truth was shown
18 by his ascension after death, whereby he arose above
the illusion of matter.

The First Commandment, "Thou shalt have no other
21 gods before me," suggests the inquiry, What meaneth
this Me, — Spirit, or matter?  It certainly does not
signify a graven idol, and must mean Spirit.  Then
24 the commandment means, Thou shalt recognize no
intelligence nor life in matter; and find neither pleasure
nor pain therein.  The Master's practical knowledge
27 of this grand verity, together with his divine Love,
healed the sick and raised the dead.  He literally
annulled the claims of physique and of physical law,
30 by the superiority of the higher law; hence his declaration, "These signs shall follow them that believe; . . .
if they drink any deadly thing, it shall not hurt them;

they shall lay hands on the sick, and they shall re- 1
cover."

Do you believe his words?  I do, and that his prom- 3
ise is perpetual.  Had it been applicable only to his
immediate disciples, the pronoun would be *you*, not *them*.
The purpose of his life-work touches universal human- 6
ity.  At another time he prayed, not for the twelve
only, but "for them also which shall believe on me through
their word."                                              9

The Christ-healing was practised even before the Christian era; "the Word was with God, and the Word was
God."  There is, however, no analogy between Christian 12
Science and spiritualism, or between it and any speculative theory.

In 1867, I taught the first student in Christian Science. 15
Since that date I have known of but fourteen deaths
in the ranks of my about five thousand students.  The
census since 1875 (the date of the first publication of 18
my work, "Science and Health with Key to the Scriptures") shows that longevity has *increased*.  Daily letters
inform me that a perusal of my volume is healing the 21
writers of chronic and acute diseases that had defied medical skill.

Surely the people of the Occident know that esoteric 24
magic and Oriental barbarisms will neither flavor Christianity nor advance health and length of days.

Miracles are no infraction of God's laws;  on the 27
contrary, they fulfil His laws;  for they are the signs following Christianity, whereby matter is proven powerless and subordinate to Mind.  Christians, like students 30
in mathematics, should be working up to those higher
rules of Life which Jesus taught and proved.  Do we

1 really understand the divine Principle of Christianity
before we prove it, in at least some feeble demonstra-
3 tion thereof, according to Jesus' example in healing the
sick? Should we adopt the "simple addition" in Christian Science and doubt its higher rules, or despair of
6 ultimately reaching them, even though failing at first to
demonstrate all the possibilities of Christianity?

St. John spiritually discerned and revealed the sum
9 total of transcendentalism. He saw the real earth and
heaven. They were spiritual, not material; and they
were without pain, sin, or death. Death was not the
12 door to this heaven. The gates thereof he declared were
inlaid with pearl, — likening them to the priceless understanding of man's real existence, to be recognized here
15 and now.

The great Way-shower illustrated Life unconfined, un-
contaminated, untrammelled, by matter. He proved the
18 superiority of Mind over the flesh, opened the door to
the captive, and enabled man to demonstrate the law of
Life, which St. Paul declares "hath made me free from
21 the law of sin and death."

The stale saying that Christian Science "is neither
Christian nor science!" is to-day the fossil of wisdom-
24 less wit, weakness, and superstition. "The fool hath
said in his heart, There is no God."

Take courage, dear reader, for any seeming mysti-
27 cism surrounding realism is explained in the Scripture,
"There went up a mist from the earth [matter];" and
the mist of materialism will vanish as we approach spirit-
30 uality, the realm of reality; cleanse our lives in Christ's
righteousness; bathe in the baptism of Spirit, and awake
in His likeness.

# CHAPTER III

## QUESTIONS AND ANSWERS

*What do you consider to be mental malpractice?*  1

MENTAL malpractice is a bland denial of Truth, and is the antipode of Christian Science.  To 3
mentally argue in a manner that can disastrously affect the happiness of a fellow-being — harm him morally, physically, or spiritually — breaks the Golden 6
Rule and subverts the scientific laws of being.  This, therefore, is not the use but the abuse of mental treatment, and is mental malpractice.  It is needless to 9
say that such a subversion of right is not scientific.  Its claim to power is in proportion to the faith in evil, and consequently to the lack of faith in good.  Such false 12
faith finds no place in, and receives no aid from, the Principle or the rules of Christian Science;  for it denies the grand verity of this Science, namely, that God, good, 15
has *all* power.

This leaves the individual no alternative but to relinquish his faith in evil, or to argue against his own 18
convictions of good and so destroy his power to be or to do good, because he has no faith in the *omnipotence* of God, good.  He parts with his understanding of good, 21
in order to retain his faith in evil and so succeed with his

1 wrong argument, — if indeed he desires success in this
broad road to destruction.

3  *How shall we demean ourselves towards the students
of disloyal students?  And what about that clergyman's
remarks on "Christ and Christmas"?*

6  From this question, I infer that some of my students
seem not to know in what manner they should act towards
the students of false teachers, or such as have strayed
9 from the rules and divine Principle of Christian Science.
The query is abnormal, when "precept upon precept;
line upon line" are to be found in the Scriptures, and in
12 my books, on this very subject.

In Mark, ninth chapter, commencing at the thirty-
third verse, you will find my views on this subject; love
15 alone is admissible towards friend and foe.  My sympathies extend to the above-named class of students more
than to many others.  If I had the time to talk with all
18 students of Christian Science, and correspond with them,
I would gladly do my best towards helping those unfortunate seekers after Truth whose teacher is straying
21 from the straight and narrow path.  But I have not moments enough in which to give to my own flock all the
time and attention that they need, — and charity must
24 begin at home.

Distinct denominational and social organizations and
societies are at present necessary for the individual,
27 and for our Cause.  But all people can and should be
just, merciful; they should never envy, elbow, slander,
hate, or try to injure, but always should try to bless their
30 fellow-mortals.

To the query in regard to some clergyman's com-

ments on my illustrated poem, I will say: It is the righteous 1
prayer that avails with God.   Whatever is wrong will
receive its own reward.   The high priests of old caused 3
the crucifixion of even the great Master;  and thereby
they lost, and he won, heaven.   I love all ministers and
ministries of Christ, Truth.                                      6

All clergymen may not understand the illustrations
in "Christ and Christmas;"  or that these refer not to
personality, but present the type and shadow of Truth's 9
appearing in the womanhood as well as in the manhood
of God, our divine Father and Mother.

*Must I have faith in Christian Science in order to be* 12
*healed by it?*

This is a question that is being asked every day.   It
has not proved impossible to heal those who, when they 15
began treatment, had no faith whatever in the Science,
— other than to place themselves under my care, and
follow the directions given.   Patients naturally gain con- 18
fidence in Christian Science as they recognize the help
they derive therefrom.

*What are the advantages of your system of healing, over* 21
*the ordinary methods of healing disease?*

Healing by Christian Science has the following advantages: —                                                       24
*First:* It does away with all material medicines, and
recognizes the fact that, as mortal mind is the cause of
all "the ills that flesh is heir to," the antidote for sickness, 27
as well as for sin, may and must be found in mortal mind's
opposite, — the divine Mind.
*Second:* It is more effectual than drugs;  curing where 30

1 these fail, and leaving none of the harmful "after effects"
of these in the system; thus proving that metaphysics
3 is above physics.

*Third:* One who has been healed by Christian Science is not only healed of the disease, but is improved
6 morally. The body is governed by mind; and mortal
mind must be improved, before the body is renewed
and harmonious, — since the physique is simply thought
9 made manifest.

*Is spiritualism or mesmerism included in Christian
Science?*

12 They are wholly apart from it. Christian Science is
based on divine Principle; whereas spiritualism, so far
as I understand it, is a mere speculative opinion and
15 human belief. If the departed were to communicate
with us, we should see them as they were before death,
and have them with us; after death, they can no more
18 come to those they have left, than we, in our present state
of existence, can go to the departed or the adult can return to his boyhood. We may pass on to their state
21 of existence, but they cannot return to ours. Man is
*im*-mortal, and there is not a moment when he ceases to
exist. All that are called "communications from spirits,"
24 lie within the realm of mortal thought on this present plane
of existence, and are the antipodes of Christian Science;
the immortal and mortal are as direct opposites as light
27 and darkness.

*Who is the Founder of mental healing?*

The author of "Science and Health with Key to the
30 Scriptures," who discovered the Science of healing em-

bodied in her works. Years of practical proof, through ₁
homœopathy, revealed to her the fact that Mind, instead of matter, is the Principle of pathology; and ₃
subsequently her recovery, through the supremacy of
Mind over matter, from a severe casualty pronounced
by the physicians incurable, sealed that proof with the ₆
signet of Christian Science. In 1883, a million of people acknowledge and attest the blessings of this mental
system of treating disease. Perhaps the following ₉
words of her husband, the late Dr. Asa G. Eddy,
afford the most concise, yet complete, summary of the
matter: — 12

"Mrs. Eddy's works are the outgrowths of her life.
I never knew so unselfish an individual."

*Will the book Science and Health, that you offer for sale* 15
*at three dollars, teach its readers to heal the sick, — or is*
*one obliged to become a student under your personal in-*
*struction? And if one is obliged to study under you, of* 18
*what benefit is your book?*

Why do we read the Bible, and then go to church to
hear it expounded? Only because both are important. 21
Why do we read moral science, and then study it at
college?

You are benefited by reading Science and Health, but 24
it is greatly to your advantage to be taught its Science
by the author of that work, who explains it in detail.

*What is immortal Mind?* 27

In reply, we refer you to "Science and Health with
Key to the Scriptures," ¹ Vol. I. page 14: "That which

---

¹ Quoted from the sixth edition. 30

1 is erring, sinful, sick, and dying, termed material or
mortal man, is neither God's man nor Mind; but to be
3 understood, we shall classify evil and error as mortal
mind, in contradistinction to good and Truth, or the
Mind which is immortal."

6 *Do animals and beasts have a mind?*

Beasts, as well as men, express Mind as their origin;
but they manifest less of Mind. The first and only
9 cause is the eternal Mind, which is God, and there is
but one God. The ferocious mind seen in the beast is
mortal mind, which is harmful and proceeds not from
12 God; for His beast is the lion that lieth down with
the lamb. Appetites, passions, anger, revenge, subtlety,
are the animal qualities of sinning mortals; and the
15 beasts that have these propensities express the lower
qualities of the so-called animal man; in other words,
the nature and quality of mortal mind, — not immortal
18 Mind.

*What is the distinction between mortal mind and im-*
*mortal Mind?*

21 Mortal mind includes all evil, disease, and death;
also, all beliefs relative to the so-called material laws,
and all material objects, and the law of sin and death.
24 The Scripture says, "The carnal mind [in other words,
mortal mind] is enmity against God; for it is not subject to the law of God, neither indeed can be." Mortal
27 mind is an illusion; as much in our waking moments
as in the dreams of sleep. The belief that intelligence,
Truth, and Love, are in matter and separate from God,
30 is an error; for there is no intelligent evil, and no power

besides God, good.  God would not be omnipotent if  1
there were in reality another mind creating or governing
man or the universe.                                         3

Immortal Mind is God;  and this Mind is made
manifest in all thoughts and desires that draw mankind toward purity, health, holiness, and the spiritual  6
facts of being.

Jesus recognized this relation so clearly that he said,
"I and my Father are one."  In proportion as we oppose  9
the belief in material sense, in sickness, sin, and death,
and recognize ourselves under the control of God,
spiritual and immortal Mind, shall we go on to leave the  12
animal for the spiritual, and learn the meaning of those
words of Jesus, "Go ye into all the world . . . heal the
sick."                                                       15

*Can your Science cure intemperance?*

Christian Science lays the axe at the root of the tree.
Its antidote for all ills is God, the perfect Mind, which  18
corrects mortal thought, whence cometh all evil.  God
can and does destroy the thought that leads to moral
or physical death.  Intemperance, impurity, sin of every  21
sort, is destroyed by Truth.  The appetite for alcohol
yields to Science as directly and surely as do sickness
and sin.                                                     24

*Does Mrs. Eddy take patients?*

She now does not.  Her time is wholly devoted to instruction, leaving to her students the work of healing;  27
which, at this hour, is in reality the least difficult of the
labor that Christian Science demands.

1  *Why do you charge for teaching Christian Science, when
all the good we can do must be done freely?*

3  When teaching imparts the ability to gain and maintain health, to heal and elevate man in every line of
life, — as this teaching certainly does, — is it un-
6 reasonable to expect in return something to support
one's self and a Cause?  If so, our whole system
of education, secular and religious, is at fault, and the
9 instructors and philanthropists in our land should expect no compensation.  "If we have sown unto you
spiritual things, is it a great thing if we shall reap your
12 carnal things?"


*How happened you to establish a college to instruct in
metaphysics, when other institutions find little interest in
15 such a dry and abstract subject?*

Metaphysics, as taught by me at the Massachusetts
Metaphysical College, is far from dry and abstract.  It
18 is a Science that has the animus of Truth.  Its practical
application to benefit the race, heal the sick, enlighten
and reform the sinner, makes divine metaphysics need-
21 ful, indispensable.  Teaching metaphysics at other colleges means, mainly, elaborating a man-made theory,
or some speculative view too vapory and hypothetical
24 for questions of practical import.


*Is it necessary to study your Science in order to be healed
by it and keep well?*

27  It is not necessary to make each patient a student
in order to cure his present disease, if this is what
you mean.  Were it so, the Science would be of less

practical value. Many who apply for help are not 1
prepared to take a course of instruction in Christian
Science. 3

To avoid being *subject* to disease, would require the
understanding of how you are healed. In 1885, this
knowledge can be obtained in its genuineness at the 6
Massachusetts Metaphysical College. There are abroad
at this early date some grossly incorrect and false
teachers of what they term Christian Science; of such 9
beware. They have risen up in a day to make this claim;
whereas the Founder of genuine Christian Science has
been all her years in giving it birth. 12

*Can you take care of yourself?*

God giveth to every one this *puissance;* and I have
faith in His promise, "Lo, I am with you alway" — 15
*all the way.* Unlike the M. D.'s, Christian Scientists
are not afraid to take their own medicine, for this
medicine is divine Mind; and from this saving, ex- 18
haustless source they intend to fill the human mind with
enough of the leaven of Truth to leaven the whole lump.
There may be exceptional cases, where one Christian 21
Scientist who has more to meet than others needs support
at times; then, it is right to bear "one another's burdens,
and so fulfil the law of Christ." 24

*In what way is a Christian Scientist an instrument by*
*which God reaches others to heal them, and what most*
*obstructs the way?* 27

A Christian, or a Christian Scientist, assumes no more
when claiming to work with God in healing the sick,
than in converting the sinner. Divine help is as neces- 30
3

1 sary in the one case as in the other.  The scientific Principle of healing demands such cooperation;  but this
3 unison and its power would be arrested if one were to
mix material methods with the spiritual, — were to mingle hygienic rules, drugs, and prayers in the same pro-
6 cess, — and thus serve "other gods."  Truth is as
effectual in destroying sickness as in the destruction
of sin.

9    It is often asked, "If Christian Science is the same
method of healing that Jesus and the apostles used,
why do not its students perform as instantaneous cures
12 as did those in the first century of the Christian era?"

In some instances the students of Christian Science
equal the ancient prophets as healers.  All true healing
15 is governed by, and demonstrated on, the same Principle as theirs; namely, the action of the divine Spirit,
through the power of Truth to destroy error, discord
18 of whatever sort.  The reason that the same results follow not in every case, is that the student does not in
every case possess sufficiently the Christ-spirit and its
21 power to cast out the disease.  The Founder of Christian Science teaches her students that they must possess
the spirit of Truth and Love, must gain the power
24 over sin in themselves, or they cannot be instantaneous
healers.

In this Christian warfare the student or practitioner
27 has to master those elements of evil too common to other
minds.  If it is hate that is holding the purpose to kill
his patient by mental means, it requires more divine
30 understanding to conquer this sin than to nullify either
the disease itself or the ignorance by which one unin-
tentionally harms himself or another.  An element of

brute-force that only the cruel and evil can send forth, is given vent in the diabolical practice of one who, having learned the power of liberated thought to do good, perverts it, and uses it to accomplish an evil purpose. This mental malpractice would disgrace Mind-healing, were it not that God overrules it, and causes "the wrath of man" to praise Him. It deprives those who practise it of the power to heal, and destroys their own possibility of progressing.

The honest student of Christian Science is purged through Christ, Truth, and thus is ready for victory in the ennobling strife. The good fight must be fought by those who keep the faith and finish their course. Mental purgation must go on: it promotes spiritual growth, scales the mountain of human endeavor, and gains the summit in Science that otherwise could not be reached, — where the struggle with sin is forever done.

*Can all classes of disease be healed by your method?*

We answer, Yes. Mind is the architect that builds its own idea, and produces all harmony that appears. There is no other healer in the case. If mortal mind, through the action of fear, manifests inflammation and a belief of chronic or acute disease, by removing the cause in that so-called mind the effect or disease will disappear and health will be restored; for health, *alias* harmony, is the normal manifestation of man in Science. The divine Principle which governs the universe, including man, if demonstrated, is sufficient for all emergencies. But the practitioner may not always prove equal to bringing out the result of the Principle that he knows to be true.

1 *After the change called death takes place, do we meet*
*those gone before? — or does life continue in thought only*
3 *as in a dream?*

Man is not annihilated, nor does he lose his identity,
by passing through the belief called death. After the
6 momentary belief of dying passes from mortal mind, this
mind is still in a conscious state of existence; and the individual has but passed through a moment of extreme
9 mortal fear, to awaken with thoughts, and being, as
material as before. Science and Health clearly states
that spiritualization of thought is not attained by the death
12 of the body, but by a conscious union with God. When
we shall have passed the ordeal called death, or destroyed
this last enemy, and shall have come upon the same plane
15 of conscious existence with those gone before, then we
shall be able to communicate with and to recognize them.

If, before the change whereby we meet the dear de-
18 parted, our life-work proves to have been well done, we
shall not have to repeat it; but our joys and means of advancing will be proportionately increased.

21 The difference between a belief of material existence
and the spiritual fact of Life is, that the former is a dream
and unreal, while the latter is real and eternal. Only
24 as we understand God, and learn that good, not evil,
lives and is immortal, that immortality exists only in
spiritual perfection, shall we drop our false sense of Life
27 in sin or sense material, and recognize a better state of
existence.

*Can I be treated without being present during treatment?*

30 Mind is not confined to limits; and nothing but our
own false admissions prevent us from demonstrating this

great fact. Christian Science, recognizing the capabili- 1
ties of Mind to act of itself, and independent of matter,
enables one to heal cases without even having seen the 3
individual, — or simply after having been made acquainted with the mental condition of the patient.

*Do all who at present claim to be teaching Christian* 6
*Science, teach it correctly?*

By no means: Christian Science is not sufficiently understood for that. The student of this Science who under- 9
stands it best, is the one least likely to pour into other
minds a trifling sense of it as being adequate to make safe
and successful practitioners. The simple sense one gains 12
of this Science through careful, unbiased, contemplative
reading of my books, is far more advantageous to the
sick and to the learner than is or can be the spurious 15
teaching of those who are spiritually unqualified. The
sad fact at this early writing is, that the letter is gained
sooner than the spirit of Christian Science: time is re- 18
quired thoroughly to qualify students for the great ordeal
of this century.

If one student tries to undermine another, such sinister 21
rivalry does a vast amount of injury to the Cause. To
fill one's pocket at the expense of his conscience, or to
build on the downfall of others, incapacitates one to 24
practise or teach Christian Science. The occasional temporary success of such an one is owing, in part, to the impossibility for those unacquainted with the mighty Truth 27
of *Christian* Science to recognize, as such, the barefaced
errors that are taught — and the damaging effects these
leave on the practice of the learner, on the Cause, and 30
on the health of the community.

1 Honest students speak the truth "according to the pattern showed to thee in the mount," and live it: these
3 are not working for emoluments, and may profitably teach people, who are ready to investigate this subject, the rudiments of Christian Science.

6 *Can Christian Science cure acute cases where there is necessity for immediate relief, as in membranous croup?*

The remedial power of Christian Science is positive,
9 and its application direct. It cannot fail to heal in every case of disease, when conducted by one who understands this Science sufficiently to demonstrate its
12 highest possibilities.

*If I have the toothache, and nothing stops it until I have the tooth extracted, and then the pain ceases, has*
15 *the mind, or extracting, or both, caused the pain to cease?*

What you thought was pain in the bone or nerve, could
18 only have been a belief of pain in matter; for matter has no sensation. It was a state of mortal thought made manifest in the flesh. You call this body matter, when
21 awake, or when asleep in a dream. That matter can report pain, or that mind is *in* matter, reporting sensations, is but a dream at all times. You believed that if
24 the tooth were extracted, the pain would cease: this demand of mortal thought once met, your belief assumed a new form, and said, There is no more pain. When
27 your belief in pain ceases, the pain stops; for matter has no intelligence of its own. By applying this mental remedy or antidote directly to your belief, you scien-

tifically prove the fact that Mind is supreme.  This is not 1
done by will-power, for that is not Science but mesmerism.
The full understanding that God is Mind, and that mat- 3
ter is but a belief, enables you to control pain.  Christian Science, by means of its Principle of metaphysical
healing, is able to do more than to heal a toothache; 6
although its power to allay fear, prevent inflammation,
and destroy the necessity for ether — thereby avoiding
the fatal results that frequently follow the use of that 9
drug — render this Science invaluable in the practice
of dentistry.

*Can an atheist or a profane man be cured by metaphysics,* 12
*or Christian Science?*

The moral status of the man demands the remedy of
Truth more in this than in most cases;  therefore, under 15
the deific law that supply invariably meets demand, this
Science is effectual in treating moral ailments.  Sin is
not the master of divine Science, but *vice versa;* and 18
when Science in a single instance decides the conflict,
the patient is better both morally and physically.

*If God made all that was made, and it was good, where* 21
*did evil originate?*

It never originated or existed as an entity.  It is but a
false belief;  even the belief that God is not what the 24
Scriptures imply Him to be, All-in-all, but that there
is an opposite intelligence or mind termed evil.  This
error of belief is idolatry, having "other gods before me." 27
In John i. 3 we read, "All things were made by Him;
and without Him was not anything made that was made."

1 The admission of the reality of evil perpetuates the belief
or faith in evil. The Scriptures declare, "To whom ye
3 yield yourselves servants to obey, his servants ye are."
The leading self-evident proposition of Christian Science
is: good being real, evil, good's opposite, is unreal. This
6 truism needs only to be tested scientifically to be found
true, and adapted to destroy the appearance of evil to an
extent beyond the power of any doctrine previously
9 entertained.

### *Do you teach that you are equal with God?*

A reader of my writings would not present this ques-
12 tion. There are no such indications in the premises or
conclusions of Christian Science, and such a misconception of Truth is not scientific. Man is not equal with
15 his Maker; that which is formed is not cause, but effect,
and has no power underived from its creator. It is possible, and it is man's duty, so to throw the weight of his
18 thoughts and acts on the side of Truth, that he be ever
found in the scale *with* his creator; not weighing
equally with Him, but comprehending at every point, in
21 divine Science, the full significance of what the apostle
meant by the declaration, "The Spirit itself beareth witness with our spirit, that we are the children of God: and
24 if children, then heirs; heirs of God, and joint-heirs with
Christ." In Science, man represents his divine Principle, — the Life and Love that are God, — even as the
27 idea of sound, in tones, represents harmony; but thought
has not yet wholly attained unto the Science of being,
wherein man is perfect even as the Father, his divine
30 Principle, is perfect.

*How can I believe that there is no such thing as matter,* 1
*when I weigh over two hundred pounds and carry about*
*this weight daily?* 3

By learning that matter is but manifest mortal mind.
You entertain an adipose belief of yourself as substance;
whereas, substance means more than matter: it is the 6
glory and permanence of Spirit: it is that which is
hoped for but unseen, that which the material senses
cannot take in. Have you never been so preoccupied in 9
thought when moving your body, that you did this without consciousness of its weight? If never in your waking
hours, you have been in your night-dreams; and these 12
tend to elucidate your day-dream, or the mythical nature
of matter, and the possibilities of mind when let loose
from its own beliefs. In sleep, a sense of the body ac- 15
companies thought with less impediment than when
awake, which is the truer sense of being. In Science,
body is the servant of Mind, not its master: Mind is 18
supreme. Science reverses the evidence of material
sense with the spiritual sense that God, Spirit, is the only
substance; and that man, His image and likeness, is 21
spiritual, not material. This great Truth does not destroy but substantiates man's identity, — together with
his immortality and preexistence, or his spiritual co- 24
existence with his Maker. That which has a beginning
must have an ending.

*What should one conclude as to Professor Carpenter's* 27
*exhibitions of mesmerism?*

That largely depends upon what one accepts as either
useful or true. I have no knowledge of mesmerism, 30

1 practically or theoretically, save as I measure its demonstrations as a false belief, and avoid all that works ill. If
3 mesmerism has the power attributed to it by the gentleman referred to, it should neither be taught nor practised,
but should be conscientiously condemned.   One thing
6 is quite apparent;  namely, that its so-called power is
despotic, and Mr. Carpenter deserves praise for his public
exposure of it.   If such be its power, I am opposed to it,
9 as to every form of error, — whether of ignorance or
fanaticism, prompted by money-making or malice.   It
is enough for me to know that animal magnetism is neither
12 of God nor Science.

It is alleged that at one of his recent lectures in Boston Mr. Carpenter made a man drunk on water, and
15 then informed his audience that he could produce the
effect of alcohol, or of any drug, on the human system,
through the action of mind alone.   This honest declara-
18 tion as to the animus of animal magnetism and the possible purpose to which it can be devoted, has, we trust,
been made in season to open the eyes of the people to the
21 hidden nature of some tragic events and sudden deaths
at this period.

*Was ever a person made insane by studying meta-*
24 *physics?*

Such an occurrence would be impossible, for the
proper study of Mind-healing would cure the insane.
27 That persons have gone away from the Massachusetts
Metaphysical College "made insane by Mrs. Eddy's
teachings," like a hundred other stories, is a baseless
30 fabrication offered solely to injure her or her school.
The enemy is trying to make capital out of the follow-

ing case. A young lady entered the College class who, 1
I quickly saw, had a tendency to monomania, and requested her to withdraw before its close. We are cred- 3
ibly informed that, before entering the College, this
young lady had manifested some mental unsoundness,
and have no doubt she could have been restored by 6
Christian Science treatment. Her friends employed a
homœopathist, who had the skill and honor to state, as his
opinion given to her friends, that "Mrs. Eddy's teach- 9
ings had not produced insanity." This is the only case
that could be distorted into the claim of insanity ever
having occurred in a class of Mrs. Eddy's; while ac- 12
knowledged and notable cases of insanity have been
cured in her class.

*If all that is mortal is a dream or error, is not* 15
*our capacity for formulating a dream, real; is it not*
*God-made; and if God-made, can it be wrong, sinful, or*
*an error?* 18

The spirit of Truth leads into all truth, and enables
man to discern between the real and the unreal. Entertaining the common belief in the opposite of goodness, 21
and that evil is as real as good, opposes the leadings of
the divine Spirit that are helping man Godward: it prevents a recognition of the nothingness of the dream, or 24
belief, that Mind is in matter, intelligence in non-intel-
ligence, sin, and death. This belief presupposes not
only a power opposed to God, and that God is not All- 27
in-all, as the Scriptures imply Him to be, but that the
capacity to err proceeds from God.

That God is Truth, the Scriptures aver; that Truth 30
never created error, or such a capacity, is self-evident;

1 that God made all that was made, is again Scriptural;
therefore your answer is, that error is an illusion of
3 mortals; that God is not its author, and it cannot be
real.

*Does "Science and Health with Key to the Scriptures"*
6 *explain the entire method of metaphysical healing, or is*
*there a secret back of what is contained in that book, as*
*some say?*

9 "Science and Health with Key to the Scriptures"
is a complete textbook of Christian Science; and its
metaphysical method of healing is as lucid in presenta-
12 tion as can be possible, under the necessity to express
the metaphysical in physical terms. There is absolutely
no additional secret outside of its teachings, or that gives
15 one the power to heal; but it is essential that the student
gain the spiritual understanding of the contents of this
book, in order to heal.

18 *Do you believe in change of heart?*

We do believe, and understand — which is more —
that there must be a change from human affections, de-
21 sires, and aims, to the divine standard, "Be ye therefore
perfect;" also, that there must be a change from the belief that the heart is matter and sustains life, to the
24 understanding that God is our Life, that we exist in
Mind, live thereby, and have being. This change of
heart would deliver man from heart-disease, and ad-
27 vance Christianity a hundredfold. The human affections
need to be changed from self to benevolence and love
for God and man; changed to having but *one* God and
30 loving Him supremely, and helping our brother man.

This change of heart is essential to Christianity, and 1
will have its effect physically as well as spiritually,
healing disease.   Burnt offerings and drugs, God does 3
not require.

*Is a belief of nervousness, accompanied by great mental
depression, mesmerism?*                                       6

All mesmerism is of one of three kinds;   namely, the
ignorant, the fraudulent, or the malicious workings of
error or mortal mind.   We have not the particulars of 9
the case to which you may refer, and for this reason cannot answer your question professionally.

*How can I govern a child metaphysically?   Doesn't the* 12
*use of the rod teach him life in matter?*

The use of the rod is virtually a declaration to the
child's mind that sensation belongs to matter.   Motives 15
govern acts, and Mind governs man.   If you make clear
to the child's thought the right motives for action, and
cause him to love them, they will lead him aright:  if you 18
educate him to love God, good, and obey the Golden
Rule, he will love and obey you without your having to
resort to corporeal punishment.                              21

> "When from the lips of Truth one mighty breath
> Shall, like a whirlwind, scatter in its breeze
> The whole dark pile of human mockeries;                     24
> Then shall the reign of Mind commence on earth,
> And starting fresh, as from a second birth,
> Man in the sunshine of the world's new spring,             27
> Shall walk transparent like some holy thing."

*Are both prayer and drugs necessary to heal?*

The apostle James said, "Ye ask, and receive not, 30
because ye ask amiss, that ye may consume it upon your

1 lusts." This text may refer to such as seek the material
to aid the spiritual, and take drugs to support God's
3 power to heal them.  It is difficult to say how much
one can do for himself, whose faith is divided between catnip and Christ;  but not so difficult to know
6 that if he were to serve one master, he could do vastly
more.  Whosoever understands the power of Spirit, has
no doubt of God's power, — even the might of Truth, —
9 to heal, through divine Science, beyond all human means
and methods.

*What do you think of marriage?*

12    That it is often convenient, sometimes pleasant, and
occasionally a love affair.  Marriage is susceptible of
many definitions.  It sometimes presents the most
15 wretched condition of human existence.  To be normal,
it must be a union of the affections that tends to lift
mortals higher.

18   *If this life is a dream not dispelled, but only changed,*
*by death, — if one gets tired of it, why not commit*
*suicide?*

21    Man's existence is a problem to be wrought in divine
Science.  What progress would a student of science
make, if, when tired of mathematics or failing to dem-
24 onstrate one rule readily, he should attempt to work
out a rule farther on and more difficult — and this,
because the first rule was not easily demonstrated?  In
27 that case he would be obliged to turn back and work
out the previous example, before solving the advanced
problem.  Mortals have the sum of being to work out,
30 and up, to its spiritual standpoint.  They must work

out of this dream or false claim of sensation and life 1
in matter, and up to the spiritual realities of existence,
before this false claim can be wholly dispelled. Com- 3
mitting suicide to dodge the question is not working
it out. The error of supposed life and intelligence in
matter, is dissolved only as we master error with Truth. 6
Not through sin or suicide, but by *overcoming* temptation and sin, shall we escape the weariness and wickedness of mortal existence, and gain heaven, the harmony 9
of being.

*Do you sometimes find it advisable to use medicine to
assist in producing a cure, when it is difficult to start the* 12
*patient's recovery?*

You only weaken your power to heal through Mind,
by any compromise with matter; which is virtually ac- 15
knowledging that under difficulties the former is not equal
to the latter. He that resorts to physics, seeks what is
below instead of above the standard of metaphysics; 18
showing his ignorance of the meaning of the term and
of Christian Science.

*If Christian Science is the same as Jesus taught, why is* 21
*it not more simple, so that all can readily understand it?*

The teachings of Jesus were simple; and yet he found
it difficult to make the rulers understand, because of 24
their great lack of spirituality. Christian Science is
simple, and readily understood by the children; only
the thought educated away from it finds it abstract or 27
difficult to perceive. Its seeming abstraction is the
mystery of godliness; and godliness is simple to the
godly; but to the unspiritual, the ungodly, it is dark 30

1 and difficult.  The carnal mind cannot discern spiritual
things.

3   *Has Mrs. Eddy lost her power to heal?*

Has the sun forgotten to shine, and the planets to
revolve around it?  Who is it that discovered, dem-
6 onstrated, and teaches Christian Science?  That one,
whoever it be, does understand something of what cannot be lost.  Thousands in the field of metaphysical
9 healing, whose lives are worthy testimonials, are her
students, and they bear witness to this fact.  Instead
of losing her power to heal, she is demonstrating the
12 power of Christian Science over all obstacles that envy
and malice would fling in her path.  The reading of her
book, "Science and Health with Key to the Scriptures,"
15 is curing hundreds at this very time;  and the sick, un-
asked, are testifying thereto.

*Must I study your Science in order to keep well all my*
18 *life?  I was healed of a chronic trouble after one month's*
*treatment by one of your students.*

When once you are healed by Science, there is no rea-
21 son why you should be liable to a return of the disease
that you were healed of.  But not to be subject again to
any disease whatsoever, would require an understanding
24 of the Science by which you were healed.

*Because none of your students have been able to perform*
*as great miracles in healing as Jesus and his disciples did,*
27 *does it not suggest the possibility that they do not heal on*
*the same basis?*

You would not ask the pupil in simple equations to
30 solve a problem involving logarithms;  and then, because

he failed to get the right answer, condemn the pupil ₁
and the science of numbers. The simplest problem
in Christian Science is healing the sick, and the least ₃
understanding and demonstration thereof prove all its
possibilities. The ability to demonstrate to the extent
that Jesus did, will come when the student possesses as ₆
much of the divine Spirit as he shared, and utilizes its
power to overcome sin.

Opposite to good, is the universal claim of evil that ₉
seeks the proportions of good. There may be those
who, having learned the power of the unspoken thought,
use it to harm rather than to heal, and who are using ₁₂
that power against Christian Scientists. This giant sin
is the sin against the Holy Ghost spoken of in Matt.
xii. 31, 32. ₁₅

*Is Christian Science based on the facts of both Spirit
and matter?*

Christian Science is based on the facts of Spirit and ₁₈
its forms and representations, but these facts are the
direct antipodes of the so-called facts of matter; and
the eternal verities of Spirit assert themselves over their ₂₁
opposite, or matter, in the final destruction of all that
is unlike Spirit.

Man knows that he can have one God only, when ₂₄
he regards God as the only Mind, Life, and substance.
If God is Spirit, as the Scriptures declare, and All-in-
all, matter is mythology, and its laws are mortal ₂₇
beliefs.

If Mind is in matter and beneath a skull bone, it is
in something unlike Him; hence it is either a godless and ₃₀
material Mind, or it is God in matter, — which are theo-

1 ries of agnosticism and pantheism, the very antipodes
of Christian Science.

3   *What is organic life?*

Life is inorganic, infinite Spirit; if Life, or Spirit,
were organic, disorganization would destroy Spirit and
6 annihilate man.

If Mind is not substance, form, and tangibility, God
is substanceless; for the substance of Spirit is divine
9 Mind.   Life is God, the only creator, and Life is immortal Mind, not matter.

Every indication of matter's constituting life is mortal,
12 the direct opposite of immortal Life, and infringes the
rights of Spirit.   Then, to conclude that Spirit constitutes or ever has constituted laws to that effect, is a mor-
15 tal error, a human conception opposed to the divine
government.   Mind and matter mingling in perpetual
warfare is a kingdom divided against itself, that shall be
18 brought to desolation.   The final destruction of this
false belief in matter will appear at the full revelation
of Spirit, — one God, and the brotherhood of man.
21 Organic life is an error of statement that Truth destroys.
The Science of Life needs only to be understood; its demonstration proves the correctness of my statements, and
24 brings blessings infinite.

*Why did God command, "Be fruitful, and multiply,
and replenish the earth," if all minds (men) have existed
27 from the beginning, and have had successive stages of
existence to the present time?*

Your question implies that Spirit, which first spirit-
30 ually created the universe, including man, created man

over again materially; and, by the aid of mankind, all
was later made which *He had made.* If the first record
is true, what evidence have you — apart from the evidence of that which you admit cannot discern spiritual
things — of any other creation? The creative "Us"
made all, and Mind was the creator. Man originated
not from dust, materially, but from Spirit, spiritually.
This work had been done; the true creation was finished,
and its spiritual Science is alluded to in the first chapter
of Genesis.

Jesus said of error, "That thou doest, do quickly."
By the law of opposites, after the truth of man had been
demonstrated, the postulate of error must appear. That
this addendum was untrue, is seen when Truth, God,
denounced it, and said: "I will greatly multiply thy
sorrow." "In the day that thou eatest thereof thou shalt
surely die." The opposite error said, "I am true," and
declared, "God doth know . . . that your eyes shall be
opened, and ye shall be as gods," creators. This was false;
and the Lord God never said it. This history of a falsity
must be told in the name of Truth, or it would have no
seeming. The Science of creation is the universe with man
created spiritually. The false sense and error of creation
is the sense of man and the universe created materially.

*Why does the record make man a creation of the sixth
and last day, if he was coexistent with God?*

In its genesis, the Science of creation is stated in mathematical order, beginning with the lowest form and ascending the scale of being up to man. But all that really is,
always was and forever is; for it existed in and of the Mind
that is God, wherein man is foremost.

1 *If one has died of consumption, and he has no remem-*
*brance of that disease or dream, does that disease have any*
3 *more power over him?*

Waking from a dream, one learns its *unreality;* then
it has no power over one. Waking from the dream of
6 death, proves to him who thought he died that it was a
dream, and that he did not die; then he learns that consumption did not kill him. When the belief in the power
9 of disease is destroyed, disease cannot return.

*How does Mrs. Eddy know that she has read and studied*
*correctly, if one must deny the evidences of the senses?*
12 *She had to use her eyes to read.*

Jesus said, "Having eyes, see ye not?" I read the inspired page through a higher than mortal sense. As
15 matter, the eye cannot see; and as mortal mind, it is a
belief that sees. I may read the Scriptures through a
belief of eyesight; but I must spiritually understand
18 them to interpret their Science.

*Does the theology of Christian Science aid its heal-*
*ing?*

21 Without its theology there is no mental science, no
order that proceeds from God. All Science is divine,
not human, in origin and demonstration. If God does
24 not govern the action of man, it is inharmonious: if He
does govern it, the action is Science. Take away the
theology of mental healing and you take away its science,
27 leaving it a human "mind-cure," nothing more nor less,
— even one human mind governing another; by which,
if you agree that God is Mind, you admit that there is

more than one government and God. Having no true 1
sense of the healing theology of Mind, you can neither
understand nor demonstrate its Science, and will prac- 3
tise your belief of it in the name of Truth. This is the
mortal "mind-cure" that produces the effect of mesmerism. It is using the power of human will, instead 6
of the divine power understood, as in Christian Science;
and without this Science there had better be no "mind-
cure," — in which the last state of patients is worse than 9
the first.

*Is it wrong to pray for the recovery of the sick?*

Not if we pray Scripturally, with the understanding 12
that God *has* given all things to those who love Him;
but pleading with infinite Love to love us, or to restore
health and harmony, and then to admit that it has been 15
lost under His government, is the prayer of doubt and
mortal belief that is unavailing in divine Science.

*Is not all argument mind over mind?* 18

The Scriptures refer to God as saying, "Come now, and
let us reason together." There is but one right Mind, and
that one should and does govern man. Any copartnership 21
with that Mind is impossible; and the only benefit in
speaking often one to another, arises from the success that
one individual has with another in leading his thoughts 24
away from the human mind or body, and guiding them
with Truth. That individual is the best healer who as-
serts himself the least, and thus becomes a transparency 27
for the divine Mind, who is the only physician; the divine
Mind is the scientific healer.

1 *How can you believe there is no sin, and that God does*
*not recognize any, when He sent His Son to save from*
3 *sin, and the Bible is addressed to sinners? How can you*
*believe there is no sickness, when Jesus came healing the*
*sick?*

6 To regard sin, disease, and death with less deference,
and only as the woeful unrealities of being, is the only
way to destroy them; Christian Science is proving this by
9 healing cases of disease and sin after all other means have
failed. The Nazarene Prophet could make the unreality
of both apparent in a moment.

12 *Does it not limit the power of Mind to deny the possi-*
*bility of communion with departed friends — dead only in*
*belief?*

15 Does it limit the power of Mind to say that addition
is not subtraction in mathematics? The Science of Mind
reveals the impossibility of two individual sleepers, in
18 different phases of thought, communicating, even if touching each other corporeally; or for one who sleeps to
communicate with another who is awake. Mind's possi-
21 bilities are not lessened by being confined and conformed
to the Science of being.

*If mortal mind and body are myths, what is the con-*
24 *nection between them and real identity, and why are there*
*as many identities as mortal bodies?*

Evil in the beginning claimed the power, wisdom, and
27 utility of good; and every creation or idea of Spirit has
its counterfeit in some matter belief. Every material belief hints the existence of spiritual reality; and if mortals
30 are instructed in spiritual things, it will be seen that ma-

terial belief, in all its manifestations, reversed, will be 1
found the type and representative of verities priceless,
eternal, and just at hand. 3

The education of the future will be instruction, in spiritual Science, against the material symbolic counterfeit
sciences. All the knowledge and vain strivings of mortal 6
mind, that lead to death, — even when aping the wisdom
and magnitude of immortal Mind, — will be swallowed
up by the reality and omnipotence of Truth over error, 9
and of Life over death.

*"Dear Mrs. Eddy:* — In the October *Journal* I read
the following: 'But the real man, who was created in the 12
image of God, does not commit sin.' *What then does sin?*
*What commits theft? Or who does murder?* For instance,
the man is held responsible for the crime; for I went once 15
to a place where a man was said to be 'hanged for murder' — and certainly I saw him, or his effigy, dangling
at the end of a rope. This 'man' was held responsible 18
for the 'sin.' "

*What sins?*

According to the Word, man is the image and likeness 21
of God. Does God's essential likeness sin, or dangle at
the end of a rope? If not, what does? A culprit, a sinner,
— anything but a man! Then, what is a sinner? A 24
mortal; but man is *immortal.*

Again: mortals are the embodiments (or bodies, if
you please) of error, not of Truth; of sickness, sin, and 27
death. Naming these His embodiment, can neither make
them so nor overthrow the logic that man is God's likeness. Mortals seem very material; man in the likeness 30

1 of Spirit is spiritual. Holding the *right* idea of man in my
mind, I can improve my own, and other people's individ-
3 uality, health, and morals; whereas, the opposite image
of man, a sinner, kept constantly in mind, can no more
improve health or morals, than holding in thought the
6 form of a boa-constrictor can aid an artist in painting a
landscape.

Man is seen only in the true likeness of his Maker.
9 Believing a lie veils the truth from our vision; even as
in mathematics, in summing up positive and negative
quantities, the negative quantity offsets an equal positive
12 quantity, making the aggregate positive, or true quantity,
by that much, less available.

*Why do Christian Scientists hold that their theology is*
15 *essential to heal the sick, when the mind-cure claims to heal*
*without it?*

The theology of Christian Science is Truth; opposed
18 to which is the error of sickness, sin, and death, that
Truth destroys.

A "mind-cure" is a matter-cure. An adherent to this
21 method honestly acknowledges this fact in her work
entitled "Mind-cure on a Material Basis." In that
work the author grapples with Christian Science, attempts
24 to solve its divine Principle by the rule of human mind,
fails, and ends in a parody on this Science which is amus-
ing to astute readers, — especially when she tells them
27 that she is practising this Science.

The theology of Christian Science is based on the action
of the divine Mind over the human mind and body;
30 whereas, "mind-cure" rests on the notion that the human
mind can cure its own disease, or that which it causes,

and the *sickness of matter,* — which is infidel in the one 1
case, and anomalous in the other. It was said of old by
Truth-traducers, that Jesus healed through Beelzebub; 3
but the claim that one erring mind cures another one was
at first gotten up to hinder his benign influence and to hide
his divine power. 6

Our Master understood that Life, Truth, Love are the
triune Principle of all pure theology; also, that this divine
trinity is one infinite remedy for the opposite triad, sick- 9
ness, sin, and death.

*If there is no sin, why did Jesus come to save sinners?*

If there is no reality in sickness, why does a Chris- 12
tian Scientist go to the bedside and address himself to
the healing of disease, on the basis of its unreality?
Jesus came to seek and to save such as believe in the 15
reality of the unreal; to save them from *this false belief;*
that they might lay hold of eternal Life, the great reality
that concerns man, and understand the final fact, — that 18
God is omnipotent and omnipresent; yea, "that the Lord
He is God; there is none else beside Him," as the Scriptures declare. 21

*If Christ was God, why did Jesus cry out, "My God,
why hast Thou forsaken me?"*

Even as the struggling heart, reaching toward a higher 24
goal, appeals to its hope and faith, Why failest thou
me? Jesus as the son of man was human: Christ as
the Son of God was divine. This divinity was reaching 27
humanity through the crucifixion of the human, — that
momentous demonstration of God, in which Spirit proved
its supremacy over matter. Jesus assumed for mortals the 30

1 weakness of flesh, that Spirit might be found "All-in-all."
Hence, the human cry which voiced that struggle;
3 thence, the way he made for mortals' escape. Our
Master bore the cross to show his power over death;
then relinquished his earth-task of teaching and dem-
6 onstrating the nothingness of sickness, sin, and death,
and rose to his native estate, man's indestructible eternal
life in God.

9 *What can prospective students of the College take for*
*preliminary studies? Do you regard the study of litera-*
*ture and languages as objectionable?*

12 Persons contemplating a course at the Massachusetts
Metaphysical College, can prepare for it through no
books except the Bible, and "Science and Health with
15 Key to the Scriptures." Man-made theories are narrow, else extravagant, and are always materialistic.
The ethics which guide thought spiritually must bene-
18 fit every one; for the only philosophy and religion that
afford instruction are those which deal with facts and
resist speculative opinions and fables.

21 Works on science are profitable; for science is not
human. It is spiritual, and not material. Literature
and languages, to a limited extent, are aids to a student
24 of the Bible and of Christian Science.

*Is it possible to know why we are put into this condition*
*of mortality?*

27 It is quite as possible to know wherefore man is thus
conditioned, as to be certain that he *is* in a state of
mortality. The only evidence of the existence of a mor-
30 tal man, or of a material state and universe, is gathered

from the five personal senses. This delusive evidence, 1
Science has dethroned by repeated proofs of its falsity.

We have no more proof of human discord, — sin, 3
sickness, disease, or death, — than we have that the
earth's surface is flat, and her motions imaginary. If
man's *ipse dixit* as to the stellar system is correct, this 6
is because Science is true, and the evidence of the senses
is false. Then why not submit to the affirmations of
Science concerning the greater subject of human weal 9
and woe? Every question between Truth and error,
Science must and will decide. Left to the decision of
Science, your query concerns a negative which the posi- 12
tive Truth destroys; for God's universe and man are
immortal. We must not consider the false side of existence in order to gain the true solution of Life and its 15
great realities.

*Have you changed your instructions as to the right way*
*of treating disease?* 18

I have not; and this important fact must be, and already is, apprehended by those who understand my instructions on this question. Christian Science demands 21
both law and gospel, in order to demonstrate healing,
and I have taught them both in its demonstration, and
with signs following. They are a unit in restoring the 24
equipoise of mind and body, and balancing man's account with his Maker. The sequence proves that strict
adherence to one is inadequate to compensate for the 27
absence of the other, since both constitute the divine law
of healing.

The Jewish religion demands that "whoso sheddeth 30
man's blood, by man shall his blood be shed." But this

1 law is not infallible in wisdom; and obedience thereto may be found faulty, since false testimony or mistaken
3 evidence may cause the innocent to suffer for the guilty. Hence the gospel that fulfils the law in righteousness, the genius whereof is displayed in the surprising wisdom
6 of these words of the New Testament: "Whatsoever a man soweth, that shall he also reap." No possible injustice lurks in this mandate, and no human mis-
9 judgment can pervert it; for the offender alone suffers, and always according to divine decree. This sacred, solid precept is verified in all directions in Mind-
12 healing, and is supported in the Scripture by parallel proof.

The law and gospel of Truth and Love teach, through
15 divine Science, that sin is identical with suffering, and that suffering is the lighter affliction. To reach the summit of Science, whence to discern God's perfect ways
18 and means, the material sense must be controlled by the higher spiritual sense, and Truth be enthroned, while "we look not at the things which are seen, but at
21 the things which are not seen."

Cynical critics misjudge my meaning as to the scientific treatment of the sick. Disease that is superin-
24 duced by sin is not healed like the more physical ailment. The beginner in sin-healing must know this, or he never can reach the Science of Mind-healing, and
27 so "overcome evil with good." Error in premise is met with error in practice; yea, it is "the blind leading the blind." Ignorance of the cause of disease can neither
30 remove that cause nor its effect.

I endeavor to accommodate my instructions to the present capability of the learner, and to support the

liberated thought until its altitude reaches beyond the 1
mere alphabet of Mind-healing. Above physical wants,
lie the higher claims of the law and gospel of healing. 3
First is the law, which saith: —

"Thou shalt not commit adultery;" in other words,
thou shalt not adulterate Life, Truth, or Love, — men- 6
tally, morally, or physically. "Thou shalt not steal;"
that is, thou shalt not rob man of money, which is but
trash, compared with his rights of mind and character. 9
"Thou shalt not kill;" that is, thou shalt not strike at the
eternal sense of Life with a malicious aim, but shalt
know that by doing thus thine own sense of Life shall be 12
forfeited. "Thou shalt not bear false witness;" that is,
thou shalt not utter a lie, either mentally or audibly, nor
cause it to be thought. Obedience to these command- 15
ments is indispensable to health, happiness, and length
of days.

The gospel of healing demonstrates the law of Love. 18
Justice uncovers sin of every sort; and mercy demands
that if you see the danger menacing others, you shall,
*Deo volente,* inform them thereof. Only thus is the right 21
practice of Mind-healing achieved, and the wrong practice discerned, disarmed, and destroyed.

*Do you believe in translation?* 24

If your question refers to language, whereby one expresses the sense of words in one language by equiva-
lent words in another, I do. If you refer to the removal 27
of a person to heaven, without his subjection to death,
I modify my affirmative answer. I believe in this
removal being possible after all the footsteps requisite 30
have been taken up to the very throne, up to the

spiritual sense and fact of divine substance, intelligence, Life, and Love. This translation is not the work of mo-
3 ments; it requires both time and eternity. It means more than mere disappearance to the human sense; it must include also man's changed appearance and diviner form
6 visible to those beholding him here.

*The Rev. —— said in a sermon: A true Christian would protest against metaphysical healing being called*
9 *Christian Science. He also maintained that pain and disease are not illusions but realities; and that it is not Christian to believe they are illusions. Is this so?*

12 It is unchristian to believe that pain and sickness are anything *but* illusions. My proof of this is, that the penalty for believing in their reality is the very pain and
15 disease. Jesus cast out a devil, and the dumb spake; hence it is right to know that the works of Satan are the illusion and error which Truth casts out.

18 Does the gentleman above mentioned know the meaning of divine metaphysics, or of metaphysical theology?

21 According to Webster, metaphysics is defined thus: "The science of the conceptions and relations which are necessary to thought and knowledge; science of the
24 mind." Worcester defines it as "the philosophy of mind, as distinguished from that of matter; a science of which the object is to explain the principles and causes of
27 all things existing." Brande calls metaphysics "the science which regards the ultimate grounds of being, as distinguished from its phenomenal modifications." "A
30 speculative science, which soars beyond the bounds of experience," is a further definition.

Divine metaphysics is that which treats of the existence of God, His essence, relations, and attributes. A sneer at metaphysics is a scoff at Deity; at His goodness, mercy, and might.

Christian Science is the unfolding of true metaphysics; that is, of Mind, or God, and His attributes. Science rests on Principle and demonstration. The Principle of Christian Science is divine. Its rule is, that man shall utilize the divine power.

In Genesis i. 26, we read: "Let us make man in our image, after our likeness: and let them have dominion over the fish of the sea, and over the fowl of the air."

I was once called to visit a sick man to whom the regular physicians had given three doses of Croton oil, and then had left him to die. Upon my arrival I found him barely alive, and in terrible agony. In one hour he was well, and the next day he attended to his business. I removed the stoppage, healed him of enteritis, and neutralized the bad effects of the poisonous oil. His physicians had failed even to move his bowels, — though the wonder was, with the means used in their effort to accomplish this result, that they had not quite killed him. According to their diagnosis, the exciting cause of the inflammation and stoppage was — eating smoked herring. The man is living yet; and I will send his address to any one who may wish to apply to him for information about his case.

Now comes the question: Had that sick man dominion over the fish in his stomach?

His want of control over "the fish of the sea" must

1 have been an illusion, or else the Scriptures misstate man's power. That the Bible is true I believe, not 3 only, but I *demonstrated* its truth when I exercised my power over the fish, cast out the sick man's illusion, and healed him. Thus it was shown that the 6 healing action of Mind upon the body has its only explanation in divine metaphysics. As a man "thinketh in his heart, so is he." When the mortal thought, or be-9 lief, was removed, the man was well.

*What did Jesus mean when he said to the dying thief, "To-day shalt thou be with me in paradise"?*

12 Paradisaical rest from physical agony would come to the criminal, if the dream of dying should startle him from the dream of suffering. The paradise of Spirit 15 would come to Jesus, in a spiritual sense of Life and power. Christ Jesus lived and reappeared. He was too good to die; for goodness is immortal. The thief was 18 not equal to the demands of the hour; but sin was destroying itself, and had already begun to die, — as the poor thief's prayer for help indicated. The dy-21 ing malefactor and our Lord were inevitably separated through Mind. The thief's body, as matter, must dissolve into its native nothingness; whereas the 24 body of the holy Spirit of Jesus was eternal. That day the thief would be with Jesus only in a finite and material sense of relief; while our Lord would 27 soon be rising to the supremacy of Spirit, working out, even in the silent tomb, those wonderful demonstrations of divine power, in which none could equal his 30 glory.

*Is it right for me to treat others, when I am not entirely* 1
*well myself?*

The late John B. Gough is said to have suffered from 3
an appetite for alcoholic drink until his death; yet he
saved many a drunkard from this fatal appetite. Paul
had a thorn in the flesh: one writer thinks that he was 6
troubled with rheumatism, and another that he had sore
eyes; but this is certain, that he healed others who were
sick. It is unquestionably right to do right; and heal- 9
ing the sick is a very right thing to do.

*Does Christian Science set aside the law of transmission,*
*prenatal desires, and good or bad influences on the unborn* 12
*child?*

Science never averts law, but supports it. All actual
causation must interpret omnipotence, the all-knowing 15
Mind. Law brings out Truth, not error; unfolds divine
Principle, — but neither human hypothesis nor matter.
Errors are based on a mortal or material formation; they 18
are suppositional modes, not the factors of divine presence
and power.

Whatever is humanly conceived is a departure from 21
divine law; hence its mythical origin and certain end.
According to the Scriptures, — St. Paul declares astutely,
"For of Him, and through Him, and to Him, are all 24
things," — man is incapable of originating: nothing can
be formed apart from God, good, the all-knowing Mind.
What seems to be of human origin is the counterfeit 27
of the divine, — even human concepts, mortal shadows
flitting across the dial of time.

Whatever is real is right and eternal; hence the im- 30
mutable and just law of Science, that God is good only,
4

1 and can transmit to man and the universe nothing evil,
or unlike Himself.  For the innocent babe to be born a
3 lifelong sufferer because of his parents' mistakes or sins,
were sore injustice.  Science sets aside man as a creator,
and unfolds the eternal harmonies of the only living and
6 true origin, God.

According to the beliefs of the flesh, both good and
bad traits of the parents are transmitted to their help-
9 less offspring, and God is supposed to impart to man
this fatal power.  It is cause for rejoicing that this belief
is as false as it is remorseless.  The immutable Word
12 saith, through the prophet Ezekiel, "What mean ye, that
ye use this proverb concerning the land of Israel, saying,
The fathers have eaten sour grapes, and the children's
15 teeth are set on edge?  As I live, saith the Lord God,
ye shall not have occasion any more to use this proverb
in Israel."

18 *Are material things real when they are harmonious, and
do they disappear only to the natural sense?  Does this
Scripture, "Your heavenly Father knoweth that ye have
21 need of all these things," imply that Spirit takes note of
matter?*

The Science of Mind, as well as the material uni-
24 verse, shows that nothing which is material is in
perpetual harmony.  Matter is manifest mortal mind,
and it exists only to material sense.  Real sensation
27 is not material; it is, and must be, mental: and Mind
is not mortal, it is immortal.  Being is God, infinite
Spirit; therefore it cannot cognize aught material, or
30 outside of infinity.

The Scriptural passage quoted affords no evidence of

the reality of matter, or that God is conscious of it. 1
The so-called material body is said to suffer, but this
supposition is proven erroneous when Mind casts out 3
the suffering. The Scripture saith, "Whom the Lord
loveth He chasteneth;" and again, "He doth not
afflict willingly." Interpreted materially, these pas- 6
sages conflict; they mingle the testimony of immortal Science with mortal sense; but once discern their
spiritual meaning, and it separates the false sense from 9
the true, and establishes the reality of what is spiritual,
and the unreality of materiality.

Law is never material: it is always mental and moral, 12
and a commandment to the wise. The foolish disobey
moral law, and are punished. Human wisdom therefore
can get no farther than to say, He knoweth that we have 15
need of experience. Belief fulfils the conditions of a belief, and these conditions destroy the belief. Hence the
verdict of experience: We have need of *these* things; we 18
have need to know that the so-called pleasures and pains
of matter — yea, that all subjective states of false sensation — are *unreal*. 21

*"And Jesus said unto them, Verily I say unto you,*
*That ye which have followed me, in the regeneration when*
*the Son of man shall sit in the throne of his glory,* 24
*ye also shall sit upon twelve thrones, judging the*
*twelve tribes of Israel."* (Matt. xix. 28.) *What is meant*
*by regeneration?* 27

It is the appearing of divine law to human understanding; the spiritualization that comes from spiritual
sense in contradistinction to the testimony of the so- 30
called material senses. The phenomena of Spirit in

1 Christian Science, and the divine correspondence of
noumenon and phenomenon understood, are here signi-
3 fied. This new-born sense subdues not only the false
sense of generation, but the human will, and the unnatural enmity of mortal man toward God. It quickly
6 imparts a new apprehension of the true basis of being,
and the spiritual foundation for the affections which en-
throne the Son of man in the glory of his Father; and
9 judges, through the stern mandate of Science, all human
systems of etiology and teleology.

*If God does not recognize matter, how did Jesus, who was*
12 *"the way, the truth, and the life," cognize it?*

Christ Jesus' sense of matter was the opposite of that
which mortals entertain: his nativity was a spiritual and
15 immortal sense of the ideal world. His earthly mission
was to translate substance into its original meaning,
Mind. He walked upon the waves; he turned the water
18 into wine; he healed the sick and the sinner; he raised
the dead, and rolled away the stone from the door of his
own tomb. His demonstration of Spirit virtually van-
21 quished matter and its supposed laws. Walking the
wave, he proved the fallacy of the theory that matter is
substance; healing through Mind, he removed any sup-
24 position that matter is intelligent, or can recognize or
express pain and pleasure. His triumph over the grave
was an everlasting victory for Life; it demonstrated the
27 lifelessness of matter, and the power and permanence
of Spirit. He met and conquered the resistance of the
world.

30    If you will admit, with me, that matter is neither
substance, intelligence, nor Life, you may have all that

is left of it;  and you will have touched the hem of the 1
garment of Jesus' idea of matter.  Christ was "the way;"
since Life and Truth were the way that gave us, through 3
a human person, a spiritual revelation of man's possible
earthly development.

*Why do you insist that there is but one Soul, and that* 6
*Soul is not in the body?*

*First:* I urge this fundamental fact and grand verity
of Christian Science, because it includes a rule that must 9
be understood, or it is impossible to demonstrate the Science.  Soul is a synonym of Spirit, and God is Spirit.
There is but one God, and the infinite is not within the 12
finite;  hence Soul is one, and is God;  and God is not in
matter or the mortal body.

*Second:* Because Soul is a term for Deity, and this 15
term should seldom be employed except where the word
*God* can be used and make complete sense.  The word
*Soul* may sometimes be used metaphorically;  but if this 18
term is warped to signify human quality, a substitution
of *sense* for *soul* clears the meaning, and assists one to
understand Christian Science.  Mary's exclamation, 21
"My *soul* doth magnify the Lord," is rendered in Science, "My *spiritual sense* doth magnify the Lord;"
for the name of Deity used in that place does not bring 24
out the meaning of the passage.  It was evidently an
illuminated sense through which she discovered the
spiritual origin of man.  "The soul that sinneth, it shall 27
die," means, that mortal man (*alias* material sense) that
sinneth, shall die;  and the commonly accepted view is
that *soul* is deathless.  Soul is the divine Mind, — for 30
Soul cannot be formed or brought forth by human

1 thought, — and must proceed from God; hence it must
be sinless, and destitute of self-created or derived capacity
3 to sin.

*Third:* Jesus said, "If a man keep my saying, he
shall never see death." This statement of our Master
6 is true, and remains to be demonstrated; for it is the
ultimatum of Christian Science; but this immortal saying
can never be tested or proven true upon a false premise,
9 such as the mortal belief that soul is in body, and life
and intelligence are in matter. That doctrine is not
theism, but pantheism. According to human belief the
12 bodies of mortals are mortal, but they contain immortal
souls! hence these bodies must die for these souls to
escape and be immortal. The theory that death must
15 occur, to set a human soul free from its environments,
is rendered void by Jesus' divine declaration, who spake
as never man spake, — and no man can rationally reject
18 his authority on this subject and accept it on other topics
less important.

Now, exchange the term *soul* for *sense* whenever this
21 word means the so-called soul in the body, and you will
find the right meaning indicated. The misnamed human
soul is material sense, which sinneth and shall die; for
24 it is an error or false sense of mentality in matter, and
matter has no sense. You will admit that Soul is the
Life of man. Now if Soul sinned, it would die; for "the
27 wages of sin is death." The Scripture saith, "When
Christ, who is our life, shall appear, then shall ye also
appear with him in glory." The Science of Soul, Spirit,
30 involves this appearing, and is essential to the fulfilment
of this glorious prophecy of the master Metaphysician,
who overcame the last enemy, death.

*Did the salvation of the eunuch depend merely on his* 1
*believing that Jesus Christ was the Son of God?*

It did; but this believing was more than faith in the 3
fact that Jesus was the Messiah.  Here the verb *believe*
took its original meaning, namely, to be *firm,* — yea, to
*understand* those great truths asserted of the Messiah: 6
it meant to discern and consent to that infinite demand
made upon the eunuch in those few words of the apostle.
Philip's requirement was, that he should not only ac- 9
knowledge the incarnation, — God made manifest through
man, — but even the eternal unity of man and God, as
the divine Principle and spiritual idea; which is the in- 12
dissoluble bond of union, the power and presence, in
divine Science, of Life, Truth, and Love, to support their
ideal man.  This is the Father's great Love that He 15
hath bestowed upon us, and it holds man in endless
Life and one eternal round of harmonious being.  It
guides him by Truth that knows no error, and with 18
supersensual, impartial, and unquenchable Love.  To
*believe* is to *be firm.*  In adopting all this vast idea of
Christ Jesus, the eunuch was to *know* in whom he be- 21
lieved.  To *believe* thus was to enter the spiritual sanctuary
of Truth, and there learn, in divine Science, somewhat
of the All-Father-Mother God.  It was to understand 24
God and man: it was sternly to rebuke the mortal
belief that man has fallen away from his first estate; that
man, made in God's own likeness, and reflecting Truth, 27
could fall into mortal error; or, that man is the father
of man.  It was to enter unshod the Holy of Holies, where
the miracle of grace appears, and where the miracles of 30
Jesus had their birth, — healing the sick, casting out
evils, and resurrecting the human *sense* to the belief

1 that Life, God, is not buried in matter. This is the spiritual dawn of the Messiah, and the overture of the
3 angels. This is when God is made manifest in the
flesh, and thus it destroys all sense of sin, sickness, and
death, — when the brightness of His glory encompasseth
6 all being.

*Can Christian Science Mind-healing be taught to those
who are absent?*

9 The Science of Mind-healing can no more be taught
thus, than can science in any other direction. I know
not how to teach either Euclid or the Science of Mind
12 silently; and never dreamed that either of these partook
of the nature of occultism, magic, alchemy, or necromancy. These "ways that are vain" are the inventions
15 of animal magnetism, which would deceive, if possible,
the very elect. We will charitably hope, however, that
some people employ the *et cetera* of ignorance and self-
18 conceit unconsciously, in their witless ventilation of false
statements and claims. Misguiding the public mind and
taking its money in exchange for this abuse, has become
21 too common: we will hope it is the froth of error passing
off; and that Christian Science will some time appear all
the clearer for the purification of the public thought con-
24 cerning it.

*Has man fallen from a state of perfection?*

If God is the Principle of man (and He is), man is the
27 idea of God; and this idea cannot fail to express the exact nature of its Principle, — any more than goodness,
to present the quality of good. Human hypotheses are
30 always human vagaries, formulated views antagonistic

to the divine order and the nature of Deity. All these 1
mortal beliefs will be purged and dissolved in the crucible of Truth, and the places once knowing them will 3
know them no more forever, having been swept clean
by the winds of history. The grand verities of Science
will sift the chaff from the wheat, until it is clear to hu- 6
man comprehension that man was, and is, God's perfect
likeness, that reflects all whereby we can know God. In
Him we live, move, and have being. Man's origin and 9
existence being in Him, man is the ultimatum of perfection, and by no means the medium of imperfection.
Immortal man is the eternal idea of Truth, that cannot 12
lapse into a mortal belief or error concerning himself
and his origin: he cannot get out of the focal distance of
infinity. If God is upright and eternal, man as His like- 15
ness is erect in goodness and perpetual in Life, Truth,
and Love. If the great cause is perfect, its effect is perfect also; and cause and effect in Science are immutable 18
and immortal. A mortal who is sinning, sick, and dying,
is not immortal man; and never was, and never can be,
God's image and likeness, the true ideal of immortal 21
man's divine Principle. The spiritual man is that perfect and unfallen likeness, coexistent and coeternal with
God. "As in Adam all die, even so in Christ shall all be 24
made alive."

*What course should Christian Scientists take in regard
to aiding persons brought before the courts for violation of 27
medical statutes?*

Beware of joining any medical league which in any
way obligates you to assist — because they chance to be 30
under arrest — vendors of patent pills, mesmerists,

1 occultists, sellers of impure literature, and authors of
spurious works on mental healing. By rendering error
3 such a service, you lose much more than can be gained
by mere unity on the single issue of opposition to unjust
medical laws.

6    A league which obligates its members to give money
and influence in support and defense of medical charlatans in general, and possibly to aid individual rights
9 in a wrong direction — which Christian Science eschews
— should be avoided. Anybody and everybody, who
will fight the medical faculty, can join this league. It is
12 better to be friendly with cultured and conscientious
medical men, who leave Christian Science to rise or fall
on its own merit or demerit, than to affiliate with a wrong
15 class of people.

Unconstitutional and unjust coercive legislation and
laws, infringing individual rights, must be "of few days,
18 and full of trouble." The *vox populi*, through the providence of God, promotes and impels all true reform; and,
at the best time, will redress wrongs and rectify injus-
21 tice. Tyranny can thrive but feebly under our Government. God reigns, and will "turn and overturn" until
right is found supreme.

24    In a certain sense, we should commiserate the lot of
regular doctors, who, in successive generations for centuries, have planted and sown and reaped in the fields
27 of what they deem pathology, hygiene, and therapeutics,
but are now elbowed by a new school of practitioners,
outdoing the healing of the old. The old will not patronize
30 the new school, at least not until it shall come to understand the medical system of the new.

Christian Science Mind-healing rests demonstrably on

the broad and sure foundation of Science; and this is  1
not the basis of *materia medica,* as some of the most skilful and scholarly physicians openly admit.  3

To prevent all unpleasant and unchristian action — as
we drift, by right of God's dear love, into more spiritual
lines of life — let each society of practitioners, the matter-  6
physicians and the metaphysicians, agree to disagree, and
then patiently wait on God to decide, as surely He will,
which is the true system of medicine.  9

*Do we not see in the commonly accepted teachings of the
day, the Christ-idea mingled with the teachings of John
the Baptist? or, rather, Are not the last eighteen centuries*  12
*but the footsteps of Truth being baptized of John, and com-
ing up straightway out of the ceremonial (or ritualistic)
waters to receive the benediction of an honored Father, and*  15
*afterwards to go up into the wilderness, in order to over-
come mortal sense, before it shall go forth into all the cities
and towns of Judea, or see many of the people from beyond*  18
*Jordan? Now, if all this be a fair or correct view of this
question, why does not John hear this voice, or see the
dove, — or has not Truth yet reached the shore?*  21

Every individual character, like the individual John
the Baptist, at some date must cry in the desert of
earthly joy; and his voice be heard divinely and  24
humanly. In the desolation of human understanding,
divine Love hears and answers the human call for help;
and the voice of Truth utters the divine verities of being  27
which deliver mortals out of the depths of ignorance
and vice. This *is* the Father's benediction. It gives
lessons to human life, guides the understanding, peoples  30

1 the mind with spiritual ideas, reconstructs the Judean
religion, and reveals God and man as the Principle and
3 idea of all good.

Understanding this fact in Christian Science, brings
the peace symbolized by a dove; and this peace floweth
6 as a river into a shoreless eternity. He who knew the
foretelling Truth, beheld the forthcoming Truth, as it
came up out of the baptism of Spirit, to enlighten and
9 redeem mortals. Such Christians as John cognize the
symbols of God, reach the sure foundations of time, stand
upon the shore of eternity, and grasp and gather — in all
12 glory — what eye hath not seen.

*Is there infinite progression with man after the destruction of mortal mind?*

15 Man is the offspring and idea of the Supreme Being,
whose law is perfect and infinite. In obedience to this
law, man is forever unfolding the endless beatitudes of
18 Being; for he is the image and likeness of infinite Life,
Truth, and Love.

Infinite progression is concrete being, which finite
21 mortals see and comprehend only as abstract glory. As
mortal mind, or the material sense of life, is put off,
the spiritual sense and Science of being is brought to
24 light.

Mortal mind is a myth; the one Mind is immortal.
A mythical or mortal sense of existence is consumed
27 as a moth, in the treacherous glare of its own flame —
the errors which devour it. Immortal Mind is God,
immortal good; in whom the Scripture saith "we live,
30 and move, and have our being." This Mind, then, is not
subject to growth, change, or diminution, but is the divine

# Questions and Answers 83

intelligence, or Principle, of all real being; holding 1
man forever in the rhythmic round of unfolding bliss,
as a living witness to and perpetual idea of inexhaustible 3
good.

*In your book, Science and Health,[1] page* 181, *you
say:* "*Every sin is the author of itself, and every* 6
*invalid the cause of his own sufferings.*" *On page*
182 *you say:* "*Sickness is a growth of illusion, springing from a seed of thought, — either your own thought* 9
*or another's.*" *Will you please explain this seeming
contradiction?*

No person can accept another's belief, except it be 12
with the consent of his own belief. If the error which
knocks at the door of your own thought originated in
another's mind, you are a free moral agent to reject or 15
to accept this error; hence, you are the arbiter of your
own fate, and sin is the author of sin. In the words
of our Master, you are "a liar, and the father of it 18
[the lie]."

*Why did Jesus call himself* "*the Son of man*"?

In the life of our Lord, meekness was as conspicuous 21
as might. In John xvii. he declared his sonship with
God: "These words spake Jesus, and lifted up his
eyes to heaven, and said, Father, the hour is come; 24
glorify Thy Son, that Thy Son also may glorify Thee."
The hour had come for the avowal of this great truth,
and for the proof of his eternal Life and sonship. Jesus' 27

---

[1] Quoted from the sixteenth edition.

1 wisdom ofttimes was shown by his forbearing to speak, as well as by speaking, the whole truth. Haply he waited 3 for a preparation of the human heart to receive startling announcements. This wisdom, which characterized his sayings, did not prophesy his death, and thereby 6 hasten or permit it.

The disciples and prophets thrust disputed points on minds unprepared for them. This cost them their lives, 9 and the world's temporary esteem; but the prophecies were fulfilled, and their motives were rewarded by growth and more spiritual understanding, which dawns 12 by degrees on mortals. The spiritual Christ was infallible; Jesus, as material manhood, was not Christ. The "man of sorrows" knew that the man of joys, his spiritual 15 self, or Christ, was the Son of God; and that the mortal mind, not the immortal Mind, suffered. The human manifestation of the Son of God was called the Son of 18 man, or Mary's son.

*Please explain Paul's meaning in the text, "For to me to live is Christ, and to die is gain."*

21 The Science of Life, overshadowing Paul's sense of life in matter, so far extinguished the latter as forever to quench his love for it. The discipline of the flesh is 24 designed to turn one, like a weary traveller, to the home of Love. To lose error thus, is to live in Christ, Truth. A true sense of the falsity of material joys and sorrows, 27 pleasures and pains, takes them away, and teaches Life's lessons aright. The transition from our lower sense of Life to a new and higher sense thereof, even though it be 30 through the door named death, yields a clearer and nearer sense of Life to those who have utilized the present,

and are ripe for the harvest-home. To the battle- 1
worn and weary Christian hero, Life eternal brings
blessings. 3

*Is a Christian Scientist ever sick, and has he who is
sick been regenerated?*

The Christian Scientist learns spiritually all that he 6
knows of Life, and demonstrates what he understands.
God is recognized as the divine Principle of his being,
and of every thought and act leading to good. His pur- 9
pose must be right, though his power is temporarily limited. Perfection, the goal of existence, is not won in a
moment; and regeneration leading thereto is gradual, 12
for it culminates in the fulfilment of this divine rule in
Science: "Be ye therefore perfect, even as your Father
which is in heaven is perfect." 15

The last degree of regeneration rises into the rest of
perpetual, spiritual, individual existence. The first
feeble flutterings of mortals Christward are infantile 18
and more or less imperfect. The new-born Christian
Scientist must mature, and work out his own salvation.
Spirit and flesh antagonize. Temptation, that mist of 21
mortal mind which seems to be matter and the environment of mortals, suggests pleasure and pain in matter;
and, so long as this temptation lasts, the warfare is not 24
ended and the mortal is not regenerated. The pleasures — more than the pains — of sense, retard regeneration; for pain compels human consciousness to escape 27
from sense into the immortality and harmony of Soul.
Disease in error, more than ease in it, tends to destroy
error: the sick often are thereby led to Christ, Truth, 30
and to learn their way out of both sickness and sin.

1 The material and physical are imperfect. The individual and spiritual are perfect; these have no fleshly
3 nature. This final degree of regeneration is saving, and the Christian will, must, attain it; but it doth not yet appear. Until this be attained, the Christian Scientist
6 must continue to strive with sickness, sin, and death — though in lessening degrees — and manifest growth at every experience.

9 *Is it correct to say of material objects, that they are nothing and exist only in imagination?*

*Nothing* and *something* are words which need correct
12 definition. They either mean formations of indefinite and vague human opinions, or scientific classifications of the unreal and the real. My sense of the beauty of
15 the universe is, that beauty typifies holiness, and is something to be desired. Earth is more spiritually beautiful to my gaze now than when it was more earthly to the
18 eyes of Eve. The pleasant sensations of human belief, of form and color, must be spiritualized, until we gain the glorified sense of substance as in the new heaven and
21 earth, the harmony of body and Mind.

Even the human conception of beauty, grandeur, and utility is something that defies a sneer. It is more than
24 imagination. It is next to divine beauty and the grandeur of Spirit. It lives with our earth-life, and is the subjective state of high thoughts. The atmos-
27 phere of mortal mind constitutes our mortal environment. What mortals hear, see, feel, taste, smell, constitutes their present earth and heaven: but we must
30 grow out of even this pleasing thraldom, and find wings to reach the glory of supersensible Life; then we shall

soar above, as the bird in the clear ether of the blue tem- 1
poral sky.

To take all earth's beauty into one gulp of vacuity 3
and label beauty nothing, is ignorantly to caricature
God's creation, which is unjust to human sense and
to the divine realism. In our immature sense of spirit- 6
ual things, let us say of the beauties of the sensuous
universe: "I love your promise; and shall know, some
time, the spiritual reality and substance of form, light, 9
and color, of what I now through you discern dimly; and
knowing this, I shall be satisfied. Matter is a frail conception of mortal mind; and mortal mind is a poorer 12
representative of the beauty, grandeur, and glory of the
immortal Mind."

*Please inform us, through your Journal, if you sent* 15
*Mrs. —— to ——. She said that you sent her there to look
after the students; and also, that no one there was working
in Science, — which is certainly a mistake.* 18

I never commission any one to teach students of mine.
After class teaching, he does best in the investigation of
Christian Science who is most reliant on himself and 21
God. My students are taught the divine Principle and
rules of the Science of Mind-healing. What they need
thereafter is to study thoroughly the Scriptures and 24
"Science and Health with Key to the Scriptures." To
watch and pray, to be honest, earnest, loving, and truth-
ful, is indispensable to the demonstration of the truth 27
they have been taught.

If they are haunted by obsequious helpers, who, un-
called for, imagine they can help anybody and steady 30
God's altar — this interference prolongs the struggle

1 and tends to blight the fruits of my students.  A faithful student may even sometimes feel the need of
3 physical help, and occasionally receive it from others;
but the less this is required, the better it is for that
student.

6 *Please give us, through your Journal, the name of
the author of that genuine critique in the September
number, "What Quibus Thinks."*

9    I am pleased to inform this inquirer, that the author
of the article in question is a Boston gentleman whose
thought is appreciated by many liberals.  Patience, ob-
12 servation, intellectual culture, reading, writing, exten-
sive travel, and twenty years in the pulpit, have equipped
him as a critic who knows whereof he speaks.  His allu-
15 sion to Christian Science in the following paragraph,
glows in the shadow of darkling criticism like a midnight sun.  Its manly honesty follows like a benediction
18 after prayer, and closes the task of talking to deaf ears
and dull debaters.

"We have always insisted that this Science is natural,
21 spiritually natural;  that Jesus was the highest type of
real nature;  that Christian healing is supernatural, or
extra-natural, only to those who do not enter into its
24 sublimity or understand its modes — as imported ice
was miraculous to the equatorial African, who had never
seen water freeze."

27 *Is it right for a Scientist to treat with a doctor?*

This depends upon what kind of a doctor it is.  Mind-
healing, and healing with drugs, are opposite modes of
30 medicine.  As a rule, drop one of these doctors when you

employ the other. The Scripture saith, "No man can serve two masters;" and, "Every kingdom divided against itself is brought to desolation." 3

*If Scientists are called upon to care for a member of the family, or a friend in sickness, who is employing a regular physician, would it be right to treat this patient 6 at all; and ought the patient to follow the doctor's directions?*

When patients are under material medical treatment, 9 it is advisable in most cases that Scientists do not treat them, or interfere with *materia medica.* If the patient is in peril, and you save him or alleviate his sufferings, 12 although the medical attendant and friends have no faith in your method, it is humane, and not unchristian, to do him all the good you can; but your good will gen- 15 erally "be evil spoken of." The hazard of casting "pearls before swine" caused our Master to refuse help to some who sought his aid; and he left this precaution for 18 others.

*If mortal man is unreal, how can he be saved, and why does he need to be saved? I ask for information, not for 21 controversy, for I am a seeker after Truth.*

You will find the proper answer to this question in my published works. Man is immortal. Mortal man 24 is a false concept that is not spared or prolonged by being saved from itself, from whatever is false. This salvation means: saved from error, or error overcome. Im- 27 mortal man, in God's likeness, is safe in divine Science. Mortal man is saved on this divine Principle, if he will only avail himself of the efficacy of Truth, and recog- 30

1 nize his Saviour. He must know that God is omnipotent; hence, that sin is impotent. He must know that
3 the power of sin is the pleasure in sin. Take away this pleasure, and you remove all reality from its power. Jesus demonstrated sin and death to be powerless. This
6 practical Truth saves from sin, and will save all who understand it.

*Is it wrong for a wife to have a husband treated for*
9 *sin, when she knows he is sinning, or for drinking and smoking?*

It is always right to act rightly; but sometimes, under
12 circumstances exceptional, it is inexpedient to attack evil. This rule is forever golden: "As ye would that men should do to you, do ye even so to them." Do you
15 desire to be freed from sin? Then help others to be free; but in your measures, obey the Scriptures, "Be ye wise as serpents." Break the yoke of bondage in every wise
18 way. First, be sure that your means for doing good are equal to your motives; then judge them by their fruits.

21 *If not ordained, shall the pastor of the Church of Christ, Scientist, administer the communion, — and shall members of a church not organized receive the*
24 *communion?*

Our great Master administered to his disciples the Passover, or last supper, without this prerogative being
27 conferred by a visible organization and ordained priesthood. His spiritually prepared breakfast, after his resurrection, and after his disciples had left their nets
30 to follow him, is the spiritual communion which Chris-

tian Scientists celebrate in commemoration of the Christ. 1
This ordinance is significant as a type of the true worship,
and it should be observed at present in our churches. 3

It is not indispensable to organize materially Christ's
church. It is not absolutely necessary to ordain pastors and to dedicate churches; but if this be done, 6
let it be in concession to the period, and not as a perpetual or indispensable ceremonial of the church. If
our church is organized, it is to meet the demand, 9
"Suffer it to be so now." The real Christian compact
is love for one another. This bond is wholly spiritual
and inviolate. 12

It is imperative, at all times and under every circumstance, to perpetuate no ceremonials except as
types of these mental conditions, — remembrance and 15
love; a real affection for Jesus' character and example.
Be it remembered, that all types employed in the service of Christian Science should represent the most spir- 18
itual forms of thought and worship that can be made
visible.

*Should not the teacher of Christian Science have our* 21
*textbook, "Science and Health with Key to the Scriptures,"*
*in his schoolroom and teach from it?*

I never dreamed, until informed thereof, that a loyal 24
student did not take his textbook with him into the class-
room, ask questions from it, answer them according to
it, and, as occasion required, read from the book as au- 27
thority for what he taught. I supposed that students
had followed my example, and that of other teachers,
sufficiently to do this, and also to require their pupils to 30
study the lessons before recitations.

1   To omit these important points is anomalous, considering the necessity for understanding Science, and
3 the present liability of deviating from Christian Science. Centuries will intervene before the statement of the inexhaustible topics of that book become sufficiently under-
6 stood to be absolutely demonstrated.  The teacher of Christian Science needs continually to study this textbook. His work is to replenish thought, and to spiritualize human
9 life, from this open fount of Truth and Love.

He who sees most clearly and enlightens other minds most readily, keeps his own lamp trimmed and burning.
12 He will take the textbook of Christian Science into his class, repeat the questions in the chapter on Recapitulation, and his students will answer them from the same
15 source.  Throughout his entire explanations, the teacher should strictly adhere to the questions and answers contained in that chapter of "Science and Health with Key
18 to the Scriptures."  It is important to point out the lesson to the class, and to require the students thoroughly to study it before the recitations;  for this spirit-
21 ualizes their thoughts.  When closing his class, the teacher should require each member to own a copy of the above-named book and to continue the study of this
24 textbook.

The opinions of men cannot be substituted for God's revelation.  It must not be forgotten that in times past,
27 arrogant ignorance and pride, in attempting to steady the ark of Truth, have dimmed the power and glory of the Scriptures, to which this Christian Science textbook
30 is the Key.

That teacher does most for his students who most divests himself of pride and self, spiritualizes his own

thought, and by reason thereof is able to empty his stu- 1
dents' minds, that they may be filled with Truth.

Beloved students, *so* teach that posterity shall call 3
you blessed, and the heart of history shall be made
glad!

*Can fear or sin bring back old beliefs of disease that have* 6
*been healed by Christian Science?*

The Scriptures plainly declare the allness and oneness
of God to be the premises of Truth, and that God is 9
good: in Him dwelleth no evil. Christian Science authorizes the logical conclusion drawn from the Scriptures,
that there is in reality none besides the eternal, infinite 12
God, good. Evil is temporal: it is the illusion of time
and mortality.

This being true, sin has no power; and fear, its coeval, 15
is without divine authority. Science sanctions only what
is supported by the unerring Principle of being. Sin can
do nothing: all cause and effect are in God. Fear is a 18
belief of sensation in matter: this belief is neither maintained by Science nor supported by facts, and exists only
as fable. Your answer is, that neither fear nor sin can 21
bring on disease or bring back disease, since there is in
reality no disease.

Bear in mind, however, that human consciousness does 24
not test sin and the fact of its nothingness, by believing
that sin is pardoned without repentance and reformation. Sin punishes itself, because it cannot go unpun- 27
ished either here or hereafter. Nothing is more fatal than
to indulge a sinning sense or consciousness for even one
moment. Knowing this, obey Christ's Sermon on the 30
Mount, even if you suffer for it in the first instance, —

1 are misjudged and maligned; in the second, you will
reign with him.

3    I never knew a person who knowingly indulged evil,
to be grateful; to understand me, or himself.  He must
first see himself and the hallucination of sin;  then he
6 must repent, and love good in order to understand God.
The sinner and the sin are the twain that are one flesh, —
but which God hath not joined together.

# CHAPTER IV

## ADDRESSES

FROM the platform of the Monday lectureship in Tremont Temple, on Monday, March 16, 1885, as 3 will be seen by what follows, Reverend Mary Baker G. Eddy was presented to Mr. Cook's audience, and allowed ten minutes in which to reply to his public letter con- 6 demning her doctrines; which reply was taken in full by a shorthand reporter who was present, and is transcribed below. 9

Mrs. Eddy responding, said: —

As the time so kindly allotted me is insufficient for even a synopsis of Christian Science, I shall confine my- 12 self to questions and answers.

Am I a spiritualist?

I am not, and never was. I understand the impossi- 15 bility of intercommunion between the so-called dead and living. There have always attended my life phenomena of an uncommon order, which spiritualists have mis- 18 called mediumship; but I clearly understand that no human agencies were employed, — that the divine Mind reveals itself to humanity through spiritual law. And 21 to such as are "waiting for the adoption, to wit, the re- demption of our body," Christian Science reveals the in-

1 finitude of divinity and the way of man's salvation from
sickness and death, as wrought out by Jesus, who robbed
3 the grave of victory and death of its sting.  I understand
that God is an ever-present help in all times of trouble, —
have found Him so;  and would have no other gods, no
6 remedies in drugs, no material medicine.

Do I believe in a personal God?

I believe in God as the Supreme Being.  I know not
9 what the person of omnipotence and omnipresence is,
or what the infinite includes;  therefore, I worship that
of which I can conceive, first, as a loving Father and
12 Mother;  then, as thought ascends the scale of being to
diviner consciousness, God becomes to me, as to the
apostle who declared it, "God is Love," — divine Prin-
15 ciple, — which I worship;  and "after the manner of my
fathers, so worship I God."

Do I believe in the atonement of Christ?

18 I do;  and this atonement becomes more to me since
it includes man's redemption from sickness as well as
from sin.  I reverence and adore Christ as never before.

21 It brings to my sense, and to the sense of all who entertain this understanding of the Science of God, a *whole*
salvation.

24 How is the healing done in Christian Science?

This answer includes too much to give you any conclusive idea in a brief explanation.  I can name some
27 means by which it is not done.

It is not one mind acting upon another mind;  it is
not the transference of human images of thought to
30 other minds;  it is not supported by the evidence before
the personal senses, — Science contradicts this evidence;
it is not of the flesh, but of the Spirit.  It is Christ come

to destroy the power of the flesh; it is Truth over error;  1
that understood, gives man ability to rise above the evidence of the senses, take hold of the eternal energies of  3
Truth, and destroy mortal discord with immortal harmony, — the grand verities of being.   It is not one mortal
thought transmitted to another's thought from the human  6
mind that holds within itself all evil.

Our Master said of one of his students, "He is a devil,"
and repudiated the idea of casting out devils through  9
Beelzebub.   Erring human mind is by no means a desirable or efficacious healer.   Such suppositional healing
I deprecate.   It is in no way allied to divine power.   All  12
human control is animal magnetism, more despicable
than all other methods of treating disease.

Christian Science is not a remedy of faith alone, but  15
combines faith with understanding, through which we
may touch the hem of His garment;  and know that omnipotence has all power.   "I am the Lord, and there is  18
none else, there is no God beside me."

Is there a personal man?

The Scriptures inform us that man was made in the  21
image and likeness of God.   I commend the Icelandic
translation: "He created man in the image and likeness
of Mind, in the image and likeness of Mind created  24
He him."   To my sense, we have not seen all of man;
he is more than personal sense can cognize, who is the
image and likeness of the infinite.   I have not seen a  27
perfect man in mind or body, — and such must be the
personality of him who is the true likeness: the lost
image is not this personality, and corporeal man is this  30
lost image;  hence, it doth not appear what is the real
personality of man.   The only cause for making this

1 question of personality a point, or of any importance, is
that man's perfect model should be held in mind, whereby
3 to improve his present condition; that his contemplation
regarding himself should turn away from inharmony, sickness, and sin, to that which is the image of his Maker.

6        SCIENCE AND THE SENSES

Substance of my Address at the National Convention in Chicago,
June 13, 1888

9    The National Christian Scientist Association has
brought us together to minister and to be ministered
unto; mutually to aid one another in finding ways and
12 means for helping the whole human family; to quicken
and extend the interest already felt in a higher mode of
medicine; to watch with eager joy the individual growth
15 of Christian Scientists, and the progress of our common
Cause in Chicago, — the miracle of the Occident. We
come to strengthen and perpetuate our organizations
18 and institutions; and to find strength in union, — strength
to build up, through God's right hand, that pure and
undefiled religion whose Science demonstrates God and
21 the perfectibility of man. This purpose is immense,
and it must begin with individual growth, a "consummation devoutly to be wished." The lives of all re-
24 formers attest the authenticity of their mission, and call
the world to acknowledge its divine Principle. Truly
is it written: —

27    "Thou must be true thyself, if thou the truth would'st teach;
Thy heart must overflow, if thou another's heart would'st
reach."

Science is absolute and final.  It is revolutionary in 1
its very nature; for it upsets all that is not upright.
It annuls false evidence, and saith to the five material 3
senses, "Having eyes ye see not, and ears ye hear not;
neither can you understand."  To weave one thread of
Science through the looms of time, is a miracle in itself. 6
The risk is stupendous.  It cost Galileo, what?  This
awful price:  the temporary loss of his self-respect.  His
fear overcame his loyalty;  the courage of his convictions 9
fell before it.  Fear is the weapon in the hands of
tyrants.

Men and women of the nineteenth century, are you 12
called to voice a higher order of Science?  Then obey
this call.  Go, if you must, to the dungeon or the scaffold, but take not back the words of Truth.  How many 15
are there ready to suffer for a righteous cause, to stand
a long siege, take the front rank, face the foe, and be
in the battle every day? 18

In no other one thing seemed Jesus of Nazareth more
divine than in his faith in the immortality of his words.
He said, "Heaven and earth shall pass away, but my 21
words shall not pass away;"  and they have not.  The
winds of time sweep clean the centuries, but they can
never bear into oblivion his words.  They still live, and 24
to-morrow speak louder than to-day.  They are to-day
as the voice of one crying in the wilderness, "Make
straight God's paths;  make way for health, holiness, 27
universal harmony, and come up hither."  The grandeur of the word, the power of Truth, is again casting
out evils and healing the sick;  and it is whispered, "This 30
is Science."

Jesus taught by the wayside, in humble homes.  He

1 spake of Truth and Love to artless listeners and dull
disciples.   His immortal words were articulated in a
3 decaying language, and then left to the providence of
God.   Christian Science was to interpret them;   and
woman, "last at the cross," was to awaken the dull senses,
6 intoxicated with pleasure or pain, to the infinite meaning of those words.

Past, present, future, will show the word and might of
9 Truth — healing the sick and reclaiming the sinner —
so long as there remains a claim of error for Truth to
deny or to destroy.   Love's labors are not lost.   The
12 five personal senses, that grasp neither the meaning nor
the magnitude of self-abnegation, may lose sight thereof;
but Science voices unselfish love, unfolds infinite good,
15 leads on irresistible forces, and will finally show the fruits
of Love.   Human reason is inaccurate;   and the scope
of the senses is inadequate to grasp the word of Truth,
18 and teach the eternal.

Science speaks when the senses are silent, and then
the evermore of Truth is triumphant.   The spiritual mon-
21 itor understood is coincidence of the divine with the
human, the acme of Christian Science.   Pure humanity,
friendship, home, the interchange of love, bring to earth
24 a foretaste of heaven.   They unite terrestrial and celestial joys, and crown them with blessings infinite.

The Christian Scientist loves man more because he
27 loves God most.   He understands this Principle, — Love.
Who is sufficient for these things?   Who remembers that
patience, forgiveness, abiding faith, and affection, are
30 the symptoms by which our Father indicates the different stages of man's recovery from sin and his entrance into Science?   Who knows how the feeble lips

are made eloquent, how hearts are inspired, how heal- 1
ing becomes spontaneous, and how the divine Mind is
understood and demonstrated? He alone knows these 3
wonders who is departing from the thraldom of the
senses and accepting spiritual truth, — that which blesses
its adoption by the refinement of joy and the dismissal of 6
sorrow.

Christian Science and the senses are at war. It is a
revolutionary struggle. We already have had two in 9
this nation; and they began and ended in a contest for
the true idea, for human liberty and rights. Now cometh
a third struggle; for the freedom of health, holiness, and 12
the attainment of heaven.

The scientific sense of being which establishes harmony, enters into no compromise with finiteness and 15
feebleness. It undermines the foundations of mortality,
of physical law, breaks their chains, and sets the captive
free, opening the doors for them that are bound. 18

He who turns to the body for evidence, bases his conclusions on mortality, on imperfection; but Science saith
to man, "God hath all-power." 21

The Science of omnipotence demonstrates but one
power, and this power is good, not evil; not matter,
but Mind. This virtually destroys matter and evil, in- 24
cluding sin and disease.

If God is All, and God is good, it follows that all
must be good; and no other power, law, or intelligence 27
can exist. On this proof rest premise and conclusion in
Science, and the facts that disprove the evidence of the
senses. 30

God is individual Mind. This one Mind and His
individuality comprise the elements of all forms and

1 individualities, and prophesy the nature and stature of
Christ, the ideal man.

3   A corporeal God, as often defined by lexicographers
and scholastic theologians, is only an infinite finite being,
an unlimited man, — a theory to me inconceivable.   If
6 the unlimited and immortal Mind could originate in a
limited body, Mind would be chained to finity, and the
infinite forever finite.

9   In this limited and lower sense God is not personal.
His infinity precludes the possibility of corporeal personality.   His being is individual, but not physical.

12   God is like Himself and like nothing else.   He is universal and primitive.   His character admits of no degrees
of comparison.   God is not part, but the whole.   In His
15 individuality I recognize the loving, divine Father-Mother
God.   Infinite personality must be incorporeal.

God's ways are not ours.   His pity is expressed in
18 modes above the human.   His chastisements are the
manifestations of Love.   The sympathy of His eternal
Mind is fully expressed in divine Science, which blots
21 out all our iniquities and heals all our diseases.   Human
pity often brings pain.

Science supports harmony, denies suffering, and de-
24 stroys it with the divinity of Truth.   Whatever seems material, seems thus only to the material senses, and is but the
subjective state of mortal and material thought.

27   Science has inaugurated the irrepressible conflict between sense and Soul.   Mortal thought wars with this
sense as one that beateth the air, but Science outmasters
30 it, and ends the warfare.   This proves daily that "one
on God's side is a majority."

Science defines *omnipresence* as universality, that which

precludes the presence of evil. This verity annuls the tes- 1
timony of the senses, which say that sin is an evil power,
and substance is perishable. Intelligent Spirit, Soul, is 3
substance, far more impregnable and solid than matter; for
one is temporal, while the other is eternal, the ultimate
and predicate of being. 6

Mortality, materiality, and destructive forces, such as
sin, disease, and death, mortals virtually name *substance;*
but these are the substance of things *not* hoped for. For 9
lack of knowing what substance is, the senses say vaguely:
"The substance of life is sorrow and mortality; for who
knoweth the substance of good?" In Science, form and 12
individuality are never lost, thoughts are outlined, indi-
vidualized ideas, which dwell forever in the divine Mind
as tangible, true substance, because eternally conscious. 15
Unlike mortal mind, which must be ever in bondage,
the eternal Mind is free, unlimited, and knows not the
temporal. 18

Neither does the temporal know the eternal. Mortal
man, as mind or matter, is neither the pattern nor Maker
of immortal man. Any inference of the divine derived 21
from the human, either as mind or body, hides the actual
power, presence, and individuality of God.

Jesus' personality in the flesh, so far as material sense 24
could discern it, was like that of other men; but Science
exchanges this human concept of Jesus for the divine
ideal, his spiritual individuality that reflected the Im- 27
manuel, or "God with us." This God was not outlined.
He was too mighty for that. He was eternal Life, infinite
Truth and Love. The individuality is embraced in Mind, 30
therefore is forever with the Father. Hence the Scripture, "I am a God at hand, saith the Lord." Even while
5

1 his personality was on earth and in anguish, his individual
being, the Christ, was at rest in the eternal harmony.
3 His unseen individuality, so superior to that which was
seen, was not subject to the temptations of the flesh, to
laws material, to death, or the grave.   Formed and gov-
6 erned by God, this individuality was safe in the substance
of Soul, the substance of Spirit, — yea, the substance of
God, the one inclusive good.

9    In Science all being is individual; for individuality is
endless in the calculus of forms and numbers.   Herein
sin is miraculous and supernatural; for it is not in the
12 nature of God, and good is forever good.   According to Christian Science, perfection is normal, — not
miraculous.   Clothed, and in its right Mind, man's
15 individuality is sinless, deathless, harmonious, eternal.
His materiality, clad in a false mentality, wages feeble
fight with his individuality, — his physical senses with
18 his spiritual senses.   The latter move in God's grooves
of Science:  the former revolve in their own orbits, and
must stand the friction of false selfhood until self-
21 destroyed.

In obedience to the divine nature, man's individuality
reflects the divine law and order of being.   How shall
24 we reach our true selves?   Through Love.   The Principle of Christian Science is Love, and its idea represents
Love.   This divine Principle and idea are demonstrated,
27 in healing, to be God and the real man.

. Who wants to be mortal, or would not gain the true
ideal of Life and recover his own individuality?   I will
30 love, if another hates.   I will gain a balance on the side of
good, my true being.   This alone gives me the forces of
God wherewith to overcome all error.   On this rests the

implicit faith engendered by Christian Science, which 1
appeals intelligently to the facts of man's spirituality, individuality, to disdain the fears and destroy the discords 3
of this material personality.

On our Master's individual demonstrations over sin,
sickness, and death, rested the anathema of priesthood 6
and the senses; yet this demonstration is the foundation
of Christian Science. His physical sufferings, which
came from the testimony of the senses, were over when 9
he resumed his individual spiritual being, after showing
us the way to escape from the material body.

Science would have no conflict with Life or common 12
sense, if this sense were consistently sensible. Man's real
life or existence is in harmony with Life and its glorious
phenomena. It upholds being, and destroys the too 15
common sense of its opposites — death, disease, and sin.
Christian Science is an everlasting victor, and vanquish-
ment is unknown to the omnipresent Truth. I must ever 18
follow this line of light and battle.

Christian Science is my only ideal; and the individual
and his ideal can never be severed. If either is misunder- 21
stood or maligned, it eclipses the other with the shadow
cast by this error.

Truth destroys error. Nothing appears to the physi- 24
cal senses but their own subjective state of thought. The
senses join issue with error, and pity what has no right
either to be pitied or to exist, and what does not exist in 27
Science. Destroy the thought of sin, sickness, death, and
you destroy their existence. "Whatsoever a man soweth,
that shall he also reap."                                    30

Because God is Mind, and this Mind is good, all
is good and all is Mind. God is the sum total of the

1 universe.   Then what and where are sin, sickness, and
death?

3   Christian Science and Christian Scientists will, *must,*
have a history;  and if I could write the history in poor
parody on Tennyson's grand verse, it would read
6 thus: —

> Traitors to right of them,
> M. D.'s to left of them,
> Priestcraft in front of them,
>    Volleyed and thundered!
> Into the jaws of hate,
> Out through the door of Love,
> On to the blest above,
>    Marched the one hundred.

15 EXTRACT FROM MY FIRST ADDRESS IN THE MOTHER
CHURCH, MAY 26, 1895

*Friends and Brethren:* — Your Sunday Lesson, com-
18 posed of Scripture and its correlative in "Science and
Health with Key to the Scriptures," has fed you.   In addition, I can only bring crumbs fallen from this table of
21 Truth, and gather up the fragments.

It has long been a question of earnest import, How
shall mankind worship the most adorable, but most
24 unadored, — and where shall begin that praise that shall
never end?   Beneath, above, beyond, methinks I hear
the soft, sweet sigh of angels answering, "So live, that
27 your lives attest your sincerity and resound His praise."

Music is the harmony of being;  but the music of Soul
affords the only strains that thrill the chords of feeling
30 and awaken the heart's harpstrings.   Moved by mind,
your many-throated organ, in imitative tones of many

instruments, praises Him; but even the sweetness and 1
beauty in and of this temple that praise Him, are earth's
accents, and must not be mistaken for the oracles of God. 3
Art must not prevail over Science.   Christianity is not
superfluous.   Its redemptive power is seen in sore trials,
self-denials, and crucifixions of the flesh.   But these come 6
to the rescue of mortals, to admonish them, and plant
the feet steadfastly in Christ.   As we rise above the seeming mists of sense, we behold more clearly that all the 9
heart's homage belongs to God.

More love is the great need of mankind.   A pure affection, concentric, forgetting self, forgiving wrongs and 12
forestalling them, should swell the lyre of human love.

Three cardinal points must be gained before poor
humanity is regenerated and Christian Science is dem- 15
onstrated: (1) A proper sense of sin; (2) repentance;
(3) the understanding of good.   Evil is a negation: it
never started with time, and it cannot keep pace with 18
eternity.   Mortals' false senses pass through three states
and stages of human consciousness before yielding error.
The deluded sense must first be shown its falsity through 21
a knowledge of evil as evil, so-called.   Without a sense
of one's oft-repeated violations of divine law, the individual may become morally blind, and this deplorable 24
mental state is moral idiocy.   The lack of seeing one's
deformed mentality, and of *repentance* therefor, deep,
never to be repented of, is retarding, and in certain mor- 27
bid instances stopping, the growth of Christian Scientists.
Without a knowledge of his sins, and repentance so severe
that it destroys them, no person is or can be a Christian 30
Scientist.

Mankind thinks either too much or too little of sin.

1 The sensitive, sorrowing saint thinks too much of it: the
sordid sinner, or the so-called Christian asleep, thinks too
3 little of sin.

To allow sin of any sort is anomalous in Christian
Scientists, claiming, as they do, that good is infinite, All.
6 Our Master, in his definition of Satan as a liar from the
beginning, attested the absolute powerlessness — yea,
nothingness — of evil: since a lie, being without founda-
9 tion in fact, is merely a falsity; spiritually, literally, it
*is nothing.*

Not to know that a false claim is false, is to be in danger
12 of believing it; hence the utility of knowing evil aright,
then reducing its claim to its proper denominator, —
nobody and nothing. Sin should be conceived of only
15 as a delusion. This true conception would remove mortals'
ignorance and its consequences, and advance the second
stage of human consciousness, repentance. The first
18 state, namely, the knowledge of one's self, the proper
knowledge of evil and its subtle workings wherein evil
seems as real as good, is indispensable; since that which
21 is truly conceived of, we can handle; but the misconception of what we need to know of evil, — or the conception of it at all as something real, — costs much. Sin
24 needs only to be known for what it is not; then we are
its master, not servant. Remember, and act on, Jesus'
definition of sin as a *lie.* This cognomen makes it less
27 dangerous; for most of us would not be seen believing
in, or adhering to, that which we know to be untrue.
What would be thought of a Christian Scientist who be-
30 lieved in the use of drugs, while declaring that they have
no intrinsic quality and that there is no matter? What
should be thought of an individual believing in that

which is untrue, and at the same time declaring the unity 1
of Truth, and its allness?  Beware of those who misrepresent facts;  or tacitly assent where they should dis- 3
sent;  or who take me as authority for what I disapprove,
or mayhap never have thought of, and try to reverse, in-
vert, or controvert, Truth;  for this is a sure pretext of 6
moral defilement.

Examine yourselves, and see what, and how much, sin
claims of you;  and how much of this claim you admit 9
as valid, or comply with.  The knowledge of evil that
brings on repentance is the most hopeful stage of mortal
mentality.  Even a mild mistake must be seen as a mis- 12
take, in order to be corrected;  how much more, then,
should one's sins be seen and repented of, before they
can be reduced to their native nothingness!                    15

Ignorance is only blest by reason of its nothingness;
for seeing the need of somethingness in its stead, blesses
mortals.  Ignorance was the first condition of sin in the 18
allegory of Adam and Eve in the garden of Eden.  Their
mental state is not desirable, neither is a knowledge of
sin and its consequences, repentance, *per se;* but, ad- 21
mitting the existence of both, mortals must hasten through
the second to the third stage, — the knowledge of good;
for without this the valuable sequence of knowledge 24
would be lacking, — even the power to escape from the
false claims of sin.  To understand good, one must discern
the nothingness of evil, and consecrate one's life anew.     27

Beloved brethren, Christ, Truth, saith unto you, "Be
not afraid!" — fear not sin, lest thereby it master you;
but only *fear to sin.*  Watch and pray for self-knowledge; 30
since then, and thus, cometh repentance, — and your
superiority to a delusion is won.

1 Repentance is better than sacrifice. The costly balm
of Araby, poured on our Master's feet, had not the value
3 of a single *tear*.

Beloved children, the world has need of you, — and
more as children than as men and women: it needs your
6 innocence, unselfishness, faithful affection, uncontami-
nated lives. You need also to watch, and pray that you
preserve these virtues unstained, and lose them not through
9 contact with the world. What grander ambition is there
than to maintain in yourselves what Jesus loved, and to
know that your example, more than words, makes morals
12 for mankind!

## ADDRESS BEFORE THE ALUMNI OF THE MASSACHUSETTS METAPHYSICAL COLLEGE, 1895

15 *My Beloved Students:* — Weeks have passed into
months, and months into years, since last we met; but
time and space, when encompassed by divine presence,
18 do not separate us. Our hearts have kept time together,
and our hands have wrought steadfastly at the same
object-lesson, while leagues have lain between us.

21 We may well unite in thanksgiving for the continued
progress and unprecedented prosperity of our Cause. It
is already obvious that the world's acceptance and the
24 momentum of Christian Science, increase rapidly as
years glide on.

As Christian Scientists, you have dared the perilous de-
27 fense of Truth, and have succeeded. You have learned
how fleeting is that which men call great; and how permanent that which God calls good.

You have proven that the greatest piety is scarcely 1
sufficient to demonstrate what you have adopted and
taught; that your work, well done, would dignify angels. 3

Faithfully, as meekly, you have toiled all night; and
at break of day caught much. At times, your net has
been so full that it broke: human pride, creeping into 6
its meshes, extended it beyond safe expansion; then,
losing hold of divine Love, you lost your fishes, and possibly blamed others more than yourself. But those whom 9
God makes "fishers of men" will not pull for the shore;
like Peter, they launch into the depths, cast their nets
on the right side, compensate loss, and gain a higher sense 12
of the true idea. Nothing is lost that God gives: had He
filled the net, it would not have broken.

Leaving the seed of Truth to its own vitality, it propa- 15
gates: the tares cannot hinder it. Our Master said,
"Heaven and earth shall pass away, but my words shall
not pass away;" and Jesus' faith in Truth must not ex- 18
ceed that of Christian Scientists who prove its power to
be immortal.

The Christianity that is merely of sects, the pulpit, and 21
fashionable society, is brief; but the Word of God abideth.
Plato was a pagan; but no greater difference existed between his doctrines and those of Jesus, than to-day exists 24
between the Catholic and Protestant sects. I love the
orthodox church; and, in time, that church will love
Christian Science. Let me specially call the attention of 27
this Association to the following false beliefs inclining
mortal mind more deviously: —

The belief in anti-Christ: that somebody in the flesh 30
is the son of God, or is another Christ, or is a spiritually
adopted child, or is an incarnated babe, is the evil one—

1 in other words, the one evil — disporting itself with the subtleties of sin!

3 Even honest thinkers, not knowing whence they come, may deem these delusions verities, before they know it, or really look the illusions in the face. The ages are bur-
6 dened with material modes. Hypnotism, microbes, X-rays, and ex-common sense, occupy time and thought; and error, given new opportunities, will improve them. The
9 most just man can neither defend the innocent nor detect the guilty, unless he knows *how* to be just; and this knowledge demands our time and attention.

12 The mental stages of crime, which seem to belong to the latter days, are strictly classified in metaphysics as some of the many features and forms of what is properly
15 denominated, in extreme cases, moral idiocy. I visited in his cell the assassin of President Garfield, and found him in the mental state called moral idiocy. He had no
18 sense of his crime; but regarded his act as one of simple justice, and himself as the victim. My few words touched him; he sank back in his chair, limp and pale; his flip-
21 pancy had fled. The jailer thanked me, and said, "Other visitors have brought to him bouquets, but you have brought what will do him good."

24 This mental disease at first shows itself in extreme sensitiveness; then, in a loss of self-knowledge and of self-condemnation, — a shocking inability to see one's
27 own faults, but an exaggerating sense of other people's. Unless this mental condition be overcome, it ends in a total loss of moral, intellectual, and spiritual discernment,
30 and is characterized in this Scripture: "The fool hath said in his heart, There is no God." This state of mind is the exemplification of total depravity, and the result

of sensuous mind in matter. Mind that is God is not in 1
matter; and God's presence gives spiritual light, wherein
is no darkness. 3

If, as is indisputably true, "God is Spirit," and Spirit
is our Father and Mother, and that which it includes is
all that is real and eternal, when evil seems to predomi- 6
nate and divine light to be obscured, free moral agency
is lost; and the Revelator's vision, that "no man might
buy or sell, save he that had the mark, or the name of the 9
beast, or the number of his name," is imminent.

Whoever is mentally manipulating human mind, and
is not gaining a higher sense of Truth by it, is losing in 12
the scale of moral and spiritual being, and may be carried to the depths of perdition by his own consent. He
who refuses to be influenced by any but the divine Mind, 15
commits his way to God, and rises superior to suggestions from an evil source. Christian Science shows that
there is a way of escape from the latter-day ultimatum 18
of evil, through scientific truth; so that all are without
excuse.

Already I clearly recognize that mental malpractice, 21
if persisted in, will end in insanity, dementia, or moral
idiocy. Thank God! this evil can be resisted by true
Christianity. Divine Love is our hope, strength, and 24
shield. We have nothing to fear when Love is at the
helm of thought, but everything to enjoy on earth and
in heaven. 27

The systematized centres of Christian Science are life-
giving fountains of truth. Our churches, *The Christian
Science Journal,* and the *Christian Science Quarterly,* 30
are prolific sources of spiritual power whose intellectual,
moral, and spiritual animus is felt throughout the land.

1 Our Publishing Society, and our Sunday Lessons, are
of inestimable value to all seekers after Truth. The Com-
3 mittee on Sunday School Lessons cannot give too much
time and attention to their task, and should spare no
research in the preparation of the *Quarterly* as an educa-
6 tional branch.

The teachers of Christian Science need to watch inces-
santly the trend of their own thoughts; watch that these
9 be not secretly robbed, and themselves misguided, and
so made to misteach others. Teachers must conform
strictly to the rules of divine Science announced in the
12 Bible and their textbook, "Science and Health with Key
to the Scriptures." They must themselves practise, and
teach others to practise, the Hebrew Decalogue, the Ser-
15 mon on the Mount, and the understanding and enuncia-
tion of these according to Christ.

They must always have on armor, and resist the foe
18 within and without. They cannot arm too thoroughly
against original sin, appearing in its myriad forms: passion, appetites, hatred, revenge, and all the *et cetera* of
21 evil. Christian Scientists cannot watch too sedulously,
or bar their doors too closely, or pray to God too fer-
vently, for deliverance from the claims of evil. Thus
24 doing, Scientists will silence evil suggestions, uncover
their methods, and stop their hidden influence upon the
lives of mortals. Rest assured that God in His wisdom
27 will test all mankind on all questions; and then, if found
faithful, He will deliver us from temptation and show us
the powerlessness of evil, — even its utter nothingness.

30 The teacher in Christian Science who does not specially instruct his pupils how to guard against evil and
its silent modes, and to be able, through Christ, the liv-

ing Truth, to protect themselves therefrom, is commit- 1
ting an offense against God and humanity. With Science
and Health for their textbook, I am astounded at the 3
apathy of some students on the subject of sin and mental
malpractice, and their culpable ignorance of the workings of these — and even the teacher's own deficiency in 6
this department. I can account for this state of mind in
the teacher only as the result of sin; otherwise, his own
guilt as a mental malpractitioner, and fear of being found 9
out.

The helpless ignorance of the community on this subject is pitiable, and plain to be seen. May God enable 12
my students to take up the cross as I have done, and meet
the pressing need of a proper preparation of heart to practise, teach, and live Christian Science! Your means of 15
protection and defense from sin are, constant watchfulness and prayer that you enter not into temptation and
are delivered from every claim of evil, till you intelligently 18
know and demonstrate, in Science, that evil has neither
prestige, power, nor existence, since God, good, is All-
in-all.                                                    21

The increasing necessity for relying on God to defend us against the subtler forms of evil, turns us more
unreservedly to Him for help, and thus becomes a means 24
of grace. If one lives rightly, every effort to hurt one
will only help that one; for God will give the ability to
overcome whatever tends to impede progress. Know 27
this: that you cannot overcome the baneful effects of
sin on yourself, if you in any way indulge in sin; for,
sooner or later, you will fall the victim of your own as 30
well as of others' sins. Using mental power in the right
direction only, doing to others as you would have them

1 do to you, will overcome evil with good, and destroy
your own sensitiveness to the power of evil.

3 The God of all grace be with you, and save you from
"spiritual wickedness in high places."

PLEASANT VIEW, CONCORD, N. H.,
6     June 3, 1895


ADDRESS BEFORE THE CHRISTIAN SCIENTIST ASSOCIA-
TION OF THE MASSACHUSETTS METAPHYSICAL COL-
9 LEGE, IN 1893

SUBJECT: *Obedience*

*My Beloved Students:* — This question, ever nearest
12 to my heart, is to-day uppermost: Are we filling the
measures of life's music aright, emphasizing its grand
strains, swelling the harmony of being with tones whence
15 come glad echoes? As *crescendo* and *diminuendo* accent
music, so the varied strains of human chords express
life's loss or gain, — loss of the pleasures and pains and
18 pride of life: gain of its sweet concord, the courage of
honest convictions, and final obedience to spiritual law.
The ultimate of scientific research and attainment in
21 divine Science is not an argument: it is not merely saying, but doing, the Word — demonstrating Truth — even
as the fruits of watchfulness, prayer, struggles, tears, and
24 triumph.

Obeying the divine Principle which you profess to understand and love, demonstrates Truth. Never absent
27 from your post, never off guard, never ill-humored, never
unready to work for God, — is obedience; being "faithful over a few things." If in one instance obedience be
30 lacking, you lose the scientific rule and its reward: namely,

to be made "ruler over many things." A progressive 1
life is the reality of Life that unfolds its immortal Principle. 3

The student of Christian Science must first separate the
tares from the wheat; discern between the thought,
motive, and act superinduced by the wrong motive or 6
the true — the God-given intent and volition — arrest
the former, and obey the latter. This will place him on
the safe side of practice. We always know where to look 9
for the real Scientist, and always find him there. I agree
with Rev. Dr. Talmage, that "there are wit, humor, and
enduring vivacity among God's people." 12

Obedience is the offspring of Love; and Love is the
Principle of unity, the basis of all right thinking and
acting; it fulfils the law. We see eye to eye and know as we 15
are known, reciprocate kindness and work wisely, in
proportion as we love.

It is difficult for me to carry out a divine commission 18
while participating in the movements, or *modus operandi*,
of other folks. To point out every step to a student and
then watch that each step be taken, consumes time, — 21
and experiments ofttimes are costly. According to my
calendar, God's time and mortals' differ. The neophyte is inclined to be too fast or too slow: he works 24
somewhat in the dark; and, sometimes out of season,
he would replenish his lamp at the midnight hour and
borrow oil of the more provident watcher. God is the 27
fountain of light, and He illumines one's way when one
is obedient. The disobedient make their moves before
God makes His, or make them too late to follow Him. 30
Be sure that God *directs* your way; then, hasten to follow
under every circumstance.

1  Human will must be subjugated. We cannot obey
both God, good, and evil, — in other words, the ma-
3 terial senses, false suggestions, self-will, selfish motives,
and human policy. We shall have no faith in evil
when faith finds a resting-place and scientific under-
6 standing guides man. Honesty in every condition,
under every circumstance, is the indispensable rule of
obedience. To obey the principle of mathematics ninety-
9 nine times in one hundred and then allow one numeral
to make incorrect your entire problem, is neither Science
nor obedience.

12  However keenly the human affections yearn to forgive a mistake, and pass a friend over it smoothly, one's
sympathy can neither atone for error, advance individual
15 growth, nor change this immutable decree of Love: "Keep
My commandments." The guerdon of meritorious
faith or trustworthiness rests on being willing to work
18 alone with God and for Him, — willing to suffer patiently
for error until all error is destroyed and His rod and His
staff comfort you.

21  Self-ignorance, self-will, self-righteousness, lust, covetousness, envy, revenge, are foes to grace, peace, and
progress; they must be met manfully and overcome,
24 or they will uproot all happiness. Be of good cheer;
the warfare with one's self is grand; it gives one plenty
of employment, and the divine Principle worketh with
27 you, — and obedience crowns persistent effort with
everlasting victory. Every attempt of evil to harm good
is futile, and ends in the fiery punishment of the
30 evil-doer.

Jesus said, "Not that which goeth into the mouth
defileth a man; but that which cometh out of the mouth,

this defileth a man." If malicious suggestions whisper evil through the mind's tympanum, this were no apology for acting evilly. We are responsible for our thoughts and acts; and instead of aiding other people's devices by obeying them, — and then whining over misfortune, — rise and overthrow both. If a criminal coax the unwary man to commit a crime, our laws punish the dupe as accessory to the fact. Each individual is responsible for himself.

Evil is impotent to turn the righteous man from his uprightness. The nature of the individual, more stubborn than the circumstance, will always be found arguing for itself, — its habits, tastes, and indulgences. This material nature strives to tip the beam against the spiritual nature; for the flesh strives against Spirit, — against whatever or whoever opposes evil, — and weighs mightily in the scale against man's high destiny. This conclusion is not an argument either for pessimism or for optimism, but is a plea for free moral agency, — full exemption from all necessity to obey a power that should be and is found powerless in Christian Science.

Insubordination to the law of Love even in the least, or strict obedience thereto, tests and discriminates between the real and the unreal Scientist. Justice, a prominent statute in the divine law, demands of all trespassers upon the sparse individual rights which one justly reserves to one's self, — Would you consent that others should tear up your landmarks, manipulate your students, nullify or reverse your rules, countermand your orders, steal your possessions, and escape the penalty therefor? No! "Therefore all things whatsoever ye would that men should do to you, do ye even

1 so to them." The professors of Christian Science must take off their shoes at our altars; they must unclasp
3 the material sense of things at the very threshold of Christian Science: they must obey implicitly each and every injunction of the divine Principle of life's long
6 problem, or repeat their work in tears. In the words of St. Paul, "Know ye not, that to whom ye yield yourselves servants to obey, his servants ye are to whom ye
9 obey; whether of sin unto death, or of *obedience* unto righteousness?"

Beloved students, loyal laborers are ye that have wrought
12 valiantly, and achieved great guerdons in the vineyard of our Lord; but a mighty victory is yet to be won, a great freedom for the race; and Christian success is
15 under arms, — with armor on, not laid down. Let us rejoice, however, that the clarion call of peace will at length be heard above the din of battle, and come more
18 sweetly to our ear than sound of vintage bells to villagers on the Rhine.

I recommend that this Association hereafter meet tri-
21 ennially: many of its members reside a long distance from Massachusetts, and they are members of The Mother Church who would love to be with you on Sunday, and
24 once in three years is perhaps as often as they can afford to be away from their own fields of labor.

COMMUNION ADDRESS, JANUARY, 1896

27 *Friends and Brethren:* — The Biblical record of the great Nazarene, whose character we to-day commemorate, is scanty; but what is given, puts to flight every doubt as
30 to the immortality of his words and works. Though

written in a decaying language, his words can never pass 1
away: they are inscribed upon the hearts of men: they
are engraved upon eternity's tablets. 3

Undoubtedly our Master partook of the Jews' feast
of the Passover, and drank from their festal wine-cup.
This, however, is not the cup to which I call your at- 6
tention, — even the cup of martyrdom: wherein Spirit
and matter, good and evil, seem to grapple, and the
human struggles against the divine, up to a point of 9
discovery; namely, the impotence of evil, and the omnipotence of good, as divinely attested. Anciently, the
blood of martyrs was believed to be the seed of the Church. 12
Stalled theocracy would make this fatal doctrine just
and sovereign, even a divine decree, a law of Love! That
the innocent shall suffer for the guilty, is inhuman. The 15
prophet declared, "Thou shalt put away the guilt of
innocent blood from Israel." This is plain: that whatever belittles, befogs, or belies the nature and essence of 18
Deity, is not divine. Who, then, shall father or favor
this sentence passed upon innocence? thereby giving the
signet of God to the arrest, trial, and crucifixion of His 21
beloved Son, the righteous Nazarene, — christened by
John the Baptist, "the Lamb of God."

Oh! shameless insult to divine royalty, that drew 24
from the great Master this answer to the questions of the
rabbinical rabble: "If I tell you, ye will not believe; and
if I also ask you, ye will not answer me, nor let me go." 27

Infinitely greater than human pity, is divine Love, —
that cannot be unmerciful. Human tribunals, if just,
borrow their sense of justice from the divine Principle 30
thereof, which punishes the guilty, not the innocent. The
Teacher of both law and gospel construed the substitution

1 of a good man to suffer for evil-doers — a *crime!* When
foretelling his own crucifixion, he said, "Woe unto the
3 world because of offenses! for it must needs be that
offenses come; but woe to that man by whom the offense
cometh!"

6 Would Jesus thus have spoken of what was indispensable for the salvation of a world of sinners, or of the
individual instrument in this holy (?) alliance for accom-
9 plishing such a monstrous work? or have said of him
whom God foreordained and predestined to fulfil a divine
decree, "It were better for him that a millstone were
12 hanged about his neck, and that he were drowned in the
depth of the sea"?

The divine order is the acme of mercy: it is neither
15 questionable nor assailable: it is not evil producing good,
nor good ultimating in evil. Such an inference were
impious. Holy Writ denounces him that declares, "Let
18 us do evil, that good may come! whose damnation is
just."

Good is not educed from its opposite: and Love divine
21 spurned, lessens not the hater's hatred nor the criminal's
crime; nor reconciles justice to injustice; nor substitutes
the suffering of the Godlike for the suffering due to sin.
24 Neither spiritual bankruptcy nor a religious chancery can
win high heaven, or the "Well done, good and faithful
servant, . . . enter thou into the joy of thy Lord."

27 Divine Love knows no hate; for hate, or the hater, is
nothing: God never made it, and He made all that was
made. The hater's pleasures are unreal; his sufferings,
30 self-imposed; his existence is a parody, and he ends —
with suicide.

The murder of the just Nazarite was incited by the

same spirit that in our time massacres our missionaries, 1
butchers the helpless Armenians, slaughters innocents.
Evil was, and is, the illusion of breaking the First Com- 3
mandment, "Thou shalt have no other gods before me:"
it is either idolizing something and somebody, or hating
them: it is the spirit of idolatry, envy, jealousy, covet- 6
ousness, superstition, lust, hypocrisy, *witchcraft*.

That man can break the forever-law of infinite Love,
was, and is, the serpent's biggest lie! and ultimates in 9
a religion of pagan priests bloated with crime; a religion
that demands human victims to be sacrificed to human
passions and human gods, or tortured to appease the 12
anger of a so-called god or a miscalled man or woman!
The Assyrian Merodach, or the god of sin, was the "lucky
god;" and the Babylonian Yawa, or Jehovah, was the 15
Jewish tribal deity. The *Christian's* God is neither, and
is too pure to behold iniquity.

Divine Science has rolled away the stone from the sepul- 18
chre of our Lord; and there has risen to the awakened
thought the majestic atonement of divine Love. The
at-one-ment with Christ has appeared — not through 21
vicarious suffering, whereby the just obtain a pardon for
the unjust, — but through the eternal law of justice;
wherein sinners suffer for their own sins, repent, forsake 24
sin, love God, and keep His commandments, thence to
receive the reward of righteousness: salvation from sin,
not through the *death* of a man, but through a divine *Life*, 27
which is our Redeemer.

Holy Writ declares that God is Love, is Spirit; hence
it follows that those who worship Him, must worship 30
Him spiritually, — far apart from physical sensation
such as attends eating and drinking corporeally. It is

1 plain that aught unspiritual, intervening between God
and man, would tend to disturb the divine order, and
3 countermand the Scripture that those who worship the
Father must worship Him in spirit.  It is also plain,
that we should not seek and cannot find God in mat-
6 ter, or through material methods;  neither do we love
and obey Him by means of matter, or the flesh, — which
warreth against Spirit, and will not be reconciled
9 thereto.

We turn, with sickened sense, from a pagan Jew's
or Moslem's misconception of Deity, for peace; and find
12 rest in the spiritual ideal, or Christ.  For "who is so
great a God as our God!" unchangeable, all-wise, all-
just, all-merciful;  the ever-loving, ever-living Life, Truth,
15 Love:  comforting such as mourn, opening the prison
doors to the captive, marking the unwinged bird, pitying
with more than a father's pity;  healing the sick, cleansing
18 the leper, raising the dead, saving sinners.  As we think
thereon, man's true sense is filled with peace, and power;
and we say, It is well that Christian Science has taken
21 expressive silence wherein to muse His praise, to kiss the
feet of Jesus, adore the white Christ, and stretch out our
arms to God.

24     The last act of the tragedy on Calvary rent the veil
of matter, and unveiled Love's great legacy to mortals:
*Love forgiving its enemies.*  This grand act crowned
27 and still crowns Christianity: it manumits mortals; it
translates love;  it gives to suffering, inspiration;  to
patience, experience;  to experience, hope;  to hope, faith;
30 to faith, understanding;  and to understanding, Love triumphant!

In proportion to a man's spiritual progress, he will

indeed drink of our Master's cup, and be baptized with his baptism! be purified as by fire, — the fires of suffering; then hath he part in Love's atonement, for "whom the Lord loveth He chasteneth." Then shall he also reign with him: he shall rise to know that there is no sin, that there is no suffering; since all that is *real* is *right.* This knowledge enables him to overcome the world, the flesh, and all evil, to have dominion over his own sinful sense and self. Then shall he drink anew Christ's cup, in the kingdom of God — the reign of righteousness — within him; he shall sit down at the Father's right hand: *sit down;* not stand waiting and weary; but rest on the bosom of God; rest, in the understanding of divine Love that passeth all understanding; rest, in that which "to know aright is Life eternal," and whom, not having seen, we love.

Then shall he press on to Life's long lesson, the eternal lore of Love; and learn forever the infinite meanings of these short sentences: "God is Love;" and, All that is real is divine, for God is All-in-all.

## MESSAGE TO THE ANNUAL MEETING OF THE MOTHER CHURCH, BOSTON, 1896

*Beloved Brethren, Children, and Grandchildren:* — Apart from the common walks of mankind, revolving oft the hitherto untouched problems of being, and oftener, perhaps, the controversies which baffle it, Mother, thought-tired, turns to-day to you; turns to her dear church, to tell the towers thereof the remarkable achievements that have been ours within the past few years: the rapid transit from halls to churches, from un-

1 settled questions to permanence, from danger to escape,
from fragmentary discourses to one eternal sermon; yea,
3 from darkness to daylight, in physics and metaphysics.

Truly, I half wish for society again; for once, at least,
to hear the soft music of our Sabbath chimes saluting the
6 ear in tones that leap for joy, with love for God and
man.

Who hath not learned that when alone he has his
9 own thoughts to guard, and when struggling with mankind his temper, and in society his tongue? We also
have gained higher heights; have learned that trials lift
12 us to that dignity of Soul which sustains us, and finally
conquers them; and that the ordeal refines while it
chastens.

15 Perhaps our church is not yet quite sensible of what
we owe to the strength, meekness, honesty, and obedience of the Christian Science Board of Directors; to
18 the able editors of *The Christian Science Journal,* and
to our efficient Publishing Society.

No reproof is so potent as the silent lesson of a good
21 example. Works, more than words, should characterize
Christian Scientists. Most people condemn evil-doing,
evil-speaking; yet nothing circulates so rapidly: even gold
24 is less current. Christian Scientists have a strong race to
run, and foes in ambush; but bear in mind that, in the
long race, honesty always defeats dishonesty.

27 God hath indeed smiled on my church, — this
daughter of Zion: she sitteth in high places; and to de-
ride her is to incur the penalty of which the Hebrew
30 bard spake after this manner: "He that sitteth in the
heavens shall laugh: the Lord shall have them in
derision."

Hitherto, I have observed that in proportion as this 1
church has smiled on His "little ones," He has blessed
her. Throughout my entire connection with The Mother 3
Church, I have seen, that in the ratio of her love for
others, hath His love been bestowed upon her; watering
her waste places, and enlarging her borders. 6

One thing I have greatly desired, and again earnestly
request, namely, that Christian Scientists, here and
elsewhere, pray daily for themselves; not verbally, nor 9
on bended knee, but mentally, meekly, and importu-
nately. When a hungry heart petitions the divine Father-
Mother God for bread, it is not given a stone, — but 12
more grace, obedience, and love. If this heart, humble
and trustful, faithfully asks divine Love to feed it with the
bread of heaven, health, holiness, it will be conformed to 15
a fitness to receive the answer to its desire; then will flow
into it the "river of His pleasure," the tributary of divine
Love, and great growth in Christian Science will follow, — 18
even that joy which finds one's own in another's good.

To love, and to be loved, one must do good to others.
The inevitable condition whereby to become blessed, is to 21
bless others: but here, you must so know yourself, under
God's direction, that you will do His will even though
your pearls be downtrodden. Ofttimes the rod is His 24
means of grace; then it must be ours, — we cannot avoid
wielding it if we reflect Him.

Wise sayings and garrulous talk may fall to the ground, 27
rather than on the ear or heart of the hearer; but a tender
sentiment felt, or a kind word spoken, at the right moment,
is never wasted. Mortal mind presents phases of charac- 30
ter which need close attention and examination. The
human heart, like a feather bed, needs often to be *stirred,*

1 sometimes roughly, and given a variety of *turns,* else it grows hard and uncomfortable whereon to repose.

3    The lessons of this so-called life in matter are too vast and varied to learn or to teach briefly; and especially within the limits of a letter.  Therefore I close here, 6 with the apostle's injunction: "Finally, brethren, whatsoever things are true, whatsoever things are honest, whatsoever things are just, whatsoever things are pure, 9 whatsoever things are lovely, whatsoever things are of good report; if there be any virtue, and if there be any praise, think on these things.  Those things, which ye 12 have both learned, and received, and heard, and seen in me, do: and the God of peace shall be with you."

With love, Mother,

MARY BAKER G. EDDY

# CHAPTER V

## LETTERS

1

MY BELOVED BRETHREN:— If a member of the church
is inclined to be uncharitable, or to condemn his 3
brother without cause, let him put his finger to his lips,
and forgive others as he would *be* forgiven. One's first
lesson is to learn one's self; having done this, one will 6
naturally, through grace from God, forgive his brother and
love his enemies. To avenge an imaginary or an actual
wrong, is suicidal. The law of our God and the rule of 9
our church is to tell thy brother his fault and thereby help
him. If this rule fails in effect, then take the next Scriptural step: drop this member's name from the church, and 12
thereafter "let the dead bury their dead," — let silence
prevail over his remains.

If a man is jealous, envious, or revengeful, he will seek 15
occasion to balloon an atom of another man's indis-
cretion, inflate it, and send it into the atmosphere of mortal
mind — for other green eyes to gaze on: he will always 18
find somebody in his way, and try to push him aside;
will see somebody's faults to magnify under the lens that
he never turns on himself. 21

What have been your Leader's precepts and example!
Were they to save the sinner, and to spare his exposure

1 so long as a hope remained of thereby benefiting him?
Has her life exemplified long-suffering, meekness, charity,
3 purity?

She readily leaves the answer to those who know
her.

6   Do we yet understand how much better it is to be
wronged, than to commit wrong? What do we find in
the Bible, and in the Christian Science textbook, on this
9 subject? Does not the latter instruct you that looking
continually for a fault in somebody else, talking about it,
thinking it over, and how to meet it, — "rolling sin as a
12 sweet morsel under your tongue," — has the same power
to make you a sinner that acting thus regarding disease
has to make a man sick? Note the Scripture on this
15 subject: "Vengeance is mine;  I will repay, saith the
Lord."

The Christian Science Board of Directors has borne
18 the burden in the heat of the day, and it ought not to
be expected that they could have accomplished, without
one single mistake, such Herculean tasks as they have
21 accomplished. He who judges others should know well
whereof he speaks. Where the motive to do right exists,
and the majority of one's acts are right, we should avoid
24 referring to past mistakes. The greatest sin that one can
commit against himself is to wrong one of God's "little
ones."

27   Know ye not that he who exercises the largest charity,
and waits on God, renews his strength, and is exalted?
Love is not puffed up;  and the meek and loving, God
30 anoints and appoints to lead the line of mankind's tri-
umphal march out of the wilderness, out of darkness
into light.

Whoever challenges the errors of others and cherishes 1
his own, can neither help himself nor others; he will be
called a moral nuisance, a fungus, a microbe, a mouse 3
gnawing at the vitals of humanity. The darkness in
one's self must first be cast out, in order rightly to discern
darkness or to reflect light. 6

If the man of more than average avoirdupois kneels on
a stool in church, let the leaner sort console this brother's
necessity by doing likewise. Christian Scientists preserve 9
unity, and so shadow forth the substance of our sublime
faith, and the evidence of its being built upon the rock of
divine oneness, — one faith, one God, one baptism. 12

If our Board of Directors is prepared to itemize a report
of the first financial year since the erection of the edifice of
The First Church of Christ, Scientist, let it do so; other- 15
wise, I recommend that you waive the church By-law
relating to finances this year of your firstfruits. This
Board did not act under that By-law; it was not in ex- 18
istence all of the year. It is but just to consider the great
struggles with perplexities and difficulties which the
Directors encountered in Anno Domini 1894, and which 21
they have overcome. May God give unto us all that loving sense of gratitude which delights in the opportunity to
cancel accounts. I, for one, would be pleased to have the 24
Christian Science Board of Directors itemize a bill of this
church's gifts to Mother; and then to have them let her
state the value thereof, if, indeed, it could be estimated. 27

After this financial year, when you call on the members
of the Christian Science Board of Directors to itemize or
audit their accounts, these will be found already itemized, 30
and last year's records immortalized, with perils past and
victories won.

1   A motion was made, and a vote passed, at your last
meeting, on a subject the substance whereof you had al-
3 ready accepted as a By-law.  But, I shall take this as a
favorable omen, a fair token that heavy lids are opening,
even wider than before, to the light of Love — and By-laws.
6                    Affectionately yours,
                              MARY BAKER EDDY


                   TO ——, ON PRAYER

9              MASSACHUSETTS METAPHYSICAL COLLEGE,
                    571 COLUMBUS AVENUE,
                      BOSTON, March 21, 1885

12   *Dear Sir:* — In your communication to *Zion's Herald*,
March 18, under the heading, "Prayer and Healing; sup-
plemental," you state that you would "like to hear from
15 Dr. Cullis; and, by the way, from Mrs. Eddy, also."
  Because of the great demand upon my time, consisting
in part of dictating answers through my secretary, or an-
18 swering personally manifold letters and inquiries from all
quarters, — having charge of a church, editing a magazine, teaching Christian Science, receiving calls, etc., — I
21 find it inconvenient to accept your invitation to answer
you through the medium of a newspaper; but, for information as to what I believe and teach, would refer you to
24 the Holy Scriptures, to my various publications, and to my
Christian students.
  It was with a thrill of pleasure that I read in your arti-
27 cle these words: "If we have in any way misrepresented
either Dr. Cullis or Mrs. Eddy, we are sorry."  Even the
desire to be just is a vital spark of Christianity.  And those
30 words inspire me with the hope that you wish to be just.

If this is so, you will not delay corrections of the statement 1
you make at the close of your article, when referring to
me, "the pantheistic and prayerless Mrs. Eddy, of Boston." 3

It would be difficult to build a sentence of so few words
conveying ideas more opposite to the fact.

In refutation of your statement that I am a pantheist, 6
I request you to read my sermons and publications.

As to being "prayerless," I call your attention and
deep consideration to the following Scripture, that voices 9
my impressions of prayer: —

"When thou prayest, thou shalt not be as the hypocrites
are: for they love to pray standing in the synagogues and 12
in the corners of the streets, that they may be seen of men.
. . . But thou, when thou prayest, enter into thy closet,
and when thou hast shut thy door, pray to thy Father 15
which is in secret; and thy Father which seeth in secret
shall reward thee openly."

I hope I am not wrong in literally following the dictum 18
of Jesus; and, were it not because of my desire to set
you right on this question, I should feel a delicacy in making the following statement: — 21

Three times a day, I retire to seek the divine blessing
on the sick and sorrowing, with my face toward the Jerusalem of Love and Truth, in silent prayer to the Father 24
which "seeth in secret," and with childlike confidence that
He will reward "openly." In the midst of depressing care
and labor I turn constantly to divine Love for guidance, 27
and find rest. It affords me great joy to be able to attest to
the truth of Jesus' words. Love makes all burdens light,
it giveth a peace that passeth understanding, and with 30
"signs following." As to the peace, it is unutterable; as
to "signs," behold the sick who are healed, the sorrowful

1 who are made hopeful, and the sinful and ignorant who
have become "wise unto salvation"!

3 And now, dear sir, as you have expressed contrition for
an act which you have immediately repeated, you are
placed in this dilemma: To reiterate such words of
6 apology as characterize justice and Christianity.

Very truly,<br>
MARY BAKER G. EDDY

9 TO THE NATIONAL CHRISTIAN SCIENTIST ASSOCIATION

*Beloved Students:*— Meet together and meet *en masse,*
in 1888, at the annual session of the National Christian
12 Scientist Association. Be "of one mind," "in one place,"
and God will pour you out a blessing such as you never
before received. He who dwelleth in eternal light is
15 bigger than the shadow, and will guard and guide His
own.

Let no consideration bend or outweigh your purpose
18 to be in Chicago on June 13. Firm in your allegiance to
the reign of universal harmony, go to its rescue. In God's
hour, the powers of earth and hell are proven powerless.
21 The reeling ranks of *materia medica,* with poisons, nos-
trums, and knives, are impotent when at war with the
omnipotent! Like Elisha, look up, and behold: "They
24 that be with us, are more than they that be with them."

Error is only fermenting, and its heat hissing at the
"still, small voice" of Truth; but it can neither silence
27 nor disarm God's voice. Spiritual wickedness is standing in high places; but, blind to its own fate, it will tumble
into the bottomless.

Christians, and all *true* Scientists, marching under what- 1
soever ensign, come into the ranks!  Again I repeat, person is not in the question of Christian Science.  Principle, 3
instead of person, is next to our hearts, on our lips, and
in our lives.  Our watchwords are Truth and Love; and
if we abide in these, they will abound in us, and we shall 6
be one in heart, — one in motive, purpose, pursuit.  Abiding in Love, not one of you can be separated from me; and
the sweet sense of journeying on together, doing unto 9
others as ye would they should do unto you, conquers all
opposition, surmounts all obstacles, and secures success.
If you falter, or fail to fulfil this Golden Rule, though you 12
should build to the heavens, you would build on sand.

Is it a cross to give one week's time and expense to the
jubilee of Spirit?  Then take this cross, and the crown 15
with it.  Sending forth currents of Truth, God's methods
and means of healing, and so spreading the gospel of
Love, is in itself an eternity of joy that outweighs an 18
hour.  Add one more noble offering to the unity of good,
and so cement the bonds of Love.

With love,                                           21
MARY BAKER EDDY

## TO THE COLLEGE ASSOCIATION

Letter read at the meeting of the Massachusetts Metaphysical 24
College Association, June 3, 1891

TO THE MEMBERS OF THE CHRISTIAN SCIENTISTS' ASSOCIATION OF
THE MASSACHUSETTS METAPHYSICAL COLLEGE 27

*My Beloved Students:* — You may be looking to see me
in my accustomed place with you, but this you must no
6

1 longer expect. When I retired from the field of labor,
it was a departure, socially, publicly, and finally, from
3 the routine of such material modes as society and our
societies demand. Rumors are rumors, — nothing more.
I am still with you on the field of battle, taking forward
6 marches, broader and higher views, and with the hope
that you will follow.

The eternal and infinite, already brought to your
9 earnest consideration, so grow upon my vision that I
cannot feel justified in turning aside for one hour from
contemplation of them and of the faith unfeigned.
12 When the verities of being seem to you as to me, — as
they must some time, — you will understand the necessity for my seclusion, and its fulfilment of divine order.
15 "Wherefore come out from among them, and be ye separate, saith the Lord."

All our thoughts should be given to the absolute
18 demonstration of Christian Science. You can well
afford to give me up, since you have in my last revised edition of Science and Health your teacher and
21 guide.

I recommend that the June session of this honorable
body shall close your meetings for the summer; also, that
24 hereafter you hold three sessions annually, convening
once in four months; oftener is not requisite, and the
members coming from a distance will be accommodated
27 by this arrangement.

Yours affectionately,<br>
MARY B. G. EDDY

TO THE NATIONAL CHRISTIAN SCIENTIST ASSOCIATION 1

*My Dear Students and Friends:* — Accept my thanks
for your card of invitation, your badge, and order of exer- 3
cise, all of which are complete.

When I gave you a meagre reception in Boston at the
close of the first convention of the National Christian 6
Scientist Association, it was simply to give you the privilege, poor as it was, of speaking a few words aside to your
teacher.  I remember my regret, when, having asked in 9
general assembly if you had any questions to propose, I
received no reply.  Since then you have doubtless realized
that such opportunity might have been improved;  but 12
that time has passed.

I greatly rejoice over the growth of my students within
the last few years.  It was kind of you to part so gently 15
with the protecting wings of the mother-bird, and to spread
your own so bravely.  Now, dear ones, if you take my
advice again, you will do — what?                          18

Even this: Disorganize the National Christian Scientist Association! and each one return to his place of
labor, to work out individually and alone, for himself and 21
for others, the sublime ends of human life.

To accomplish this, you must give much time to self-
examination and correction; you must control appetite, 24
passion, pride, envy, evil-speaking, resentment, and each
one of the innumerable errors that worketh or maketh
a lie.  Then you can give to the world the benefit of all 27
this, and heal and teach with increased confidence.  My
students can *now* organize their students into associations, form churches, and hold these organizations of their 30

1 own, — until, in turn, their students will sustain themselves and work for others.

3 The time it takes yearly to prepare for this national
convention is worse than wasted, if it causes thought to
wander in the wilderness or ways of the world.  The de-
6 tail of conforming to society, in any way, costs you what
it would to give time and attention to hygiene in your
ministry and healing.

9 For students to work together is not always to cooperate, but sometimes to coelbow!  Each student should
seek alone the guidance of our common Father — even
12 the divine Principle which he claims to demonstrate, —
and especially should he prove his faith by works, ethi-
cally, physically, and spiritually.  Remember that the
15 first and last lesson of Christian Science is love, perfect
love, and love made perfect through the cross.

I once thought that in unity was human strength; but
18 have grown to know that human strength is weakness, —
that unity is divine might, giving to human power, peace.

My counsel is applicable to the state of general growth
21 in the members of the National Christian Scientist Association, but it is not so adapted to the members of
students' organizations.  And wherefore?  Because the
24 growth of these at first is more gradual; but whenever
they are equal to the march triumphant, God will give
to all His soldiers of the cross the proper command, and
27 under the banner of His love, and with the "still, small
voice" for the music of our march, we all shall take step
and march on in spiritual organization.

30          Your loving teacher,
               MARY BAKER G. EDDY
CONCORD, N. H., May 23, 1890

N. B. I recommend this honorable body to adjourn, 1
if it does not disorganize, to three years from this date;
or, if it does disorganize, to meet again in three years. 3
Then bring your tithes into the storehouse, and God will
pour you out a blessing such as you even yet have not
received. 6

M. B. G. E.

## TO THE FIRST CHURCH OF CHRIST, SCIENTIST, BOSTON 9

*(For the weapons of our warfare are not carnal, but mighty through God to the pulling down of strong holds;) casting down imaginations, and every high thing that exalteth itself against the 12 knowledge of God, and bringing into captivity every thought to the obedience of Christ.* — 2 COR. X. 4, 5.

In April, 1883, I started the *Journal* of Christian 15
Science, with a portion of the above Scripture for its
motto.

On December 10, 1889, I gave a lot of land — in 18
Boston, situated near the beautiful Back Bay Park, now
valued at $20,000 and rising in value — for the purpose
of having erected thereon a church edifice to be called The 21
Church of Christ, Scientist.

I had this desirable site transferred in a circuitous,
novel way, at the wisdom whereof a few persons have 24
since scrupled; but to my spiritual perception, like all
true wisdom, this transaction will in future be regarded
as greatly wise, and it will be found that this act was in 27
advance of the erring mind's apprehension.

As with all former efforts in the interest of Christian
Science, I took care that the provisions for the land and 30

1 building were such as error could not control. I knew
that to God's gift, foundation and superstructure, no one
3 could hold a wholly material title. The land, and the
church standing on it, must be conveyed through a type
representing the true nature of the gift; a type morally
6 and spiritually inalienable, but materially questionable
— even after the manner that all spiritual good comes
to Christian Scientists, to the end of taxing their faith
9 in God, and their adherence to the superiority of the
claims of Spirit over matter or merely legal titles.

No one could buy, sell, or mortgage my gift as I had
12 it conveyed. Thus the case rested, and I supposed the
trustee-deed was legal; but this was God's business, not
mine. Our church was prospered by the right hand of
15 His righteousness, and contributions to the Building Fund
generously poured into the treasury. Unity prevailed, —
till mortal man sought to know who owned God's temple,
18 and adopted and urged only the material side of this
question.

The lot of land which I donated I redeemed from under
21 mortgage. The foundation on which our church was to
be built had to be rescued from the grasp of legal power,
and now it must be put back into the arms of Love, if we
24 would not be found fighting against God.

The diviner claim and means for upbuilding the Church
of Christ were prospered. Our title to God's acres will
27 be safe and sound — when we can "read our title clear"
to heavenly mansions. Built on the rock, our church
will stand the storms of ages: though the material super-
30 structure should crumble into dust, the fittest would survive, — the spiritual idea would live, a perpetual type of
the divine Principle it reflects.

The First Church of Christ, Scientist, our prayer in 1
stone, will be the prophecy fulfilled, the monument up-
reared, of Christian Science.  It will speak to you of the 3
Mother, and of your hearts' offering to her through whom
was revealed to you God's all-power, all-presence, and
all-science.  This building begun, will go up, and no one 6
can suffer from it, for no one can resist the power that
is behind it;  and against this church temple "the gates
of hell" cannot prevail.                                      9

All loyal Christian Scientists hail with joy this proposed type of universal Love;  not so, however, with
error, which hates the bonds and methods of Truth, and 12
shudders at the freedom, might, and majesty of Spirit,
— even the annihilating law of Love.

I vindicate both the law of God and the laws of our 15
land.  I believe, — yea, I understand, — that with the
spirit of Christ actuating all the parties concerned about
the legal quibble, it can easily be corrected to the satis- 18
faction of all.  Let this be speedily done.  Do not, I im-
plore you, stain the early history of Christian Science by
the impulses of human will and pride;  but let the divine 21
will and the nobility of human meekness rule this business transaction, in obedience to the law of Love and the
laws of our land.                                             24

As the ambassador of Christ's teachings, I admonish
you:  Delay not longer to commence building our church
in Boston;  or else return every dollar that you yourselves 27
declare you have had no legal authority for obtaining, to
the several contributors, — and let them, not you, say
what shall be done with their money.                          30

Of our first church in Boston, O recording angel!
write:  God is in the midst of her:  how beautiful are her

feet! how beautiful are her garments! how hath He enlarged her borders! how hath He made her wildernesses
to bud and blossom as the rose!

With love,

MARY BAKER EDDY

6 TO DONORS OF BOAT, FROM TORONTO, CANADA

*Written on receipt of a beautiful boat presented by Christian Scientists in Toronto, for the little pond at Pleasant View. The boat displays, among other beautiful decorations, a number of masonic symbols.*

*Beloved Students and Friends:* — Accept my thanks for the beautiful boat and presentation poem. Each day since they arrived I have said, Let me write to the donors, — and what?

My first impression was to indite a poem; my second, a psalm; my third, a letter. Why the letter alone? Be- cause your dear hearts expressed in their lovely gift such varying types of true affection, shaded as autumn leaves with bright hues of the spiritual, that my Muse lost her lightsome lyre, and imagery of thought gave place to chords of feeling too deep for words.

A boat song seemed more Olympian than the psalm in spiritual strains of the Hebrew bard. So I send my answer in a commonplace letter. Poor return, is it not?

The symbols of freemasonry depicted on the boat wakened memory, touched tender fibres of thought, and I longed to say to the masonic brothers: If as a woman I may not unite with you in freemasonry, nor you with me in Christian Science, yet as friends we can feel the

touch of heart to heart and hand to hand, on the broad 1
basis and sure foundation of true friendship's "level"
and the "square" of moral sentiments. 3

My dear students may have explained to the kind participants in beautifying this boat our spiritual points,
above the plane of matter. If so, I may hope that a 6
closer link hath bound us. Across lakes, into a kingdom,
I reach out my hand to clasp yours, with this silent benediction: May the kingdom of heaven come in each of 9
your hearts!

With love,

MARY BAKER EDDY    12

## ADDRESS, — LAYING THE CORNER-STONE

*Beloved Students:* — On the 21st day of May, A. D.
1894, with quiet, imposing ceremony, is laid the corner- 15
stone of "The First Church of Christ, Scientist," in
Boston.

It gives me great pleasure to say that you, principally 18
the Normal class graduates of my College, well known
physicians, teachers, editors, and pastors of churches,
by contributions of one thousand dollars each, husband 21
and wife reckoned as one, have, within about three
months, donated the munificent sum of forty-two thousand dollars toward building The Mother Church. A 24
quiet call from me for this extra contribution, in aid of
our Church Building Fund, found you all "with one
accord in one place." Each donation came promptly; 27
sometimes at much self-sacrifice, but always accompanied
with a touching letter breathing the donor's privileged joy.

1 The granite for this church was taken from the quarries in New Hampshire, my native State. The money
3 for building "Mother's Room," situated in the second story of the tower on the northeast corner of this building, and the name thereof, came from the dear children
6 of Christian Scientists; a little band called Busy Bees, organized by Miss Maurine R. Campbell.

On this memorable day there are laid away a copy of
9 this address, the subscription list on which appear your several names in your own handwriting, your textbook, "Science and Health with Key to the Scriptures," and
12 other works written by the same author, your teacher, the Discoverer and Founder of Christian Science; * without pomp or pride, laid away as a sacred secret in the
15 heart of a rock, there to typify the prophecy, "And a man shall be as an hiding place from the wind, and a covert from the tempest; . . . as the shadow of a great rock in
18 a weary land:" henceforth to whisper our Master's promise, "Upon this rock I will build my church; and the gates of hell shall not prevail against it."
21 To-day, be this hope in each of our hearts, — precious in God's sight as shall be the assembling of His people in this temple, sweet as the rest that remaineth for the
24 righteous, and fresh as a summer morn, — that, from earth's pillows of stone, our visible lives are rising to God. As in the history of a seed, so may our earthly
27 sowing bear fruit that exudes the inspiration of the wine poured into the cup of Christ.

To-day I pray that divine Love, the life-giving Principle
30 of Christianity, shall speedily wake the long night of materialism, and the universal dawn shall break upon the spire of this temple. The Church, more than any

---

* A copy of the Bible was included among the books placed in the corner-stone.

other institution, at present is the cement of society, and 1
it should be the bulwark of civil and religious liberty.
But the time cometh when the religious element, or Church 3
of Christ, shall exist alone in the affections, and need no
organization to express it.   Till then, this form of godliness seems as requisite to manifest its spirit, as individ- 6
uality to express Soul and substance.

Does a single bosom burn for fame and power?  Then
when that person shall possess these, let him ask him- 9
self, and answer to his name in this corner-stone of our
temple: Am I greater for them?  And if he thinks that
he is, then is he less than man to whom God gave "do- 12
minion over all the earth," less than the meek who "inherit the earth."   Even vanity forbids man to be vain;
and pride is a hooded hawk which flies in darkness.  Over 15
a wounded sense of its own error, let not mortal thought
resuscitate too soon.

In our rock-bound friendship, delicate as dear, our 18
names may melt into one, and common dust, and their
modest sign be nothingness.  Be this as it may, the visible
unity of spirit remains, to quicken even dust into sweet 21
memorial such as Isaiah prophesied: "The wolf also shall
dwell with the lamb, and the leopard shall lie down with
the kid;  and the calf and the young lion and the fatling 24
together;  and a little child shall lead them."

When the *hearts* of Christian Scientists are woven together as are their names in the web of history, earth will 27
float majestically heaven's heraldry, and echo the song
of angels: "Glory to God in the highest, and on earth
peace, good will toward men."                              30

To The Church of Christ, Scientist, in Boston, and to
the dear children that my heart folds within it, let me

1 say, 'Tis sweet to remember thee, and God's Zion, with
healing on her wings.  May her walls be vocal with sal-
3 vation; and her gates with praise!

TO THE FIRST CHURCH OF CHRIST, SCIENTIST,
BOSTON

6  *My Beloved Students:* — I cannot conscientiously lend
my counsel to direct your action on receiving or dismiss-
ing candidates.  To do this, I should need to be with
9 you.  I cannot accept hearsay, and would need to know
the circumstances and facts regarding both sides of the
subject, to form a proper judgment.  This is not my
12 present province; hence I have hitherto declined to be
consulted on these subjects, and still maintain this
position.

15  These are matters of grave import; and you cannot
be indifferent to this, but will give them immediate attention, and be governed therein by the spirit and the
18 letter of this Scripture: "Whatsoever ye would that men
should do unto you, do ye even so to them."

I cannot be the conscience for this church; but if I
21 were, I would gather every reformed mortal that desired
to come, into its fold, and counsel and help him to walk
in the footsteps of His flock.  I feel sure that as Chris-
24 tian Scientists you will act, relative to this matter, up to
your highest understanding of justice and mercy.

Affectionately yours,

MARY BAKER EDDY

27

Feb. 12, 1895

THE FIRST MEMBERS OF THE FIRST CHURCH OF CHRIST, SCIENTIST, BOSTON, MASSACHUSETTS

*My Beloved Students:* — Another year has rolled on, another annual meeting has convened, another space of time has been given us, and has another duty been done and another victory won for time and eternity? Do you meet in unity, preferring one another, and demonstrating the divine Principle of Christian Science? Have you improved past hours, and ladened them with records worthy to be borne heavenward? Have you learned that sin is inadmissible, and indicates a small mind? Do you manifest love for those that hate you and despitefully use you?

The man of integrity is one who makes it his constant rule to follow the road of duty, according as Truth and the voice of his conscience point it out to him. He is not guided merely by affections which may some time give the color of virtue to a loose and unstable character.

The upright man is guided by a fixed Principle, which destines him to do nothing but what is honorable, and to abhor whatever is base or unworthy; hence we find him ever the same, — at all times the trusty friend, the affectionate relative, the conscientious man of business, the pious worker, the public-spirited citizen.

He assumes no borrowed appearance. He seeks no mask to cover him, for he acts no studied part; but he is indeed what he appears to be, — full of truth, candor, and humanity. In all his pursuits, he knows no path but the fair, open, and direct one, and would much rather fail of success than attain it by reproachable means. He

1 never shows us a smiling countenance while he meditates
evil against us in his heart.  We shall never find one part
3 of his character at variance with another.

Lovingly yours,<br>MARY BAKER EDDY

6 Sept. 30, 1895

EXTRACT FROM A LETTER

The Rules and By-laws in the Manual of The First
9 Church of Christ, Scientist, Boston, originated not in
solemn conclave as in ancient Sanhedrim.  They were
not arbitrary opinions nor dictatorial demands, such as
12 one person might impose on another.  They were impelled by a power not one's own, were written at different dates, and as the occasion required.  They sprang
15 from necessity, the logic of events, — from the immediate demand for them as a help that must be supplied to
maintain the dignity and defense of our Cause;  hence
18 their simple, scientific basis, and detail so requisite to
demonstrate genuine Christian Science, and which will
do for the race what absolute doctrines destined for future
21 generations might not accomplish.

TO THE MOTHER CHURCH

*Beloved Brethren:* — Until recently, I was not aware
24 that the contribution box was presented at your Friday
evening meetings.  I specially desire that you collect no
moneyed contributions from the people present on these
27 occasions.

Let the invitation to this sweet converse be in the words
of the prophet Isaiah: "Ho, every one that thirsteth,

come ye to the waters, and he that hath no money; come 1
ye, buy, and eat; yea, come, buy wine and milk without
money and without price." 3

Invite all cordially and freely to this banquet of Christian Science, this feast and flow of Soul. Ask them to bring what they possess of love and light to help leaven 6 your loaf and replenish your scanty store. Then, after presenting the various offerings, and one after another has opened his lips to discourse and distribute what God 9 has given him of experience, hope, faith, and understanding, gather up the fragments, and count the baskets full of accessions to your love, and see that nothing has 12 been lost.

With love,
MARY BAKER EDDY 15

## TO FIRST CHURCH OF CHRIST, SCIENTIST, IN OCONTO

*My Beloved Brethren:* — Lips nor pen can ever ex- 18 press the joy you give me in parting so promptly with your beloved pastor, Rev. Mr. Norcross, to send him to aid me. It is a refreshing demonstration of Christianity, 21 brotherly love, and all the rich graces of the Spirit. May this sacrifice bring to your beloved church a vision of the new church, that cometh down from heaven, whose altar 24 is a loving heart, whose communion is fellowship with saints and angels. This example of yours is a light that cannot be hid. 27

Guided by the pillar and the cloud, this little church that built the first temple for Christian Science worship shall abide steadfastly in the faith of Jesus' words: "Fear 30

1 not, little flock; for it is your Father's good pleasure to
give you the kingdom." May He soon give you a pastor;
3 already you have the great Shepherd of Israel watching over you. Give my forever-love to your dear church.

Yours in bonds of Christ,

6               MARY BAKER G. EDDY
Boston, Mass., 1889

## TO FIRST CHURCH OF CHRIST, SCIENTIST, IN
9                     SCRANTON

*Beloved Brethren:* — Space is no separator of hearts.
Spiritually, I am with all who are with Truth, and whose
12 hearts to-day are repeating their joy that God dwelleth
in the congregation of the faithful, and loveth the gates
of Zion.

15    The outlook is cheering. We have already seen the
salvation of many people by means of Christian Science.
Chapels and churches are dotting the entire land. Con-
18 venient houses and halls can now be obtained wherein, as
whereout, Christian Scientists may worship the Father
"in spirit and in truth," as taught by our great Master.

21    "If God be for us, who can be against us?" If He
be with us, the wayside is a sanctuary, and the desert a
resting-place peopled with living witnesses of the fact
24 that "God is Love."

God is universal; confined to no spot, defined by no
dogma, appropriated by no sect. Not more to one than
27 to all, is God demonstrable as divine Life, Truth, and
Love; and His people are they that reflect Him — that
reflect Love. Again, this infinite Principle, with its uni-
30 versal manifestation, is all that really is or can be;
hence God is our Shepherd. He guards, guides, feeds,

and folds the sheep of His pasture; and their ears are attuned to His call.   In the words of the loving disciple, "My sheep hear my voice, . . . and they follow me; . . . neither shall any man pluck them out of my hand."

God is a consuming fire.   He separates the dross from the gold, purifies the human character, through the furnace of affliction.   Those who bear fruit He purgeth, that they may bear more fruit.   Through the sacred law, He speaketh to the unfruitful in tones of Sinai: and, in the gospel, He saith of the barren fig-tree, "Cut it down; why cumbereth it the ground?"

God is our Father and our Mother, our Minister and the great Physician:  He is man's only real relative on earth and in heaven.   David sang, "Whom have I in heaven but thee? and there is none upon earth that I desire beside thee."

Brother, sister, beloved in the Lord, knowest thou thyself, and art thou acquainted with God?  If not, I pray thee as a Christian Scientist, delay not to make Him thy first acquaintance.

Glorious things are spoken of you in His Word.  Ye are a chosen people, whose God is — what?  Even *All*. May mercy and truth go before you: may the lamp of your life continually be full of oil, and you be wedded to the spiritual idea, Christ;  then will you heal, and teach, and preach, on the ascending scale of everlasting Life and Love.

Affectionately yours in Christ,

MARY BAKER EDDY

1    TO FIRST CHURCH OF CHRIST, SCIENTIST,
                    IN DENVER

3    *Beloved Pastor and Brethren:* — "As in water face
answereth to face," and in love continents clasp hands, so
the oneness of God includes also His presence with those
6 whose hearts unite in the purposes of goodness.  Of this
we may be sure: that thoughts winged with peace and
love breathe a silent benediction over all the earth, co-
9 operate with the divine power, and brood unconsciously
o'er the work of His hand.

I, as a corporeal person, am not in your midst: I, as a
12 dictator, arbiter, or ruler, am not present;  but I, as a
mother whose heart pulsates with every throb of theirs
for the welfare of her children, am present, and rejoice
15 with them that rejoice.

May meekness, mercy, and love dwell forever in the
hearts of those who worship in this tabernacle:  then
18 will they receive the heritage that God has prepared for
His people, — made ready for the pure in affection, the
meek in spirit, the worshipper in truth, the follower of
21 good.

Thus founded upon the rock of Christ, when storm
and tempest beat against this sure foundation, you,
24 safely sheltered in the strong tower of hope, faith, and
Love, are God's nestlings;  and He will hide you in His
feathers till the storm has passed.   Into His haven of
27 Soul there enters no element of earth to cast out angels,
to silence the right intuition which guides you safely
home.

30    Exercise more faith in God and His spiritual means

and methods, than in man and his material ways and means, of establishing the Cause of Christian Science. If right yourself, God will confirm His inheritance. "Be not weary in well doing." Truth is restful, and Love is triumphant.

When God went forth before His people, they were fed with manna: they marched through the wilderness: they passed through the Red Sea, untouched by the billows. At His command, the rock became a fountain; and the land of promise, green isles of refreshment. In the words of the Psalmist, when "the Lord gave the word: great was the company of those that published it."

God is good to Israel, — washed in the waters of Meribah, cleansed of the flesh, — good to His Israel encompassed not with pride, hatred, self-will, and self-justification; wherein violence covereth men as a garment, and as captives are they enchained.

Christian Scientists bring forth the fruits of Spirit, not flesh; and God giveth this "new name" to no man who honors Him not by positive proof of trustworthiness. May you be able to say, "I have not cleansed my heart in vain."

Sir Edwin Arnold, to whom I presented a copy of my first edition of "Science and Health with Key to the Scriptures," writes: —

> Peace on earth and Good-will!
> Souls that are gentle and still
> Hear the first music of this
> Far-off, infinite, Bliss!

So may the God of peace be and abide with this church.

Affectionately yours,

MARY BAKER EDDY

1    TO FIRST CHURCH OF CHRIST, SCIENTIST,
IN LAWRENCE

3    *Beloved Brethren:* — The spreading branches of The
Church of Christ, Scientist, are fast reaching out their
broad shelter to the entire world.  Your faith has not
6 been without works, — and God's love for His flock is
manifest in His care.  He will dig about this little church,
prune its encumbering branches, water it with the dews
9 of heaven, enrich its roots, and enlarge its borders with
divine Love.  God only waits for man's worthiness to
enhance the means and measure of His grace.  You
12 have already proof of the prosperity of His Zion.  You
sit beneath your own vine and fig-tree as the growth
of spirituality — even that vine whereof our Father is
15 husbandman.

It is the purpose of divine Love to resurrect the understanding, and the kingdom of God, the reign of har-
18 mony already within us.  Through the word that is
spoken unto you, are you made free.  Abide in His word,
and it shall abide in you; and the healing Christ will
21 again be made manifest in the flesh — understood and
glorified.

Honor thy Father and Mother, God.  Continue in
24 His love.  Bring forth fruit — "signs following" — that
your prayers be not hindered.  Pray without ceasing.
Watch diligently; never desert the post of spiritual ob-
27 servation and self-examination.  Strive for self-abnegation, justice, meekness, mercy, purity, love.  Let your
light reflect Light.  Have no ambition, affection, nor
30 aim apart from holiness.  Forget not for a moment, that

God is All-in-all — therefore, that in reality there is but 1
one cause and effect.

The pride of circumstance or power is the prince of 3
this world that has nothing in Christ. All power and
happiness are spiritual, and proceed from goodness.
Sacrifice self to bless one another, even as God has 6
blessed you. Forget self in laboring for mankind; then
will you woo the weary wanderer to your door, win the
pilgrim and stranger to your church, and find access to 9
the heart of humanity. While pressing meekly on, be
faithful, be valiant in the Christian's warfare, and peace
will crown your joy.                                          12

Lovingly yours,

MARY BAKER EDDY

TO CORRESPONDENTS                    15

*Beloved Students:* — Because Mother has not the time
even to read all of her interesting correspondence, and
less wherein to answer it (however much she desires 18
thus to do), she hereby requests: First, that you, her
students' students, who write such excellent letters to
her, will hereafter, as a general rule, send them to the 21
editors of *The Christian Science Journal* for publication,
and thereby give to us all the pleasure of hearing from you.

If my own students cannot spare time to write to God, 24
— when they address me I shall be apt to forward their
letters to Him as our common Parent, and by way of
*The Christian Science Journal;* thus fulfilling their moral 27
obligation to furnish some reading-matter for our denominational organ. Methinks, were they to contemplate the
universal charge wherewith divine Love has entrusted us, 30

1 in behalf of a suffering race, they would contribute oftener
to the pages of this swift vehicle of scientific thought;
3 for it reaches a vast number of earnest readers, and seekers after Truth.        With love,

MARY BAKER EDDY

6                      TO STUDENTS

*Beloved Christian Scientists:* — Please send in your
contributions as usual to our *Journal.*  All is well at head-
9 quarters, and when the mist shall melt away you will see
clearly the signs of Truth and the heaven of Love within
your hearts.  Let the reign of peace and harmony be
12 supreme and forever yours.

I proposed to merge the adjourned meeting in the one
held at Chicago, because I saw no advantage, but great
15 disadvantage, in one student's opinions or *modus operandi* becoming the basis for others: read "Retrospection"
on this subject.  Science is absolute, and best under-
18 stood through the study of my works and the daily Christian demonstration thereof.  It is their *materiality* that
clogs the progress of students, and "this kind goeth not
21 forth but by prayer and fasting."  It is materialism through
which the animal magnetizer preys, and in turn becomes
a prey.  Spirituality is the basis of all true thought and
24 volition.  Assembling themselves together, and listening
to each other amicably, or contentiously, is no aid to
students in acquiring solid Christian Science.  Experi-
27 ence and, above all, *obedience,* are the aids and tests of
growth and understanding in this direction.

With love,
30                      MARY B. G. EDDY

## TO A STUDENT

*My Dear Student:* — It is a great thing to be found worthy to suffer for Christ, Truth. Paul said, "If we suffer, we shall also reign with him." Reign then, my beloved in the Lord. He that marketh the sparrow's fall will direct thy way.

I have written, or caused my secretary to write, to Mr. and Mrs. Stewart, of Toronto, Canada (you will find their card in *The C. S. Journal*), that you or your lawyer will ask them all questions important for your case, and requested that they furnish all information possible. They will be glad to help you. Every true Christian Scientist will feel "as bound with you," but as free in Truth and Love, safe under the shadow of His wing.

Yes, my student, my Father is your Father; and He helps us most when help is most needed, for He is the ever-present help.

I am glad that you are in good cheer. I enclose you the name of Mr. E. A. Kimball, C. S. D., of Chicago, — 5020 Woodlawn Ave., — for items relative to Mrs. Stebbin's case.

"Commit thy way unto the Lord; trust also in Him; and He shall bring it to pass. And He shall bring forth thy righteousness as the light, and thy judgment as the noonday." This I know, for God is for us.

Write me when you need me. Error has no power but to destroy itself. It *cannot harm you;* it cannot stop the eternal currents of Truth.

Ever with love,

MARY B. G. EDDY

1 TO A STUDENT

*My Beloved Student:* — In reply to your letter I will
3 say: God's ways are not as our ways; but higher far
than the heavens above the earth is His wisdom above
ours. When I requested you to be ordained, I little
6 thought of the changes about to be made. When I insisted on your speaking without notes, I little knew that
so soon another change in your pulpit would be demanded.
9 But now, after His messenger has obeyed the message
of divine Love, comes the interpretation thereof. But you
see we both had first to obey, and to do this through faith,
12 not sight.

The meaning of it all, as now shown, is this: when
you were bidden to be ordained, it was in reward for your
15 faithful service, thus to honor it. The second command,
to drop the use of notes, was to rebuke a lack of faith in
divine help, and to test your humility and obedience in
18 bearing this cross.

All God's servants are minute men and women. As
of old, I stand with sandals on and staff in hand, wait-
21 ing for the watchword and the revelation of what, how,
whither. Let us be faithful and obedient, and God will
do the rest.

24 In the April number of *The Christian Science Journal*
you will find the forthcoming completion (as I now think)
of the divine directions sent out to the churches. It is
27 satisfactory to note, however, that the order therein given
corresponds to the example of our Master. Jesus was
not ordained as our churches ordain ministers. We
30 have no record that he used notes when preaching. He

spake in their synagogues, reading the Scriptures and expounding them; and God has given to this age "Science and Health with Key to the Scriptures," to elucidate His Word.

You may read this letter to your church, and then send it to Rev. Mr. Norcross, and he will understand. May the God of all grace give you peace.

With love,

MARY BAKER EDDY

### EXTRACT FROM A CHRISTMAS LETTER

*Beloved Students:* — My heart has many rooms: one of these is sacred to the memory of my students. Into this upper chamber, where all things are pure and of good report, — into this sanctuary of love, — I often retreat, sit silently, and ponder. In this chamber is memory's wardrobe, where I deposit certain recollections and rare grand collections once in each year. This is my Christmas storehouse. Its goods commemorate, — not so much the Bethlehem babe, as the man of God, the risen Christ, and the adult Jesus. Here I deposit the gifts that my dear students offer at the shrine of Christian Science, and to their lone Leader. Here I talk once a year, — and this is a bit of what I said in 1890: "O glorious Truth! O Mother Love! how has the sense of Thy children grown to behold *Thee!* and how have many weary wings sprung upward! and how has our Model, Christ, been unveiled to us, and to the age!"

I look at the rich devices in embroidery, silver, gold, and jewels, — all gifts of Christian Scientists from all parts of our nation, and some from abroad, — then al-

1 most marvel at the power and permanence of affection
under the *régime* of Christian Science! Never did grati-
3 tude and love unite more honestly in uttering the word
*thanks,* than ours at this season. But a mother's love
behind words has no language; it may give no material
6 token, but lives steadily on, through time and circumstance, as part and paramount portion of her being.

Thus may our lives flow on in the same sweet rhythm
9 of head and heart, till they meet and mingle in bliss supernal. There is a special joy in knowing that one is gaining
constantly in the knowledge of Truth and divine Love.
12 Your progress, the past year, has been marked. It satisfies my present hope. Of this we rest assured, that every
trial of our faith in God makes us stronger and firmer in
15 understanding and obedience.

Lovingly yours,<br>
MARY BAKER G. EDDY

# CHAPTER VI

## SERMONS

### A CHRISTMAS SERMON

Delivered in Chickering Hall, Boston, Mass., on the
Sunday before Christmas, 1888

Subject: *The Corporeal and Incorporeal Saviour*

Text: *For unto us a child is born, unto us a son is given: and the
government shall be upon his shoulder: and his name shall be called
Wonderful, Counsellor, The mighty God, The everlasting Father, The
Prince of Peace.* — Isaiah ix. 6.

TO the senses, Jesus was the son of man: in Science,
man is the son of God. The material senses could
not cognize the Christ, or Son of God: it was Jesus'
approximation to this state of being that made him the
Christ-Jesus, the Godlike, the anointed.

The prophet whose words we have chosen for our
text, prophesied the appearing of this dual nature, as
both human and divinely endowed, the personal and the
impersonal Jesus.

The only record of our Master as a public benefactor,
or personal Saviour, opens when he was thirty years of
age; owing in part, perhaps, to the Jewish law that none
should teach or preach in public under that age. Also,
it is natural to conclude that at this juncture he was
specially endowed with the Holy Spirit; for he was given
the new name, Messiah, or Jesus Christ, — the God-

1 anointed;  even as, at times of special enlightenment,
Jacob was called Israel;  and Saul, Paul.

3    The third event of this eventful period, — a period of
such wonderful spiritual import to mankind! — was the
advent of a higher Christianity.

6    From this dazzling, God-crowned summit, the Nazarene stepped suddenly before the people and their schools
of philosophy;  Gnostic, Epicurean, and Stoic.  He must
9 stem these rising angry elements, and walk serenely over
their fretted, foaming billows.

Here the cross became the emblem of Jesus' history;
12 while the central point of his Messianic mission was peace,
good will, love, teaching, and healing.

Clad with divine might, he was ready to stem the tide
15 of Judaism, and prove his power, derived from Spirit, to
be supreme;  lay himself as a lamb upon the altar of
materialism, and therefrom rise to his nativity in Spirit.

18    The corporeal Jesus bore our infirmities, and through
his stripes we are healed.  He was the Way-shower, and
suffered in the flesh, showing mortals how to escape from
21 the sins of the flesh.

There was no incorporeal Jesus of Nazareth.  The
spiritual man, or Christ, was after the similitude of the
24 Father, without corporeality or finite mind.

Materiality, worldliness, human pride, or self-will, by
demoralizing his motives and Christlikeness, would have
27 dethroned his power as the Christ.

To carry out his holy purpose, he must be oblivious of
human self.

30    Of the lineage of David, like him he went forth, simple
as the shepherd boy, to disarm the Goliath.  Panoplied
in the strength of an exalted hope, faith, and understand-

ing, he sought to conquer the three-in-one of error: the world, the flesh, and the devil.

Three years he went about doing good. He had for thirty years been preparing to heal and teach divinely; but his three-years mission was a marvel of glory: its chaplet, a grave to mortal sense dishonored — from which sprang a sublime and everlasting victory!

He who dated time, the Christian era, and spanned eternity, was the meekest man on earth. He healed and taught by the wayside, in humble homes: to arrant hypocrite and to dull disciples he explained the Word of God, which has since ripened into interpretation through Science.

His words were articulated in the language of a declining race, and committed to the providence of God. In no one thing seemed he less human and more divine than in his unfaltering faith in the immortality of Truth. Referring to this, he said, "Heaven and earth shall pass away, but my words shall not pass away!" and they have not: they still live; and are the basis of divine liberty, the medium of Mind, the hope of the race.

Only three years a personal Saviour! yet the foundations he laid are as eternal as Truth, the chief cornerstone.

After his brief brave struggle, and the crucifixion of the corporeal man, the incorporeal Saviour — the Christ or spiritual idea which leadeth into all Truth — must needs come in Christian Science, demonstrating the spiritual healing of body and mind.

This idea or divine essence was, and is, forever about the Father's business; heralding the Principle of health, holiness, and immortality.

1 Its divine Principle interprets the incorporeal idea, or
Son of God; hence the incorporeal and corporeal are
3 distinguished thus: the former is the spiritual idea that
represents divine good, and the latter is the human
presentation of goodness in man. The Science of Chris-
6 tianity, that has appeared in the ripeness of time, reveals the incorporeal Christ; and this will continue
to be seen more clearly until it be acknowledged, under-
9 stood, — and the Saviour, which is Truth, be compre-
hended.

To the vision of the Wisemen, this spiritual idea of the
12 Principle of man or the universe, appeared as a star. At
first, the babe Jesus seemed small to mortals; but from
the mount of revelation, the prophet beheld it from the
15 beginning as the Redeemer, who would present a wonderful manifestation of Truth and Love.

In our text Isaiah foretold, "His name shall be called
18 Wonderful, Counsellor, The mighty God, The everlasting
Father, The Prince of Peace."

As the Wisemen grew in the understanding of Christ,
21 the spiritual idea, it grew in favor with them. Thus it
will continue, as it shall become understood, until man
be found in the actual likeness of his Maker. Their
24 highest human concept of the man Jesus, that portrayed
him as the only Son of God, the only begotten of the
Father, full of grace and Truth, will become so magnified
27 to human sense, by means of the lens of Science, as to
reveal man collectively, as individually, to be the son of
God.

30 The limited view of God's ideas arose from the testimony
of the senses. Science affords the evidence that God is the
Father of man, of all that is real and eternal. This spir-

itual idea that the personal Jesus demonstrated, casting 1
out evils and healing, more than eighteen centuries ago,
disappeared by degrees; both because of the ascension 3
of Jesus, in which it was seen that he had grown beyond
the human sense of him, and because of the corruption of
the Church. 6

The last appearing of Truth will be a wholly spiritual
idea of God and of man, without the fetters of the flesh, or
corporeality. This infinite idea of infinity will be, is, as 9
eternal as its divine Principle. The daystar of this appearing is the light of Christian Science — the Science which
rends the veil of the flesh from top to bottom. The light 12
of this revelation leaves nothing that is material; neither
darkness, doubt, disease, nor death. The material corporeality disappears; and individual spirituality, perfect 15
and eternal, appears — never to disappear.

The truth uttered and lived by Jesus, who passed on
and left to mortals the rich legacy of what he said and 18
did, makes his followers the heirs to his example; but
they can neither appreciate nor appropriate his treasures
of Truth and Love, until lifted to these by their own 21
growth and experiences. His goodness and grace purchased the means of mortals' redemption from sin; but,
they never paid the price of sin. This cost, none but the 24
sinner can pay; and accordingly as this account is settled
with divine Love, is the sinner ready to avail himself of
the rich blessings flowing from the teaching, example, 27
and suffering of our Master.

The secret stores of wisdom must be discovered, their
treasures reproduced and given to the world, before man 30
can truthfully conclude that he has been found in the
order, mode, and virgin origin of man according to divine

1 Science, which alone demonstrates the divine Principle
and spiritual idea of being.

3     The monument whose finger points upward, commem-
orates the earthly life of a martyr; but this is not all of
the philanthropist, hero, and Christian.   The Truth he
6 has taught and spoken lives, and moves in our midst a
divine afflatus.   Thus it is that the ideal Christ — or
impersonal infancy, manhood, and womanhood of Truth
9 and Love — is still with us.

And what of *this* child? — "For unto us a child *is*
born, unto us a son *is* given:  and the government shall
12 be upon his shoulder."

This child, or spiritual idea, has evolved a more ready
ear for the overture of angels and the scientific under-
15 standing of Truth and Love.   When Christ, the incorporeal idea of God, was nameless, and a Mary knew not
how to declare its spiritual origin, the idea of man was
18 not understood.   The Judæan religion even required the
Virgin-mother to go to the temple and be purified, for
having given birth to the corporeal child Jesus, whose
21 origin was more spiritual than the senses could interpret.   Like the leaven that a certain woman hid in three
measures of meal, the Science of God and the spiritual
24 idea, named in this century Christian Science, is leaven-
ing the lump of human thought, until the whole shall
be leavened and all materialism disappear.   This action
27 of the divine energy, even if not acknowledged, has
come to be seen as diffusing richest blessings.   This
spiritual idea, or Christ, entered into the minutiæ of the
30 life of the personal Jesus.   It made him an honest man,
a good carpenter, and a good man, before it could make
him the glorified.

The material questions at this age on the reappearing 1
of the infantile thought of God's man, are after the manner of a mother in the flesh, though their answers per- 3
tain to the spiritual idea, as in Christian Science: —

Is he deformed?
He is wholly symmetrical; the one altogether lovely. 6

Is the babe a son, or daughter?
Both son and daughter: even the compound idea of
all that resembles God. 9

How much does he weigh?
His substance outweighs the material world.

How old is he? 12
Of his days there is no beginning and no ending.

What is his name?
Christ Science. 15

Who are his parents, brothers, and sisters?
His Father and Mother are divine Life, Truth, and
Love; and they who do the will of his Father are his 18
brethren.

Is he heir to an estate?
"The government shall be upon his shoulder!" He 21
has dominion over the whole earth; and in admiration
of his origin, he exclaims, "I thank Thee, O Father, Lord
of heaven and earth, that Thou hast hid these things 24
from the wise and prudent, and hast revealed them unto
babes!"

Is he wonderful? 27
His works thus prove him. He giveth power, peace,
and holiness; he exalteth the lowly; he giveth liberty

7

1 to the captive, health to the sick, salvation from sin to the sinner — and overcometh the world!

3   Go, and tell what things ye shall see and hear:  how the blind, spiritually and physically, receive sight;  how the lame, those halting between two opinions or hob-
6 bling on crutches, walk;  how the physical and moral lepers are cleansed;  how the deaf — those who, having ears, hear not, and are afflicted with "tympanum on the
9 brain" — hear;  how the dead, those buried in dogmas and physical ailments, are raised;  that to the poor — the lowly in Christ, not the man-made rabbi — the
12 gospel is preached.  Note this:  only such as are pure in spirit, emptied of vainglory and vain knowledge, re-ceive Truth.

15   Here ends the colloquy;  and a voice from heaven seems to say, "Come and see."

The nineteenth-century prophets repeat, "Unto us a
18 son is given."

The shepherds shout, "We behold the appearing of the star!" — and the pure in heart clap their hands.


21     EDITOR'S EXTRACTS FROM SERMON

TEXT:  *Ye do err, not knowing the Scriptures, nor the power of God.* — MATT. xxii. 29.

24   *The Christian Science Journal* reported as follows: —
The announcement that the Rev. Mary B. G. Eddy would speak before the Scientist denomination on the
27 afternoon of October 26, drew a large audience.  Haw-thorne Hall was densely packed, and many had to go away unable to obtain seats.  The distinguished speaker
30 began by saying: —

Within Bible pages she had found all the divine Science 1
she preaches; noticing, all along the way of her researches
therein, that whenever her thoughts had wandered into 3
the bypaths of ancient philosophies or pagan literatures,
her spiritual insight had been darkened thereby, till
she was God-driven back to the inspired pages. Early 6
training, through the misinterpretation of the Word,
had been the underlying cause of the long years of invalidism she endured before Truth dawned upon her 9
understanding, through right interpretation. With the
understanding of Scripture-meanings, had come physical
rejuvenation. The uplifting of spirit was the upbuild- 12
ing of the body.

She affirmed that the Scriptures cannot properly be
interpreted in a literal way. The truths they teach must 15
be spiritually discerned, before their message can be
borne fully to our minds and hearts. That there is a
dual meaning to every Biblical passage, the most eminent 18
divines of the world have concluded; and to get at the
highest, or metaphysical, it is necessary rightly to read
what the inspired writers left for our spiritual instruction. 21
The literal rendering of the Scriptures makes them nothing valuable, but often is the foundation of unbelief and
hopelessness. The metaphysical rendering is health and 24
peace and hope for all. The literal or material reading is
the reading of the carnal mind, which is enmity toward
God, Spirit.                                          27

Taking several Bible passages, Mrs. Eddy showed how
beautiful and inspiring are the thoughts when rightly
understood. "Let the dead bury their dead; follow 30
thou me," was one of the passages explained metaphysically. In their fullest meaning, those words are salvation

1 from the belief of death, the last enemy to be overthrown;
for by following Christ truly, resurrection and life im-
3 mortal are brought to us.   If we follow him, to us there
can be no dead.   Those who know not this, may still
believe in death and weep over the graves of their beloved;
6 but with him is Life eternal, which never changes to
death.   The eating of bread and drinking of wine at the
Lord's supper, merely symbolize the spiritual refresh-
9 ment of God's children having rightly read His Word,
whose entrance into their understanding is healthful life.
This is the reality behind the symbol.

12    So, also, she spoke of the hades, or hell of Scripture,
saying, that we make our own heavens and our own hells,
by right and wise, or wrong and foolish, conceptions of
15 God and our fellow-men.   Jesus interpreted all spiritually: "I have bread to eat that ye know not of," he
said.   The bread he ate, which was refreshment of divine
18 strength, we also may all partake of.

The material record of the Bible, she said, is no more
important to our well-being than the history of Europe
21 and America;   but the spiritual application bears upon
our eternal life.   The method of Jesus was purely metaphysical;   and no other method is Christian Science.   In
24 the passage recording Jesus' proceedings with the blind
man (Mark viii.) he is said to have spat upon the dust.
Spitting was the Hebrew method of expressing the utmost
27 contempt.   So Jesus is recorded as having expressed
contempt for the belief of material eyes as having any
power to see.   Having eyes, ye see not;   and ears, ye hear
30 not, he had just told them.   The putting on of hands
mentioned, she explained as the putting forth of power.
"Hand," in Bible usage, often means spiritual power.

"His hand is not shortened that it cannot save," can 1
never be wrested from its true meaning to signify human
hands.  Jesus' first effort to realize Truth was not wholly 3
successful;  but he rose to the occasion with the second
attempt, and the blind saw clearly.  To suppose that
Jesus did actually anoint the blind man's eyes with his 6
spittle, is as absurd as to think, according to the report
of some, that Christian Scientists sit in back-to-back
seances with their patients, for the divine power to filter 9
from vertebræ to vertebræ.  When one comes to the age
with spiritual translations of God's messages, expressed
in literal or physical terms, our right action is not to con- 12
demn and deny, but to "try the spirits" and see what
manner they are of.  This does not mean communing
with spirits supposed to have departed from the earth, 15
but the seeking out of the basis upon which are accomplished the works by which the new teacher would prove
his right to be heard.  By these signs are the true disciples 18
of the Master known:  the sick are healed;  to the poor
the gospel is preached.

EXTRACT FROM A SERMON DELIVERED IN BOSTON, 21
JANUARY 18, 1885

TEXT: *The kingdom of heaven is like unto leaven, which a woman
took, and hid in three measures of meal, till the whole was leavened.* — 24
MATT. xiii. 33.

Few people at present know aught of the Science of
mental healing;  and so many are obtruding upon the 27
public attention their ignorance or false knowledge in
the name of Science, that it behooves all clad in the shining mail to keep bright their invincible armor; to keep 30

1 their demonstrations modest, and their claims and lives steadfast in Truth.

3 Dispensing the Word charitably, but separating the tares from the wheat, let us declare the positive and the negative of metaphysical Science; what it is, and 6 what it is not. Intrepid, self-oblivious Protestants in a higher sense than ever before, let us meet and defeat the claims of sense and sin, regardless of the bans or 9 clans pouring in their fire upon us; and white-winged charity, brooding over all, shall cover with her feathers the veriest sinner.

12 Divine and unerring Mind measures man, until the three measures be accomplished, and he arrives at fulness of stature; for "the Lord God omnipotent 15 reigneth."

Science is divine: it is neither of human origin nor of human direction. That which is termed "natural science," 18 the evidences whereof are taken in by the five personal senses, presents but a finite, feeble sense of the infinite law of God; which law is written on the heart, received 21 through the affections, spiritually understood, and demonstrated in our lives.

This law of God is the Science of mental healing, 24 spiritually discerned, understood, and obeyed.

Mental Science, and the five personal senses, are at war; and peace can only be declared on the side of im- 27 mutable right, — the health, holiness, and immortality of man. To gain this scientific result, the first and fundamental rule of Science must be understood and adhered 30 to; namely, the oft-repeated declaration in Scripture that God is good; hence, good is omnipotent and omnipresent.

Ancient and modern philosophy, human reason, or 1
man's theorems, misstate mental Science, its Principle
and practice. The most enlightened sense herein sees 3
nothing but a law of matter.

Who has ever learned of the schools that there is but
one Mind, and that this is God, who healeth all our sick- 6
ness and sins?

Who has ever learned from the schools, pagan philosophy, or scholastic theology, that Science is the law of 9
Mind and not of matter, and that this law has no relation
to, or recognition of, matter?

Mind is its own great cause and effect. Mind is God, 12
omnipotent and omnipresent. What, then, of an opposite so-called science, which says that man is both matter
and mind, that Mind is in matter? Can the infinite 15
be within the finite? And must not man have preexisted
in the All and Only? Does an evil mind exist without
space to occupy, power to act, or vanity to pretend that 18
it is man?

If God is Mind and fills all space, is everywhere, matter
is nowhere and sin is obsolete. If Mind, God, is all-power 21
and all-presence, man is not met by another power
and presence, that — obstructing his intelligence —
pains, fetters, and befools him. The perfection of man 24
is intact; whence, then, is something besides Him that
is not the counterpart but the counterfeit of man's creator?
Surely not from God, for He made man in His own 27
likeness. Whence, then, is the atom or molecule called
matter? Have attraction and cohesion formed it?
But are these forces laws of matter, or laws of 30
Mind?

For matter to be matter, it must have been self-created.

1 Mind has no more power to evolve or to create matter
than has good to produce evil. Matter is a misstatement
3 of Mind; it is a lie, claiming to talk and disclaim against
Truth; idolatry, having other gods; evil, having presence
and power over omnipotence!

6  Let us have a clearing up of abstractions. Let us
come into the presence of Him who removeth all iniquities, and healeth all our diseases. Let us attach our sense
9 of Science to what touches the religious sentiment within
man. Let us open our affections to the Principle that
moves all in harmony, — from the falling of a sparrow
12 to the rolling of a world. Above Arcturus and his sons,
broader than the solar system and higher than the atmosphere of our planet, is the Science of mental
15 healing.

What is the kingdom of heaven? The abode of Spirit,
the realm of the real. No matter is there, no night is
18 there — nothing that maketh or worketh a lie. Is this
kingdom afar off? No: it is ever-present here. The
first to declare against this kingdom is matter. Shall
21 that be called heresy which pleads for Spirit — the All of
God, and His omnipresence?

The kingdom of heaven is the reign of divine Science:
24 it is a mental state. Jesus said it is within you, and
taught us to pray, "Thy kingdom come;" but he did
not teach us to pray for death whereby to gain heaven.
27 We do not look into darkness for light. Death can never
usher in the dawn of Science that reveals the spiritual
facts of man's Life here and now.

30  The leaven which a woman took and hid in three
measures of meal, is Divine Science; the Comforter;
the Holy Ghost that leadeth into all Truth; the "still,

small voice" that breathes His presence and power, cast- 1
ing out error and healing the sick. And woman, the
spiritual idea, takes of the things of God and showeth 3
them unto the creature, until the whole sense of being
is leavened with Spirit. The three measures of meal
may well be likened to the false sense of life, substance, 6
and intelligence, which says, I am sustained by bread,
matter, instead of Mind. The spiritual leaven of divine
Science changes this false sense, giving better views of 9
Life; saying, Man's Life is God; and when this shall
appear, it shall be "the substance of things hoped for."

The measure of Life shall increase by every spiritual 12
touch, even as the leaven expands the loaf. Man shall
keep the feast of Life, not with the old leaven of the
scribes and Pharisees, neither with "the leaven of malice 15
and wickedness; but the unleavened bread of sincerity
and truth."

Thus it can be seen that the Science of mental healing 18
must be understood. There are false Christs that would
"deceive, if it were possible, the very elect," by institut-
ing matter and its methods in place of God, Mind. Their 21
supposition is, that there are other minds than His; that
one mind controls another; that one belief takes the
place of another. But this ism of to-day has nothing 24
to do with the Science of mental healing which acquaints
us with God and reveals the one perfect Mind and His
laws. 27

The attempt to mix matter and Mind, to work by
means of both animal magnetism and divine power, is
literally saying, Have we not in thy name cast out devils, 30
and done many wonderful works?

But remember God in all thy ways, and thou shalt

1 find the truth that breaks the dream of sense, letting the
harmony of Science that declares *Him,* come in with
3 healing, and peace, and perfect love.

## SUNDAY SERVICES ON JULY FOURTH

### EXTEMPORE REMARKS

6 The great theme so deeply and solemnly expounded
by the preacher, has been exemplified in all ages, but
chiefly in the great crises of nations or of the human race.
9 It is then that supreme devotion to Principle has especially been called for and manifested. It is then that we
learn a little more of the nothingness of evil, and more
12 of the divine energies of good, and strive valiantly for the
liberty of the sons of God.

The day we celebrate reminds us of the heroes and
15 heroines who counted not their own lives dear to them,
when they sought the New England shores, not as the
flying nor as conquerors, but, steadfast in faith and love,
18 to build upon the rock of Christ, the true idea of God —
the supremacy of Spirit and the nothingness of matter.
When first the Pilgrims planted their feet on Plymouth
21 Rock, frozen ritual and creed should forever have melted
away in the fire of love which came down from heaven.
The Pilgrims came to establish a nation in true freedom,
24 in the rights of conscience.

But what of ourselves, and our times and obligations?
Are we duly aware of our own great opportunities and
27 responsibilities? Are we prepared to meet and improve
them, to act up to the acme of divine energy wherewith
we are armored?

Never was there a more solemn and imperious call 1
than God makes to us all, right here, for fervent devotion and an absolute consecration to the greatest and 3
holiest of all causes. The hour is come. The great
battle of Armageddon is upon us. The powers of evil
are leagued together in secret conspiracy against the 6
Lord and against His Christ, as expressed and operative in Christian Science. Large numbers, in desperate
malice, are engaged day and night in organizing action 9
against us. Their feeling and purpose are deadly, and
they have sworn enmity against the lives of our standard-
bearers. 12

What will you do about it? Will you be equally in
earnest for the truth? Will you doff your lavender-kid
zeal, and become real and consecrated warriors? Will 15
you give yourselves wholly and irrevocably to the great
work of establishing the truth, the gospel, and the Science
which are necessary to the salvation of the world from 18
error, sin, disease, and death? Answer at once and practically, and answer aright!

EASTER SERVICES 21

The editor of *The Christian Science Journal* said that
at three o'clock, the hour for the church service proper,
the pastor, Rev. Mary Baker G. Eddy, accompanied 24
by Rev. D. A. Easton, who was announced to preach
the sermon, came on the platform. The pastor introduced Mr. Easton as follows: — 27

*Friends:* — The homesick traveller in foreign lands
greets with joy a familiar face. I am constantly homesick for heaven. In my long journeyings I have met 30

1 one who comes from the place of my own sojourning
for many years, — the Congregational Church.  He is
3 a graduate of Bowdoin College and of Andover The-
ological School.  He has left his old church, as I did,
from a yearning of the heart;  because he was not sat-
6 isfied with a manlike God, but wanted to become a Godlike man.  He found that the new wine could not be
put into old bottles without bursting them, and he came
9 to us.

Mr. Easton then delivered an interesting discourse
from the text, "If ye then be risen with Christ, seek
12 those things which are above, where Christ sitteth on the
right hand of God" (Col. iii. 1), which he prefaced by
saying: —

15   "I think it was about a year ago that I strayed into
this hall, a stranger, and wondered what sort of people
you were, and of what you were worshippers.  If any
18 one had said to me that to-day I should stand before
you to preach a sermon on Christian Science, I should
have replied, 'Much learning' — or something else —
21 'hath made thee mad.'  If I had not found Christian
Science a new gospel, I should not be standing before you:
if I had not found it truth, I could not have stood up
24 again *to* preach, here or elsewhere."

At the conclusion of the sermon, the pastor again came
forward, and added the following: —

27 My friends, I wished to be excused from speaking
to-day, but will yield to circumstances.  In the flesh, we
are as a partition wall between the old and the new;
30 between the old religion in which we have been educated,
and the new, living, impersonal Christ-thought that has
been given to the world to-day.

The old churches are saying, "He is not here;" and, 1
"Who shall roll away the stone?"

The stone has been rolled away by human suffer- 3
ing. The first rightful desire in the hour of loss, when
believing we have lost sight of Truth, is to know where
He is laid. This appeal resolves itself into these 6
questions: —

Is our consciousness in matter or in God? Have we
any other consciousness than that of good? If we have, 9
He is saying to us to-day, "Adam, where art thou?" We
are wrong if our consciousness is in sin, sickness, and
death. This is the old consciousness. 12

In the new religion the teaching is, "He is not here;
Truth is not in matter; he is risen; Truth has become
more to us, — more true, more spiritual." 15

Can we say this to-day? Have we left the consciousness of sickness and sin for that of health and
holiness? 18

What is it that seems a stone between us and the
resurrection morning?

It is the belief of mind in matter. We can only come 21
into the spiritual resurrection by quitting the old consciousness of Soul in sense.

These flowers are floral apostles. God does all this 24
through His followers; and He made every flower in
Mind before it sprang from the earth: yet we look into
matter and the earth to give us these smiles of God! 27

We must lay aside material consciousness, and then
we can perceive Truth, and say with Mary, "Rabboni!"
— Master! 30

In 1866, when God revealed to me this risen Christ,
this Life that knows no death, that saith, "Because he

1 lives, I live," I awoke from the dream of Spirit in the
flesh so far as to take the side of Spirit, and strive to cease
3 my warfare.

When, through this consciousness, I was delivered from
the dark shadow and portal of death, my friends were
6 frightened at beholding me restored to health.

A dear old lady asked me, "How is it that you are
restored to us?  Has Christ come again on earth?"
9 "Christ never left," I replied; "Christ is Truth, and
Truth is always here, — the impersonal Saviour."

Then another person, more material, met me, and I
12 said, in the words of my Master, "Touch me not."   I
shuddered at her material approach;  then my heart went
out to God, and I found the open door from this sepulchre
15 of matter.

I *love* the Easter service:  it speaks to me of Life, and
not of death.

18 Let us do our work;  then we shall have part in his
resurrection.


### BIBLE LESSONS

21 *But as many as received him, to them gave he power to become the*
*sons of God, even to them that believe on his name:  which were born,*
*not of blood, nor of the will of the flesh, nor of the will of man, but of*
24 *God.* — JOHN i. 12, 13.

Here, the apostle assures us that man has power to
become the son of God.  In the Hebrew text, the word
27 "son" is defined variously;  a month is called the son
of a year.  This term, as applied to man, is used in both
a material and a spiritual sense.  The Scriptures speak
30 of Jesus as the Son of God and the Son of man;  but

Jesus said to call no man father; "for one is your Father," 1
even God.

Is man's spiritual sonship a personal gift to man, or 3
is it the reality of his being, in divine Science? Man's
knowledge of this grand verity gives him power to demonstrate his divine Principle, which in turn is requisite 6
in order to understand his sonship, or unity with God,
good. A personal requirement of blind obedience to
the law of being, would tend to obscure the order of 9
Science, unless that requirement should express the claims
of the divine Principle. Infinite Principle and infinite
Spirit must be one. What avail, then, to quarrel over 12
what is the person of Spirit, — if we recognize infinitude
as personality, — for who can tell what is the form of
infinity? When we understand man's true birthright, that 15
he is "born, not . . . of the will of the flesh, nor of the
will of man, but of God," we shall understand that man
is the offspring of Spirit, and not of the flesh; recognize 18
him through spiritual, and not material laws; and regard
him as spiritual, and not material. His sonship, referred
to in the text, is his spiritual relation to Deity: it is not, 21
then, a personal gift, but is the order of divine Science.
The apostle urges upon our acceptance this great fact:
"But as many as received him, to them gave he power 24
to become the sons of God." Mortals will lose their sense
of mortality — disease, sickness, sin, and death — in
the proportion that they gain the sense of man's spirit- 27
ual preexistence as God's child; as the offspring of
good, and not of God's opposite, — evil, or a fallen
man. 30

John the Baptist had a clear discernment of divine
Science: being born not of the human will or flesh, he

1 antedated his own existence, began spiritually instead
of materially to reckon himself logically; hence the im-
3 possibility of putting him to death, only in belief, through
violent means or material methods.

"As many as received him;" that is, as many as per-
6 ceive man's actual existence in and of his divine Principle, receive the Truth of existence; and these have no
other God, no other Mind, no other origin; therefore, in
9 time they lose their false sense of existence, and find
their adoption with the Father; to wit, the redemption
of the body. Through divine Science man gains the
12 power to become the son of God, to recognize his perfect
and eternal estate.

"Which were born, not of blood, nor of the will of
15 the flesh." This passage refers to man's primal, spiritual existence, created neither from dust nor carnal desire. "Nor of the will of man." Born of no doctrine,
18 no human faith, but beholding the truth of being; even
the understanding that man was never lost in Adam,
since he is and ever was the image and likeness of God,
21 good. But no mortal hath seen the spiritual man, more
than he hath seen the Father. The apostle indicates
no personal plan of a personal Jehovah, partial and finite;
24 but the possibility of all finding their place in God's great
love, the eternal heritage of the Elohim, His sons and
daughters. The text is a metaphysical statement of exist-
27 ence as Principle and idea, wherein man and his Maker
are inseparable and eternal.

When the Word is made flesh, — that is, rendered
30 practical, — this eternal Truth will be understood; and
sickness, sin, and death will yield to it, even as they did
more than eighteen centuries ago. The lusts of the flesh

and the pride of life will then be quenched in the divine 1
Science of being; in the ever-present good, omnipotent
Love, and eternal Life, that know no death.  In the great 3
forever, the verities of being exist, and must be acknowledged and demonstrated.  Man must love his neighbor
as himself, and the power of Truth must be seen and 6
felt in health, happiness, and holiness: then it will be
found that Mind is All-in-all, and there is no matter to
cope with.                                                      9

Man is free born: he is neither the slave of sense, nor a
silly ambler to the so-called pleasures and pains of self-
conscious matter.  Man is God's image and likeness; 12
whatever is possible to God, is possible to man *as God's
reflection*.  Through the transparency of Science we learn
this, and receive it: learn that man can fulfil the Scrip- 15
tures in every instance; that if he open his mouth it shall
be filled — not by reason of the schools, or learning, but
by the natural ability, that reflection already has bestowed 18
on him, to give utterance to Truth.

"Who hath believed our report?"  Who understands
these sayings?  He to whom the arm of the Lord is re- 21
vealed; to whom divine Science unfolds omnipotence,
that equips man with divine power while it shames human
pride.  Asserting a selfhood apart from God, is a denial 24
of man's spiritual sonship; for it claims another father.
As many as do receive a knowledge of God through
Science, will have power to reflect His power, in proof of 27
man's "dominion over all the earth."  He is bravely
brave who dares at this date refute the evidence of material
sense with the facts of Science, and will arrive at the true 30
status of man because of it.  The material senses would
make man, that the Scriptures declare reflects his Maker,

1 the very opposite of that Maker, by claiming that God is
Spirit, while man is matter; that God is good, but man is
3 evil; that Deity is deathless, but man dies.   Science and
sense conflict, from the revolving of worlds to the death
of a sparrow.

6    The Word will be made flesh and dwell among mortals,
only when man reflects God in body as well as in mind.
The child born of a woman has the formation of his
9 parents; the man born of Spirit is spiritual, not material.
Paul refers to this when speaking of presenting our bodies
holy and acceptable, which is our reasonable service;
12 and this brings to remembrance the Hebrew strain,
"Who healeth all thy diseases."

If man should say of the power to be perfect which he
15 possesses, "I am the power," he would trespass upon
divine Science, yield to material sense, and lose his power;
even as when saying, "I have the power to sin and be
18 sick," and persisting in believing that he is sick and a
sinner.   If he says, "I am of God, therefore good," yet
persists in evil, he has denied the power of Truth, and
21 must suffer for this error until he learns that all power is
good because it is of God, and so destroys his self-deceived sense of power in evil.   The Science of being gives
24 back the lost likeness and power of God as the seal of
man's adoption.   Oh, for that light and love ineffable,
which casteth out all fear, all sin, sickness, and death;
27 that seeketh not her own, but another's good; that saith
Abba, Father, and *is* born of God!

John came baptizing with water.   He employed a type
30 of physical cleanliness to foreshadow metaphysical purity,
even mortal mind purged of the animal and human, and
submerged in the humane and divine, giving back the

lost sense of man in unity with, and reflecting, his Maker. 1
None but the pure in heart shall see God, — shall be able
to discern fully and demonstrate fairly the divine Principle 3
of Christian Science.   The will of God, or power of Spirit,
is made manifest as Truth, and through righteousness, —
not as or through matter, — and it strips matter of all 6
claims, abilities or disabilities, pains or pleasures.   Self-
renunciation of all that constitutes a so-called material
man, and the acknowledgment and achievement of his 9
spiritual identity as the child of God, is Science that
opens the very flood-gates of heaven; whence good
flows into every avenue of being, cleansing mortals of 12
all uncleanness, destroying all suffering, and demonstrating the true image and likeness.   There is no other
way under heaven whereby we can be saved, and man 15
be clothed with might, majesty, and immortality.

"As many as received him," — as accept the truth
of being, — "to them gave he power to become the sons 18
of God."   The spiritualization of our sense of man opens
the gates of paradise that the so-called material senses
would close, and reveals man infinitely blessed, upright, 21
pure, and free;   having no need of statistics by which to
learn his origin and age, or to measure his manhood, or to
know how much of a man he ever has been: for, "as 24
many as received him, to them gave he power to become
the sons of God."

*And so it is written, The first man Adam was made a living soul;* 27
*the last Adam was made a quickening spirit.* — 1 Cor. xv. 45.

When reasoning on this subject of man with the Corin-
thian brethren, the apostle first spake from their stand- 30
point of thought; namely, that creation is material:

1 he was not at this point giving the history of the spiritual
man who originates in God, Love, who created man
3 in His own image and likeness.   In the creation of Adam
from dust, — in which Soul is supposed to enter the
embryo-man after his birth, — we see the material self-
6 constituted belief of the Jews as referred to by St. Paul.
Their material belief has fallen far below man's original
standard, the spiritual man made in the image and like-
9 ness of God;  for this erring belief even separates its
conception of man from God, and ultimates in the opposite of *im*mortal man, namely, in a sick and sinning
12 mortal.

We learn in the Scriptures, as in divine Science, that
God made all;  that He is the universal Father and Mother
15 of man;  that God is divine Love:  therefore divine Love
is the divine Principle of the divine idea named man;
in other words, the spiritual Principle of spiritual man.
18 Now let us not lose this Science of man, but gain it clearly;
then we shall see that man cannot be separated from
his perfect Principle, God, inasmuch as an idea cannot
21 be torn apart from its fundamental basis.   This scientific knowledge affords self-evident proof of immortality;
proof, also, that the Principle of man cannot produce a
24 less perfect man than it produced in the beginning.   A
material sense of existence is not the scientific fact of
being;  whereas, the spiritual sense of God and His uni-
27 verse is the immortal and true sense of being.

As the apostle proceeds in this line of thought, he
undoubtedly refers to the last Adam represented by the
30 Messias, whose demonstration of God restored to mortals
the lost sense of man's perfection, even the sense of the
real man in God's likeness, who restored this sense by

the spiritual regeneration of both mind and body, — 1
casting out evils, *healing the sick,* and raising the dead.
The man Jesus demonstrated over sin, sickness, disease, 3
and death.    The great Metaphysician wrought, over and
above every sense of matter, into the proper sense of the
possibilities of Spirit.    He established health and har- 6
mony, the perfection of mind and body, as the reality of
man;   while discord, as seen in disease and death, was to
him the opposite of man, hence the unreality;   even as in 9
Science a chord is manifestly the reality of music, and
discord the unreality.    This rule of harmony must be accepted as true relative to man.                                        12

The translators of the older Scriptures presuppose a
material man to be the first man, solely because their
transcribing thoughts were not lifted to the inspired sense 15
of the spiritual man, as set forth in original Holy Writ.
Had both writers and translators in that age fully com-
prehended the later teachings and demonstrations of 18
our human and divine Master, the Old Testament might
have been as spiritual as the New.

The origin, substance, and life of man are one, and 21
that one is God, — Life, Truth, Love.    The self-existent,
perfect, and eternal are God;   and man is their reflection
and glory.    Did the substance of God, Spirit, become a 24
clod, in order to create a sick, sinning, dying man?    The
primal facts of being are eternal;   they are never extinguished in a night of discord.                                        27

That man must be evil before he can be good;   dying,
before deathless;   material, before spiritual;   sick and a
sinner in order to be healed and saved, is but the declara- 30
tion of the material senses transcribed by pagan religionists, by wicked mortals such as crucified our Master, —

1 whose teachings opposed the doctrines of Christ that
demonstrated the opposite, Truth.

3 Man is as perfect now, and henceforth, and forever,
as when the stars first sang together, and creation joined
in the grand chorus of harmonious being. It is the trans-
6 lator, not the original Word, who presents as being first
that which appears second, material, and mortal; and
as last, that which is primal, spiritual, and eternal. Be-
9 cause of human misstatement and misconception of God
and man, of the divine Principle and idea of being, there
seems to be a war between the flesh and Spirit, a contest
12 between Truth and error; but the apostle says, "There
is therefore now no condemnation to them which are in
Christ Jesus, who walk not after the flesh, but after the
15 Spirit."

On our subject, St. Paul first reasons upon the basis
of what is seen, the effects of Truth on the material senses;
18 thence, up to the unseen, the testimony of spiritual sense;
and right there he leaves the subject.

Just there, in the intermediate line of thought, is where
21 the present writer found it, when she discovered Christian
Science. And she has *not* left it, but continues the explanation of the power of Spirit up to its infinite meaning,
24 its allness. The recognition of this power came to her
through a spiritual sense of the real, and of the unreal
or mortal sense of things; not that there is, or can
27 be, an actual change in the realities of being, but
that we can discern more of them. At the moment
of her discovery, she knew that the last Adam, namely,
30 the true likeness of God, was the first, the only man.
This knowledge did become to her "a quickening
spirit;" for she beheld the meaning of those words

of our Master, "The last shall be first, and the first last."

When, as little children, we are receptive, become willing to accept the divine Principle and rule of being, as unfolded in divine Science, the interpretation therein will be found to be the Comforter that leadeth into all truth.

The meek Nazarene's steadfast and true knowledge of preexistence, of the nature and the inseparability of God and man, — made him mighty. Spiritual insight of Truth and Love antidotes and destroys the errors of flesh, and brings to light the true reflection: man as God's image, or "the first man," for Christ plainly declared, through Jesus, "Before Abraham was, I am."

The supposition that Soul, or Mind, is breathed into matter, is a pantheistic doctrine that presents a false sense of existence, and the quickening spirit takes it away: revealing, in place thereof, the power and perfection of a released sense of Life in God and Life *as* God. The Scriptures declare Life to be the infinite I AM, — not a dweller in matter. For man to know Life as it is, namely God, the eternal good, gives him not merely a sense of existence, but an accompanying consciousness of spiritual power that subordinates matter and destroys sin, disease, and death. This, Jesus demonstrated; insomuch that St. Matthew wrote, "The people were astonished at his doctrine: for he taught them as one having authority, and not as the scribes." This spiritual power, healing sin and sickness, was not confined to the first century; it extends to all time, inhabits eternity, and demonstrates Life without beginning or end.

1 Atomic action is Mind, not matter. It is neither the
energy of matter, the result of organization, nor the out-
3 come of life infused into matter: it is infinite Spirit, Truth,
Life, defiant of error or matter. Divine Science demonstrates Mind as dispelling a false sense and giving the
6 true sense of itself, God, and the universe; wherein the
mortal evolves not the immortal, nor does the material
ultimate in the spiritual; wherein man is coexistent with
9 Mind, and is the recognized reflection of infinite Life and
Love.

*And he was casting out a devil, and it was dumb. And it came to*
12 *pass, when the devil was gone out, the dumb spake.* — LUKE xi. 14.

The meaning of the term "devil" needs yet to be
learned. Its definition as an individual is too limited
15 and contradictory. When the Scripture is understood,
the spiritual signification of its terms will be understood,
and will contradict the interpretations that the senses
18 give them; and these terms will be found to include the
inspired meaning.

It could not have been a person that our great Master
21 cast out of another person; therefore the devil herein
referred to was an impersonal evil, or whatever worketh
ill. In this case it was the evil of dumbness, an error of
24 material sense, cast out by the spiritual truth of being;
namely, that speech belongs to Mind instead of matter,
and the wrong power, or the lost sense, must yield to the
27 right sense, and exist in Mind.

In the Hebrew, "devil" is denominated Abaddon; in
the Greek, Apollyon, serpent, liar, the god of this world,
30 etc. The apostle Paul refers to this personality of evil
as "the god of this world;" and then defines this god

as "dishonesty, craftiness, handling the word of God   1
deceitfully." The Hebrew embodies the term "devil"
in another term, serpent, — which the senses are supposed   3
to take in, — and then defines this serpent as "more
subtle than all the beasts of the field." Subsequently,
the ancients changed the meaning of the term, to their   6
sense, and then the serpent became a symbol of wisdom.

The Scripture in John, sixth chapter and seventieth
verse, refers to a wicked man as the devil: "Have not   9
I chosen you twelve, and one of you is a devil?" According to the Scripture, if devil is an individuality, there is
more than one devil. In Mark, ninth chapter and thirty-   12
eighth verse, it reads: "Master, we saw one casting out
devils in thy name." Here is an assertion indicating
the existence of more than one devil; and by omitting the   15
first letter, the name of his satanic majesty is found
to be evils, apparent wrong traits, that Christ, Truth,
casts out. By no possible interpretation can this passage   18
mean several individuals cast out of another individual
no bigger than themselves. The term, being here employed in its plural number, destroys all consistent sup-   21
position of the existence of one personal devil. Again,
our text refers to the devil as dumb; but the original
devil was a great talker, and was supposed to have out-   24
talked even Truth, and carried the question with Eve.
Also, the original texts define him as an "accuser," a
"calumniator," which would be impossible if he were   27
speechless. These two opposite characters ascribed to
him could only be possible as evil beliefs, as different
phases of sin or disease made manifest.                   30

Let us obey St. Paul's injunction to reject fables, and
accept the Scriptures in their broader, more spiritual

1 and practical sense. When we speak of a good man, we
do not mean that man is God because the Hebrew term
3 for Deity was "good," and *vice versa;* so, when referring
to a liar, we mean not that he is a personal devil, because
the original text defines devil as a "liar."
6   It is of infinite importance to man's spiritual progress,
and to his demonstration of Truth in casting out error,
— sickness, sin, disease, and death, in all their forms, —
9 that the terms and nature of Deity and devil be understood.

*He that believeth on me, the works that I do shall he do also; and*
*greater works than these shall he do;  because I go unto my Father. —*
12 JOHN xiv. 12.

Such are the words of him who spake divinely, well
knowing the omnipotence of Truth.  The Hebrew bard
15 saith, "His name shall endure forever:  His name shall
be continued as long as the sun."  Luminous with the
light of divine Science, his words reveal the great Principle
18 of a full salvation.  Neither can we question the practi-
cability of the divine Word, who have learned its adaptability to human needs, and man's ability to prove the
21 truth of prophecy.

The fulfilment of the grand verities of Christian healing
belongs to every period;  as the above Scripture plainly
24 declares, and as primitive Christianity confirms.  Also,
the last chapter of Mark is emphatic on this subject;
making healing a condition of salvation, that extends to
27 all ages and throughout all Christendom.  Nothing can
be more conclusive than this:  "And these signs shall
follow them that believe; . . . they shall lay hands on
30 the sick, and they shall recover."  This declaration of
our Master settles the question;  else we are entertaining

the startling inquiries, Are the Scriptures inspired? Are 1
they true? Did Jesus mean what he said?

If this be the cavil, we reply in the affirmative that the 3
Scripture is true; that Jesus did mean all, and even more
than he said or deemed it safe to say at that time. His
words are unmistakable, for they form propositions of 6
self-evident demonstrable truth. Doctrines that deny
the substance and practicality of all Christ's teachings
cannot be evangelical; and evangelical religion can be 9
established on no other claim than the authenticity of
the Gospels, which support unequivocally the proof that
Christian Science, as defined and practised by Jesus, 12
heals the sick, casts out error, and will destroy death.

Referring to The Church of Christ, Scientist, in Boston,
of which I am pastor, a certain clergyman charitably 15
expressed it, "the so-called Christian Scientists."

I am thankful even for his allusion to truth; it being
a modification of silence on this subject, and also of what 18
had been said when critics attacked me for supplying the
word Science to Christianity, — a word which the people
are now adopting. 21

The next step for ecclesiasticism to take, is to admit
that all Christians are properly called Scientists who
follow the commands of our Lord and His Christ, Truth; 24
and that no one is following his full command without
this enlarged sense of the spirit and power of Christianity.
"He that believeth on me, the works that I do shall he do," 27
is a radical and unmistakable declaration of the right and
power of Christianity to heal; for this is Christlike,
and includes the understanding of man's capabilities and 30
spiritual power. The condition insisted upon is, first,
"belief;" the Hebrew of which implies understanding.

1 How many to-day believe that the power of God equals
even the power of a drug to heal the sick! Divine Science
3 reveals the Principle of this power, and the rule whereby
sin, sickness, disease, and death are destroyed; and God
is this Principle. Let us, then, seek this Science; that we
6 may know Him better, and love Him more.

Though a man were begirt with the Urim and Thum-
mim of priestly office, yet should deny the validity or
9 permanence of Christ's command to heal in all ages,
this denial would dishonor that office and misinterpret
evangelical religion. Divine Science is not an interpo-
12 lation of the Scriptures, but is redolent with love, health,
and holiness, for the whole human race. It only needs
the prism of this Science to divide the rays of Truth, and
15 bring out the entire hues of Deity, which scholastic theology has hidden. The lens of Science magnifies the divine
power to human sight; and we then see the supremacy
18 of Spirit and the nothingness of matter.

The context of the foregoing Scriptural text explains
Jesus' words, "because I go unto my Father." "Because"
21 in following him, you understand God and *how* to turn
from matter to Spirit for healing; *how* to leave self, the
sense material, for the sense spiritual; *how* to accept
24 God's power and guidance, and become imbued with
divine Love that casts out all fear. Then are you baptized in the Truth that destroys all error, and you receive
27 the sense of Life that knows no death, and you *know* that
God is the only Life.

To reach the consummate naturalness of the Life that
30 is God, good, we must comply with the first condition
set forth in the text, namely, believe; in other words,
understand God sufficiently to exclude all faith in any

other remedy than Christ, the Truth that antidotes all 1
error. Thence will follow the absorption of all action,
motive, and mind, into the rules and divine Principle of 3
metaphysical healing.

Whosoever learns the letter of Christian Science but
possesses not its spirit, is unable to demonstrate this 6
Science; or whosoever hath the spirit without the letter,
is held back by reason of the lack of understanding. Both
the spirit and the letter are requisite; and having these, 9
every one can prove, in some degree, the validity of those
words of the great Master, "For the Son of man is come
to save that which was lost." 12

It has been said that the New Testament does not au-
thorize us to expect the ministry of healing at this period.

We ask what is the authority for such a conclusion, 15
the premises whereof are not to be found in the Scriptures.
The Master's divine logic, as seen in our text, contradicts
this inference, — these are his words: "He that believeth 18
on me, the works that I do shall he do also." That perfect syllogism of Jesus has but one correct premise and
conclusion, and it cannot fall to the ground beneath the 21
stroke of unskilled swordsmen. He who never unsheathed
his blade to try the edge of truth in Christian Science, is
unequal to the conflict, and unfit to judge in the case; 24
the shepherd's sling would slay this Goliath. I once believed that the practice and teachings of Jesus relative to
healing the sick, were spiritual abstractions, impractical 27
and impossible to us; but deed, not creed, and practice
more than theory, have given me a higher sense of
Christianity. 30

The "I" will go to the Father when meekness, purity,
and love, informed by divine Science, the Comforter,

1 lead to the one God: then the ego is found not in matter but in Mind, for there is but one God, one
3 Mind; and man will then claim no mind apart from God. Idolatry, the supposition of the existence of many minds and more than one God, has repeated itself in all manner
6 of subtleties through the entire centuries, saying as in the beginning, "Believe in me, and I will make you as gods;" that is, I will give you a separate mind from God
9 (good), named evil; and this so-called mind shall open your eyes and make you know evil, and thus become material, sensual, evil. But bear in mind that a serpent
12 said that; therefore that saying came not from Mind, good, or Truth. God was not the author of it; hence the words of our Master: "He is a liar, and the father of it;"
15 also, the character of the votaries to "other gods" which sprung from it.

The sweet, sacred sense and permanence of man's
18 unity with his Maker, in Science, illumines our present existence with the ever-presence and power of God, good. It opens wide the portals of salvation from sin, sickness,
21 and death. When the Life that is God, good, shall appear, "we shall be like Him;" we shall do the works of Christ, and, in the words of David, "the stone which the
24 builders refused is become the head stone of the corner," because the "I" does go unto the Father, the ego does arise to spiritual recognition of being, and is exalted, —
27 not through death, but Life, God understood.

*Believe on the Lord Jesus Christ, and thou shalt be saved.* — ACTS xvi. 31.

30 The Scriptures require more than a simple admission and feeble acceptance of the truths they present; they

require a living faith, that so incorporates their lessons 1
into our lives that these truths become the motive-power
of every act. 3

Our chosen text is one more frequently used than
many others, perhaps, to exhort people to turn from sin
and to strive after holiness; but we fear the full import 6
of this text is not yet recognized. It means a *full* salvation, — man saved from sin, sickness, and death; for,
unless this be so, no man can be wholly fitted for heaven 9
in the way which Jesus marked out and bade his followers
pursue.

In order to comprehend the meaning of the text, let 12
us see what it is to believe. It means more than an opinion
entertained concerning Jesus as a man, as the Son of God,
or as God; such an action of mind would be of no more 15
help to save from sin, than would a belief in any historical
event or person. But it does mean so to understand the
beauty of holiness, the character and divinity which Jesus 18
presented in his power to heal and to save, that it will
compel us to pattern after both; in other words, to "let
this Mind be in you, which was also in Christ Jesus." 21
(Phil. ii. 5.)

Mortal man believes in, but does not understand life
in, Christ. He believes there is another power or intelli- 24
gence that rules over a kingdom of its own, that is both
good and evil; yea, that is divided against itself, and therefore cannot stand. This belief breaks the First Command- 27
ment of God.

Let man abjure a theory that is in opposition to God,
recognize God as omnipotent, having all-power; and, 30
placing his trust in this grand Truth, and working from
no other Principle, he can neither be sick nor forever a

1 sinner.  When wholly governed by the one perfect Mind,
man has no sinful thoughts and will have no desire
3 to sin.

To arrive at this point of unity of Spirit, God, one must
commence by turning away from material gods;  denying
6 material so-called laws and material sensation, — or mind
in matter, in its varied forms of pleasure and pain.  This
must be done with the understanding that matter has no
9 sense;  thus it is that consciousness silences the mortal
claim to life, substance, or mind in matter, with the words
of Jesus: "When he speaketh a lie, he speaketh of his
12 own."  (John viii. 44.)

When tempted to sin, we should know that evil pro-
ceedeth not from God, good, but is a false belief of the
15 personal senses;  and if we deny the claims of these senses
and recognize man as governed by God, Spirit, not by
material laws, the temptation will disappear.

18    On this Principle, disease also is treated and healed.
We know that man's body, as matter, has no power to
govern itself;  and a belief of disease is as much the prod-
21 uct of mortal thought as sin is.  All suffering is the fruit
of the tree of the knowledge of *both* good and evil;  of
adherence to the "doubleminded" senses, to some belief,
24 fear, theory, or bad deed, based on physical material law,
so-called as opposed to good, — all of which is corrected
alone by Science, divine Principle, and its spiritual laws.
27 Suffering is the supposition of another intelligence than
God;  a belief in self-existent evil, opposed to good;  and
in whatever seems to punish man for doing good, —
30 by saying he has overworked, suffered from inclement
weather, or violated a law of matter in doing good, therefore he must suffer for it.

God does not reward benevolence and love with pen- 1
alties; and because of this, we have the right to deny the
supposed power of matter to do it, and to allege that only 3
mortal, erring mind can claim to do thus, and dignify the
result with the name of law: thence comes man's ability
to annul his own erring mental law, and to hold himself 6
amenable only to moral and spiritual law, — God's government. By so doing, male and female come into their
rightful heritage, "into the glorious liberty of the children 9
of God."

*Therefore I take pleasure in infirmities, in reproaches, in neces-*
*sities, in persecutions, in distresses for Christ's sake.* — 2 COR. 12
xii. 10.

The miracles recorded in the Scriptures illustrate the
life of Jesus as nothing else can; but they cost him the 15
hatred of the rabbis. The rulers sought the life of Jesus;
they would extinguish whatever denied and defied their
superstition. We learn somewhat of the qualities of the 18
divine Mind through the human Jesus. The power of
his transcendent goodness is manifest in the control it
gave him over the qualities opposed to Spirit which mor- 21
tals name matter.

The Principle of these marvellous works is divine; but
the actor was human. This divine Principle is discerned 24
in Christian Science, as we advance in the spiritual understanding that all substance, Life, and intelligence are
God. The so-called miracles contained in Holy Writ are 27
neither supernatural nor preternatural; for God is good,
and goodness is more natural than evil. The marvellous
healing-power of goodness is the outflowing life of Chris- 30
tianity, and it characterized and dated the Christian era.

8

1    It was the consummate naturalness of Truth in the
mind of Jesus, that made his healing easy and instan-
3 taneous. Jesus regarded good as the normal state of man,
and evil as the abnormal; holiness, life, and health as
the better representatives of God than sin, disease, and
6 death. The master Metaphysician understood omnipotence to be All-power: because Spirit was to him All-
in-all, matter was palpably an error of premise and
9 conclusion, while God was the only substance, Life,
and intelligence of man.

The apostle Paul insists on the rare rule in Christian
12 Science that we have chosen for a text; a rule that is susceptible of proof, and is applicable to every stage and
state of human existence. The divine Science of this rule
15 is quite as remote from the general comprehension of mankind as are the so-called miracles of our Master, and for
the sole reason that it is their basis. The foundational
18 facts of Christian Science are gathered from the supremacy
of spiritual law and its antagonism to every supposed material law. Christians to-day should be able to say, with
21 the sweet sincerity of the apostle, "I take pleasure in
infirmities," — I enjoy the touch of weakness, pain, and
all suffering of the flesh, *because* it compels me to seek the
24 remedy for it, and to find happiness, apart from the personal senses. The holy calm of Paul's well-tried hope
met no obstacle or circumstances paramount to the tri-
27 umph of a reasonable faith in the omnipotence of good,
involved in its divine Principle, God: the so-called pains
and pleasures of matter were alike unreal to Jesus; for he
30 regarded matter as only a vagary of mortal belief, and subdued it with this understanding.

The abstract statement that all is Mind, supports the

entire wisdom of the text;  and this statement receives 1
the mortal scoff only because it meets the immortal demands of Truth.   The Science of Paul's declaration re- 3
solves the element misnamed matter into its original sin,
or human will; that will which would oppose bringing the
qualities of Spirit into subjection to Spirit.   Sin brought 6
death;  and death is an element of matter, or material
falsity, never of Spirit.

When Jesus reproduced his body after its burial, he 9
revealed the myth or material falsity of evil;  its powerlessness to destroy good, and the omnipotence of the
Mind that knows this:  he also showed forth the error 12
and nothingness of supposed life in matter, and the great
somethingness of the good we possess, which is of Spirit,
and immortal.                                                          15

Understanding this, Paul took pleasure in infirmities,
for it enabled him to triumph over them, — he declared
that "the law of the Spirit of life in Christ Jesus hath 18
made me free from the law of sin and death;"  he took
pleasure in "reproaches" and "persecutions," because
they were so many proofs that he had wrought the prob- 21
lem of being beyond the common apprehension of sinners;
he took pleasure in "necessities," for they tested and developed latent power.                                                   24

We protect our dwellings more securely after a robbery,
and our jewels have been stolen;  so, after losing those
jewels of character, — temperance, virtue, and truth, — 27
the young man is awakened to bar his door against further
robberies.

Go to the bedside of pain, and there you can demon- 30
strate the triumph of good that has pleasure in infirmities;
because it illustrates through the flesh the divine power

1 of Spirit, and reaches the basis of all supposed miracles;
   whereby the sweet harmonies of Christian Science are
3 found to correct the discords of sense, and to lift man's
   being into the sunlight of Soul.

> "The chamber where the good man meets his fate
6    Is privileged beyond the walks of common life,
>     Quite on the verge of heaven."

# CHAPTER VII

## POND AND PURPOSE

BELOVED STUDENTS: — In thanking you for your 1
gift of the pretty pond contributed to Pleasant View,
in Concord, New Hampshire, I make no distinction be- 3
tween my students and your students; for here, thine
becomes mine through gratitude and affection.

From my tower window, as I look on this smile of 6
Christian Science, this gift from my students and their
students, it will always mirror their love, loyalty, and
good works. Solomon saith, "As in water face answereth 9
to face, so the heart of man to man."

The waters that run among the valleys, and that
you have coaxed in their course to call on me, have 12
served the imagination for centuries. Theology religiously
bathes in water, medicine applies it physically, hydrology
handles it with so-called science, and metaphysics appro- 15
priates it topically as type and shadow. Metaphysically,
baptism serves to rebuke the senses and illustrate Christian
Science. 18

*First:* The baptism of repentance is indeed a stricken
state of human consciousness, wherein mortals gain
severe views of themselves; a state of mind which rends 21
the veil that hides mental deformity. Tears flood the eyes,

1 agony struggles, pride rebels, and a mortal seems a monster, a dark, impenetrable cloud of error; and falling 3 on the bended knee of prayer, humble before God, he cries, "Save, or I perish." Thus Truth, searching the heart, neutralizes and destroys error.

6 This mental period is sometimes chronic, but oftener acute. It is attended throughout with doubt, hope, sorrow, joy, defeat, and triumph. When the good fight is fought, 9 error yields up its weapons and kisses the feet of Love, while white-winged peace sings to the heart a song of angels.

12 *Second:* The baptism of the Holy Ghost is the spirit of Truth cleansing from all sin; giving mortals new motives, new purposes, new affections, all pointing up- 15 ward. This mental condition settles into strength, free-dom, deep-toned faith in God; and a marked loss of faith in evil, in human wisdom, human policy, ways, and means. 18 It develops individual capacity, increases the intellectual activities, and so quickens moral sensibility that the great demands of spiritual sense are recognized, and they 21 rebuke the material senses, holding sway over human consciousness.

By purifying human thought, this state of mind per- 24 meates with increased harmony all the minutiæ of human affairs. It brings with it wonderful foresight, wisdom, and power; it unselfs the mortal purpose, gives steadi- 27 ness to resolve, and success to endeavor. Through the accession of spirituality, God, the divine Principle of Christian Science, literally governs the aims, ambition, 30 and acts of the Scientist. The divine ruling gives pru-dence and energy; it banishes forever all envy, rivalry, evil thinking, evil speaking and acting; and mortal

mind, thus purged, obtains peace and power outside of 1
itself.

This practical Christian Science is the divine Mind, 3
the incorporeal Truth and Love, shining through the mists
of materiality and melting away the shadows called sin,
disease, and death. 6

In mortal experience, the fire of repentance first separates the dross from the gold, and reformation brings
the light which dispels darkness.  Thus the operation 9
of the spirit of Truth and Love on the human thought,
in the words of St. John, "shall take of mine and show it
unto you." 12

*Third:* The baptism of Spirit, or final immersion of
human consciousness in the infinite ocean of Love, is the
last scene in corporeal sense.  This omnipotent act drops 15
the curtain on material man and mortality.  After this,
man's identity or consciousness reflects only Spirit, good,
whose visible being is invisible to the physical senses: eye 18
hath not seen it, inasmuch as it is the disembodied individual Spirit-substance and consciousness termed in
Christian metaphysics the ideal man — forever permeated 21
with eternal life, holiness, heaven.  This order of Science
is the chain of ages, which maintain their obvious correspondence, and unites all periods in the divine design. 24
Mortal man's repentance and absolute abandonment of
sin finally dissolves all supposed material life or physical
sensation, and the corporeal or mortal man disappears 27
forever.  The encumbering mortal molecules, called man,
vanish as a dream; but man born of the great Forever,
lives on, God-crowned and blest. 30

Mortals who on the shores of time learn Christian
Science, and live what they learn, take rapid transit to

1 heaven, — the hinge on which have turned all revolu-
tions, natural, civil, or religious, the former being servant
3 to the latter, — from flux to permanence, from foul to
pure, from torpid to serene, from extremes to intermediate.
Above the waves of Jordan, dashing against the receding
6 shore, is heard the Father and Mother's welcome, saying
forever to the baptized of Spirit: "This is my beloved
Son." What but divine Science can interpret man's
9 eternal existence, God's allness, and the scientific inde-
structibility of the universe?

The advancing stages of Christian Science are gained
12 through growth, not accretion; idleness is the foe of
progress. And scientific growth manifests no weakness,
no emasculation, no illusive vision, no dreamy absentness,
15 no insubordination to the laws that be, no loss nor lack
of what constitutes true manhood.

Growth is governed by intelligence; by the active,
18 all-wise, law-creating, law-disciplining, law-abiding Principle, God. The real Christian Scientist is constantly
accentuating harmony in word and deed, mentally and
21 orally, perpetually repeating this diapason of heaven:
"Good is my God, and my God is good. Love is my God,
and my God is Love."

24 Beloved students, you have entered the path. Press
patiently on; God is good, and good is the reward of all
who diligently seek God. Your growth will be rapid, if
27 you love good supremely, and understand and obey the
Way-shower, who, going before you, has scaled the steep
ascent of Christian Science, stands upon the mount of
30 holiness, the dwelling-place of our God, and bathes in the
baptismal font of eternal Love.

As you journey, and betimes sigh for rest "beside the

still waters," ponder this lesson of love. Learn its pur- 1
pose; and in hope and faith, where heart meets heart
reciprocally blest, drink with me the living waters of the 3
spirit of my life-purpose, — to impress humanity with
the genuine recognition of practical, operative Christian
Science. 6

# CHAPTER VIII

## PRECEPT UPON PRECEPT

### "THY WILL BE DONE"

THIS is the law of Truth to error, "Thou shalt surely
die." This law is a divine energy. Mortals cannot
prevent the fulfilment of this law; it covers all sin and
its effects. God is All, and by virtue of this nature and
allness He is cognizant only of good. Like a legislative
bill that governs millions of mortals whom the legislators
know not, the universal law of God has no knowledge
of evil, and enters unconsciously the human heart and
governs it.

Mortals have only to submit to the law of God, come
into sympathy with it, and to let His will be done. This
unbroken motion of the law of divine Love gives, to the
weary and heavy-laden, rest. But who is willing to do
His will or to let it be done? Mortals obey their own
wills, and so disobey the divine order.

All states and stages of human error are met and
mastered by divine Truth's negativing error in the way
of God's appointing. Those "whom the Lord loveth He
chasteneth." His rod brings to view His love, and interprets to mortals the gospel of healing. David said, "Before I was afflicted I went astray: but now have I
kept Thy word." He who knows the end from the be-

ginning, attaches to sin due penalties as its antidotes and  1
remedies.

Who art thou, vain mortal, that usurpest the preroga-  3
tive of divine wisdom, and wouldst teach God not to punish sin? that wouldst shut the mouth of His prophets,
and cry, "Peace, peace; when there is no peace," — yea,  6
that healest the wounds of my people slightly?

The Principle of divine Science being Love, the divine
rule of this Principle demonstrates Love, and proves that  9
human belief fulfils the law of belief, and dies of its own
physics. Metaphysics also demonstrates this Principle of
cure when sin is self-destroyed. Short-sighted physics  12
admits the so-called pains of matter that destroy its more
dangerous pleasures.

Insomnia compels mortals to learn that neither obliv-  15
ion nor dreams can recuperate the life of man, whose
Life is God, for God neither slumbers nor sleeps. The
loss of gustatory enjoyment and the ills of indigestion  18
tend to rebuke appetite and destroy the peace of a false
sense. False pleasure will be, is, chastened; it has no
right to be at peace. To suffer for having "other gods  21
before me," is divinely wise. Evil passions die in their
own flames, but are punished before extinguished. Peace
has no foothold on the false basis that evil should be  24
concealed and that life and happiness should still attend
it. Joy is self-sustained; goodness and blessedness are
one: suffering is self-inflicted, and good is the master of  27
evil.

To this scientific logic and the logic of events, egotism
and false charity say, " 'Not so, Lord;' it is wise to  30
cover iniquity and punish it not, then shall mortals have
peace." Divine Love, as unconscious as incapable of

1 error, pursues the evil that hideth itself, strips off its disguises, and — behold the result: evil, uncovered, is 3 self-destroyed.

Christian Science never healed a patient without proving with mathematical certainty that error, when found 6 out, is two-thirds destroyed, and the remaining third kills itself. Do men whine over a nest of serpents, and post around it placards warning people not to stir up 9 these reptiles because they have stings? Christ said, "They shall take up serpents;" and, "Be ye therefore wise as serpents and harmless as doves." The wisdom 12 of a serpent is to hide itself. The wisdom of God, as revealed in Christian Science, brings the serpent out of its hole, handles it, and takes away its sting. Good deeds 15 are harmless. He who has faith in woman's special adaptability to lead on Christian Science, will not be shocked when she puts her foot on the head of the serpent, as it 18 biteth at the heel.

Intemperance begets a belief of disordered brains, membranes, stomach, and nerves; and this belief serves 21 to uncover and kill this lurking serpent, intemperance, that hides itself under the false pretense of human need, innocent enjoyment, and a medical prescription. The 24 belief in venereal diseases tears the black mask from the shameless brow of licentiousness, torments its victim, and thus may save him from his destroyer.

27 Charity has the courage of conviction; it may suffer long, but has neither the cowardice nor the foolhardiness to cover iniquity. Charity is Love; and Love opens 30 the eyes of the blind, rebukes error, and casts it out. Charity never flees before error, lest it should suffer from an encounter. Love your enemies, or you will not

lose them; and if you love them, you will help to reform 1
them.

Christ points the way of salvation. His mode is not 3
cowardly, uncharitable, nor unwise, but it teaches mortals to handle serpents and cast out evil. Our own vision
must be clear to open the eyes of others, else the blind 6
will lead the blind and both shall fall. The sickly charity
that supplies criminals with bouquets has been dealt
with summarily by the good judgment of people in 9
the old Bay State. Inhuman medical bills, class legislation, and Salem witchcraft, are not indigenous to her
soil. 12

"Out of the depths have I delivered thee." The
drowning man just rescued from the merciless wave is
unconscious of suffering. Why, then, do you break his 15
peace and cause him to suffer in coming to life? Because
you wish to save him from death. Then, if a criminal
is at peace, is he not to be pitied and brought back to 18
life? Or, are you afraid to do this lest he suffer, trample
on your pearls of thought, and turn on you and rend you?
Cowardice is selfishness. When one protects himself at 21
his neighbor's cost, let him remember, "Whosoever will
save his life shall lose it." He risks nothing who obeys
the law of God, and shall find the Life that cannot be 24
lost.

Our Master said, "Ye shall drink indeed of my cup."
Jesus stormed sin in its citadels and kept peace with 27
God. He drank this cup giving thanks, and he said to
his followers, "Drink ye all of it," — drink it all, and let
all drink of it. He lived the spirit of his prayer, — "Thy 30
kingdom come." Shall we repeat our Lord's Prayer
when the heart denies it, refuses to bear the cross and

1 to fulfil the conditions of our petition? Human policy
is a fool that saith in his heart, "No God" — a caressing
3 Judas that betrays you, and commits suicide. This godless policy never knows what happiness is, and how it is
obtained.

6 Jesus did his work, and left his glorious career for our
example. On the shore of Gennesaret he tersely re-
minded his students of their worldly policy. They had
9 suffered, and seen their error. This experience caused
them to remember the reiterated warning of their Master and cast their nets on the right side. When they
12 were fit to be blest, they received the blessing. The
ultimatum of their human sense of ways and means
ought to silence ours. One step away from the direct
15 line of divine Science cost them — what? A speedy return under the reign of difficulties, darkness, and unre-
quited toil.

18 The currents of human nature rush in against the right
course; health, happiness, and life flow not into one of
their channels. The law of Love saith, "Not my will,
21 but Thine, be done," and Christian Science proves that
human will is lost in the divine; and Love, the white
Christ, is the remunerator.

24 If, consciously or unconsciously, one is at work in a
wrong direction, who will step forward and open his
eyes to see this error? He who *is* a Christian Scientist,
27 who has cast the beam out of his own eye, speaks plainly
to the offender and tries to show his errors to him before
letting another know it.

30 Pitying friends took down from the cross the fainting
form of Jesus, and buried it out of their sight. His disciples, who had not yet drunk of his cup, lost sight of

him; they could not behold his immortal being in the 1
form of Godlikeness.

All that I have written, taught, or lived, that is good, 3
flowed through cross-bearing, self-forgetfulness, and my
faith in the right. Suffering or Science, or both, in the
proportion that their instructions are assimilated, will 6
point the way, shorten the process, and consummate the
joys of acquiescence in the methods of divine Love. The
Scripture saith, "He that covereth his sins shall not pros- 9
per." No risk is so stupendous as to neglect opportunities which God giveth, and not to forewarn and forearm
our fellow-mortals against the evil which, if seen, can 12
be destroyed.

May my friends and my enemies so profit by these
waymarks, that what has chastened and illumined 15
another's way may perfect their own lives by gentle
benedictions. In every age, the pioneer reformer must
pass through a baptism of fire. But the faithful adher- 18
ents of Truth have gone on rejoicing. Christian Science
gives a fearless wing and firm foundation. These are
its inspiring tones from the lips of our Master, "My 21
sheep hear my voice, and I know them, and they follow
me: and I give unto them eternal life; and they shall
never perish, neither shall any man pluck them out of 24
my hand." He is but "an hireling" who fleeth when he
seeth the wolf coming.

Loyal Christian Scientists, be of good cheer: the night 27
is far spent, the day dawns; God's universal kingdom
will appear, Love will reign in every heart, and *His* will
be done on earth as in heaven. 30

1          "PUT UP THY SWORD"

While Jesus' life was full of Love, and a demonstra-
3 tion of Love, it appeared hate to the carnal mind, or
mortal thought, of his time.  He said, "Think not that
I am come to send peace on earth: I came not to send
6 peace, but a sword.  For I am come to set a man at
variance against his father, and the daughter against her
mother, and the daughter-in-law against her mother-in-
9 law.  And a man's foes shall be they of his own household."

This action of Jesus was stimulated by the same Love
12 that closed — to the senses — that wondrous life, and
that summed up its demonstration in the command,
"Put up thy sword."  The very conflict his Truth brought,
15 in accomplishing its purpose of Love, meant, all
the way through, "Put up thy sword;" but the sword
must have been drawn before it could be returned into
18 the scabbard.

My students need to search the Scriptures and "Science
and Health with Key to the Scriptures," to understand
21 the personal Jesus' labor in the flesh for their salvation:
they need to do this even to understand my works, their
motives, aims, and tendency.
24    The attitude of mortal mind in being healed morally,
is the same as its attitude physically.  The Christian
Scientist cannot heal the sick, and take error along with
27 Truth, either in the recognition or approbation of it.
This would prevent the possibility of destroying the
tares: they must be separated from the wheat before
30 they can be burned, and Jesus foretold the harvest hour

and the final destruction of error through this very pro- 1
cess, — the sifting and the fire. The tendency of mortal
mind is to go from one extreme to another: Truth comes 3
into the intermediate space, saying, "I wound to heal;
I punish to reform; I do it all in love; my peace I leave
with thee: not as the world giveth, give I unto thee. 6
Arise, let us go hence; let us depart from the material
sense of God's ways and means, and gain a spiritual
understanding of them." 9

But let us not seek to climb up some other way, as we
shall do if we take the end for the beginning or start
from wrong motives. Christian Science demands order 12
and truth. To abide by these we must first understand
the Principle and object of our work, and be clear that
it is Love, peace, and good will toward men. Then we 15
shall demonstrate the Principle in the way of His ap-
pointment, and not according to the infantile conception of our way; as when a child in sleep walks on the 18
summit of the roof of the house because he is a som-
nambulist, and thinks he is where he is not, and would
fall immediately if he knew where he was and what he 21
was doing.

My students are at the beginning of their demonstration; they have a long warfare with error in themselves 24
and in others to finish, and they must at this stage use
the sword of Spirit.

They cannot in the beginning take the attitude, nor 27
adopt the words, that Jesus used at the *end* of his
demonstration.

If you would follow in his footsteps, you must not try 30
to gather the harvest while the corn is in the blade, nor
yet when it is in the ear; a wise spiritual discernment

1 must be used in your application of his words and inference from his acts, to guide your own state of combat
3 with error. There *remaineth,* it is true, a Sabbath rest
for the people of God; but we must first have done our
work, and entered into our rest, as the Scriptures give
6 example.

### SCIENTIFIC THEISM

In the May number of our *Journal,* there appeared a
9 review of, and some extracts from, "Scientific Theism,"
by Phare Pleigh.

Now, Phare Pleigh evidently means more than "hands
12 off." A live lexicographer, given to the Anglo-Saxon
tongue, might add to the above definition the "laying
on of hands," as well. Whatever his *nom de plume*
15 means, an acquaintance with the author justifies one
in the conclusion that he is a power in criticism, a
big protest against injustice; but, the best may be
18 mistaken.

One of these extracts is the story of the Cheshire Cat,
which "vanished quite slowly, beginning with the end
21 of the tail, and ending with the grin, which remained
some time after the rest of it had gone." Was this a witty
or a happy hit at idealism, to illustrate the author's fol-
24 lowing point? —

"When philosophy becomes fairy-land, in which neither
laws of nature nor the laws of reason hold good, the
27 attempt of phenomenism to conceive the universe as a
*phenomenon without a noumenon* may succeed, but not
before; for it is an attempt to conceive a grin without
30 a cat."

True idealism is a divine Science, which combines in 1
logical sequence, nature, reason, and revelation. An
effect without a cause is inconceivable; neither philoso- 3
phy nor reason attempts to find one; but all should conceive and understand that Spirit cannot become less than
Spirit; hence that the universe of God is spiritual, — even 6
the ideal world whose cause is the self-created Principle,
with which its ideal or phenomenon must correspond in
quality and quantity. 9

The fallacy of an unscientific statement is this: that
matter and Spirit are one and eternal; or, that the phenomenon of Spirit is the antipode of Spirit, namely, mat- 12
ter. Nature declares, throughout the mineral, vegetable,
and animal kingdoms, that the specific nature of all things
is unchanged, and that nature is constituted of and by 15
Spirit.

Sensuous and material realistic views presuppose that
nature is matter, and that Deity is a finite person con- 18
taining infinite Mind; and that these opposites, in suppositional unity and personality, produce matter, — a
third quality unlike God. Again, that matter is both 21
cause and effect, but that the effect is antagonistic to its
cause; that death is at war with Life, evil with good, —
and man a rebel against his Maker. This is neither 24
Science nor theism. According to Holy Writ, it is a
kingdom divided against itself, that shall be brought
to desolation. 27

The nature of God must change in order to become
matter, or to become both finite and infinite; and matter
must *dis*appear, for Spirit to appear. To the material 30
sense, everything is matter; but spiritualize human
thought, and our convictions change: for spiritual sense

1 takes in new views, in which nature becomes Spirit; and
Spirit is God, and God is good. Science unfolds the fact
3 that Deity was forever Mind, Spirit; that matter never
produced Mind, and *vice versa.*

The visible universe declares the invisible only by re-
6 version, as error declares Truth. The testimony of material sense in relation to existence is false; for matter can
neither see, hear, nor feel, and mortal mind must change
9 all its conceptions of life, substance, and intelligence,
before it can reach the immortality of Mind and its ideas.
It is erroneous to accept the evidence of the material
12 senses whence to reason out God, when it is conceded
that the five personal senses can take no cognizance of
Spirit or of its phenomena. False realistic views sap the
15 Science of Principle and idea; they make Deity unreal
and inconceivable, either as mind or matter; but Truth
comes to the rescue of reason and immortality, and un-
18 folds the real nature of God and the universe to the spiritual sense, which beareth witness of things spiritual, and
not material.

21    To begin with, the notion of Spirit as cause and end,
with matter as its effect, is more ridiculous than the "grin
without a cat;" for a grin expresses the nature of a cat,
24 and this nature may linger in memory: but matter does
not express the nature of Spirit, and matter's graven
grins are neither eliminated nor retained by Spirit. What
27 can illustrate Dr. ——'s views better than Pat's echo,
when he said "How do you do?" and echo answered,
"Pretty well, I thank you!"

30    Dr. —— says: "The recognition of teleology in nature
is necessarily the recognition of purely spiritual personality in God."

According to lexicography, teleology is the science of the final cause of things; and divine Science (and all Science is divine) neither reveals God in matter, cause in effect, nor teaches that nature and her laws are the *material* universe, or that the personality of infinite Spirit is finite or material. Jesus said, "Ye do err, not knowing the Scriptures, nor the power of God." Now, what saith the Scripture? "God is a Spirit: and they that worship Him must worship Him in spirit and in truth."

## MENTAL PRACTICE

It is admitted that mortals think wickedly and act wickedly: it is beginning to be seen by thinkers, that mortals think also after a sickly fashion. In common parlance, one person feels sick, another feels wicked. A third person knows that if he would remove this feeling in either case, in the one he must change his patient's consciousness of dis-ease and suffering to a consciousness of ease and loss of suffering; while in the other he must change the patient's sense of sinning at ease to a sense of discomfort in sin and peace in goodness.

This is Christian Science: that mortal mind makes sick, and immortal Mind makes well; that mortal mind makes sinners, while immortal Mind makes saints; that a state of health is but a state of consciousness made manifest on the body, and *vice versa;* that while one person feels wickedly and acts wickedly, another knows that if he can change this evil sense and consciousness to a good sense, or conscious goodness, the fruits of goodness will follow, and he has reformed the sinner.

1    Now, demonstrate this rule, which obtains in every
line of mental healing, and you will find that a good rule
3 works one way, and a false rule the opposite way.

Let us suppose that there is a sick person whom another would heal mentally.  The healer begins by mental
6 argument.  He mentally says, "You are well, and you
know it;" and he supports this silent mental force by
audible explanation, attestation, and precedent.  His
9 mental and oral arguments aim to refute the sick man's
thoughts, words, and actions, in certain directions, and
turn them into channels of Truth.  He persists in this
12 course until the patient's mind yields, and the harmonious
thought has the full control over this mind on the point
at issue.  The end is attained, and the patient says and
15 feels, "I am well, and I know it."

This mental practitioner has changed his patient's
consciousness from sickness to health.  The patient's
18 mental state is now the diametrical opposite of what it
was when the mental practitioner undertook to transform
it, and he is improved morally and physically.

21    That this mental method has power and bears fruit,
is patent both to the conscientious Christian Scientist and
the observer.  Both should understand with equal clear-
24 ness, that if this mental process and power be reversed,
and people believe that a man is sick and knows it, and
speak of him as being sick, put it into the minds of others
27 that he is sick, publish it in the newspapers that he is
failing, and persist in this action of mind over mind, it
follows that he will believe that he is sick, — and Jesus
30 said it would be according to the woman's belief; but if
with the certainty of Science he knows that an error of
belief has not the power of Truth, and cannot, does

not, produce the slightest effect, it has no power over 1
him.  Thus a mental malpractitioner may lose his
power to harm by a false mental argument; for it 3
gives one opportunity to handle the error, and when
mastering it one gains in the rules of metaphysics, and
thereby learns more of its divine Principle.  Error pro- 6
duces physical sufferings, and these sufferings show
the fundamental Principle of Christian Science; namely,
that error and sickness are one, and Truth is their 9
remedy.

The evil-doer can do little at removing the effect of sin
on himself, unless he believes that sin has produced the 12
effect and knows he is a sinner; or, knowing that he is a
sinner, if he denies it, the good effect is lost.  Either of
these states of mind will stultify the power to heal men- 15
tally.  This accounts for many helpless mental practitioners and mysterious diseases.

Again:  If error is the cause of disease, Truth being 18
the cure, denial of this fact in one instance and
acknowledgment of it in another saps one's understanding of the Science of Mind-healing.  Such denial 21
dethrones demonstration, baffles the student of Mind-
healing, and divorces his work from Science.  Such denial also contradicts the doctrine that we must mentally 24
struggle against both evil and disease, and is like saying
that five times ten are fifty while ten times five are not
fifty; as if the multiplication of the same two numbers 27
would not yield the same product whichever might serve
as the multiplicand.

Who would tell another of a crime that he himself is 30
committing, or call public attention to that crime?  The
belief in evil and in the process of evil, holds the issues

1 of death to the evil-doer.   It takes away a man's proper
sense of good, and gives him a false sense of both evil
3 and good.   It inflames envy, passion, evil-speaking, and
strife.   It reverses Christian Science in all things.   It
causes the victim to believe that he is advancing while
6 injuring himself and others.   This state of false consciousness in many cases causes the victim great physical suffering;  and conviction of his wrong state of feeling reforms
9 him, and so heals him:  or, failing of conviction and reform, he becomes morally paralyzed — in other words,
a moral idiot.

12      In this state of misled consciousness, one is ready to
listen complacently to audible falsehoods that once he
would have resisted and loathed;  and this, because the
15 false seems true.   The malicious mental argument and
its action on the mind of the perpetrator, is fatal, morally
and physically.   From the effects of mental malpractice
18 the subject scarcely awakes in time, and must suffer its
full penalty after death.   This sin against divine Science
is cancelled only through human agony:  the measure it
21 has meted must be remeasured to it.

The crimes committed under this new *régime* of mind-
power, when brought to light, will make stout hearts quail.
24 Its mystery protects it now, for it is not yet known.   Error
is more abstract than Truth.   Even the healing Principle,
whose power seems inexplicable, is not so obscure;  for
27 this is the power of God, and good should seem more
natural than evil.

I shall not forget the cost of investigating, for this age,
30 the methods and power of error.   While the ways, means,
and potency of Truth had flowed into my consciousness
as easily as dawns the morning light and shadows flee,

the metaphysical mystery of error — its hidden paths, 1
purpose, and fruits — at first defied me.  I was saying all the time, "Come not thou into the secret" — 3
but at length took up the research according to God's
command.

Streams which purify, necessarily have pure fountains; 6
while impure streams flow from corrupt sources.  Here,
divine light, logic, and revelation coincide.

Science proves, beyond cavil, that the tree is known 9
by its fruit; that mind reaches its own ideal, and cannot
be separated from it.  I respect that moral sense which
is sufficiently strong to discern what it believes, and to say, 12
if it must, "I discredit Mind with having the power to
heal."  This individual disbelieves in Mind-healing, and
is consistent.  But, alas! for the mistake of believing in 15
mental healing, claiming full faith in the divine Principle,
and saying, "I am a Christian Scientist," while doing
unto others what we would resist to the hilt if done unto 18
ourselves.

May divine Love so permeate the affections of all those
who have named the name of Christ in its fullest sense, 21
that no counteracting influence can hinder their growth
or taint their examples.

## TAKING OFFENSE    24

There is immense wisdom in the old proverb, "He
that is slow to anger is better than the mighty."  Hannah
More said, "If I wished to punish my enemy, I should 27
make him hate somebody."

To punish ourselves for others' faults, is superlative
folly.  The mental arrow shot from another's bow is 30

1 practically harmless, unless our own thought barbs it. It is our pride that makes another's criticism rankle, our
3 self-will that makes another's deed offensive, our egotism that feels hurt by another's self-assertion. Well may we feel wounded by our own faults; but we can hardly afford
6 to be miserable for the faults of others.

A courtier told Constantine that a mob had broken the head of his statue with stones. The emperor lifted
9 his hands to his head, saying: "It is very surprising, but I don't feel hurt in the least."

We should remember that the world is wide; that there
12 are a thousand million different human wills, opinions, ambitions, tastes, and loves; that each person has a different history, constitution, culture, character, from all the
15 rest; that human life is the work, the play, the ceaseless action and reaction upon each other of these different atoms. Then, we should go forth into life with the smallest
18 expectations, but with the largest patience; with a keen relish for and appreciation of everything beautiful, great, and good, but with a temper so genial that the friction
21 of the world shall not wear upon our sensibilities; with an equanimity so settled that no passing breath nor accidental disturbance shall agitate or ruffle it; with a
24 charity broad enough to cover the whole world's evil, and sweet enough to neutralize what is bitter in it, — determined not to be offended when no wrong is meant, nor
27 even when it is, unless the offense be against God.

Nothing short of our own errors should offend us. He who can wilfully attempt to injure another, is an object
30 of pity rather than of resentment; while it is a question in my mind, whether there is enough of a flatterer, a fool, or a liar, *to* offend a whole-souled woman.

## HINTS TO THE CLERGY                    1

At the residence of Mr. Rawson, of Arlington, Massachusetts, a happy concourse of friends had gathered to 3 celebrate the eighty-second birthday of his mother — a friend of mine, and a Christian Scientist.

Among the guests, were an orthodox clergyman, his 6 wife and child.

In the course of the evening, conversation drifted to the seventh modern wonder, Christian Science; where- 9 upon the mother, Mrs. Rawson, who had drunk at its fount, firmly bore testimony to the power of Christ, Truth, to heal the sick.                                          12

Soon after this conversation, the clergyman's son was taken violently ill. Then was the clergyman's opportunity to demand a proof of what the Christian 15 Scientist had declared; and he said to this venerable Christian: —

"If you heal my son, when seeing, I may be led to 18 believe."

Mrs. Rawson then rose from her seat, and sat down beside the sofa whereon lay the lad with burning brow, 21 moaning in pain.

Looking away from all material aid, to the spiritual source and ever-present help, silently, through the divine 24 power, she healed him.

The deep flush faded from the face, a cool perspiration spread over it, and he slept.                          27

In about one hour he awoke, and was hungry.

The parents said: —

"Wait until we get home, and you shall have some 30 gruel."

1   But Mrs. Rawson said: —

"Give the child what he relishes, and doubt not that
3 the Father of all will care for him."

Thus, the unbiased youth and the aged Christian
carried the case on the side of God; and, after eating
6 several ice-creams, the clergyman's son returned home
— *well.*

### PERFIDY AND SLANDER

9   What has an individual gained by losing his own self-
respect? or what has he lost when, retaining his own,
he loses the homage of fools, or the pretentious praise of
12 hypocrites, false to themselves as to others?

Shakespeare, the immortal lexicographer of mortals,
writes: —

15                     To thine own self be true,
           And it must follow, as the night the day,
           Thou canst not then be false to any man.

18   When Aristotle was asked what a person could gain
by uttering a falsehood, he replied, "Not to be credited
when he shall tell the truth."

21   The character of a liar and hypocrite is so contempti-
ble, that even of those who have lost their honor it might
be expected that from the violation of truth they should
24 be restrained by their pride.

Perfidy of an inferior quality, such as manages to evade
the law, and which dignified natures cannot stoop to
27 notice, except legally, disgraces human nature more than
do most vices.

Slander is a midnight robber; the red-tongued assas-
30 sin of radical worth; the conservative swindler, who

sells himself in a traffic by which he can gain nothing. 1
It can retire for forgiveness to no fraternity where its
crime may stand in the place of a virtue; but must at 3
length be given up to the hisses of the multitude, without friend and without apologist.

Law has found it necessary to offer to the innocent, 6
security from slanderers — those pests of society — when
their crime comes within its jurisdiction. Thus, to evade
the penalty of law, and yet with malice aforethought to 9
extend their evil intent, is the nice distinction by which
they endeavor to get their weighty stuff into the hands
of gossip! Some uncharitable one may give it a forward 12
move, and, ere that one himself become aware, find
himself responsible for kind (?) endeavors.

Would that my pen or pity could raise these weak, 15
pitifully poor objects from their choice of self-degrada-
tion to the nobler purposes and wider aims of a life made
honest: a life in which the fresh flowers of feeling blos- 18
som, and, like the camomile, the more trampled upon,
the sweeter the odor they send forth to benefit mankind;
a life wherein calm, self-respected thoughts abide in 21
tabernacles of their own, dwelling upon a holy hill, speaking the truth in the heart; a life wherein the mind can
rest in green pastures, beside the still waters, on isles 24
of sweet refreshment. The sublime summary of an
honest life satisfies the mind craving a higher good, and
bathes it in the cool waters of peace on earth; till it 27
grows into the full stature of wisdom, reckoning its
own by the amount of happiness it has bestowed upon
others.                                                                          30

Not to avenge one's self upon one's enemies, is the
command of almighty wisdom; and we take this to be

1 a safer guide than the promptings of human nature.
To know that a deception dark as it is base has been
3 practised upon thee, — by those deemed at least indebted
friends whose welfare thou hast promoted, — and yet
not to avenge thyself, is to do good to thyself; is to take
6 a new standpoint whence to look upward; is to be calm
amid excitement, just amid lawlessness, and pure amid
corruption.

9 To be a great man or woman, to have a name whose
odor fills the world with its fragrance, is to bear with
patience the buffetings of envy or malice — even while
12 seeking to raise those barren natures to a capacity for a
higher life. We should look with pitying eye on the
momentary success of all villainies, on mad ambition
15 and low revenge. This will bring us also to look on a
kind, true, and just person, faithful to conscience and
honest beyond reproach, as the only suitable fabric out
18 of which to weave an existence fit for earth and
heaven.

### CONTAGION

21 Whatever man sees, feels, or in any way takes cognizance of, must be caught through mind; inasmuch
as perception, sensation, and consciousness belong to
24 mind and not to matter. Floating with the popular
current of mortal thought without questioning the re-
liability of its conclusions, we do what others do,
27 believe what others believe, and say what others say.
Common consent is contagious, and it makes disease
catching.

30 People believe in infectious and contagious diseases,

and that any one is liable to have them under certain 1
predisposing or exciting causes. This mental state pre-
pares one to have any disease whenever there appear the 3
circumstances which he believes produce it. If he believed
as sincerely that health is catching when exposed to contact with healthy people, he would catch their state of 6
feeling quite as surely and with better effect than he does
the sick man's.

If only the people would believe that good is more 9
contagious than evil, since God is omnipresence, how
much more certain would be the doctor's success, and
the clergyman's conversion of sinners. And if only the 12
pulpit would encourage faith in God in this direction,
and faith in Mind over all other influences governing
the receptivity of the body, theology would teach man 15
as David taught: "Because thou hast made the Lord,
which is my refuge, even the most High thy habitation;
there shall no evil befall thee, neither shall any plague 18
come nigh thy dwelling."

The confidence of mankind in contagious disease would
thus become beautifully less; and in the same propor- 21
tion would faith in the power of God to heal and to save
mankind increase, until the whole human race would
become healthier, holier, happier, and longer lived. A 24
calm, Christian state of mind is a better preventive of
contagion than a drug, or than any other possible sana-
tive method; and the "perfect Love" that "casteth out 27
fear" is a sure defense.

1    IMPROVE YOUR TIME

Success in life depends upon persistent effort, upon
3 the improvement of moments more than upon any other
one thing.  A great amount of time is consumed in talking
nothing, doing nothing, and indecision as to what one
6 should do.  If one would be successful in the future, let
him make the most of the present.

Three ways of wasting time, one of which is con-
9 temptible, are gossiping mischief, making lingering calls,
and mere motion when at work, thinking of nothing or
planning for some amusement, — travel of limb more
12 than mind.  Rushing around smartly is no proof of accomplishing much.

All successful individuals have become such by hard
15 work; by improving moments before they pass into hours,
and hours that other people may occupy in the pursuit
of pleasure.  They spend no time in sheer idleness, in
18 talking when they have nothing to say, in building air-
castles or floating off on the wings of sense: all of which
drop human life into the ditch of nonsense, and worse
21 than waste its years.

> "Let us, then, be up and doing,
>     With a heart for any fate;
24      Still achieving, still pursuing,
>     Learn to labor and to wait."


THANKSGIVING DINNER

27    It was a beautiful group! needing but canvas and the
touch of an artist to render it pathetic, tender, gorgeous.

Age, on whose hoary head the almond-blossom formed a 1
crown of glory; middle age, in smiles and the full fruition
of happiness; infancy, exuberant with joy, — ranged side 3
by side. The sober-suited grandmother, rich in experience, had seen sunshine and shadow fall upon ninety-
six years. Four generations sat at that dinner-table. 6
The rich viands made busy many appetites; but, what
of the poor! Willingly — though I take no stock in
spirit-rappings — would I have had the table give a 9
spiritual groan for the unfeasted ones.

Under the skilful carving of the generous host, the
mammoth turkey grew beautifully less. His was the 12
glory to vie with guests in the dexterous use of knife and
fork, until delicious pie, pudding, and fruit caused un-
conditional surrender.                                  15

And the baby! Why, he made a big hole, with two
incisors, in a big pippin, and bit the finger presump-
tuously poked into the little mouth to arrest the peel! 18
Then he was caught walking! one, two, three steps, —
and papa knew that he could walk, but grandpa was
taken napping. Now! baby has tumbled, soft as thistle- 21
down, on the floor; and instead of a real set-to at crying,
a look of cheer and a toy from mamma bring the soft
little palms patting together, and pucker the rosebud 24
mouth into saying, "Oh, pretty!" That was a scientific
baby; and his first sitting-at-table on Thanksgiving Day
— yes, and his little rainbowy life — brought sunshine 27
to every heart. How many homes echo such tones of
heartfelt joy on Thanksgiving Day! But, alas! for the
desolate home; for the tear-filled eyes looking longingly 30
at the portal through which the loved one comes not, or
gazing silently on the vacant seat at fireside and board —

9

1 God comfort them all! we inwardly prayed — but the
memory was too much; and, turning from it, in a bumper
3 of pudding-sauce we drank to peace, and plenty, and
happy households.

## CHRISTIAN SCIENCE

6 This age is reaching out towards the perfect Principle
of things; is pushing towards perfection in art, inven-
tion, and manufacture. Why, then, should religion be
9 stereotyped, and we not obtain a more perfect and practical Christianity? It will never do to be behind the
times in things most essential, which proceed from the
12 standard of right that regulates human destiny. Human
skill but foreshadows what is next to appear as its divine
origin. Proportionately as we part with material systems
15 and theories, personal doctrines and dogmas, meekly to
ascend the hill of Science, shall we reach the maximum
of perfection in all things.
18 Spirit is omnipotent; hence a more spiritual Christianity will be one having more power, having perfected
in Science that most important of all arts, — healing.
21 Metaphysical healing, or Christian Science, is a demand of the times. Every man and every woman would
desire and demand it, if he and she knew its infinite
24 value and firm basis. The unerring and fixed Principle
of all healing is God; and this Principle should be
sought from the love of good, from the most spiritual
27 and unselfish motives. Then will it be understood to be
of God, and not of man; and this will prevent mankind
from striking out promiscuously, teaching and practising

in the *name* of Science without knowing its fundamental 1
Principle.

It is important to know that a malpractice of the best 3
system will result in the worst form of medicine. More-
over, the feverish, disgusting pride of those who call
themselves metaphysicians or Scientists, — but are such 6
in name only, — fanned by the breath of mental malpractice, is the death's-head at the feast of Truth; the
monkey in harlequin jacket that will retard the onward 9
march of life-giving Science, if not understood and with-
stood, and so strangled in its attempts.

The standard of metaphysical healing is traduced by 12
thinking to put into the old garment of drugging the new
cloth of metaphysics; or by trying to twist the fatal
magnetic force of mortal mind, termed hypnotism, into 15
a more fashionable cut and naming that "mind-cure,"
or — which is still worse in the eyes of Truth — terming
it metaphysics! Substituting good words for a good life, 18
fair-seeming for straightforward character, mental malpractice for the practice of true medicine, is a poor shift
for the weak and worldly who think the standard of 21
Christian Science too high for them.

What think you of a scientist in mathematics who finds
fault with the exactness of the rule because unwilling to 24
work hard enough to practise it? The perfection of the
rule of Christian Science is what constitutes its utility:
having a true standard, if some fall short, others will 27
approach it; and these are they only who adhere to that
standard.

Matter must be understood as a false belief or product 30
of mortal mind: whence we learn that sensation is not
in matter, but in this so-called mind; that we see and

1 feel disease only by reason of our belief in it: then shall
matter remain no longer to blind us to Spirit, and clog
3 the wheels of progress. We spread our wings in vain when
we attempt to mount above error by speculative views
of Truth.

6     Love is the Principle of divine Science; and Love is
not learned of the material senses, nor gained by a culpable attempt to seem what we have not lifted ourselves
9 to *be,* namely, a Christian. In love for man, we gain a
true sense of Love as God; and in no other way can we
reach this spiritual sense, and rise — and still rise — to
12 things most essential and divine. What hinders man's
progress is his vain conceit, the Phariseeism of the times,
also his effort to steal from others and avoid hard work;
15 errors which can never find a place in Science. Empiri-
cal knowledge is worse than useless: it never has advanced
man a single step in the scale of being.

18     That one should have ventured on such unfamiliar
ground, and, self-forgetful, should have gone on to establish this mighty system of metaphysical healing, called
21 Christian Science, against such odds, — even the entire
current of mortality, — is matter of grave wonderment to
profound thinkers. That, in addition to this, she has made
24 some progress, has seen far into the spiritual facts of being which constitute physical and mental perfection, in
the midst of an age so sunken in sin and sensuality, seems
27 to them still more inconceivable.

In this new departure of metaphysics, God is regarded
more as absolute, supreme; and Christ is clad with a
30 richer illumination as our Saviour from sickness, sin,
and death. God's fatherliness as Life, Truth, and Love,
makes His sovereignty glorious.

By this system, too, man has a changed recognition 1
of his relation to God. He is no longer obliged to sin,
be sick, and die to reach heaven, but is required and em- 3
powered to conquer sin, sickness, and death; thus, as
image and likeness, to reflect Him who destroys death
and hell. By this reflection, man becomes the partaker 6
of that Mind whence sprang the universe.

In Christian Science, progress is demonstration, not
doctrine. This Science is ameliorative and regenerative, 9
delivering mankind from all error through the light and
love of Truth. It gives to the race loftier desires and new
possibilities. It lays the axe at the root of the tree of 12
knowledge, to cut down all that bringeth not forth good
fruit; "and blessed is he, whosoever shall not be offended
in me." It touches mind to more spiritual issues, sys- 15
tematizes action, gives a keener sense of Truth and a
stronger desire for it.

Hungering and thirsting after a better life, we shall 18
have it, and become Christian Scientists; learn God
aright, and know something of the ideal man, the real
man, harmonious and eternal. This movement of thought 21
must push on the ages: it must start the wheels of reason
aright, educate the affections to higher resources, and
leave Christianity unbiased by the superstitions of a 24
senior period.

## INJUSTICE

Who that has tried to follow the divine precept, "All 27
things whatsoever ye would that men should do unto
you, do ye even so to them," has not suffered from the

1 situation? — has not found that human passions in their reaction have misjudged motives?

3    Throughout our experience since undertaking the labor of uplifting the race, we have been made the repository of little else than the troubles, indiscretions, 6 and errors of others; until thought has shrunk from contact with family difficulties, and become weary with study to counsel wisely whenever giving advice on per9 sonal topics.

   To the child complaining of his parents we have said, "Love and honor thy parents, and yield obedience to 12 them in all that is right; but you have the rights of conscience, as we all have, and must follow God in all your ways."

15    When yielding to constant solicitations of husband or wife to give, to one or the other, advice concerning difficulties and the best way to overcome them, we have done 18 this to the best of our ability, — and always with the purpose to restore harmony and prevent dishonor. In such cases we have said, "Take no counsel of a mortal, even 21 though it be your best friend; but be guided by God alone;" meaning by this, Be not estranged from each other by anything that is said to you, but seek in divine 24 Love the remedy for all human discord.

   Yet, notwithstanding one's good intentions, in some way or at some step in one's efforts to help another, as 27 a general rule, one will be blamed for all that is not right: but this must not deter us from doing our duty, whatever else may appear, and at whatever cost.

## REFORMERS 1

The olden opinion that hell is fire and brimstone, has yielded somewhat to the metaphysical fact that suffering 3 is a thing of mortal mind instead of body: so, in place of material flames and odor, mental anguish is generally accepted as the penalty for sin. This changed belief 6 has wrought a change in the actions of men. Not a few individuals serve God (or try to) from fear; but remove that fear, and the worst of human passions belch forth 9 their latent fires. Some people never repent until earth gives them such a cup of gall that conscience strikes home; then they are brought to realize how impossible it is to 12 sin and not suffer. All the different phases of error in human nature the reformer must encounter and help to eradicate. 15

This period is not essentially one of conscience: few feel and live now as when this nation began, and our forefathers' prayers blended with the murmuring winds 18 of their forest home. This is a period of doubt, inquiry, speculation, selfishness; of divided interests, marvellous good, and mysterious evil. But sin can only work out 21 its own destruction; and reform does and must push on the growth of mankind.

Honor to faithful merit is delayed, and always has 24 been; but it is sure to follow. The very streets through which Garrison was dragged were draped in honor of the dead hero who did the hard work, the immortal work, 27 of loosing the fetters of one form of human slavery. I remember, when a girl, and he visited my father, how a childish fear clustered round his coming. I had heard 30

1 the awful story that "he helped 'niggers' kill the white
folks!" Even the loving children are sometimes made
3 to believe a lie, and to hate reformers. It is pleasant,
now, to contrast with that childhood's wrong the reverence
of my riper years for all who dare to be true, honest to
6 their convictions, and strong of purpose.

The reformer has no time to give in defense of his
own life's incentive, since no sacrifice is too great for the
9 silent endurance of his love. What has not unselfed love
achieved for the race? All that ever was accomplished,
and more than history has yet recorded. The reformer
12 works on unmentioned, save when he is abused or his
work is utilized in the interest of somebody. He may
labor for the establishment of a cause which is fraught
15 with infinite blessings, — health, virtue, and heaven;
but what of all that? Who should care for everybody?
It is enough, say they, to care for a few. Yet the good
18 done, and the love that foresees more to do, stimulate
philanthropy and are an ever-present reward. Let one's
life answer well these questions, and it already hath a
21 benediction:

Have you renounced self? Are you faithful? Do
you love?

24                    MRS. EDDY SICK

The frequent public allegement that I am "sick, unable
to speak a loud word," or that I died of palsy, and am
27 dead, — is but another evidence of the falsehoods kept
constantly before the public.

While I accord these evil-mongers due credit for their

desire, let me say to you, dear reader: Call at the 1
Massachusetts Metaphysical College, in 1889, and judge
for yourself whether I can talk — and laugh too! I 3
never was in better health. I have had but four
days' vacation for the past year, and am about to commence a large class in Christian Science. Lecturing, 6
writing, preaching, teaching, etc., give fair proof that
my shadow is not growing less; and substance is taking
larger proportions. 9

## "I'VE GOT COLD"

Out upon the sidewalk one winter morning, I observed
a carriage draw up before a stately mansion; a portly 12
gentleman alight, and take from his carriage the ominous
hand-trunk.

"Ah!" thought I, "somebody has to take it; and what 15
may the potion be?"

Just then a tiny, sweet face appeared in the vestibule,
and red nose, suffused eyes, cough, and tired look, told 18
the story; but, looking up quaintly, the poor child said, —

"I've got cold, doctor."

Her apparent pride at sharing in a popular influenza 21
was comical. However, her dividend, when compared
with that of the household stockholders, was new; and
doubtless their familiarity with what the stock paid, made 24
them more serious over it.

What if that sweet child, so bravely confessing that
she had something that she ought not to have, and which 27
mamma thought must be gotten rid of, had been taught
the value of saying even more bravely, and believing
it, — 30

1 "I have *not* got cold."

Why, the doctor's squills and bills would have been
3 avoided; and through the cold air the little one would
have been bounding with sparkling eyes, and ruby cheeks
painted and fattened by metaphysical hygiene.

6 Parents and doctors must not take the sweet freshness
out of the children's lives by that flippant caution, "You
will get cold."

9 Predicting danger does not dignify life, whereas fore-
casting liberty and joy does; for these are strong pro-
moters of health and happiness. All education should
12 contribute to moral and physical strength and freedom.
If a cold could get into the body without the assent of
mind, nature would take it out as gently, or let it remain
15 as harmlessly, as it takes the frost out of the ground or
puts it into the ice-cream to the satisfaction of all.

The sapling bends to the breeze, while the sturdy oak,
18 with form and inclination fixed, breasts the tornado. It
is easier to incline the early thought rightly, than the
biased mind. Children not mistaught, naturally love
21 God; for they are pure-minded, affectionate, and generally brave. Passions, appetites, pride, selfishness, have
slight sway over the fresh, unbiased thought.

24 Teach the children early self-government, and teach
them nothing that is wrong. If they see their father with
a cigarette in his mouth — suggest to them that the habit
27 of smoking is not nice, and that nothing but a loathsome
worm *naturally* chews tobacco. Likewise soberly inform
them that "Battle-Axe Plug" takes off men's heads; or,
30 leaving these on, that it takes from their bodies a sweet
something which belongs to nature, — namely, pure
odors.

From a religious point of view, the faith of both youth 1
and adult should centre as steadfastly in God to benefit
the body, as to benefit the mind. Body and mind are 3
correlated in man's salvation; for man will no more
enter heaven sick than as a sinner, and Christ's Christianity casts out sickness as well as sin of every sort. 6

Test, if you will, metaphysical healing on two patients:
one having morals to be healed, the other having a physical ailment. Use as your medicine the great alterative, 9
Truth: give to the immoralist a mental dose that says,
"You have no pleasure in sin," and witness the effects.

Either he will hate you, and try to make others do like- 12
wise, so taking a dose of error big enough apparently to
neutralize your Truth, else he will doubtingly await the
result; during which interim, by constant combat and 15
direful struggles, you get the victory and Truth heals him
of the moral malady.

On the other hand, to the bedridden sufferer admin- 18
ister this alterative Truth: "God never made you sick:
there is no necessity for pain; and Truth destroys the
error that insists on the necessity of any man's bondage 21
to sin and sickness. 'Ye shall know the truth, and the
truth shall make you free.'"

Then, like blind Bartimeus, the doubting heart looks 24
up through faith, and your patient rejoices in the gospel
of health.

Thus, you see, it is easier to heal the physical than the 27
moral ailment. When divine Truth and Love heal, of
sin, the sinner who is at ease in sin, how much more should
these heal, of sickness, the sick who are dis-eased, dis- 30
comforted, and who long for relief!

1          "PRAYER AND HEALING"

The article of Professor T——, having the above cap-
3 tion, published in *Zion's Herald,* December third, came
not to my notice until January ninth.  In it the Professor
offered me, as President of the Metaphysical College in
6 Boston, or one of my students, the liberal sum of one
thousand dollars if either would reset certain dislocations
without the use of hands, and two thousand dollars if
9 either would give sight to one born blind.

Will the gentleman accept my thanks due to his gener-
osity; for, if I should accept his bid on Christianity, he
12 would lose his money.

Why?

Because I performed more difficult tasks fifteen years
15 ago.  At present, I am in another department of Christian
work, "where there shall no signs be given them," for
they shall be instructed in the Principle of Christian
18 Science that furnishes its own proof.

But, to reward his liberality, I offer him three thousand dollars if he will heal one single case of opium-eating
21 where the patient is very low and taking morphine powder
in its most concentrated form, at the rate of one ounce in
two weeks, — having taken it twenty years; and he is to
24 cure that habit in three days, leaving the patient well.  I
cured precisely such a case in 1869.

Also, Mr. C. M. H——, of Boston, formerly partner
27 of George T. Brown, pharmacist, No. 5 Beacon St., will
tell you that he was my student in December, 1884; and
that before leaving the class he took a patient thoroughly
30 addicted to the use of opium — if she went without it

twenty-four hours she would have delirium — and in 1
forty-eight hours cured her perfectly of this habit,
with no bad results, but with decided improvement in 3
health.

I have not yet made surgery one of the mental branches
taught in my college; although students treat sprains, 6
contusions, etc., successfully. In the case of sprain of the
wrist-joint, where the regular doctor had put on splints
and bandages to remain six weeks, a student of mine 9
removed these appliances the same day and effected the
cure in less than one week. Reference, Mrs. M. A. F——,
107 Eutaw Street, East Boston. 12

I agree with the Professor, that every system of medicine claims more than it practises. If the system is Science,
it includes of necessity the Principle, which the learner 15
can demonstrate only in proportion as he understands it.
Boasting is unbecoming a mortal's poor performances.
My Christian students are proverbially modest: their 18
works alone should declare them, since my system of medicine is not generally understood. There are charlatans
in "mind-cure," who practise on the basis of matter, or 21
human will, not Mind.

The Professor alludes to Paul's advice to Timothy.
Did he refer to that questionable counsel, "Take a little 24
wine for thy stomach's sake"? Even doctors disagree
on that prescription: some of the medical faculty will
tell you that alcoholic drinks cause the coats of the stomach 27
to thicken and the organ to contract; will prevent the
secretions of the gastric juice, and induce ulceration,
bleeding, vomiting, death. 30

Again, the Professor quotes, in justification of material
methods, and as veritable: "He took a bone from the

1 side of Adam, closed up the wound thereof, and builded
up the woman." (Gen. ii. 21.)

3     Here we have the Professor on the platform of Christian
Science! even a "surgical operation" that he says was
performed by divine power, — Mind alone constructing
6 the human system, before surgical instruments were
invented, and closing the incisions of the flesh.

He further states that God cannot save the soul without
9 compliance to ordained conditions.  But, we ask, have
those conditions named in Genesis been perpetuated in
the multiplication of mankind?  And, are the conditions
12 of salvation mental, or physical; are they bodily penance
and torture, or repentance and reform, which are the
action of mind?

15     He asks, "Has the law been abrogated that demands
the employment of visible agencies for specific ends?"

Will he accept my reply as derived from the life and
18 teachings of Jesus? — who annulled the so-called laws of
matter by the higher law of Spirit, causing him to walk
the wave, turn the water into wine, make the blind to see,
21 the deaf to hear, the lame to walk, and the dead to be
raised without matter-agencies.  And he did this for man's
example;  not to teach himself, but others, the way of
24 healing and salvation.  He said, "And other sheep I have,
which are not of this fold."

The teachings and demonstration of Jesus were for
27 all peoples and for all time;  not for a privileged class or
a restricted period, but for as many as should believe in
him.

30     Are the discoverers of quinine, cocaine, etc., especially the children of our Lord because of their medical
discoveries?

We have no record showing that our Master ever used, 1
or recommended others to use, drugs; but we have his
words, and the prophet's, as follows: "Take no thought, 3
saying, What shall we eat? or, What shall we drink?"
"And Asa . . . sought not to the Lord, but to the physicians. And Asa slept with his fathers." 6

## VERITAS ODIUM PARIT

The combined efforts of the materialistic portion of
the pulpit and press in 1885, to retard by misrepresen- 9
tation the stately goings of Christian Science, are giving
it new impetus and energy; calling forth the *vox populi*
and directing more critical observation to its uplifting 12
influence upon the health, morals, and spirituality of
mankind.

Their movements indicate fear and weakness, a physi- 15
cal and spiritual need that Christian Science should remove with glorious results. The conclusion cannot now
be pushed, that women have no rights that man is bound 18
to respect. This is woman's hour, in all the good tendencies, charities, and reforms of to-day. It is difficult
to say which may be most mischievous to the human 21
heart, the praise or the dispraise of men.

I have loved the Church and followed it, thinking that
it was following Christ; but, if the pulpit allows the people 24
to go no further in the direction of Christlikeness, and
rejects apostolic Christianity, seeking to stereotype infinite
Truth, it is a thing to be thankful for that one can walk 27
alone the straight and narrow way; that, in the words of
Wendell Phillips, "one with God is a majority."

1 It is the pulpit and press, clerical robes and the pro-
hibiting of free speech, that cradles and covers the sins of
3 the world, — all unmitigated systems of crime; and it
requires the enlightenment of these worthies, through
civil and religious reform, to blot out all inhuman codes.
6 It was the Southern pulpit and press that influenced the
people to wrench from man both human and divine rights,
in order to subserve the interests of wealth, religious caste,
9 civil and political power. And the pulpit had to be
purged of that sin by human gore, — when the love of
Christ would have washed it divinely away in Christian
12 Science!

The cry of the colored slave has scarcely been heard
and hushed, when from another direction there comes
15 another sharp cry of oppression. Another form of inhu-
manity lifts its hydra head to forge anew the old fetters;
to shackle conscience, stop free speech, slander, vilify;
18 to invite its prey, then turn and refuse the victim a solitary
vindication in this most unprecedented warfare.

A conflict more terrible than the battle of Gettysburg
21 awaits the crouching wrong that refused to yield its
prey the peace of a desert, when a voice was heard
crying in the wilderness, — the spiritual famine of 1866,
24 — "Prepare ye the way of the Lord, make His paths
straight."

Shall religious intolerance, arrayed against the rights
27 of man, again deluge the earth in blood? The question
at issue with mankind is: Shall we have a spiritual Christianity and a spiritual healing, or a materialistic religion
30 and a *materia medica?*

The advancing faith and hope of Christianity, the
earnest seeking after practical truth that shall cast out

error and heal the sick, wisely demand for man his God- 1
given heritage, both human and divine rights; namely,
that his honest convictions and *proofs* of advancing truth 3
be allowed due consideration, and treated not as pearls
trampled upon.

Those familiar with my history are more tolerant; those 6
who know me, know that I found health in just what I
teach. I have professed Christianity a half-century; and
now I calmly challenge the world, upon fair investigation, 9
to furnish a single instance of departure in one of my
works from the highest possible ethics.

The charges against my views are false, but natural, 12
since those bringing them do not understand my statement of the Science I introduce, and are unwilling to be
taught it, even gratuitously. If they did understand it, they 15
could demonstrate this Science by healing the sick; hence
the injustice of their interpretations.

To many, the healing force developed by Christian 18
Science seems a mystery, because they do not understand
that Spirit controls body. They acknowledge the existence of mortal mind, but believe it to reside in matter 21
of the brain; but that man is the idea of infinite Mind,
is not so easily accepted. That which is temporary
seems, to the common estimate, solid and substantial. 24
It is much easier for people to believe that the body
affects mind, than that the body is an expression of
mind, and reflects harmony or discord according to 27
thought.

Everything that God created, He pronounced good.
He never made sickness. Hence *that* is only an evil belief 30
of mortal mind, which must be met, in every instance,
with a denial by Truth.

1   This is the "new tongue," the language of them that "lay hands on the sick, and they shall recover," whose
3 spiritual interpretation they refuse to hear. For instance: the literal meaning of the passage "lay hands on the sick" would be manipulation; its moral meaning, found in the
6 "new tongue," is spiritual power, — as, in another Scripture, "I will triumph in the works of Thy hands."

## FALSEHOOD

9   The Greeks showed a just estimate of the person they called slanderer, when they made the word synonymous with devil. If the simple falsehoods uttered about me
12 were compounded, the mixture would be labelled thus: "Religionists' mistaken views of Mrs. Eddy's book, 'Science and Health with Key to the Scriptures,' and the
15 malice aforethought of sinners."

That I take opium; that I am an infidel, a mesmerist, a medium, a "pantheist;" or that my hourly life is prayer-
18 less, or not in strict obedience to the Mosaic Decalogue, — is not more true than that I am dead, as is oft reported. The *St. Louis Democrat* is alleged to have reported my
21 demise, and to have said that I died of poison, and bequeathed my property to Susan Anthony.

The opium falsehood has only this to it: Many years
24 ago my regular physician prescribed morphine, which I took, when he could do no more for me. Afterwards, the glorious revelations of Christian Science saved me
27 from that necessity and made me well, since which time I have not taken drugs, with the following exception: When the mental malpractice of poisoning people was

first undertaken by a mesmerist, to test that malprac- 1
tice I experimented by taking some large doses of morphine, to see if Christian Science could not obviate its 3
effect; and I say with tearful thanks, "The drug had
no effect upon me whatever." The hour has struck,
— "If they drink any deadly thing, it shall not hurt 6
them."

The false report that I have appropriated other people's
manuscripts in my works, has been met and answered 9
*legally*. Both in private and public life, and especially
through my teachings, it is well known that I am not a
spiritualist, a pantheist, or prayerless. The most devout 12
members of evangelical churches will say this, as well as
my intimate acquaintances. None are permitted to remain in my College building whose morals are not un- 15
questionable. I have neither purchased nor ordered a
drug since my residence in Boston; and to my knowledge,
not one has been sent to my house, unless it was something 18
to remove stains or vermin.

The report that I was dead arose no doubt from the
combined efforts of some malignant students, expelled 21
from my College for immorality, to kill me: of their mental
design to do this I have proof, but no fear. My heavenly
Father will never leave me comfortless, in the amplitude 24
of His love; coming nearer in my need, more tenderly to
save and bless.

## LOVE                                                27

What a word! I am in awe before it. Over what
worlds on worlds it hath range and is sovereign! the un-

1 derived, the incomparable, the infinite All of good, the
*alone* God, is Love.

3     By what strange perversity is the best become the most
abused, — either as a quality or as an entity?  Mortals
misrepresent and miscall affection;  they make it what
6 it is not, and doubt what it is.  The so-called affection
pursuing its victim is a butcher fattening the lamb to
slay it.  What the lower propensities express, should be
9 repressed by the sentiments.  No word is more mis-
construed;  no sentiment less understood.  The divine
significance of Love is distorted into human qualities,
12 which in their human abandon become jealousy and
hate.

Love is not something put upon a shelf, to be taken
15 down on rare occasions with sugar-tongs and laid on a
rose-leaf.  I make strong demands on love, call for active
witnesses to prove it, and noble sacrifices and grand
18 achievements as its results.  Unless these appear, I cast
aside the word as a sham and counterfeit, having no ring
of the true metal.  Love cannot be a mere abstraction, or
21 goodness without activity and power.  As a human quality,
the glorious significance of affection is more than words:
it is the tender, unselfish deed done in secret;  the silent,
24 ceaseless prayer;  the self-forgetful heart that overflows;
the veiled form stealing on an errand of mercy, out of a
side door;  the little feet tripping along the sidewalk;  the
27 gentle hand opening the door that turns toward want and
woe, sickness and sorrow, and thus lighting the dark
places of earth.

ADDRESS ON THE FOURTH OF JULY AT PLEASANT VIEW, 1
CONCORD, N. H., BEFORE 2,500 MEMBERS OF THE
MOTHER CHURCH, 1897                                           3

My beloved brethren, who have come all the way from
the Pacific to the Atlantic shore, from the Palmetto to the
Pine Tree State, I greet you; my hand may not touch 6
yours to-day, but my heart will with tenderness untalkable.

His Honor, Mayor Woodworth, has welcomed you to
Concord most graciously, voicing the friendship of this 9
city and of my native State — loyal to the heart's core to
religion, home, friends, and country.

To-day we commemorate not only our nation's civil 12
and religious freedom, but a greater even, the liberty of
the sons of God, the inalienable rights and radiant reality
of Christianity, whereof our Master said: "The works 15
that I do shall he do;" and, "The kingdom of God cometh
not with observation" (with knowledge obtained from
the senses), but "the kingdom of God is within you," — 18
within the present possibilities of mankind.

Think of this inheritance! Heaven right here, where
angels are as men, clothed more lightly, and men as angels 21
who, burdened for an hour, spring into liberty, and the
good they would do, that they do, and the evil they would
not do, that they do not.                                    24

From the falling leaves of old-time faiths men learn a
parable of the period, that all error, physical, moral, or
religious, will fall before Truth demonstrated, even as 27
dry leaves fall to enrich the soil for fruitage.

Sin, sickness, and disease flee before the evangel of
Truth as the mountain mists before the sun. Truth is 30

1 the tonic for the sick, and this medicine of Mind is not
necessarily infinitesimal but infinite. Herein the mental
3 medicine of divine metaphysics and the medical systems
of allopathy and homœopathy differ. Mental medicine gains no potency by attenuation, and its largest
6 dose is never dangerous, but the more the better in every
case.

Christian Science classifies thought thus: Right thoughts
9 are reality and power; wrong thoughts are unreality and
powerless, possessing the nature of dreams. Good thoughts
are potent; evil thoughts are impotent, and they should
12 appear thus. Continuing this category, we learn that
sick thoughts are unreality and weakness; while healthy
thoughts are reality and strength. My proof of these
15 novel propositions is demonstration, whereby any man
can satisfy himself of their verity.

Christian Science is not only the acme of Science
18 but the crown of Christianity. It is universal. It appeals to man as man; to the whole and not to a portion; to man physically, as well as spiritually, and to all
21 mankind.

It has one God. It demonstrates the divine Principle,
rules and practice of the great healer and master of meta-
24 physics, Jesus of Nazareth. It spiritualizes religion and
restores its lost element, namely, healing the sick. It
consecrates and inspires the teacher and preacher; it
27 equips the doctor with safe and sure medicine; it encourages and empowers the business man and secures
the success of honesty. It is the dear children's toy and
30 strong tower; the wise man's spiritual dictionary; the
poor man's money; yea, it is the pearl priceless whereof
our Master said, if a man findeth, he goeth and selleth

all that he hath and buyeth it. Buyeth it! Note the 1
scope of that saying, even that Christianity is not merely
a gift, as St. Paul avers, but is bought with a price, a great 3
price; and what man knoweth as did our Master its
value, and the price that he paid for it?

Friends, I am not enough the new woman of the period 6
for outdoor speaking, and the incidental platform is not
broad enough for me, but the speakers that will now address you — one a congressman — may improve our 9
platforms; and make amends for the nothingness of
matter with the allness of Mind.

## WELL DOINGE IS THE FRUITE OF DOINGE WELL   12
### HERRICK

This period is big with events. Fraught with history,
it repeats the past and portends much for the future. 15

The Scriptural metaphors, — of the woman in travail,
the great red dragon that stood ready to devour the child
as soon as it was born, and the husbandmen that said, 18
"This is the heir: come, let us kill him, that the inheritance may be ours," — are type and shadow of this
hour. 21

A mother's love touches the heart of God, and should
it not appeal to human sympathy? Can a mother tell
her child one tithe of the agonies that gave that child 24
birth? Can that child conceive of the anguish, until she
herself is become a mother?

Do the children of this period dream of the spiritual 27
Mother's sore travail, through the long night, that has
opened their eyes to the light of Christian Science? Cherish

1 these new-born children that filial obedience to which the
Decalogue points with promise of prosperity? Should not
3 the loving warning, the far-seeing wisdom, the gentle en-
treaty, the stern rebuke have been heeded, in return for
all that love which brooded tireless over their tender
6 years? for all that love that hath fed them with Truth, —
even the bread that cometh down from heaven, — as the
mother-bird tendeth her young in the rock-ribbed nest of
9 the raven's callow brood!

And what of the hope of that parent whose children
rise up against her; when brother slays brother, and
12 the strength of union grows weak with wickedness?
The victim of mad ambition that saith, "This is
the heir: come, let us kill him, that the inheritance
15 may be ours," goes on to learn that he must at last
kill this evil in "self" in order to gain the kingdom
of God.

18 Envy, the great red dragon of this hour, would obscure
the light of Science, take away a third part of the stars
from the spiritual heavens, and cast them to the earth.
21 This is not Science. *Per contra,* it is the mortal mind
sense — mental healing on a material basis — hurling
its so-called healing at random, filling with hate its
24 deluded victims, or resting in silly peace upon the
laurels of headlong human will. "What shall, therefore,
the Lord of the vineyard do? He will come and de-
27 stroy the husbandmen, and will give the vineyard unto
others."

## LITTLE GODS                                1

It is sometimes said, cynically, that Christian Scientists set themselves on pedestals, as so many petty deities; 3 but there is no fairness or propriety in the aspersion.

Man is not equal to his Maker. That which is formed is not cause, but effect; and has no underived power. 6 But it is possible, and dutiful, to throw the weight of thought and action on the side of right, and to be thus lifted up.                                        9

Man should be found not claiming equality with, but growing into, that altitude of Mind which was in Christ Jesus. He should comprehend, in divine Science, a 12 recognition of what the apostle meant when he said: "The Spirit itself beareth witness with our spirit, that we are the children of God: and if children, then heirs; 15 heirs of God, and joint-heirs with Christ."

## ADVANTAGE OF MIND-HEALING

It is sometimes asked, What are the advantages of your 18 system of healing?

I claim for healing by Christian Science the following advantages: —                                   21

*First:* It does away with material medicine, and recognizes the fact that the antidote for sickness, as well as for sin, may be found in God, the divine Mind.   24

*Second:* It is more effectual than drugs, and cures where they fail, because it is this divine antidote, and metaphysics is above physics.                        27

1 *Third:* Persons who have been healed by Christian Science are not only cured of their belief in disease, but 3 they are at the same time improved morally. The body is governed by Mind, and mortal mind must be corrected in order to make the body harmonious.

6  A CARD

While gratefully acknowledging the public confidence manifested in daily letters that protest against receiving 9 instruction in the Massachusetts Metaphysical College from any other than Mrs. Eddy, I feel, deeply, that of necessity this imposes on me the severe task of remain- 12 ing at present a public servant: also, that this must prevent my classes from forming as frequently as was announced in the October number of the *Journal,* and 15 necessitates receiving but a select number of students. To meet the old impediment, lack of time, that has occasioned the irregular intervals between my class terms, 18 I shall continue to send to each applicant a notice from one to two weeks previous to the opening term.

MARY BAKER G. EDDY

21  SPIRIT AND LAW

We are accustomed to think and to speak of gravitation as a law of matter; while every quality of matter, 24 in and of itself, is inert, inanimate, and non-intelligent. The assertion that matter is a law, or a lawgiver, is anomalous. Wherever law is, Mind is; and the notion

that Mind can be in matter is rank infidelity, which either
excludes God from the universe, or includes Him in every
mode and form of evil.   Pantheism presupposes that
God sleeps in the mineral, dreams in the animal, and
wakes in a wicked man.

The distinction between that which is and that which
is not law, must be made by Mind and as Mind.   Law is
either a moral or an immoral force.   The law of God is
the law of Spirit, a moral and spiritual force of immortal and divine Mind.   The so-called law of matter is an
immoral force of erring mortal mind, *alias* the minds of
mortals.   This so-called force, or law, at work in nature
as a power, prohibition, or license, is cruel and merciless.
It punishes the innocent, and repays our best deeds
with sacrifice and suffering.   It is a code whose modes
trifle with joy, and lead to immediate or ultimate death.
It fosters suspicion where confidence is due, fear where
courage is requisite, reliance where there should be
avoidance, a belief in safety where there is most
danger.   Our Master called it "a murderer from the
beginning."

Electricity, governed by this so-called law, sparkles
on the cloud, and strikes down the hoary saint.   Floods
swallow up homes and households; and childhood, age,
and manhood go down in the death-dealing wave.   Earth-
quakes engulf cities, churches, schools, and mortals.
Cyclones kill and destroy, desolating the green earth.
This pitiless power smites with disease the good Samari-
tan ministering to his neighbor's need.   Even the chamber
where the good man surrenders to death is not exempt
from this law.   Smoothing the pillow of pain may infect
you with smallpox, according to this lawless law which

1 dooms man to die for loving his neighbor as himself, —
when Christ has said that love is the fulfilling of the
3 law.

Our great Ensample, Jesus of Nazareth, met and abol-
ished this unrelenting false claim of matter with the
6 righteous scorn and power of Spirit. When, through
Mind, he restored sight to the blind, he figuratively and
literally spat upon matter; and, anointing the wounded
9 spirit with the great truth that God is All, he demonstrated the healing power and supremacy of the law of
Life and Love.

12 In the spiritual Genesis of creation, all law was vested
in the Lawgiver, who was a law to Himself. In divine
Science, God is One and All; and, governing Himself,
15 He governs the universe. This is the law of creation:
"My defense is of God, which saveth the upright in
heart." And that infinite Mind governs all things. On
18 this infinite Principle of freedom, God named Himself, I AM. Error, or Adam, might give names to itself,
and call Mind by the name of matter, but error could
21 neither name nor demonstrate Spirit. The name, I
AM, indicated no personality that could be paralleled
with it; but it did declare a mighty individuality,
24 even the everlasting Father, as infinite consciousness,
ever-presence, omnipotence; as all law, Life, Truth, and
Love.

27 God's interpretation of Himself furnishes man with
the only suitable or true idea of Him; and the divine
definition of Deity differs essentially from the human.
30 It interprets the law of Spirit, not of matter. It explains
the eternal dynamics of being, and shows that nature
and man are as harmonious to-day as in the beginning,

when "all things were made by Him; and without Him 1
was not any thing made."

Whatever appears to be law, but partakes not of the 3
nature of God, is not law, but is what Jesus declared
it, "a liar, and the father of it." God is the law of Life,
not of death; of health, not of sickness; of good, not 6
of evil. It is this infinitude and oneness of good that
silences the supposition that evil is a claimant or a claim.
The consciousness of good has no consciousness or knowl- 9
edge of evil; and evil is not a quality to be known or
eliminated by good: while iniquity, too evil to conceive
of good as being unlike itself, declares that God knows 12
iniquity!

When the Lawgiver was the only law of creation, freedom reigned, and was the heritage of man; but this 15
freedom was the moral power of good, not of evil: it
was divine Science, in which God is supreme, and the
only law of being. In this eternal harmony of Science, 18
man is not fallen: he is governed in the same rhythm
that the Scripture describes, when "the morning stars
sang together, and all the sons of God shouted for joy." 21

## TRUTH-HEALING

The spiritual elevator of the human race, physically,
morally, and Christianly, is the truism that Truth dem- 24
onstrates good, and is natural; while error, or evil,
is really non-existent, and must have produced its own
illusion, — for it belongs not to nature nor to God. Truth 27
is the power of God which heals the sick and the sinner,
and is applicable to all the needs of man. It is the uni-

1 versal, intelligent Christ-idea illustrated by the life of
Jesus, through whose "stripes we are healed." By con-
3 flicts, defeats, and triumphs, Christian Science has been
reduced to the understanding of mortals, and found able
to heal them.

6    Pagan mysticism, Grecian philosophy, or Jewish religion, never entered into the line of Jesus' thought or
action. His faith partook not of drugs, matter, nor of
9 the travesties of mortal mind. The divine Mind was
his only instrumentality and potency, in religion or medicine. The Principle of his cure was God, in the laws
12 of Spirit, not of matter; and these laws annulled all other
laws.

Jesus knew that erring mortal thought holds only in
15 itself the supposition of evil, and that sin, sickness, and
death are its subjective states; also, that pure Mind is
the truth of being that subjugates and destroys any sup-
18 positional or elementary opposite to Him who is All.

Truth is supreme and omnipotent. Then, whatever
else seemeth to be intelligence or power is false, delud-
21 ing reason and denying revelation, and seeking to dethrone
Deity. The truth of Mind-healing uplifts mankind, by
acknowledging pure Mind as absolute and entire, and
24 that evil is naught, although it seems to be.

Pure Mind gives out an atmosphere that heals and
saves. Words are not always the auxiliaries of Truth.
27 The spirit, and not the letter, performs the vital func-
tions of Truth and Love. Mind, imbued with this Science
of healing, is a law unto itself, needing neither license
30 nor prohibition; but lawless mind, with unseen motives,
and silent mental methods whereby it may injure the
race, is the highest attenuation of evil.

Again: evil, as *mind,* is doomed, already sentenced, 1 punished; for suffering is commensurate with evil, and lasts as long as the evil. As *mind,* evil finds no escape 3 from itself; and the sin and suffering it occasions can only be removed by reformation.

According to divine law, sin and suffering are not 6 cancelled by repentance or pardon. Christian Science not only elucidates but demonstrates this verity of being; namely, that mortals suffer from the wrong they 9 commit, whether intentionally or ignorantly; that every effect and amplification of wrong will revert to the wrongdoer, until he pays his full debt to divine law, and the 12 measure he has meted is measured to him again, full, pressed down, and running over. Surely "the way of the transgressor is hard." 15

In this law of justice, the atonement of Christ loses no efficacy. Justice is the handmaid of mercy, and showeth mercy by punishing sin. Jesus said, "I came not to 18 destroy the law," — the divine requirements typified in the law of Moses, — "but to fulfil it" in righteousness, by Truth's destroying error. No greater type of divine 21 Love can be presented than effecting so glorious a purpose. This spirit of sacrifice always has saved, and still saves mankind; but by mankind I mean mortals, or a kind 24 of men after man's own making. Man as God's idea is already saved with an everlasting salvation. It is impossible to be a Christian Scientist without apprehend- 27 ing the moral law so clearly that, for conscience' sake, one will either abandon his claim to even a knowledge of this Science, or else make the claim valid. All Science 30 is divine. Then, to be Science, it must produce physical and moral harmony.

1 Dear readers, our *Journal* is designed to bring health and happiness to all households wherein it is permitted 3 to enter, and to confer increased power to be good and to do good. If you wish to brighten so pure a purpose, you will aid our prospect of fulfilling it by your kind 6 patronage of *The Christian Science Journal,* now entering upon its fifth volume, clad in Truth-healing's new and costly spring dress.

9 HEART TO HEART

When the heart speaks, however simple the words, its language is always acceptable to those who have 12 hearts.

I just want to say, I thank you, my dear students, who are at work conscientiously and assiduously, for the good 15 you are doing. I am grateful to you for giving to the sick relief from pain; for giving joy to the suffering and hope to the disconsolate; for lifting the fallen and strength- 18 ening the weak, and encouraging the heart grown faint with hope deferred. We are made glad by the divine Love which looseth the chains of sickness and sin, open- 21 ing the prison doors to such as are bound; and we should be more grateful than words can express, even through this white-winged messenger, our *Journal.*

24 With all the homage beneath the skies, yet were our burdens heavy but for the Christ-love that makes them light and renders the yoke easy. Having his word, you 27 have little need of words of approval and encouragement from me. Perhaps it is even selfish in me sometimes to relieve my heart of its secrets, because I take so much

pleasure in thus doing; but if my motives are sinister, 1
they will harm myself only, and I shall have the unselfish joy of knowing that the wrong motives are not yours, 3
to react on yourselves.

These two words in Scripture suggest the sweetest
similes to be found in any language — *rock* and *feathers:* 6
"Upon this rock I will build my church;" "He shall
cover thee with His feathers." How blessed it is to
think of you as "beneath the shadow of a great rock in 9
a weary land," safe in His strength, building on His
foundation, and covered from the devourer by divine
protection and affection. Always bear in mind that His 12
presence, power, and peace meet all human needs and
reflect all bliss.

### THINGS TO BE THOUGHT OF          15

The need of their teacher's counsel, felt by students,
especially by those at a distance, working assiduously for
our common Cause, — and their constant petitions for 18
the same, should be met in the most effectual way.

To be responsible for supplying this want, and poise
the wavering balance on the right side, is impracticable 21
without a full knowledge of the environments. The
educational system of Christian Science lacks the aid
and protection of State laws. The Science is hampered 24
by immature demonstrations, by the infancy of its discovery, by incorrect teaching; and especially by unprincipled claimants, whose mad ambition drives them to 27
appropriate my ideas and discovery, without credit, appreciation, or a single original conception, while they
10

1 quote from other authors and give them credit for every
random thought in line with mine.

3   My noble students, who are loyal to Christ, Truth, and
human obligations, will not be disheartened in the midst
of this seething sea of sin.   They build for time and eter-
6 nity.   The others stumble over misdeeds, and their own
unsubstantiality, without the groundwork of right, till,
like camera shadows thrown upon the mists of time, they
9 melt into darkness.

Unity is the essential nature of Christian Science.   Its
Principle is One, and to demonstrate the divine One,
12 demands oneness of thought and action.

Many students enter the Normal class of my College
whom I have not fitted for it by the Primary course.
15 They are taught their first lessons by my students;   hence
the aptness to assimilate pure and abstract Science is
somewhat untested.

18 "As the twig is bent, the tree's inclined."   As mortal
mind is directed, it acts for a season.   Some students
leave my instructions before they are quite free from
21 the bias of their first impressions, whether those be correct or incorrect.   Such students are more or less subject
to the future mental influence of their former teacher.
24 Their knowledge of Mind-healing may be right theoretically, but the moral and spiritual status of thought
must be right also.   The tone of the teacher's mind must
27 be pure, grand, true, to aid the mental development of
the student;   for the tint of the instructor's mind must
take its hue from the divine Mind.   A single mistake in
30 metaphysics, or in ethics, is more fatal than a mistake in
physics.

If a teacher of Christian Science unwittingly or inten-

tionally offers his own thought, and gives me as authority 1
for it; if he diverges from Science and knows it not, or,
knowing it, makes the venture from vanity, in order to 3
be thought original, or wiser than somebody else, — this
divergence widens. He grows dark, and cannot regain,
at will, an upright understanding. This error in the 6
teacher also predisposes his students to make mistakes
and lose their way. Diverse opinions in Science are
stultifying. All must have *one* Principle and the same 9
rule; and all *who follow the Principle and rule* have but
one opinion of it.

Whosoever understands a single rule in Science, and 12
demonstrates its Principle according to rule, is master
of the situation. Nobody can gainsay this. The ego-
tistical theorist or shallow moralist may presume to 15
make innovations upon simple proof; but his mistake
is visited upon himself and his students, whose minds
are, must be, disturbed by this discord, which extends 18
along the whole line of reciprocal thought. An error
in premise can never bring forth the real fruits of Truth.
After thoroughly explaining spiritual Truth and its ethics 21
to a student, I am not morally responsible for the mis-
statements or misconduct of this student. My teachings
are uniform. Those who abide by them do well. If 24
others, who receive the same instruction, do ill, the fault
is not in the culture but the soil.

I am constantly called to settle questions and disaf- 27
fections toward Christian Science growing out of the
departures from Science of self-satisfied, unprincipled
students. If impatient of the loving rebuke, the stu- 30
dent must stop at the foot of the grand ascent, and there
remain until suffering compels the downfall of his self-

1 conceit. Then that student must struggle up, with bleeding footprints, to the God-crowned summit of unselfish
3 and pure aims and affections.

To be two-sided, when these sides are moral opposites, is neither politic nor scientific; and to abridge a
6 single human right or privilege is an error. Whoever
does this may represent me as doing it; but he mistakes
me, and the subjective state of his own mind for mine.
9 The true leader of a true cause is the unacknowledged
servant of mankind. Stationary in the background, this
individual is doing the work that nobody else can or will
12 do. An erratic career is like the comet's course, dashing through space, headlong and alone. A clear-headed
and honest Christian Scientist will demonstrate the Prin-
15 ciple of Christian Science, and hold justice and mercy as
inseparable from the unity of God.

### UNCHRISTIAN RUMOR

18 The assertion that I have said hard things about my
loyal students in Chicago, New York, or any other place,
is utterly false and groundless. I speak of them as I feel,
21 and I cannot find it in my heart not to love them. They
are essentially dear to me, who are toiling and achieving
success in unison with my own endeavors and prayers.
24 If I correct mistakes which may be made in teaching or
lecturing on Christian Science, this is in accordance with
my students' desires, and thus we mutually aid each other,
27 and obey the Golden Rule.

The spirit of lies is abroad. Because Truth has spoken
aloud, error, running to and fro in the earth, is scream-

ing, to make itself heard above Truth's voice. The 1
audible and inaudible wail of evil never harms Scientists,
steadfast in their consciousness of the nothingness of 3
wrong and the supremacy of right.

Our worst enemies are the best friends to our growth.
Charity students, for whom I have sacrificed the most 6
time, — those whose chief aim is to injure me, — have
caused me to exercise most patience. When they report
me as "*hating* those whom I do not love," let them re- 9
member that there never was a time when I saw an opportunity really to help them and failed to improve it;
and this, too, when I knew they were secretly striving 12
to injure me.

## VAINGLORY

*Comparisons are odorous.* — SHAKESPEARE 15

Through all human history, the vital outcomes of
Truth have suffered temporary shame and loss from
individual conceit, cowardice, or dishonesty. The bird 18
whose right wing flutters to soar, while the left beats its
way downward, falls to the earth. Both wings must be
plumed for rarefied atmospheres and upward flight. 21

Mankind must gravitate from sense to Soul, and human
affairs should be governed by Spirit, intelligent good.
The antipode of Spirit, which we name *matter,* or *non-* 24
*intelligent evil,* is no real aid to being. The predisposing
and exciting cause of all defeat and victory under the
sun, rests on this scientific basis: that action, in obedi- 27
ence to God, spiritualizes man's motives and methods,
and crowns them with success; while disobedience to

1 this divine Principle materializes human modes and consciousness, and defeats them.

3 Two personal queries give point to human action: Who
shall be greatest? and, Who shall be best? Earthly
glory is vain; but not vain enough to attempt pointing
6 the way to heaven, the harmony of being. The imaginary
victories of rivalry and hypocrisy are defeats. The Holy
One saith, "O that thou hadst hearkened to My com-
9 mandments! then had thy peace been as a river." He
is unfit for Truth, and the demonstration of divine power,
who departs from Mind to matter, and from Truth to
12 error, in pursuit of better means for healing the sick and
casting out error.

The Christian Scientist keeps straight to the course.
15 His whole inquiry and demonstration lie in the line of
Truth; hence he suffers no shipwreck in a starless night
on the shoals of vainglory. His medicine is Mind —
18 the omnipotent and ever-present good. His "help is
from the Lord," who heals body and mind, head and
heart; changing the affections, enlightening the mis-
21 guided senses, and curing alike the sin and the mortal
sinner. God's preparations for the sick are potions of
His own qualities. His therapeutics are antidotes for
24 the ailments of mortal mind and body. Then let us not
adulterate His preparations for the sick with material
means.

27 From lack of moral strength empires fall. Right alone
is irresistible, permanent, eternal. Remember that human pride forfeits spiritual power, and either vacillating
30 good or self-assertive error dies of its own elements.
Through patience we must possess the sense of Truth;
and Truth is used to waiting. "Commit thy way unto

the Lord; trust also in Him; and He shall bring it to 1
pass."

By using falsehood to regain his liberty, Galileo vir- 3
tually lost it. He cannot escape from barriers who commits his moral sense to a dungeon. Hear the Master
on this subject: "No man can serve two masters: for 6
either he will hate the one, and love the other; or else he
will hold to the one, and despise the other. Ye cannot
serve God and mammon." 9

Lives there a man who can better define ethics, better
elucidate the Principle of being, than he who "spake as
never man spake," and whose precepts and example have 12
a perpetual freshness in relation to human events?

Who is it that understands, unmistakably, a fraction
of the actual Science of Mind-healing? 15

It is he who has fairly proven his knowledge on a Christian, mental, scientific basis; who has made his choice
between matter and Mind, and proven the divine Mind 18
to be the only physician. These are self-evident propositions: That man can only be Christianized through Mind;
that without Mind the body is without action; that Science 21
is a law of divine Mind. The conclusion follows that the
correct Mind-healing is the proper means of Christianity,
and is Science. 24

Christian Science may be sold in the shambles. Many
are bidding for it, — but are not willing to pay the price.
Error is vending itself on trust, well knowing the will- 27
ingness of mortals to buy error at par value. The Revelator beheld the opening of this silent mental seal, and
heard the great Red Dragon *whispering* that "no man 30
might buy or sell, save he that had the mark, or the name
of the beast, or the number of his name."

1 We are in the Valley of Decision. Then, let us take the side of him who "overthrew the tables of the money-
3 changers, and the seats of them that sold doves," — of such as barter integrity and peace for money and fame. What artist would question the skill of the masters in
6 sculpture, music, or painting? Shall we depart from the example of the Master in Christian Science, Jesus of Nazareth, — than whom mankind hath no higher ideal?
9 He who demonstrated his power over sin, disease, and death, is the master Metaphysician.

To seek or employ other means than those the Master
12 used in demonstrating Life scientifically, is to lose the priceless knowledge of his Principle and practice. He said, "Seek ye first the kingdom of God, and His right-
15 eousness; and all these things shall be added unto you." Gain a pure Christianity; for that is requisite for heal-ing the sick. Then you will need no other aid, and will
18 have full faith in his prophecy, "And there shall be one fold, and one shepherd;" but, the Word must abide in us, if we would obtain that promise. We cannot depart
21 from his holy example, — we cannot leave Christ for the schools which crucify him, and yet follow him in heal-ing. Fidelity to his precepts and practice is the only pass-
24 port to his power; and the pathway of goodness and greatness runs through the modes and methods of God. "He that glorieth, let him glory in the Lord."

27                    COMPOUNDS

Homœopathy is the last link in material medicine. The next step is Mind-medicine. Among the foremost

virtues of homœopathy is the exclusion of compounds 1
from its pharmacy, and the attenuation of a drug up to
the point of its disappearance as matter and its manifesta- 3
tion in effect as a thought, instead of a thing.

Students of Christian Science (and many who are not
students) understand enough of this to keep out of their 6
heads the notion that compounded metaphysics (so-called)
is, or can be, Christian Science, — that rests on oneness;
one cause and one effect. 9

They should take our magazine, work for it, write for
it, and read it. They should eschew all magazines and
books which are less than the best. 12

"Choose you this day whom ye will serve." Cleanse
your mind of the cobwebs which spurious "compounds"
engender. Before considering a subject that is unworthy 15
of thought, take in this axiomatic truism: "Trust her
not, she's fooling thee;" and Longfellow is right.

CLOSE OF THE MASSACHUSETTS METAPHYSICAL 18
COLLEGE

Much is said at this date, 1889, about Mrs. Eddy's
Massachusetts Metaphysical College being the only 21
chartered College of Metaphysics. To make this plain,
the Publishing Committee of the Christian Scientist
Association has published in the *Boston Traveler* the 24
following: —

"To benefit the community, and more strongly mark
the difference between true and false teachers of mental 27
healing, the following history and statistics are officially
submitted: —

"Rev. Mary Baker G. Eddy obtained a college charter in January, 1881, with all the rights and privileges pertaining thereunto (*including the right to grant degrees*) under Act of 1874, Chapter 375, Section 4.

"This Act was *repealed* from and after January 31, 1882. Mrs. Eddy's grant for a college, for metaphysical purposes *only*, is the first on record in history, and no charters were granted for similar colleges, except hers, from January, 1881, till the repealing of said Act in January, 1882.

"The substance of this Act is at present incorporated in Public Statutes, Chapter 115, Section 2, with the following important restrictions: In accordance with Statutes of 1883, Chapter 268, any officer, agent, or servant of any corporation or association, who confers, or authorizes to be conferred, any diploma or degree, shall be punished by a fine not less than five hundred dollars and not more than one thousand dollars.

"All the mind-healing colleges (except Rev. Mrs. Eddy's) have simply an incorporated grant, which may be called a charter, such as any stock company may obtain for any secular purposes; but these so-called charters bestow no rights to *confer degrees*. Hence to name these institutions, under such charters, *colleges*, is a fraudulent claim. There is but one legally chartered college of metaphysics, with powers to confer diplomas and degrees, and that is the Massachusetts Metaphysical College, of which Rev. Mrs. Eddy is founder and president."

I have endeavored to act toward all students of Christian Science with the intuition and impulse of love. If certain natures have not profited by my rebukes, some time, as Christian Scientists, they will know the value of these rebukes. I am thankful that the neophyte will be benefited by experience, although it will cost him much, and in proportion to its worth.

I close my College in order to work in other directions, where I now seem to be most needed, and where none other can do the work. I withdraw from an overwhelming prosperity. My students have never expressed so grateful a sense of my labors with them as now, and never have been so capable of relieving my tasks as at present.

God bless my enemies, as well as the better part of mankind, and gather all my students, in the bonds of love and perfectness, into one grand family of Christ's followers.

Loyal Christian Scientists should go on in their present line of labor for a good and holy cause. Their institutes have not yet accomplished all the good they are capable of accomplishing; therefore they should continue, as at present, to send out students from these sources of education, to promote the growing interest in Christian Science Mind-healing.

There are one hundred and sixty applications lying on the desk before me, for the Primary class in the Massachusetts Metaphysical College, and I cannot do my best work for a class which contains that number. When these were taught, another and a larger number would be in waiting for the same class instruction; and if I should teach that Primary class, the other three classes — one Primary and two Normal — would be delayed. The work is more than one person can well accomplish, and the imperative call is for my exclusive teaching.

1   From the scant history of Jesus and of his disciples, we have no Biblical authority for a public institution.

3 This point, however, had not impressed me when I opened my College. I desire to revise my book "Science and Health with Key to the Scriptures," and in order to do 6 this I must stop teaching at present. The work that needs to be done, and which God calls me to outside of College work, if left undone might hinder the progress 9 of our Cause more than my teaching would advance it: therefore I leave all for Christ.

Deeply regretting the disappointment this will occa-12 sion, and with grateful acknowledgments to the public for its liberal patronage, I close my College.

MARY BAKER G. EDDY

15     MALICIOUS REPORTS

*Truth is fallen in the street, and equity cannot enter.* — ISAIAH lix. 14.

When the press is gagged, liberty is besieged; but 18 when the press assumes the liberty to lie, it discounts clemency, mocks morality, outrages humanity, breaks common law, gives impulse to violence, envy, and hate, 21 and prolongs the reign of inordinate, unprincipled clans. At this period, 1888, those quill-drivers whose consciences are in their pockets hold high carnival. When news-24 dealers shout for class legislation, and decapitated reputations, headless trunks, and quivering hearts are held up before the rabble in exchange for money, place, and 27 power, the *vox populi* is suffocated, individual rights are trodden under foot, and the car of the modern Inquisition rolls along the streets besmeared with blood.

Would not our Master say to the chief actors in scenes 1
like these, "Ye fools and blind!"  Oh, tardy human
justice! would you take away even woman's trembling, 3
clinging faith in divine power?  Who can roll away the
stone from the door of this sepulchre?  Who — but God's
avenging angel!                                            6

In times like these it were well to lift the veil on the
sackcloth of home, where weepeth the faithful, stricken
mother, and the bruised father bendeth his aching head; 9
where the bereft wife or husband, silent and alone, looks
in dull despair at the vacant seat, and the motherless
little ones, wondering, huddle together, and repeat with 12
quivering lips words of strange import.  May the great
Shepherd that "tempers the wind to the shorn lamb,"
and binds up the wounds of bleeding hearts, just comfort, 15
encourage, and bless all who mourn.

Father, we thank Thee that Thy light and Thy love
reach earth, open the prison to them that are bound, con- 18
sole the innocent, and throw wide the gates of heaven.


## LOYAL CHRISTIAN SCIENTISTS

Pen can never portray the satisfaction that you afforded 21
me at the grand meeting in Chicago of the National Christian Scientist Association in 1888.  Your public and
private expressions of love and loyalty were very touch- 24
ing.  They moved me to speechless thanks.

Chicago is the wonder of the western hemisphere.  The
Palmer House, where we stopped, is magnificent and 27
orderly.  The servants are well-mannered, and the fare
is appetizing.  The floral offerings sent to my apartments

1 were superb, especially the large book of rare flowers, and
the crescent with a star.

3 The reception in the spacious rooms of the Palmer
House, like all else, was purely Western in its cordiality
and largeness. I did not hold interviews with all with
6 whom I desired to, solely because so many people and
circumstances demanded my attention that my personality was not big enough to fill the order; but rest as-
9 sured my heart's desire met the demand.

My students, our delegates, about one thousand Christian Scientists, active, earnest, and loyal, formed a goodly
12 assemblage for the third convention of our National Association, — an assemblage found waiting and watching
for the full coming of our Lord and Christ.

15 In Christian Science the midnight hour will always be
the bridal hour, until "no night is there." The wise
will have their lamps aglow, and light will illumine the
18 darkness.

Out of the gloom comes the glory of our Lord, and
His divine Love is found in affliction. When a false
21 sense suffers, the true sense comes out, and the bridegroom appears. We are then wedded to a purer, higher
affection and ideal.

24 I pray that all my students shall have their lamps
trimmed and burning at the noon of night, that not one
of them be found borrowing oil, and seeking light from
27 matter instead of Spirit, or at work erroneously, thus
shutting out spiritual light. Such an error and loss will
be quickly learned when the door is shut. Error giveth
30 no light, and it closes the door on itself.

In the dark hours, wise Christian Scientists stand
firmer than ever in their allegiance to God. Wisdom

is wedded to their love, and their hearts are not 1
troubled.

Falsehood is on the wings of the winds, but Truth 3
will soar above it. Truth is speaking louder, clearer,
and more imperatively than ever. Error is walking to
and fro in the earth, trying to be heard above Truth, 6
but its voice dies out in the distance. Whosoever pro-
claims Truth loudest, becomes the mark for error's shafts.
The archers aim at Truth's mouthpiece; but a heart 9
loyal to God is patient and strong. Justice waits, and
is used to waiting; and right wins the everlasting
victory.                                                     12

The stake and scaffold have never silenced the messages of the Most High. Then can the present mode of
attempting this — namely, by slanderous falsehoods, and 15
a secret mind-method, through which to effect the purposes of envy and malice — silence Truth? Never. They
but open the eyes to the truth of Benjamin Franklin's 18
report before the French Commissioners on Mesmerism:
"It is one more fact to be recorded in the history of the
errors of the human mind."                                  21

"The Lord reigneth; let the earth rejoice."

No evidence before the material senses can close my
eyes to the scientific proof that God, good, is supreme. 24
Though clouds are round about Him, the divine justice
and judgment are enthroned. Love is especially near
in times of hate, and never so near as when one can be 27
just amid lawlessness, and render good for evil.

I thunder His law to the sinner, and sharply lighten
on the cloud of the intoxicated senses. I cannot help 30
loathing the phenomena of drunkenness produced by
animality. I rebuke it wherever I see it. The vision

1 of the Revelator is before me. The wines of fornica-
tion, envy, and hatred are the distilled spirits of evil,
3 and are the signs of these times; but I am not dismayed,
and my peace returns unto me.

Error will hate more as it realizes more the presence
6 of its tormentor. I shall fulfil my mission, fight the good
fight, and keep the faith.

There is great joy in this consciousness, that through-
9 out my labors, and in my history as connected with the
Cause of Christian Science, it can be proven that I have
never given occasion for a single censure, when my mo-
12 tives and acts are understood and seen as my Father
seeth them. I once wondered at the Scriptural declaration that Job sinned not in all he said, even when he cursed
15 the hour of his birth; but I have learned that a curse on
sin is always a blessing to the human race.

Those only who are tried in the furnace reflect the
18 image of their Father. You, my beloved students, who
are absent from me, and have shared less of my labors
than many others, seem stronger to resist temptation
21 than some of those who have had line upon line and
precept upon precept. This may be a serviceable hint,
since necessities and God's providence are foreshadowed.
24 I have felt for some time that perpetual instruction of
my students might substitute my own for their growth,
and so dwarf their experience. If they must learn by
27 the things they suffer, the sooner this lesson is gained
the better.

For two years I have been gradually withdrawing from
30 active membership in the Christian Scientist Association.
This has developed higher energies on the part of true
followers, and led to some startling departures on the

other hand. "Offenses will come: but woe unto him, 1 through whom they come."

Why does not the certainty of individual punishment 3 for sin prevent the wrong action? It is the love of God, and not the fear of evil, that is the incentive in Science. I rejoice with those who rejoice, and am too apt to weep 6 with those who weep, but over and above it all are eternal sunshine and joy unspeakable.

## THE MARCH PRIMARY CLASS 9

To the Primary Class of the Massachusetts Metaphysical College, 571 Columbus Avenue, that Assembled Feb. 25, 1889, with an Attendance of Sixty-five Students 12

My students, three picture-stories from the Bible present themselves to my thought; three of those pictures from which we learn without study. The first is that of 15 Joshua and his band before the walls of Jericho. They went seven times around these walls, the seven times corresponding to the seven days of creation: the six days 18 are to find out the nothingness of matter; the seventh is the day of rest, when it is found that evil is naught and good is all. 21

The second picture is of the disciples met together in an upper chamber; and they were of one mind. Mark, that in the case of Joshua and his band they had all to 24 shout *together* in order that the walls might fall; and the disciples, too, were of one mind.

We, to-day, in this class-room, are enough to con- 27 vert the world if we are of one Mind; for then the whole world will feel the influence of this Mind; as when the

1 earth was without form, and Mind spake and form appeared.

3 The third picture-lesson is from Revelation, where, at the opening of the seals, one of the angels presented himself with balances to weigh the thoughts and actions of

6 men; not angels with wings, but messengers of pure and holy thoughts that say, See thou hurt not the holy things of Truth.

9 You have come to be weighed; and yet, I would not weigh you, nor have you weighed. How is this? Because God does all, and there is nothing in the opposite

12 scale. There are not two, — Mind *and* matter. We must get rid of that notion. As we commonly think, we imagine all is well if we cast something into the scale of

15 Mind, but we must realize that Mind is not put into the scales with matter; then only are we working on one side and in Science.

18 The students of this Primary class, dismissed the fifth of March, at close of the lecture on the fourth presented their teacher with an elegant album costing fifty dollars,

21 and containing beautiful hand-painted flowers on each page, with their autographs. The presentation was made in a brief address by Mr. D. A. Easton, who in appro-

24 priate language and metaphor expressed his fellow-students' thanks to their teacher.

On the morning of the fifth, I met the class to answer

27 some questions before their dismissal, and allude briefly to a topic of great import to the student of Christian Science, — the rocks and sirens in their course, on and

30 by which so many wrecks are made. The doors of animal magnetism open wide for the entrance of error, sometimes just at the moment when you are ready to enter on

the fruition of your labors, and with laudable ambition 1
are about to chant hymns of victory for triumphs.

The doors that this animal element flings open are 3
those of rivalry, jealousy, envy, revenge. It is the self-
asserting mortal will-power that you must guard against.
But I find also another mental condition of yours that 6
fills me with joy. I learned long ago that the world could
neither deprive me of something nor give me anything,
and I have now one ambition and one joy. But if 9
one cherishes ambition unwisely, one will be chastened
for it.

Admiral Coligny, in the time of the French Huguenots, 12
was converted to Protestantism through a stray copy of
the Scriptures that fell into his hands. He replied to his
wife, who urged him to come out and confess his faith, 15
"It is wise to count the cost of becoming a true Christian." She answered him, "It is wiser to count the cost
of *not* becoming a true Christian." So, whatever we meet 18
that is hard in the Christian warfare we must count as
nothing, and must think instead, of our poverty and helplessness without this understanding, and count ourselves 21
always as debtors to Christ, Truth.

Among the gifts of my students, this of yours is one
of the most beautiful and the most costly, because you 24
have signed your names. I felt the weight of this yes-
terday, but it came to me more clearly this morning when
I realized what a responsibility you assume when sub- 27
scribing to Christian Science. But, whatever may come
to you, remember the words of Solomon, "Though hand
join in hand, the wicked shall not go unpunished: but 30
the seed of the righteous shall be delivered."

You will need, in future, *practice* more than theory.

1 You are going out to demonstrate a living faith, a true
sense of the infinite good, a sense that does not limit God,
3 but brings to human view an enlarged sense of Deity.
Remember, it is personality, and the sense of personality
in God or in man, that limits man.

6    OBTRUSIVE MENTAL HEALING

The question will present itself: Shall people be treated
mentally without their knowledge or consent? The
9 direct rule for practice of Christian Science is the Golden
Rule, "As ye would that men should do to you, do ye."
Who of us would have our houses broken open or our
12 locks picked? and much less would we have our minds
tampered with.

Our Master said, "When ye enter a house, salute it."
15 Prolonging the metaphysical tone of his command, I say,
When you enter mentally the personal precincts of human
thought, you should know that the person with whom
18 you hold communion desires it.  There are solitary ex-
ceptions to most given rules: the following is an exception
to the above rule of mental practice.

21    If the friends of a patient desire you to treat him without his knowing it, and they believe in the efficacy of
Mind-healing, it is sometimes wise to do so, and the end
24 justifies the means; for he is restored through Christian
Science when other means have failed.  One other occasion which may call for aid unsought, is a case from
27 accident, when there is no time for ceremony and no other
aid is near.

The abuse which I call attention to, is promiscuous

and unannounced mental practice where there is no neces- 1
sity for it, or the motive is mercenary, or one can to advantage speak the truth audibly;  then the case is not 3
exceptional.  As a rule, one has no more right to enter
the mind of a person, stir, upset, and adjust his thoughts
without his knowledge or consent, than one has to enter 6
a house, unlock the desk, displace the furniture, and suit
one's self in the arrangement and management of another
man's property.                                                        9

It would be right to break into a burning building and
rouse the slumbering inmates, but wrong to burst open
doors and break through windows if no emergency de- 12
manded this.  Any exception to the old wholesome rule,
"Mind your own business," is rare.  For a student of
mine to treat another student without his knowledge, is 15
a breach of good manners and morals;  it is nothing less
than a mistaken kindness, a culpable ignorance, or a
conscious trespass on the rights of mortals.                18

I insist on the etiquette of Christian Science, as well
as its morals and Christianity.  The Scriptural rule of
this Science may momentarily be forgotten;  but this is 21
seldom the case with loyal students, or done without
incriminating the person who did it.

Each student should, must, work out his own problem 24
of being;  conscious, meanwhile, that God worketh with
him, and that he needs no personal aid.  It is the genius
of Christian Science to demonstrate good, not evil, — 27
harmony, not discord;  for Science is the mandate of
Truth which destroys all error.

Whoever is honestly laboring to learn the principle of 30
music and practise it, seldom calls on his teacher or musician to practise for him.  The only personal help re-

1 quired in this Science is for each one to do his own work
well, and never try to hinder others from doing theirs
3 thus.

Christian Science, more than any other system of
religion, morals, or medicine, is subject to abuses. Its
6 infinite nature and uses occasion this. Even the human-
itarian at work in this field of limitless power and good
may possess a zeal without knowledge, and thus mistake
9 the sphere of his present usefulness.

Students who strictly adhere to the right, and make the
Bible and Science and Health a study, are in no danger
12 of mistaking their way.

This question is often proposed, How shall I treat
malicious animal magnetism? The hour has passed for
15 this evil to be treated personally, but it should have been
so dealt with at the outset. Christian Scientists should
have gone personally to the malpractitioner and told
18 him his fault, and vindicated divine Truth and Love
against human error and hate. This growing sin must
now be dealt with as evil, and not as an evil-doer or per-
21 sonality. It must also be remembered that neither an evil
claim nor an evil person is *real,* hence is neither to be
*feared* nor honored.

24    Evil is not something to fear and flee before, or that
becomes more real when it is grappled with. Evil let
alone grows more real, aggressive, and enlarges its claims;
27 but, met with Science, it can and will be mastered by
Science.

I deprecate personal animosities and quarrels. But if
30 one is intrusted with the rules of church government, to
fulfil that trust those rules must be carried out; thus it
is with all moral obligations. I am opposed to all personal

attacks, and in favor of combating evil only, rather than 1
person.

An edition of one thousand pamphlets I ordered to 3
be laid away and not one of them circulated, because I
had been personal in condemnation. Afterwards, by a
blunder of the gentleman who fills orders for my books, 6
some of these pamphlets were mistaken for the corrected
edition, and sold.

Love is the fulfilling of the law. Human life is too 9
short for foibles or failures. *The Christian Science Journal* will hold high the banner of Truth and Love, and be
impartial and impersonal in its tenor and tenets. 12

### WEDLOCK

It was about the year 1875 that Science and Health
first crossed swords with free-love, and the latter fell *hors* 15
*de combat;* but the whole warfare of sensuality was not
then ended. Science and Health, the book that cast the
first stone, is still at work, deep down in human conscious- 18
ness, laying the axe at the root of error.

We have taken the precaution to write briefly on marriage, showing its relation to Christian Science. In the 21
present or future, some extra throe of error may conjure
up a new-style conjugality, which, *ad libitum,* severs the
marriage covenant, puts virtue in the shambles, and 24
coolly notifies the public of broken vows. Springing
up from the ashes of free-love, this nondescript phœnix,
in the face and eyes of common law, common sense, and 27
common honesty, may appear in the *rôle* of a superfine
conjugality; but, having no Truth, it will have no past,
present, or future. 30

1 The above prophecy, written years ago, has already been fulfilled. It is seen in Christian Science that the 3 gospel of marriage is not without the law, and the solemn vow of fidelity, "until death do us part;" this verity in human economy can neither be obscured nor throttled. 6 Until time matures human growth, marriage and progeny will continue unprohibited in Christian Science. We look to future generations for ability to comply with absolute 9 Science, when marriage shall be found to be man's oneness with God, — the unity of eternal Love. At present, more spiritual conception and education of children will 12 serve to illustrate the superiority of spiritual power over sensuous, and usher in the dawn of God's creation, wherein they neither marry nor are given in marriage, 15 but are as the angels. To abolish marriage at this period, and maintain morality and generation, would put ingenuity to ludicrous shifts; yet this is possible in *Science*, 18 although it is to-day problematic.

The time cometh, and now is, for spiritual and eternal existence to be recognized and understood in Science. 21 All is Mind. Human procreation, birth, life, and death are subjective states of the human erring mind; they are the phenomena of mortality, nothingness, that illus- 24 trate mortal mind and body as *one*, and neither real nor eternal.

It should be understood that Spirit, God, is the only 27 creator: we should recognize this verity of being, and shut out all sense of other claims. Until this absolute Science of being is seen, understood, and demonstrated 30 in the offspring of divine Mind, and man is perfect even as the Father is perfect, human speculation will go on, and stop at length at the spiritual ultimate: creation understood as the most exalted divine conception. The 1 offspring of an improved generation, however, will go out before the forever fact that man is eternal and has no 3 human origin. Hence the Scripture: "It is He that hath made us, and not we ourselves;" and the Master's demand, "Call no man your father upon the earth: for one 6 is your Father, which is in heaven."

To an ill-attuned ear, discord is harmony; so personal sense, discerning not the legitimate affection of Soul, 9 may place love on a false basis and thereby lose it. Science corrects this error with the truth of Love, and restores lost Eden. Soul is the infinite source of bliss: only high 12 and holy joy can satisfy immortal cravings. The good in human affections should preponderate over the evil, and the spiritual over the animal, — until progress lifts 15 mortals to discern the Science of mental formation and find the highway of holiness.

In the order of wisdom, the higher nature of man 18 governs the lower. This lays the foundations of human affection in line with progress, giving them strength and permanence. 21

When asked by a wife or a husband important questions concerning their happiness, the substance of my reply is: God will guide you. Be faithful over home rela- 24 tions; they lead to higher joys: obey the Golden Rule for human life, and it will spare you much bitterness. It is pleasanter to do right than wrong; it makes one 27 ruler over one's self and hallows home, — which is woman's world. Please your husband, and he will be apt to please you; preserve affection on both sides. 30

Great mischief comes from attempts to steady other people's altars, venturing on valor without discretion,

1 which is virtually meddlesomeness.  Even your sincere
and courageous convictions regarding what is best for
3 others may be mistaken;  you must be demonstratively
right yourself, and work out the greatest good to the
greatest number, before you are sure of being a fit coun-
6 sellor.  Positive and imperative thoughts should be dropped
into the balances of God and weighed by spiritual Love,
and not be found wanting, before being put into action.
9 A rash conclusion that regards only one side of a question, is weak and wicked;  this error works out the results
of error.  If the premise of mortal existence is wrong,
12 any conclusion drawn therefrom is not absolutely right.
Wisdom in human action begins with what is nearest
right under the circumstances, and thence achieves the
15 absolute.

Is marriage nearer right than celibacy?

Human knowledge inculcates that it is, while Science
18 indicates that it *is not*.  But to force the consciousness
of scientific being before it is understood is impossible,
and believing otherwise would prevent scientific demon-
21 stration.  To reckon the universal cost and gain, as well
as thine own, is right in every state and stage of being.
The selfish *rôle* of a martyr is the shift of a dishonest
24 mind, nothing short of self-seeking;  and real suffering
would stop the farce.

The cause of temperance receives a strong impulse
27 from the cause of Christian Science:  temperance and
truth are allies, and their cause prospers in proportion
to the spirit of Love that nerves the struggle.  People
30 will differ in their opinions as to means to promote the
ends of temperance;  that is, abstinence from intoxicat-
ing beverages.  Whatever intoxicates a man, stultifies

and causes him to degenerate physically and morally. 1
Strong drink is unquestionably an evil, and evil cannot
be used temperately: its slightest use is abuse; hence 3
the only temperance is total abstinence. Drunkenness
is sensuality let loose, in whatever form it is made
manifest. 6

What is evil? It is suppositional absence of good.
From a human standpoint of good, mortals must first
choose between evils, and of two evils choose the less; 9
and at present the application of scientific rules to human life seems to rest on this basis.

All partnerships are formed on agreements to certain 12
compacts: each party voluntarily surrenders independent action to act as a whole and per agreement. This
fact should be duly considered when by the marriage 15
contract two are made one, and, according to the divine
precept, "they twain shall be one flesh." Oneness in
spirit is Science, compatible with home and heaven. 18
Neither divine justice nor human equity has *divorced*
two minds in one.

Rights that are bargained away must not be retaken 21
by the contractors, except by mutual consent. Human
nature has bestowed on a wife the right to become a
mother; but if the wife esteems not this privilege, by 24
mutual consent, exalted and increased affections, she
may win a higher. Science touches the conjugal question on the basis of a bill of rights. Can the bill of con- 27
jugal rights be fairly stated by a magistrate, or by a
minister? Mutual interests and affections are the spirit
of these rights, and they should be consulted, augmented, 30
and allowed to rise to the spiritual altitude whence they
can choose only good.

1 A third person is not a party to the compact of two
hearts.  Let other people's marriage relations *alone:* two
3 persons only, should be found within their precincts.
The nuptial vow is never annulled so long as the animus
of the contract is preserved intact.  Science lifts humanity
6 higher in the scale of harmony, and must ultimately break
all bonds that hinder progress.

## JUDGE NOT

9 Mistaken views ought to be dissolving views, since
whatever is false should disappear.  To suppose that human love, guided by the divine Principle, which is Love,
12 is partial, unmerciful, or unjust, indicates misapprehen-
sion of the divine Principle and its workings in the human
heart.

15 A person wrote to me, naming the time of the occurrence, "I felt the influence of your thought on my mind,
and it produced a wonderful illumination, peace, and
18 understanding;"  but, I had not thought of the writer
at that time.  I knew that this person was doing well,
and my affections involuntarily flow out towards all.

21 When will the world cease to judge of causes from a
personal sense of things, conjectural and misapprehen-
sive!  When thought dwells in God, — and it should not,
24 to our consciousness, dwell elsewhere, — one must benefit those who hold a place in one's memory, whether it
be friend or foe, and each share the benefit of that radia-
27 tion.  This individual blessedness and blessing comes
not so much from individual as from universal love:  it
emits light because it reflects;  and all who are receptive
30 share this equally.

Mistaken or transient views are human: they are not governed by the Principle of divine Science: but the notion that a mind governed by Principle can be forced into personal channels, affinities, self-interests, or obligations, is a grave mistake; it dims the true sense of God's reflection, and darkens the understanding that demonstrates above personal motives, unworthy aims and ambitions.

Too much and too little is attached to me as authority for other people's thoughts and actions. A tacit acquiescence with others' views is often construed as direct orders, — or at least it so appears in results. I desire the equal growth and prosperity of all Christian Scientists, and the world in general; each and every one has equal opportunity to be benefited by my thoughts and writings. If any are not partakers thereof, this is not my fault, and is far from my desire; the possible perversion of Christian Science is the irony of fate, if the spirit thereof be lacking. I would part with a blessing myself to bestow it upon others, but could not deprive them of it. False views, however engendered, relative to the true and unswerving course of a Christian Scientist, will at length dissolve into thin air. The dew of heaven will fall gently on the hearts and lives of all who are found worthy to suffer for righteousness, — and have taught the truth which is energizing, refreshing, and consecrating mankind.

To station justice and gratitude as sentinels along the lines of thought, would aid the solution of this problem, and counteract the influence of envious minds or the misguided individual who keeps not watch over his emotions and conclusions.

NEW COMMANDMENT

The divinity of St. John's Gospel brings to view overwhelming tides of revelation, and its spirit is baptismal;
he chronicles this teaching, "A new commandment I
give unto you, That ye love one another."

Jesus, who so loved the world that he gave his life
(in the flesh) for it, saw that Love had a new commandment even for him.  What was it?

It must have been a rare revelation of infinite Love, a
new tone on the scale ascending, such as eternity is ever
sounding.  Could I impart to the student the higher
sense I entertain of Love, it would partly illustrate the
divine energy that brings to human weakness might and
majesty.  Divine Love eventually causes mortals to turn
away from the open sepulchres of sin, and look no more
into them as realities.  It calls loudly on them to bury
the dead out of sight;  to forgive and forget whatever is
unlike the risen, immortal Love;  and to shut out all opposite sense.  Christ enjoins it upon man to help those
who know not what he is doing in their behalf, and therefore curse him;  enjoins taking them by the hand and
leading them, if *possible,* to Christ, by loving words and
deeds.  Charity thus serves as admonition and instruction, and works out the purposes of Love.

Christian Science, full of grace and truth, is accomplishing great good, both seen and unseen;  but have
mortals, with the penetration of Soul, searched the secret
chambers of sense?  I never knew a student who fully
understood my instructions on this point of handling
evil, — as to just how this should be done, — and carried

out my ideal. It is safe not to teach prematurely the 1
infant thought in Christian Science — just breathing new
Life and Love — all the claims and modes of evil;  there- 3
fore it is best to leave the righteous unfolding of error
(as a general rule) alone, and to the special care of the
unerring modes of divine wisdom. This uncovering and 6
punishing of sin must, will come, at some date, to the
rescue of humanity. The teacher of divine metaphysics
should impart to his students the general knowledge that 9
he has gained from instruction, observation, and mental
practice.

Experience weighs in the scales of God the sense and 12
power of Truth against the opposite claims of error.
If spiritual sense is not dominant in a student, he will
not understand all your instructions;  and if evil domi- 15
nates his character, he will pervert the rules of Christian
Science, and the last error will be worse than the first —
inasmuch as wilful transgression brings greater torment 18
than ignorance.

## A CRUCE SALUS

The sum total of Love reflected is exemplified, and 21
includes the whole duty of man: Truth perverted, in
belief, becomes the creator of the claim of error.  To
affirm mentally and audibly that God is All and there is 24
no sickness and no sin, makes mortals either saints or
sinners.

Truth talked and not lived, rolls on the human heart 27
a stone; consigns sensibility to the charnel-house of sensuality, ease, self-love, self-justification, there to moulder
and rot.                                                    30

1 The noblest work of God is man in the image of his Maker; the last infirmity of evil is so-called man, swayed
3 by the mælstrom of human passions, elbowing the concepts of his own creating, making place for himself and displacing his fellows.
6 A real Christian Scientist is a marvel, a miracle in the universe of mortal mind. With selfless love, he inscribes on the heart of humanity and transcribes on the page
9 of reality the living, palpable presence — the might and majesty! — of goodness. He lives for all mankind, and honors his creator.
12 The *vice versa* of this man is sometimes called a man, but he is a small animal: a hived bee, with sting ready for each kind touch, he makes honey out of
15 the flowers of human hearts and hides it in his cell of ingratitude.
O friendly hand! keep back thy offerings from asps
18 and apes, from wolves in sheep's clothing and all ravening beasts. Love such specimens of mortality just enough to reform and transform them, — if it be possible, —
21 and then, look out for their stings, and jaws, and claws; but thank God and take courage, — that you desire to help even such as these.

24     COMPARISON TO ENGLISH BARMAIDS

Since my residence in Concord, N. H., I have read the daily paper, and had become an admirer of Edgar
27 L. Wakeman's terse, graphic, and poetic style in his "Wanderings," richly flavored with the true ideas of humanity and equality. In an issue of January 17, how-

ever, were certain references to American women which 1
deserve and elicit brief comment.

Mr. Wakeman writes from London, that a noted Eng- 3
lish leader, whom he quotes without naming, avers that
the "cursed barmaid system" in England is evolved by
the same power which in America leads women "along 6
a gamut of isms and ists, from female suffrage, past a
score of reforms, to Christian Science." This anony-
mous talker further declares, that the central cause of 9
this "same original evil" is "a female passion for some
manner of notoriety."

Is Mr. Wakeman *awake,* and caught napping? While 12
praising the Scotchman's national pride and affection,
has our American correspondent lost these sentiments
from his own breast? Has he forgotten how to honor 15
his native land and defend the dignity of her daughters
with his ready pen and pathos?

The flaunting and floundering statements of the great 18
unknown for whose ability and popularity Mr. Wakeman
strongly vouches, should not only be queried, but flatly
contradicted, as both untrue and uncivil. English senti- 21
ment is not wholly represented by one man. Nor is the
world ignorant of the fact that high and pure ethical
tones do resound from Albion's shores. The most ad- 24
vanced ideas are inscribed on tablets of such an organization as the Victoria Institute, or Philosophical Society
of Great Britain, an institution which names itself after 27
her who is unquestionably the best queen on earth; who
for a half century has with such dignity, clemency, and
virtue worn the English crown and borne the English 30
sceptre.

Now, I am a Christian Scientist, — the Founder of
11

1 this system of religion, — widely known; and, by special
invitation, have allowed myself to be elected an associate
3 life-member of the Victoria Institute, which numbers
among its constituents and managers — not barmaids,
but bishops — profound philosophers, brilliant scholars.

6 Was it ignorance of American society and history,
together with unfamiliarity with the work and career
of American women, which led the unknown author
9 cited by Mr. Wakeman to overflow in shallow sarcasm,
and place the barmaids of English alehouses and rail-
ways in the same category with noble women who min-
12 ister in the sick-room, give their time and strength to
binding up the wounds of the broken-hearted, and live
on the plan of heaven?

15 This writer classes Christian Science with theosophy
and spiritualism; whereas, they are by no means identical — nor even similar. Christian Science, antagonis-
18 tic to intemperance, as to all immorality, is by no means
associated therewith. Do manly Britons patronize tap-
rooms and lazar-houses, and thus note or foster a fem-
21 inine ambition which, in this unknown gentleman's
language, "poises and poses, higgles and wriggles" itself into publicity? Why fall into such patronage, unless
24 from their affinity for the worst forms of vice?

And the barmaids! Do they enter this line of occu-
pation from a desire for notoriety and a wish to promote
27 female suffrage? or are they incited thereto by their
own poverty and the bad appetites of men? What manner of man *is* this unknown individual who utters bar-
30 maid and Christian Scientist in the same breath? If he
but knew whereof he speaks, *his* shame would not lose
its blush!

Taking into account the short time that has elapsed 1
since the discovery of Christian Science, one readily sees
that this Science has distanced all other religious and 3
pathological systems for physical and moral reformation. In the direction of temperance it has achieved far
more than has been accomplished by legally coercive 6
measures, — and because this Science bases its work on
ethical conditions and mentally destroys the appetite for
alcoholic drinks. 9

Smart journalism is allowable, nay, it is commend-
able; but the public cannot swallow reports of American
affairs from a surly censor ventilating his lofty scorn of 12
the sects, or societies, of a nation that perhaps he has
never visited.

## A CHRISTIAN SCIENCE STATUTE 15

I hereby state, in unmistakable language, the following statute in the *morale* of Christian Science: —

A man or woman, having voluntarily entered into 18
wedlock, and accepted the claims of the marriage covenant, is held in Christian Science as morally bound to
fulfil all the claims growing out of this contract, unless 21
such claims are relinquished by mutual consent of both
parties, or this contract is legally dissolved. If the man
is dominant over the animal, he will count the conse- 24
quences of his own conduct; will consider the effects,
on himself and his progeny, of selfishness, unmerciful-
ness, tyranny, or lust. 27

Trust Truth, not error; and Truth will give you all
that belongs to the rights of freedom. The Hebrew bard

1 wrote, "Trust in the Lord with all thine heart; and lean
not unto thine own understanding." Nothing is gained
3 by wrong-doing. St. Paul's words take in the situation:
"Not . . . (as we be slanderously reported, and as some
affirm that we say,) Let us do evil, that good may come?
6 whose damnation is just."

When causing others to go astray, we also are wan-
derers. "With what measure ye mete, it shall be meas-
9 ured to you again." Ask yourself: Under the same
circumstances, in the same spiritual ignorance and power
of passion, would I be strengthened by having my best
12 friend break troth with me? These words of St. Matthew
have special application to Christian Scientists; namely,
"It is not good to marry."

15   To build on selfishness is to build on sand. When
Jesus received the material rite of water baptism, he did
not say that it was God's command; but implied that
18 the period demanded it. Trials purify mortals and deliver
them from themselves, — all the claims of sensuality.
Abide by the *morale* of absolute Christian Science, —
21 self-abnegation and purity; then Truth delivers you from
the seeming power of error, and faith vested in righteousness triumphs!

24     ADVICE TO STUDENTS

The true consciousness is the true health. One says,
"I find relief from pain in unconscious sleep." I say,
27 You mistake; through unconsciousness one no more
gains freedom from pain than immunity from evil. When
unconscious of a mistake, one thinks he is not mistaken;
30 but this false consciousness does not change the fact, or

its results; suffering and mistakes recur until one is awake 1
to their cause and character.  To know the what, when,
and how of error, destroys error.  The error that is seen 3
aright as error, has received its death-blow;  but never
until then.

Let us look through the lens of Christian Science, 6
not of "self," at the following mistake, which demands
our present attention.  I have no time for detailed report
of this matter, but simply answer the following question 9
sent to me; glad, indeed, that this query has finally come
with the courage of conviction to the minds of many
students.                                                        12

"Is it right to copy your works and read them for our
public services?"

The good which the material senses see not is the only 15
absolute good;  the evil which these senses see not is the
only absolute evil.

If I enter Mr. Smith's store and take from it his gar- 18
ments that are on sale, array myself in them, and put
myself and them on exhibition, can I make this right
by saying, These garments are Mr. Smith's;  he manu- 21
factured them and owns them, but you must pay me,
not him, for this exhibit?

The spectators may ask, Did he give you permission 24
to do this, did he sell them or loan them to you?  No.
Then have you asked yourself this question on the subject, namely, What right have I to do this?  True, it 27
saves your purchasing these garments, and gives to the
public new patterns which are useful to them;  but does
this silence your conscience? or, because you have con- 30
fessed that they are the property of a noted firm, and
you wished to handle them, does it justify you in appro-

1 priating them, and so avoiding the cost of hiring or
purchasing?

3   Copying my published works *verbatim*, compiling them
in connection with the Scriptures, taking this copy into
the pulpit, announcing the author's name, then reading
6 it publicly as your own compilation, is — what?

We answer, It is a mistake; in common parlance, it
is an *ignorant* wrong.

9   If you should print and publish your copy of my works,
you would be liable to arrest for infringement of copyright, which the law defines and punishes as theft.   Read-
12 ing in the pulpit from copies of my publications gives
you the clergyman's salary and spares you the printer's
bill, but does it spare you our Master's condemnation?
15 You literally publish my works through the pulpit, instead
of the press, and thus evade the law, *but not the gospel.*
When I consent to this act, you will then be justified
18 in it.

Your manuscript copy is liable, in some way, to be
printed as your original writings, thus incurring the pen-
21 alty of the law, and increasing the record of theft in the
United States Circuit Court.

To The Church of Christ, Scientist, in Boston, which I
24 had organized and of which I had for many years been
pastor, I gave permission to cite, in the *Christian Science
Quarterly,* from my work Science and Health, passages
27 giving the spiritual meaning of Bible texts; but this was
a special privilege, and the author's gift.

Christian Science demonstrates that the patient who
30 pays whatever he is able to pay for being healed, is more
apt to recover than he who withholds a slight equiva-
lent for health.   Healing morally and physically are one.

Then, is compiling and delivering that sermon for which 1
you pay nothing, and which you deliver without the
author's consent, and receive pay therefor, the *precedent* 3
for preaching Christian Science, — and are you doing
to the author of the above-named book as you would
have others do unto you? 6

Those authors and editors of pamphlets and periodi-
cals whose substance is made up of my publications, are
morally responsible for what the law construes as crime. 9
There are startling instances of the above-named law-
breaking and gospel-opposing system of authorship, which
characterize the writings of a few professed Christian 12
Scientists. My Christian students who have read copies
of my works in the pulpit require only a word to be wise;
too sincere and morally statuesque are they to be long 15
led into temptation; but I must not leave persistent
plagiarists without this word of warning in public, since
my private counsel they disregard. 18

To the question of my true-hearted students, "Is it
right to copy your works and read them for our public
services?" I answer: It is not right to copy my book 21
and read it publicly *without my consent.* My reasons are
as follows: —

*First:* This method is an unseen form of injustice 24
standing in a holy place.

*Second:* It breaks the Golden Rule, — a divine rule
for human conduct. 27

*Third:* All error tends to harden the heart, blind
the eyes, stop the ears of understanding, and inflate
self; counter to the commands of our hillside Priest, to 30
whom Isaiah alluded thus: "I have trodden the wine-
press alone; and of the people there was none with me."

1    Behind the scenes lurks an evil which you can prevent:
it is a purpose to kill the reformation begun and increas-
3 ing through the instructions of "Science and Health with
Key to the Scriptures;" it encourages infringement of my
copyright, and seeks again to "cast lots for his vesture,"
6 — while the perverter preserves in his own consciousness
and teaching the name without the Spirit, the skeleton
without the heart, the form without the comeliness, the
9 sense without the Science, of Christ's healing.   My students are expected to know the teaching of Christian Science sufficiently to discriminate between error and Truth,
12 thus sparing their teacher a task and themselves the
temptation to be misled.

Much good has been accomplished through Christian
15 Science Sunday services.   If Christian Scientists occasionally mistake in interpreting revealed Truth, of two evils
the less would be *not* to leave the Word unspoken and
18 untaught.   I allowed, till this permission was *withdrawn,*
students working faithfully for Christ's cause on earth,
the privilege of copying and reading my works for Sunday
21 service; *provided,* they each and all destroyed the copies
at once after said service.   When I should so elect and
give suitable notice, they were to desist from further copy-
24 ing of my writings as aforesaid.

This injunction did not curtail the benefit which the
student derived from making his copy, nor detract from
27 the good that his hearers received from his reading thereof;
but it was intended to forestall the possible evil of putting
the divine teachings contained in "Science and Health
30 with Key to the Scriptures" into human hands, to sub-
vert or to liquidate.

I recommend that students stay within their own fields

of labor, to work for the race; they are lights that can- 1
not be hid, and need only to shine from their home sum-
mits to be sought and found as healers physical and 3
moral.

The kindly shepherd has his own fold and tends his
own flock. Christian students should have their own 6
institutes and, *unmolested,* be governed by divine Love
alone in teaching and guiding their students. When
wisdom garrisons these strongholds of Christian Science, 9
peace and joy, the fruits of Spirit, will rest upon us all.
We are brethren in the fullest sense of that word; therefore no queries should arise as to "who shall be great- 12
est." Let us serve instead of rule, knock instead of
push at the door of human hearts, and allow to each
and every one the same rights and privileges that we 15
claim for ourselves. If ever I wear out from serving
students, it shall be in the effort to help them to obey
the Ten Commandments and imbibe the spirit of Christ's 18
Beatitudes.

## NOTICE

*Editor of Christian Science Journal:* — You will oblige 21
me by giving place in your *Journal* to the following notice.
The idea and purpose of a Liberty Bell is pleasing, and
can be made profitable to the heart of our country. I feel 24
assured that many Christian Scientists will respond to this
letter by contributions.

MARY BAKER EDDY  27

COLUMBIAN LIBERTY BELL COMMITTEE,
1505 PENNA. AVE., WASHINGTON, D. C.

To the Daughters of the American Revolution: —

It has been determined to create a Columbian Liberty Bell, to be placed by the lovers of liberty and peace in the most appropriate place in the coming World's Exposition at Chicago. After the close of the Exhibition this bell will pass from place to place throughout the world as a missionary of freedom, coming first to the capital of the nation under the care of our society.

Then it will go to Bunker Hill or Liberty Island, to the battle-field of New Orleans (1812), to San Francisco, to the place where any great patriotic celebration is being held, until 1900, when it will be sent to the next World's Exhibition, which takes place at Paris, France. There it will continue until that Exhibition closes.

When not in use in other places, it will return to Washington under the care of the Daughters of the American Revolution. Washington will be its home, and from there it will journey from place to place, fulfilling its mission throughout the world.

The following is the proposed use of the bell: It shall ring at sunrise and sunset; at nine o'clock in the morning on the anniversaries of the days on which great events have occurred marking the world's progress toward liberty; at twelve o'clock on the birthdays of the "creators of liberty;" and at four o'clock it will toll on the anniversaries of their death. (It will always ring at nine o'clock on October 11th, in recognition of the organization on that day of the Daughters of the American Revolution.)

. . . The responsibility of its production, and the direction of its use, have been placed in the hands of a

committee of women representing each State and Ter- 1
ritory, one representative from each Republic in the
world, and a representative from the patriotic societies, 3
— Daughters and Sons of the American Revolution,
the Lyceum League of America, the Society of German Patriots, the Human Freedom League, and kindred 6
organizations.

The National Board of Management has placed upon
me the responsibility of representing the National Society 9
of the Daughters of the American Revolution upon the
General Committee, and this circular is sent to every
member of the society, asking for her personal coopera- 12
tion in making the undertaking successful. In creating
the bell it is particularly desired that the largest number
of persons possible shall have a part in it. For this reason 15
small contributions from many persons are to be asked
for, rather than large contributions from a few. They
are to be of two kinds: — 18

*First:* Material that can be made a part of the bell;
articles of historic interest will be particularly appreciated — gold, silver, bronze, copper, and nickel can be 21
fused.

*Second:* Of money with which to pay for the bell.
Each member of the society is asked to contribute one 24
cent to be fused into the bell, and twenty-five cents to
pay for it. She is also asked to collect two dollars from
others, in pennies, if possible, and send with the amount 27
the name of each contributor. In order that the bell
shall be cast April 30th, the anniversary of the inaugu-
ration of George Washington as the first President of 30
the United States, we ask every one receiving this circular *to act at once.*

1    In forwarding material to be melted into the bell, please
send fullest historical description.  This will be entered
3 carefully in a book which will accompany the bell wherever
it goes.

. . . As the motto has not yet been decided upon, any
6 ideas on that subject will be gratefully received;  we will
also welcome suggestions of events to be celebrated and
names to be commemorated.

9                    Very cordially yours,

                                   MARY DESHA,
                    ex-Vice-President General, D. A. R.


12    Contributions should be sent to the Liberty National
Bank, corner Liberty and West Streets, New York, and
a duplicate letter written, as a notification of the same,
15 to Miss Mary Desha, 1505 Penna. Ave., Washington,
D. C., or to Miss Minnie F. Mickley, Mickleys, Pa.

We would add, as being of interest, that Mrs. Eddy is
18 a member of the above organization, having been made
such by the special request of the late Mrs. Harrison,
wife of the ex-President, who was at that time the Presi-
21 dent thereof. — ED.


### ANGELS

When angels visit us, we do not hear the rustle of wings,
24 nor feel the feathery touch of the breast of a dove;  but
we know their presence by the love they create in our
hearts.  Oh, may you feel *this* touch, — it is not the
27 clasping of hands, nor a loved person present;  it is more
than this: it is a spiritual idea that lights your path!
The Psalmist saith: "He shall give His angels charge

over thee." God gives you His spiritual ideas, and in 1
turn, they give you daily supplies. Never ask for to-
morrow: it is enough that divine Love is an ever-present 3
help; and if you wait, never doubting, you will have
all you need every moment. What a glorious inheritance
is given to us through the understanding of omnipresent 6
Love! More we cannot ask: more we do not want:
more we cannot have. This sweet assurance is the
"Peace, be still" to all human fears, to suffering of every 9
sort.

## DEIFICATION OF PERSONALITY

Notwithstanding the rapid sale already of two editions 12
of "Christ and Christmas," and many orders on hand, I
have thought best to stop its publication.

In this revolutionary religious period, the increasing 15
inquiry of mankind as to Christianity and its unity —
and above all, God's love opening the eyes of the blind
— is fast fitting all minds for the proper reception of 18
Christian Science healing.

But I must stand on this absolute basis of Christian
Science; namely, Cast not pearls before the unprepared 21
thought. Idolatry is an easily-besetting sin of all peoples.
The apostle saith, "Little children, keep yourselves from
idols." 24

The illustrations were not intended for a golden calf,
at which the sick may look and be healed. Christian
Scientists should beware of unseen snares, and adhere 27
to the divine Principle and rules for demonstration.
They must guard against the deification of finite personality. Every human thought must turn instinctively to 30

1 the divine Mind as its sole centre and intelligence. Until
this be done, man will never be found harmonious and
3 immortal.

Whosoever looks to me personally for his health or
holiness, mistakes. He that by reason of human love or
6 hatred or any other cause clings to my material personality, greatly errs, stops his own progress, and loses
the path to health, happiness, and heaven. The Scrip-
9 tures and Christian Science reveal "the way," and personal revelators will take their proper place in history,
but will not be deified.

12   Advanced scientific students are ready for "Christ
and Christmas;" but those are a minority of its readers,
and even they know its practicality only by healing
15 the sick on its divine Principle. In the words of the
prophet, "Hear, O Israel: The Lord our God is one
Lord."

18   Friends, strangers, and Christian Scientists, I thank
you, each and all, for your liberal patronage and scholarly,
artistic, and scientific notices of my book. This little
21 messenger has done its work, fulfilled its mission, retired
with honor (and mayhap taught me more than it has
others), only to reappear in due season. The knowledge
24 that I have gleaned from its fruitage is, that intensely
contemplating personality impedes spiritual growth; even
as holding in mind the consciousness of disease prevents
27 the recovery of the sick.

Christian Science is taught through its divine Principle, which is invisible to corporeal sense. A material
30 human likeness is the antipode of man in the image and
likeness of God. Hence, a finite person is not the model
for a metaphysician. I earnestly advise all Christian
33 Scientists to remove from their observation or study

the personal sense of any one, and not to dwell in thought 1
upon their own or others' corporeality, either as good or
evil. 3

According to Christian Science, material personality is
an error in premise, and must result in erroneous conclusions. All will agree with me that material portraiture 6
often fails to express even mortal man, and this declares
its unfitness for fable or fact to build upon.

The face of Jesus has uniformly been so unnaturally 9
delineated that it has turned many from the true contemplation of his character. He advances most in divine
Science who meditates most on infinite spiritual sub- 12
stance and intelligence. Experience proves this true.
Pondering on the finite personality of Jesus, the son of
man, is not the channel through which we reach the 15
Christ, or Son of God, the true idea of man's divine
Principle.

I warn students against falling into the error of anti- 18
Christ. The consciousness of corporeality, and whatever is connected therewith, must be outgrown. Corporeal
falsities include all obstacles to health, holiness, and 21
heaven. Man's individual life is infinitely above a
bodily form of existence, and the human concept an-
tagonizes the divine. "Science and Health with Key 24
to the Scriptures," on page 229, third and fourth paragraphs, elucidates this topic.[1]

My Christmas poem and its illustrations are not a text- 27
book. Scientists sometimes take things too intensely.
Let them soberly adhere to the Bible and Science and
Health, which contain all and much more than they 30
have yet learned. We should prohibit ourselves the

[1] See the revised edition of 1890, or page 334 in editions subsequent to 1902.

1 childish pleasure of studying Truth through the senses,
for this is neither the intent of my works nor possible
3 in Science.

Even the teachings of Jesus would be misused by substituting personality for the Christ, or the impersonal
6 form of Truth, amplified in this age by the discovery of
Christian Science. To impersonalize scientifically the
material sense of existence — rather than cling to per-
9 sonality — is the lesson of to-day.

### A CARD

My answer to manifold letters relative to the return
12 of members that have gone out of The First Church of
Christ, Scientist, in Boston, is this: While my affections plead for all and every one, and my desire is that
15 all shall be redeemed, I am not unmindful that the Scriptures enjoin, "Let all things be done decently and in
order."
18    To continue one's connection with this church, or to
regain it, one must comply with the church rules. All
who desire its fellowship, and to become members of it,
21 must send in their petitions to this effect to the Clerk
of the church; and upon a meeting being called, the
First Members will determine the action of the church
24 on this subject.

### OVERFLOWING THOUGHTS

In this receding year of religious jubilee, 1894, I as
27 an individual would cordially invite all persons who
have left our fold, together with those who never have

been in it, — all who love God and keep His command- 1
ments, — to come and unite with The Mother Church in
Boston. The true Christian Scientists will be welcomed, 3
greeted as brethren endeavoring to walk with us hand
in hand, as we journey to the celestial city.

Also, I would extend a tender invitation to Christian 6
Scientists' students, those who are ready for the table of
our Lord: so, should we follow Christ's teachings; so,
bury the dead past; so, loving one another, go forth to 9
the full vintage-time, exemplifying what we profess. But
some of the older members are not quite ready to take
this advanced step in the full spirit of that charity which 12
thinketh no evil; and if it be not taken thus, it is impractical, unfruitful, Soul-less.

My deepest desires and daily labors go to prove that 15
I love my enemies and would help all to gain the abiding
consciousness of health, happiness, and heaven.

I hate no one; and love others more than they can 18
love me. As I now understand Christian Science, I would
as soon harm myself as another; since by breaking
Christ's command, "Thou shalt love thy neighbor as 21
thyself," I should lose my hope of heaven.

The works I have written on Christian Science contain absolute Truth, and my necessity was to tell it; 24
therefore I did this even as a surgeon who wounds
to heal. I was a scribe under orders; and who can
refrain from transcribing what God indites, and ought 27
not that one to take the cup, drink all of it, and give
thanks?

Being often reported as saying what never escaped 30
from my lips, when rehearsing facts concerning others
who were reporting false charges, I have been sorry that

1 I spoke at all, and wished I were wise enough to guard
against that temptation.  Oh, may the love that is talked,
3 be *felt!* and so *lived,* that when weighed in the scale of
God we be not found wanting.  Love is consistent, uniform, sympathetic, self-sacrificing, unutterably kind; even
6 that which lays all upon the altar, and, speechless and
alone, bears all burdens, suffers all inflictions, endures
all piercing for the sake of others, and for the kingdom
9 of heaven's sake.

### A GREAT MAN AND HIS SAYING

Hon. Charles Carrol Bonney, President of the World's
12 Congress Auxiliary, in his remarks before that body,
said, "No more striking manifestation of the interposi-
tion of divine Providence in human affairs has come in
15 recent years, than that shown in the raising up of the
body of people known as Christian Scientists, who are
called to declare the real harmony between religion and
18 Science, and to restore the waning faith of many in the
verities of the sacred Scriptures."

In honest utterance of veritable history, and his own
21 spiritual discernment, this man must have risen above
worldly schemes, human theorems or hypotheses, to
conclusions which reason too supine or misemployed
24 cannot fasten upon.  He spake inspired; he touched a
tone of Truth that will continue to reverberate and renew
its emphasis throughout the entire centuries, into the vast
27 forever.

## WORDS OF COMMENDATION 1

*Editor of The Christian Science Journal:* — Permit me to say that your editorial in the August number is *par* 3 *excellence.*

It is a digest of good manners, morals, methods, and means. It points to the scientific spiritual molecule, 6 pearl, and pinnacle, that everybody needs. May the Christlikeness it reflects rest on the dear readers, and throw the light of penetration on the page; even as the 9 dawn, kindling its glories in the east, lightens earth's landscape.

I thank the contributors to *The Christian Science* 12 *Journal* for their jewels of thought, so adapted to the hour, and without ill-humor or hyperbolic tumor. I was impressed by the articles entitled "The New Pas- 15 tor," by Rev. Lanson P. Norcross, "The Lamp," by Walter Church, "The Temptation," a poem by J. J. Rome, etc. 18

The field waves its white ensign, the reapers are strong, the rich sheaves are ripe, the storehouse is ready: pray ye therefore the God of harvest to send forth more 21 laborers of the excellent sort, and garner the supplies for a world.

## CHURCH AND SCHOOL 24

Humbly, and, as I believe, divinely directed, I hereby ordain the Bible, and "Science and Health with Key to the Scriptures," to be hereafter the only pastor of 27

1 The Church of Christ, Scientist, throughout our land and in other lands.

3    From this date the Sunday services of our denomination shall be conducted by Readers in lieu of pastors. Each church, or society formed for Sunday worship, 6 shall elect two Readers: a male, and a female. One of these individuals shall open the meeting by reading the hymns, and chapter (or portion of the chapter) in the 9 Bible, lead in silent prayer, and repeat in concert with the congregation the Lord's Prayer. Also, this First Reader shall give out any notices from the pulpit, shall 12 read the Scriptures indicated in the Sunday School Lesson of the *Christian Science Quarterly,* and shall pronounce the benediction.

15    The First Reader shall read from my book, "Science and Health with Key to the Scriptures," alternately in response to the congregation, the spiritual interpreta- 18 tion of the Lord's Prayer; also, shall read all the selections from Science and Health referred to in the Sunday Lessons.

21    The Reader of the Scriptures shall name, at each reading, the book, chapter, and verses. The Reader of "Science and Health with Key to the Scriptures" shall 24 commence by announcing the full title of this book, with the name of its author, and add to this announcement, "the Christian Science textbook." It is unnecessary to 27 repeat the title or page. This form shall also be observed at the Communion service; the selections from both the Bible and the Christian Science textbook shall be taken 30 from the *Quarterly,* as heretofore, and this Lesson shall be such as is adapted to that service. On the first Sunday of each month, except Communion Sunday, a sermon

shall be preached to the children, from selections taken 1
from the Scriptures and Science and Health, especially
adapted to the occasion, and read after the manner of 3
the Sunday service. The children's service shall be
held on the Sunday following Communion Day.

No copies from my books are allowed to be written, 6
and read from manuscripts, either in private or in public assemblies, except by their author.

Christian Scientists, all over the world, who are let- 9
terly fit and specially spiritually fitted for teachers, can
teach annually three classes only. They shall teach
from the Christian Science textbook. Each class shall 12
consist of not over thirty-three students, carefully selected,
and only of such as have promising proclivities toward
Christian Science. The teacher shall hold himself mor- 15
ally obligated to look after the welfare of his students,
not only through class term, but after it; and to watch
well that they prove sound in sentiment, health, and 18
practical Christian Science.

Teaching Christian Science shall be no question of
money, but of morals and of uplifting the race. Teachers 21
shall form associations for this purpose; and for the
first few years, convene as often as once in three months.
Teachers shall not silently mentally address the thought, 24
to handle it, nor allow their students to do thus, except
the individual needing it asks for mental treatment.
They shall steadily and patiently strive to educate their 27
students in conformity to the unerring wisdom and law
of God, and shall enjoin upon them habitually to study
His revealed Word, the Scriptures, and "Science and 30
Health with Key to the Scriptures."

They shall teach their students how to defend them-

1 selves against mental malpractice, but never to return
evil for evil; never to attack the malpractitioner, but
3 to know the truth that makes free, — and so to be a law
not unto others, but themselves.

### CLASS, PULPIT, STUDENTS' STUDENTS

6 When will you take a class in Christian Science or
speak to your church in Boston? is often asked.

I shall speak to my dear church at Boston very seldom.
9 The Mother Church must be self-sustained by God.
The date of a class in Christian Science should depend
on the fitness of things, the tide which flows heavenward,
12 the hour best for the student. Until minds become less
worldly-minded, and depart farther from the primitives
of the race, and have profited up to their present capac-
15 ity from the written word, they are not ready for the
word spoken at this date.

My juniors can tell others what they know, and turn
18 them slowly toward the haven. Imperative, accumula-
tive, sweet demands rest on my retirement from life's
bustle. What, then, of continual recapitulation of tired
21 aphorisms and disappointed ethics; of patching breaches
widened the next hour; of pounding wisdom and love
into sounding brass; of warming marble and quench-
24 ing volcanoes! Before entering the Massachusetts Metaphysical College, had my students achieved the point
whence they could have derived most benefit from their
27 pupilage, to-day there would be on earth paragons of
Christianity, patterns of humility, wisdom, and might
for the world.

To the students whom I have not seen that ask, "May 1
I call you mother?" my heart replies, *Yes,* if you are
doing God's work.  When born of Truth and Love, we 3
are all of one kindred.

The hour has struck for Christian Scientists to do their
own work;  to appreciate the signs of the times;  to dem- 6
onstrate self-knowledge and self-government;  and to
demonstrate, as this period demands, over all sin, disease,
and death.  The dear ones whom I would have great 9
pleasure in instructing, know that the door to my teaching
was shut when my College closed.

Again, it is not absolutely requisite for some people 12
to be taught in a class, for they can learn by spiritual
growth and by the study of what is written.  Scarcely a
moiety, compared with the whole of the Scriptures and 15
the Christian Science textbook, is yet assimilated spiritually by the most faithful seekers;  yet this assimilation is
indispensable to the progress of every Christian Scientist. 18
These considerations prompt my answers to the above
questions.  Human desire is inadequate to adjust the
balance on subjects of such earnest import.  These 21
words of our Master explain this hour:  "What I do
thou knowest not now;  but thou shalt know hereafter."

My sympathies are deeply enlisted for the students 24
of students;  having already seen in many instances their
talents, culture, and singleness of purpose to uplift the
race.  Such students should not pay the penalty for 27
other people's faults;  and divine Love will open the
way for them.  My soul abhors injustice, and loves
mercy.  St. John writes:  "Whom God hath sent speaketh 30
the words of God:  for God giveth not the Spirit by measure unto him."

1          MY STUDENTS AND THY STUDENTS

Mine and thine are obsolete terms in absolute Christian
3 Science, wherein and whereby the universal brotherhood
of man is stated and demands to be demonstrated.  I have
a large affection, not alone for my students, but for thy
6 students, — for students of the second generation.  I cannot but love some of those devoted students better than
some of mine who are less lovable or Christly.  This
9 natural affection for goodness must go on *ad libitum* unto
the third and fourth and final generation of those who
love God and keep His commandments.  Hence the
12 following is an amendment of the paragraph on page 47 [1]
of "Retrospection and Introspection": —

Any student, having received instructions in a Primary
15 class from me, or from a loyal student of Christian Science,
and afterwards studied thoroughly "Science and Health
with Key to the Scriptures," can enter upon the gospel
18 work of teaching Christian Science, and so fulfil the command of Christ.  Before entering this sacred field of labor,
the student must have studied faithfully the latest edi-
21 tions of my works, and be a good Bible scholar and a
devout, consecrated Christian.

These are the indispensable demands on all those who
24 become teachers.


UNSEEN SIN

Two points of danger beset mankind; namely, making
27 sin seem either too large or too little:  if too large, we

[1] See edition of 1909.

are in the darkness of all the ages, wherein the true sense 1
of the unity of good and the unreality of evil is lost.

If good is God, even as God is good, then good and 3
evil can neither be coeval nor coequal, for God is All-in-
all. This closes the argument of aught besides Him, aught
else than good. 6

If the sense of sin is too little, mortals are in danger
of not seeing their own belief in sin, but of seeing too
keenly their neighbor's. Then they are beset with 9
egotism and hypocrisy. Here Christian Scientists must
be most watchful. Their habit of mental and audible
protest against the reality of sin, tends to make sin less 12
or more to them than to other people. They must either
be overcoming sin in themselves, or they must not lose
sight of sin; else they are self-deceived sinners of the 15
worst sort.

## A WORD TO THE WISE

Will all the dear Christian Scientists accept my tender 18
greetings for the forthcoming holidays, and grant me
this request, — let the present season pass without one
gift to me. 21

Our church edifice must be built in 1894. Take thither
thy saintly offerings, and lay them in the outstretched
hand of God. The object to be won affords ample oppor- 24
tunity for the grandest achievement to which Christian
Scientists can direct attention, and feel themselves alone
among the stars. 27

No doubt must intervene between the promise and
event; faith and resolve are friends to Truth; seize them,

1 trust the divine Providence, push upward our prayer in stone, — and God will give the benediction.

3            CHRISTMAS

This interesting day, crowned with the history of Truth's idea, — its earthly advent and nativity, — is 6 especially dear to the heart of Christian Scientists; to whom Christ's appearing in a fuller sense is so precious, and fraught with divine benedictions for mankind.

9 The star that looked lovingly down on the manger of our Lord, lends its resplendent light to this hour: the light of Truth, to cheer, guide, and bless man as he 12 reaches forth for the infant idea of divine perfection dawning upon human imperfection, — that calms man's fears, bears his burdens, beckons him on to Truth and 15 Love and the sweet immunity these bring from sin, sickness, and death.

This polar star, fixed in the heavens of divine Science, 18 shall be the sign of his appearing who "healeth all our diseases;" it hath traversed night, wading through darkness and gloom, on to glory. It doth meet the 21 antagonism of error; addressing to dull ears and undisciplined beliefs words of Truth and Life.

The star of Bethlehem is the star of Boston, high in 24 the zenith of Truth's domain, that looketh down on the long night of human beliefs, to pierce the darkness and melt into dawn.

27 The star of Bethlehem is the light of all ages; is the light of Love, to-day christening religion undefiled, divine Science; giving to it a new name, and the white stone in 30 token of purity and permanence.

The wise men follow this guiding star; the watchful 1
shepherd chants his welcome over the cradle of a great
truth, and saith, "Unto us a child is born," whose birth 3
is less of a miracle than eighteen centuries ago; and "his
name shall be called Wonderful, Counsellor, The mighty
God, The everlasting Father, The Prince of Peace." 6

My heart is filled with joy, that each receding year sees
the steady gain of Truth's idea in Christian Science; that
each recurring year witnesses the balance adjusted more 9
on the side of God, the supremacy of Spirit; as shown
by the triumphs of Truth over error, of health over sickness, of Life over death, and of Soul over sense. 12

"The hour cometh, and now is, when the true worshippers shall worship the Father in spirit and in truth."
"For the law of the Spirit of life in Christ Jesus hath made 15
me free from the law of sin and death." "Fear not, little
flock; for it is your Father's good pleasure to give you
the kingdom." 18

> Press on, press on! ye sons of light,
> Untiring in your holy fight,
> Still treading each temptation down, 21
> And battling for a brighter crown.

## CARD

In reply to all invitations from Chicago to share the 24
hospitality of their beautiful homes at any time during
the great wonder of the world, the World's Fair, I say,
Do not expect me. I have no desire to see or to hear 27
what is to be offered upon this approaching occasion.

I have a world of wisdom and Love to contemplate,
that concerns me, and you, infinitely beyond all earthly 30

1 expositions or exhibitions.  In return for your kindness,
I earnestly invite you to its contemplation with me, and
3 to preparation to behold it.


### MESSAGE TO THE MOTHER CHURCH

*Beloved Brethren:* — People coming from a distance
6 expecting to hear me speak in The Mother Church,
are frequently disappointed.  To avoid this, I may hereafter notify the Directors when I shall be present to
9 address this congregation, and the Clerk of the church
can inform correspondents.  Your dual and impersonal
pastor, the Bible, and "Science and Health with Key to
12 the Scriptures," is with you;  and the Life these give, the
Truth they illustrate, the Love they demonstrate, is
the great Shepherd that feedeth my flock, and leadeth
15 them "beside the still waters."  By any personal presence, or word of mine, your thought must not be diverted
or diverged, your senses satisfied, or self be justified.
18     Therefore, beloved, my often-coming is unnecessary;
for, though I be present or absent, it is God that feedeth the hungry heart, that giveth grace for grace, that
21 healeth the sick and cleanseth the sinner.  For this
consummation He hath given you Christian Science,
and my past poor labors and love.  He hath shown you
24 the amplitude of His mercy, the justice of His judgment,
the omnipotence of His love;  and this, to compensate
your zealous affection for seeking good, and for labor-
27 ing in its widening grooves from the infinitesimal to the
infinite.

# CHAPTER IX

## THE FRUIT OF SPIRIT

### AN ALLEGORY

PICTURE to yourself "a city set upon a hill," a celestial city above all clouds, in serene azure and unfathomable glory: having no temple therein, for God is the temple thereof; nor need of the sun, neither of the moon, for God doth lighten it. Then from this sacred summit behold a Stranger wending his way downward, to where a few laborers in a valley at the foot of the mountain are working and watching for his coming.

The descent and ascent are beset with peril, privation, temptation, toil, suffering. Venomous serpents hide among the rocks, beasts of prey prowl in the path, wolves in sheep's clothing are ready to devour; but the Stranger meets and masters their secret and open attacks with serene confidence.

The Stranger eventually stands in the valley at the foot of the mountain. He saith unto the patient toilers therein: "What do ye here? Would ye ascend the mountain, — climbing its rough cliffs, hushing the hissing serpents, taming the beasts of prey, — and bathe in its streams, rest in its cool grottos, and drink from its living fountains? The way winds and widens in the valley; up the hill it is straight and narrow, and few there be that find it."

1    His converse with the watchers and workers in the valley closes, and he makes his way into the streets of a
3 city made with hands.

Pausing at the threshold of a palatial dwelling, he knocks and waits. The door is shut. He hears the
6 sounds of festivity and mirth; youth, manhood, and age gayly tread the gorgeously tapestried parlors, dancing-halls, and banquet-rooms. But a little while, and the
9 music is dull, the wine is unsipped, the footfalls abate, the laughter ceases. Then from the window of this dwelling a face looks out, anxiously surveying him who waiteth
12 at the door.

Within this mortal mansion are adulterers, fornicators, idolaters; drunkenness, witchcraft, variance, envy, emu-
15 lation, hatred, wrath, murder. Appetites and passions have so dimmed their sight that he alone who looks from that dwelling, through the clearer pane of his own heart
18 tired of sin, can see the Stranger.

Startled beyond measure at beholding him, this mortal inmate withdraws; but growing more and more troubled,
21 he seeks to leave the odious company and the cruel walls, and to find the Stranger. Stealing cautiously away from his comrades, he departs; then turns back, — he is afraid
24 to go on and to meet the Stranger. So he returns to the house, only to find the lights all wasted and the music fled. Finding no happiness within, he rushes again
27 into the lonely streets, seeking peace but finding none. Naked, hungry, athirst, this time he struggles on, and at length reaches the pleasant path of the valley at the
30 foot of the mountain, whence he may hopefully look for the reappearance of the Stranger, and receive his heavenly guidance.

The Stranger enters a massive carved stone mansion, 1
and saith unto the dwellers therein, "Blessed are the
poor in spirit: for theirs is the kingdom of heaven." But 3
they understand not his saying.

These are believers of different sects, and of no sect;
some, so-called Christian Scientists in sheep's clothing; 6
and all "drunken without wine." They have small conceptions of spiritual riches, few cravings for the immortal,
but are puffed up with the applause of the world: they 9
have plenty of pelf, and fear not to fall upon the Stranger,
seize his pearls, throw them away, and afterwards try to
kill him. 12

Somewhat disheartened, he patiently seeks another
dwelling, — only to find its inmates asleep at noontide!
Robust forms, with manly brow nodding on cushioned 15
chairs, their feet resting on footstools, or, flat on their
backs, lie stretched on the floor, dreaming away the
hours. Balancing on one foot, with eyes half open, 18
the porter starts up in blank amazement and looks at
the Stranger, calls out, rubs his eyes, — amazed beyond
measure that anybody is animated with a purpose, and 21
seen working for it!

They in this house are those that "provoke Him in
the wilderness, and grieve Him in the desert." Away 24
from this charnel-house of the so-called living, the Stranger
turns quickly, and wipes off the dust from his feet as a
testimony against sensualism in its myriad forms. As 27
he departs, he sees robbers finding ready ingress to that
dwelling of sleepers in the midst of murderous hordes,
without watchers and the doors unbarred! 30

Next he enters a place of worship, and saith unto them,
"Go ye into all the world; preach the gospel, heal the

1 sick, cast out devils, raise the dead; for the Scripture
saith the law of the Spirit of life in Christ Jesus hath
3 made you free from the law of sin and death." And *they
cast him out.*

Once more he seeks the dwelling-place of mortals and
6 knocks loudly. The door is burst open, and sufferers
shriek for help: that house is on fire! The flames caught
in the dwelling of luxury, where the blind saw them not,
9 but the flesh at length did feel them; thence they spread
to the house of slumberers who heeded them not, until
they became unmanageable; fed by the fat of hypocrisy
12 and vainglory, they consumed the next dwelling; then
crept unseen into the synagogue, licking up the blood
of martyrs and wrapping their altars in ruins. "God is a
15 consuming fire."

Thus are all mortals, under every hue of circumstances,
driven out of their houses of clay and, homeless wan-
18 derers in a beleaguered city, forced to seek the Father's
house, if they would be led to the valley and up the
mount.

21     Seeing the wisdom of withdrawing from those who
persistently rejected him, the Stranger returned to the
valley; first, to meet with joy his own, to wash their
24 feet, and take them up the mountain. Well might this
heavenly messenger exclaim, "O Jerusalem, Jerusalem,
thou that killest the prophets, and stonest them which
27 are sent unto thee, . . . Behold, your house is left unto
you desolate."

Discerning in his path the penitent one who had groped
30 his way from the dwelling of luxury, the Stranger saith
unto him, "Wherefore comest thou hither?"

He answered, "The sight of thee unveiled my sins, and

turned my misnamed joys to sorrow. When I went back 1
into the house to take something out of it, my misery
increased; so I came hither, hoping that I might follow 3
thee whithersoever thou goest."

And the Stranger saith unto him, "Wilt thou climb
the mountain, and take nothing of thine own with thee?" 6

He answered, "I will."

"Then," saith the Stranger, "thou hast chosen the
good part; follow me." 9

Many there were who had entered the valley to specu-
late in worldly policy, religion, politics, finance, and to
search for wealth and fame. These had heavy baggage 12
of their own, and insisted upon taking all of it with them,
which must greatly hinder their ascent.

The journey commences. The encumbered travellers 15
halt and disagree. They stoutly belay those who, having less baggage, ascend faster than themselves, and
betimes burden them with their own. Despairing of 18
gaining the summit, loaded as they are, they conclude to
stop and lay down a few of the heavy weights, — but
only to take them up again, more than ever determined 21
not to part with their baggage.

All this time the Stranger is pointing the way, showing them their folly, rebuking their pride, consoling their 24
afflictions, and helping them on, saying, "He that loseth
his life for my sake, shall find it."

Obstinately holding themselves back, and sore-footed, 27
they fall behind and lose sight of their guide; when,
stumbling and grumbling, and fighting each other, they
plunge headlong over the jagged rocks. 30

Then he who has no baggage goes back and kindly
binds up their wounds, wipes away the blood stains, and
12

1 would help them on; but suddenly the Stranger shouts,
"Let them alone; they must learn from the things they
3 suffer. Make thine own way; and if thou strayest, listen
for the mountain-horn, and it will call thee back to the
path that goeth upward."

6    Dear reader, dost thou suspect that the valley is humility, that the mountain is heaven-crowned Christianity,
and the Stranger the ever-present Christ, the spiritual
9 idea which from the summit of bliss surveys the vale of
the flesh, to burst the bubbles of earth with a breath of
heaven, and acquaint sensual mortals with the mystery
12 of godliness, — unchanging, unquenchable Love? Hast
not thou heard this Christ knock at the door of thine own
heart, and closed it against Truth, to "eat and drink
15 with the drunken"? Hast thou been driven by suffering to the foot of the mount, but earth-bound, burdened
by pride, sin, and self, hast thou turned back, stumbled,
18 and wandered away? Or hast thou tarried in the habitation of the senses, pleased and stupefied, until wakened
through the baptism of fire?

21    He alone ascends the hill of Christian Science who
follows the Way-shower, the spiritual presence and idea
of God. Whatever obstructs the way, — causing to
24 stumble, fall, or faint, those mortals who are striving
to enter the path, — divine Love will remove; and uplift the fallen and strengthen the weak. Therefore, give
27 up thy earth-weights; and observe the apostle's admonition, "Forgetting those things which are behind, and
reaching forth unto those which are before." Then,
30 loving God supremely and thy neighbor as thyself, thou
wilt safely bear thy cross up to the throne of everlasting
glory.

## VOICES OF SPRING                                    1

Mine is an obstinate *penchant* for nature in all her
moods and forms, a satisfaction with whatever is hers. 3
And what shall this be named, a weakness, or a —
virtue?

In spring, nature like a thrifty housewife sets the earth 6
in order; and between taking up the white carpets and
putting down the green ones, her various apartments are
dismally dirty.                                        9

Spring is my sweetheart, whose voices are sad or glad,
even as the heart may be; restoring in memory the sweet
rhythm of unforgotten harmonies, or touching tenderly 12
its tearful tones.

Spring passes over mountain and meadow, waking up
the world; weaving the wavy grass, nursing the timid 15
spray, stirring the soft breeze; rippling all nature in
ceaseless flow, with "breath all odor and cheek all bloom."
Whatever else droops, spring is gay: her little feet trip 18
lightly on, turning up the daisies, paddling the water-
cresses, rocking the oriole's cradle; challenging the sed-
entary shadows to activity, and the streams to race for the 21
sea. Her dainty fingers put the fur cap on pussy-willow,
paint in pink the petals of arbutus, and sweep in soft
strains her Orphean lyre. "The voice of the turtle is 24
heard in our land." The snow-bird that tarried through
the storm, now chirps to the breeze; the cuckoo sounds
her invisible lute, calling the feathered tribe back to their 27
summer homes. Old robin, though stricken to the heart
with winter's snow, prophesies of fair earth and sunny
skies. The brooklet sings melting murmurs to merry 30

1 meadows; the leaves clap their hands, and the winds make melody through dark pine groves.

3    What is the anthem of human life?

Has love ceased to moan over the new-made grave, and, looking upward, does it patiently pray for the per-
6 petual springtide wherein no arrow wounds the dove? Human hope and faith should join in nature's grand harmony, and, if on minor key, make music in the heart.
9 And man, more friendly, should call his race as gently to the springtide of Christ's dear love. St. Paul wrote, "Rejoice in the Lord always." And why not, since man's
12 possibilities are infinite, bliss is eternal, and the consciousness thereof is here and now?

The alders bend over the streams to shake out their
15 tresses in the water-mirrors; let mortals bow before the creator, and, looking through Love's transparency, behold man in God's own image and likeness, arranging in the
18 beauty of holiness each budding thought. It is good to talk with our past hours, and learn what report they bear, and how they might have reported more spirit-
21 ual growth. With each returning year, higher joys, holier aims, a purer peace and diviner energy, should freshen the fragrance of being. Nature's first and last
24 lessons teach man to be kind, and even pride should sanction what our natures need. Popularity, — what is it? A mere mendicant that boasts and begs, and God
27 denies charity.

When gentle violet lifts its blue eye to heaven, and crown imperial unveils its regal splendor to the sun;
30 when the modest grass, inhabiting the whole earth, stoops meekly before the blast; when the patient corn waits on the elements to put forth its slender blade, construct

the stalk, instruct the ear, and crown the full corn in the 1
ear, — then, are mortals looking up, waiting on God,
and committing their way unto Him who tosses earth's 3
mass of wonders into their hands? When downtrodden
like the grass, did it make them humble, loving, obedient, full of good odor, and cause them to wait patiently 6
on God for man's rich heritage, — "dominion over all
the earth"? Thus abiding in Truth, the warmth and
sunlight of prayer and praise and understanding will 9
ripen the fruits of Spirit, and goodness will have its springtide of freedom and greatness.

When the white-winged dove feeds her callow brood, 12
nestles them under her wings, and, in tones tremulous
with tenderness, calls them to her breast, do mortals
remember *their* cradle hymns, and thank God for those 15
redemptive words from a mother's lips which taught
them the Lord's Prayer?

> O gentle presence, peace and joy and power; 18
> O Life divine, that owns each waiting hour;
> Thou Love that guards the nestling's faltering flight!
> Keep Thou my child on upward wing to-night. 21

Midst the falling leaves of old-time faiths, above the
frozen crust of creed and dogma, the divine Mind-force,
filling all space and having all power, upheaves the earth. 24
In sacred solitude divine Science evolved nature as thought,
and thought as things. This supreme potential Principle
reigns in the realm of the real, and is "God with us," 27
the I AM.

As mortals awake from their dream of material sensation, this adorable, all-inclusive God, and all earth's 30
hieroglyphics of Love, are understood; and infinite Mind

1 is seen kindling the stars, rolling the worlds, reflecting all space and Life, — but not life in matter. Wisely
3 governing, informing the universe, this Mind is Truth, — not laws of matter. Infinitely just, merciful, and wise, this Mind is Love, — but not fallible love.

6 Spring is here! and doors that closed on Christian Science in "the long winter of our discontent," are open flung. Its seedtime has come to enrich earth and en-
9 robe man in righteousness; may its sober-suited autumn follow with hues of heaven, ripened sheaves, and harvest songs.

12 ## "WHERE ART THOU?"

In the allegory of Genesis, third chapter and ninth verse, two mortals, walking in the cool of the day midst
15 the stately palms, many-hued blossoms, perfume-laden breezes, and crystal streams of the Orient, pondered the things of man and God.

18 A sense of evil is supposed to have spoken, been listened to, and afterwards to have formed an evil sense that blinded the eyes of reason, masked with deformity the
21 glories of revelation, and shamed the face of mortals.

What was this sense? Error versus Truth: first, a supposition; second, a false belief; third, suffering;
24 fourth, death.

Is man the supposer, false believer, sufferer?

Not man, but a mortal — the antipode of immortal
27 man. Supposing, false believing, suffering are not faculties of Mind, but are qualities of error.

The supposition is, that God and His idea are not all-
30 power; that there is something besides Him; that this

something is intelligent matter; that sin — yea, self- 1
hood — is apart from God, where pleasure and pain,
good and evil, life and death, commingle, and are for- 3
ever at strife; even that every ray of Truth, of infinity,
omnipotence, omnipresence, goodness, could be absorbed
in error! God cannot be obscured, and this renders error 6
a palpable falsity, yea, nothingness; on the basis that
black is not a color because it absorbs all the rays of
light. 9

The "Alpha and Omega" of Christian Science voices
this question: Where do we hold intelligence to be? Is
it in both evil and good, in matter as well as Spirit? 12
If so, we are literally and practically denying that God,
good, is supreme, *all* power and presence, and are turning away from the only living and true God, to "lords 15
many and gods many."

Where art thou, O mortal! who turnest away from
the divine source of being, — calling on matter to work 18
out the problem of Mind, to aid in understanding and
securing the sweet harmonies of Spirit that relate to the
universe, including man? 21

Paul asked: "What communion hath light with darkness? And what concord hath Christ with Belial?" The
worshippers of Baal worshipped the sun. They believed 24
that something besides God had authority and power,
could heal and bless; that God wrought through matter
— by means of that which does not reflect Him in a single 27
quality or quantity! — the grand realities of Mind, thus
to exemplify the power of Truth and Love.

The ancient Chaldee hung his destiny out upon the 30
heavens; but ancient or modern Christians, instructed in
divine Science, know that the prophet better understood

1 Him who said: "He doeth according to His will in the
army of heaven, and among the inhabitants of the earth;
3 and none can stay His hand, or say unto Him, What doest
Thou?"

Astrology is well in its place, but this place is second-
6 ary. Necromancy has no foundation, — in fact, no
intelligence; and the belief that it has, deceives itself.
Whatever simulates power and Truth in matter, does this
9 as a lie declaring itself, that mortals' faith in matter may
have the effect of power; but when the whole fabrication
is found to be a lie, away goes all its supposed power and
12 prestige.

Why do Christian Scientists treat disease *as* disease,
since there is no disease?
15 This is done only as one gives the lie to a lie; because
it is a lie, without one word of Truth in it. You must
find error to be *nothing:* then, and *only* then, do you
18 handle it in Science. The diabolism of suppositional
evil at work in the name of good, is a lie of the highest
degree of nothingness: just reduce this falsity to its proper
21 denomination, and you have done with it.

How shall we treat a negation, or error — by means
of matter, or Mind? Is matter Truth? No! Then it
24 cannot antidote error.

Can belief destroy belief? No: understanding is required to do this. By the substitution of Truth demon-
27 strated, Science remedies the ills of material beliefs.

Because I have uncovered evil, and dis-covered for
you divine Science, which saith, "Be not overcome of
30 evil, but overcome evil with good," and you have not
loved sufficiently to understand this Golden Rule and
demonstrate the might of perfect Love that casteth out

all fear, shall you turn away from this divine Principle 1
to graven images?  Remember the Scripture: —

"But and if that evil servant shall say in his heart, 3
My lord delayeth his coming;

"And shall begin to smite his fellow-servants, and to
eat and drink with the drunken; 6

"The lord of that servant shall come in a day when
he looketh not for him, and in an hour that he is not
aware of, 9

"And shall cut him asunder, and appoint him his portion with the hypocrites."

One mercilessly assails me for opposing the subtle lie, 12
others charge upon me with full-fledged invective for, as
they say, having too much charity;  but neither moves
me from the path made luminous by divine Love. 15

In my public works I lay bare the ability, in belief, of
evil to break the Decalogue, — to murder, steal, commit
adultery, and so on.  Those who deny my wisdom or 18
right to expose error, are either willing participants in
wrong, afraid of its supposed power, or ignorant of it.

The notion that one is covering iniquity by asserting 21
its nothingness, is a fault of zealots, who, like Peter,
sleep when the Watcher bids them watch, and when the
hour of trial comes would cut off somebody's ears.  Such 24
people say, "Would you have me get out of a burning
house, or stay in it?"

I would have you already out, and *know* that you are 27
out;  also, to remember the Scripture concerning those
who do evil that good may come, — "whose damnation
is just;"  and that whoso departeth from divine Science, 30
seeking power or good aside from God, has done himself
harm.

1   Mind is supreme: Love is the master of hate; Truth,
the victor over a lie.  Hath not Science voiced this les-
3 son to you, — that evil is powerless, that a lie is never
true?  It is your province to wrestle with error, to handle
the serpent and bruise its head; but you cannot, as a
6 Christian Scientist, resort to stones and clubs, — yea, to
matter, — to kill the serpent of a material mind.

Do you love that which represents God most, His high-
9 est idea as seen to-day?  No!

Then you would hate Jesus if you saw him personally,
and knew your right obligations towards him.  He would
12 insist on the rule and demonstration of divine Science:
even that you first cast out your own dislike and hatred
of God's idea, — the beam in your own eye that hinders
15 your seeing clearly how to cast the mote of evil out of
other eyes.  You cannot demonstrate the Principle of
Christian Science and not love its idea: we gather not
18 grapes of thorns, nor figs of thistles.

Where art thou?

### DIVINE SCIENCE

21   What is it but another name for Christian Science,
the cognomen of all true religion, the quintessence of
Christianity, that heals disease and sin and destroys
24 death!  Part and parcel of Truth and Love, wherever
one ray of its effulgence looks in upon the heart, behold
a better man, woman, or child.

27   Science is the fiat of divine intelligence, which, hoary
with eternity, touches time only to take away its frailty.
That it rests on everlasting foundations, the sequence
30 proves.

Have I discovered and founded at this period Chris-  1
tian Science, that which reveals the truth of Love, — is
the question.                                          3

And how can you be certain of so momentous an
affirmative?  By proving its effect on yourself to be —
divine.                                               6

What is the Principle and rule of Christian Science?

Infinite query!  Wonder in heaven and on earth, —
who shall say?  The immaculate Son of the Blessed  9
has spoken of them as the Golden Rule and its Principle,
God who is Love.  Listen, and *he* illustrates the rule:
"Jesus called a little child unto him, and set him in the 12
midst of them, and said, . . . Whosoever . . . shall
humble himself as this little child, the same is greatest
in the kingdom of heaven."                            15

Harmony is heaven.  Science brings out harmony;
but this harmony is not understood unless it produces a
growing affection for all good, and consequent disaffec- 18
tion for all evil, hypocrisy, evil-speaking, lust, envy, hate.
Where these exist, Christian Science has no sure foothold:  they obscure its divine element, and thus seem 21
to extinguish it.  Even the life of Jesus was belittled
and belied by personalities possessing these defacing de-
formities.  Only the devout Marys, and such as lived 24
according to his precepts, understood the concrete character of him who taught — by the wayside, in humble
homes, to itching ears and to dull disciples — the words 27
of Life.

The ineffable Life and light which he reflected through
divine Science is again reproduced in the character which 30
sensualism, as heretofore, would hide or besmear.  Sin
of any sort tends to hide from an individual this grand

1 verity in Science, that the appearing of good in an individual involves the disappearing of evil. He who first
3 brings to humanity some great good, must have gained its height beforehand, to be able to lift others toward it. I first proved to myself, not by "words," — these
6 afford no proof, — but by demonstration of Christian Science, that its Principle is divine. All must go and do likewise.

9 Faith illumined by works; the spiritual understanding which cannot choose but to labor and love; hope holding steadfastly to good in the midst of seething evil;
12 charity that suffereth long and is kind, but cancels not sin until it be destroyed, — these afford the only rule I have found which demonstrates Christian Science.

15 And remember, a pure faith in humanity will subject one to deception; the uses of good, to abuses from evil; and calm strength will enrage evil. But the very heavens
18 shall laugh at them, and move majestically to your defense when the armies of earth press hard upon you.

"Thou must be true thyself,
21    If thou the truth wouldst teach;
Thy soul must overflow, if thou
   Another's soul wouldst reach;
24 It needs the overflow of heart,
   To give the lips full speech.

"Think truly, and thy thoughts
27    Shall the world's famine feed;
Speak truly, and each word of thine
   Shall be a fruitful seed;
30 Live truly, and thy life shall be
   A great and noble creed."

FIDELITY 1

If people would confine their talk to subjects that are
profitable, that which St. John informs us took place 3
once in heaven, would happen very frequently on earth,
— silence for the space of half an hour.

Experience is victor, never the vanquished; and out 6
of defeat comes the secret of victory. That to-morrow
starts from to-day and is one day beyond it, robes the
future with hope's rainbow hues. 9

In the battle of life, good is made more industrious
and persistent because of the supposed activity of evil.
The elbowing of the crowd plants our feet more firmly. 12
In the mental collisions of mortals and the strain of intellectual wrestlings, moral tension is tested, and, if it
yields not, grows stronger. The past admonishes us: 15
with finger grim and cold it points to every mortal mistake;
or smiling saith, "Thou hast been faithful over a few
things." 18

Art thou a child, and hast added one furrow to the
brow of care? Art thou a husband, and hast pierced
the heart venturing its all of happiness to thy keeping? 21
Art thou a wife, and hast bowed the o'erburdened head
of thy husband? Hast thou a friend, and forgettest to be
grateful? Remember, that for all this thou alone canst 24
and must atone. Carelessly or remorselessly thou mayest
have sent along the ocean of events a wave that will some
time flood thy memory, surge dolefully at the door of con- 27
science, and pour forth the unavailing tear.

Change and the grave may part us; the wisdom that
might have blessed the past may come too late. One 30

1 backward step, one relinquishment of right in an evil
hour, one faithless tarrying, has torn the laurel from many
3 a brow and repose from many a heart.   Good is never
the reward of evil, and *vice versa*.

There is no excellence without labor;  and the time to
6 work, is *now*.   Only by persistent, unremitting, straightforward toil;  by turning neither to the right nor to the
left, seeking no other pursuit or pleasure than that which
9 cometh from God, can you win and wear the crown of the
faithful.

That law-school is not at fault which sends forth a
12 barrister who never brings out a brief.   Why?   Because
he followed agriculture instead of litigation, forsook
Blackstone for gray stone, dug into soils instead of delv-
15 ing into suits, raised potatoes instead of pleas, and drew
up logs instead of leases.   He has not been faithful over
a few things.

18    Is a musician made by his teacher?   He makes himself a musician by practising what he was taught.   The
conscientious are successful.   They follow faithfully;
21 through evil or through good report, they work on to the
achievement of good;  by patience, they inherit the promise.   Be active, and, however slow, thy success is sure:
24 toil is triumph;  and — thou hast been faithful over a few
things.

The lives of great men and women are miracles of pa-
27 tience and perseverance.   Every luminary in the constel-
lation of human greatness, like the stars, comes out in
the darkness to shine with the reflected light of God.

30    Material philosophy, human ethics, scholastic theology,
and physics have not sufficiently enlightened mankind.
Human wrong, sickness, sin, and death still appear in

mortal belief, and they never bring out the right action 1
of mind or body.  When will the whole human race have
one God, — an undivided affection that leaves the unreal 3
material basis of things, for the spiritual foundation and
superstructure that is real, right, and eternal?

First purify thought, then put thought into words, 6
and words into deeds;  and after much slipping and
clambering, you will go up the scale of Science to the
second rule, and be made ruler over many things.  Fidelity 9
finds its reward and its strength in exalted purpose.  Seeking is not sufficient whereby to arrive at the results of
Science:  you must strive;  and the glory of the strife 12
comes of honesty and humility.

Do human hopes deceive? is joy a trembler?  Then,
weary pilgrim, unloose the latchet of thy sandals;  for the 15
place whereon thou standest is sacred.  By that, you may
know you are parting with a material sense of life and
happiness to win the spiritual sense of good.  O learn to 18
lose with God! and you find Life eternal: you gain all.
To doubt this is implicit treason to divine decree.

The parable of "the ten virgins" serves to illustrate 21
the evil of inaction and delay.  This parable is drawn
from the sad history of Vesta, — a little girl of eight
years, who takes the most solemn vow of celibacy for thirty 24
years, and is subject to terrible torture if the lamp she
tends is not replenished with oil day and night, so that the
flame never expires.  The moral of the parable is pointed, 27
and the diction purely Oriental.

We learn from this parable that neither the cares of
this world nor the so-called pleasures or pains of mate- 30
rial sense are adequate to plead for the neglect of spiritual
light, that must be tended to keep aglow the flame of

1 devotion whereby to enter into the joy of divine Science demonstrated.

3    The foolish virgins had no oil in their lamps: their way was material; thus they were in doubt and darkness. They heeded not their sloth, their fading warmth 6 of action; hence the steady decline of spiritual light, until, the midnight gloom upon them, they must borrow the better-tended lamps of the faithful. By entering 9 the guest-chamber of Truth, and beholding the bridal of Life and Love, they would be wedded to a higher understanding of God. Each moment's fair expect- 12 ancy was to behold the bridegroom, the One "altogether lovely."

   It was midnight: darkness profound brooded over 15 earth's lazy sleepers. With no oil in their lamps, no spiritual illumination to look upon him whom they had pierced, they heard the shout, "The bridegroom cometh!" 18 But how could they behold him? Hear that human cry: "Oh, lend us your oil! our lamps have gone out, — no light! earth's fables flee, and heaven is afar 21 off."

   The door is shut. The wise virgins had no oil to spare, and they said to the foolish, "Go to them that sell, and 24 buy for yourselves." Seek Truth, and pursue it. It should cost you something: you are willing to pay for error and receive nothing in return; but if you pay the price of 27 Truth, you shall receive *all*.

   "The children of this world are in their generation wiser than the children of light;" they watch the market, 30 acquaint themselves with the etiquette of the exchange, and are ready for the next move. How much more should we be faithful over the few things of Spirit, that are able to make us wise unto salvation! Let us watch and pray that we enter not into the temptation of ease in sin; and let us not forget that others before us have laid upon the altar all that we have to sacrifice, and have passed to their reward. Too soon we cannot turn from disease in the body to find disease in the mortal mind, and its cure, in working for God. Thought must be made better, and human life more fruitful, for the divine energy to move it onward and upward.

Warmed by the sunshine of Truth, watered by the heavenly dews of Love, the fruits of Christian Science spring upward, and away from the sordid soil of self and matter. Are we clearing the gardens of thought by uprooting the noxious weeds of passion, malice, envy, and strife? Are we picking away the cold, hard pebbles of selfishness, uncovering the secrets of sin and burnishing anew the hidden gems of Love, that their pure perfection shall appear? Are we feeling the vernal freshness and sunshine of enlightened faith?

The weeds of mortal mind are not always destroyed by the first uprooting; they reappear, like devastating witch-grass, to choke the coming clover. O stupid gardener! watch their reappearing, and tear them away from their native soil, until no seedling be left to propagate — and rot.

Among the manifold soft chimes that will fill the haunted chambers of memory, this is the sweetest: "Thou hast been faithful!"

1        TRUE PHILOSOPHY AND COMMUNION

It is related of Justin Martyr that, hearing of a Pythag-
3 orean professor of ethics, he expressed the wish to become one of his disciples. "Very well," the teacher
replied; "but have you studied music, astronomy, and
6 geometry, and do you think it possible for you to understand aught of that which leads to bliss, without having mastered the sciences that disengage the soul from
9 objects of sense, so rendering it a fit habitation for
the intelligences?" On Justin's confessing that he had
not studied those branches, he was dismissed by the
12 professor.

Alas for such a material science of life! Of what
avail would geometry be to a poor sinner struggling with
15 temptation, or to a man with the smallpox?

Ancient and modern philosophies are spoiled by lack
of Science. They would place Soul wholly inside of body,
18 intelligence in matter; and from error of premise would
seek a correct conclusion. Such philosophy can never
demonstrate the Science of Life, — the Science which
21 Paul understood when he spoke of willingness "to be
absent from the body, and present with the Lord." Such
philosophy is far from the rules of the mighty Nazarene
24 Prophet. His words, living in our hearts, were these:
"Whosoever shall not receive the kingdom of God as
a little child, shall in no wise enter therein." Not through
27 astronomy did he point out the way to heaven and the
reign of harmony.

We need the spirit of St. Paul, when he stood on Mars'
30 hill at Athens, bringing Christianity for the first time

into Europe. The Spirit bestows spiritual gifts, God's 1
presence and providence. St. Paul stood where Socrates
had stood four hundred years before, defending himself 3
against the charge of atheism; in the place where De-
mosthenes had pleaded for freedom in immortal strains
of eloquence. 6

We need the spirit of the pious Polycarp, who, when
the proconsul said to him, "I will set the beasts upon
you, unless you yield your religion," replied: "Let them 9
come; I cannot change from good to bad." Then they
bound him to the stake, set fire to the fagots, and his
pure and strong faith rose higher through the baptism 12
of flame.

Methinks the infidel was blind who said, "Christianity
is fit only for women and weak men;" but even infidels 15
may disagree. Bonaparte declared, "Ever since the
reign of Christianity began the loftiest intellects have had
a practical faith in God." Daniel Webster said, "My 18
heart has always assured and reassured me that Christianity must be a divine reality."

To turn the popular indignation against an advanced 21
form of religion, the pagan slanderers affirmed that
Christians took their infants to a place of worship in
order to offer them in sacrifice, — a baptism not of 24
water but of blood, thus distorting or misapprehending
the purpose of Christian sacraments. Christians met
in midnight feasts in the early days, and talked of the 27
crucified Saviour; thence arose the rumor that it was
a part of Christian worship to kill and eat a human
being. 30

Really, Christianity turned men away from the thought
of fleshly sacrifice, and directed them to spiritual attain-

1 ments.   Life, not death, was and is the very centre of
its faith.   Christian Science carries this thought even
3 higher, and insists on the demonstration of moral and
spiritual healing as eminent proof that God is understood
and illustrated.


## ORIGIN OF EVIL

6

The origin of evil is the problem of ages.   It confronts
each generation anew.   It confronts Christian Science.
9 The question is often asked, If God created only the
good, whence comes the evil?

To this question Christian Science replies:  Evil never
12 did exist as an entity.   It is but a belief that there is an
opposite intelligence to God.   This belief is a species of
idolatry, and is not more true or real than that an image
15 graven on wood or stone is God.

The mortal admission of the reality of evil perpetuates
faith in evil;  and the Scriptures declare that "to whom
18 ye yield yourselves servants to obey, his servants ye
are."   This leading, self-evident proposition of Christian
Science, that, good being real, its opposite is necessarily
21 unreal, needs to be grasped in all its divine requirements.


## TRUTH VERSUS ERROR

"A word fitly spoken is like apples of gold in pictures
24 of silver."   It is a rule in Christian Science never to repeat error unless it becomes requisite to bring out Truth.
Then lift the curtain, let in the light, and countermand

this first command of Solomon, "Answer not a fool accord- 1
ing to his folly, lest thou also be like unto him."

A distant rumbling and quivering of the earth foretell 3
the internal action of pent-up gas. To avoid danger from
this source people have to escape from their houses to the
open space. A conical cloud, hanging like a horoscope 6
in the air, foreshadows a cyclone. To escape from this
calamity people prepare shelter in caves of the earth.

They who discern the face of the skies cannot always 9
discern the mental signs of these times, and peer through
the opaque error. Where my vision begins and is clear,
theirs grows indistinct and ends. 12

There are diversities of operation by the same spirit.
Two individuals, with all the goodness of generous natures, advise me. One says, Go this way; the other 15
says, Take the opposite direction! Between the two I
stand still; or, accepting the premonition of one of them,
I follow his counsel, take a few steps, then halt. A true 18
sense not unfamiliar has been awakened. I see the way
now. The guardians of His presence go before me. I
enter the path. It may be smooth, or it may be rugged; 21
but it is always straight and narrow; and if it be up-
hill all the way, the ascent is easy and the summit can
be gained. 24

God is responsible for the mission of those whom He
has anointed. Those who know no will but His take
His hand, and from the night He leads to light. None 27
can say unto Him, What doest Thou?

*The Christian Science Journal* was the oldest and
only authenticated organ of Christian Science up to 30
1898. Loyal Scientists are targets for envy, rivalry,
slander; and whoever hits this mark is well paid by the

1 umpire. But the Scientists aim highest. They press forward towards the mark of a high calling. They recog-
3 nize the claims of the law and the gospel. They know
that whatsoever a man soweth, that shall he reap. They
infringe neither the books nor the business of others; and
6 with hearts overflowing with love for God, they help on the
brotherhood of men. It is not *mine* but *Thine* they seek.

When God bids one uncover iniquity, in order to
9 exterminate it, one should lay it bare; and divine Love
will bless this endeavor and those whom it reaches.
"Nothing is hid that shall not be revealed."
12 It is only a question of time when God shall reveal His
rod, and show the plan of battle. Error, left to itself,
accumulates. Hence, Solomon's transverse command:
15 "Answer a fool according to his folly, lest he be wise in
his own conceit."

To quench the growing flames of falsehood, once in
18 about seven years I have to repeat this, — that I use no
drugs whatever, not even coffea (coffee), thea (tea), cap-
sicum (red pepper); though every day, and especially at
21 dinner, I indulge in homœopathic doses of *Natrum muri-*
*aticum* (common salt).

When I found myself under this new *régime* of medi-
24 cine, the medicine of Mind, I wanted to satisfy my curiosity as to the effect of drugs on one who had lost all
faith in them. Hence I tried several doses of medicine,
27 and so proved to myself that drugs have no beneficial
effect on an individual in a proper state of mind.

I have by no means encouraged students of the Massa-
30 chusetts Metaphysical College to enter medical schools,
and afterwards denied this and objected to their entering
those schools. A student who consulted me on this sub-

ject, received my consent and even the offer of pecuniary 1
assistance to take lessons outside of my College, provided
he received these lessons of a certain regular-school physi- 3
cian, whose instructions included about twelve lessons,
three weeks' time, and the surgical part of midwifery. I
have students with the degree of M. D., who are skilful 6
obstetricians. Such a course with such a teacher would
not necessitate essential materialization of a student's
thought, nor detract from the metaphysical mode of 9
obstetrics taught in my College.

This student had taken the above-named course in
obstetrics when he consulted me on the feasibility of enter- 12
ing a medical school; and to this I objected on the ground
that it was inconsistent with Christian Science, which he
claimed to be practising; but I was willing, and said 15
so, that, notwithstanding my objection, he should do as
he deemed best, for I claim no jurisdiction over any students. He entered the medical school, and several other 18
students with him. My counsel to all of them was in
substance the same as the foregoing, and some of these
students have openly acknowledged this. 21

In answer to a question on the following subject, I
will state that I preached four years, and built up the
church, before I would accept the slightest remuneration. 24
When the church had sufficient members and means to
pay a salary, and refused to give me up or to receive my
gratuitous services, I accepted, for a time, fifteen dollars 27
each Sunday when I preached. I never received more
than this; and the contributions, when I preached,
doubled that amount. I have accepted no pay from my 30
church for about three years, and believe that I have
put into the church-fund about two thousand dollars of

1 my own contributions. I hold receipts for $1,489.50 paid in, and the balance was never receipted for.

3 I temporarily organized a secret society known as the P. M., the workings whereof were not "terrible and too shocking to relate." By and with advice of the very 6 student who brings up the question of this society, it was formed. The P. M. (Private Meeting) Society met only twice. The first subject given out for considera- 9 tion was this: "There is no Animal Magnetism." There was no advice given, no mental work, and there were no transactions at those meetings which I would hesi- 12 tate to have known. On the contrary, our deliberations were, as usual, Christian, and like my public instruction. The second P. M. convened in about one week from the 15 first. The subject given out at that meeting was, in sub- stance, "God is All; there is none beside Him." This proved to be our last meeting. I dissolved the society, 18 and we have not met since. If harm could come from the consideration of these two topics, it was because of the misconception of those subjects in the mind that 21 handled them. An individual state of mind sometimes occasions effects on patients which are not in harmony with Science and the soundness of the argument used. 24 Hence it prevents the normal action, and the benefit that would otherwise accrue.

I issue no arguments, and cause none to be used in 27 mental practice, which consign people to suffering. On the contrary, I cannot serve two masters; therefore I teach the use of such arguments only as promote health 30 and spiritual growth. My life, consecrated to humanity through nameless suffering and sacrifice, furnishes its own proof of my practice.

I have sometimes called on students to test their ability 1
and meet the mental malpractice, so as to lift the burdens
imposed by students. 3

The fact is, that for want of time, and for the purpose
of blessing even my enemies, I neglect myself. I never
have practised by arguments which, perverted, are the 6
weapons of the silent mental malpractice. I have no skill
in occultism; and I could not if I would, and would not
if I could, harm any one through the mental method of 9
Mind-healing, or in any manner.

The late much-ado-about-nothing arose solely from
mental malicious practice, and the audible falsehood 12
designed to stir up strife between brethren, for the purpose
of placing Christian Science in the hands of aspirants
for place and power. These repeated attempts of mad 15
ambition may retard our Cause, but they never can place
it in the wrong hands and hold it there, nor benefit
mankind by such endeavors. 18

## FALLIBILITY OF HUMAN CONCEPTS

Evil counterfeits good: it says, "I am Truth," though
it is a lie; it says, "I am Love," — but Love is spirit- 21
ual, and sensuous love is material, wherefore it is hate
instead of Love; for the five senses give to mortals pain,
sickness, sin, and death, — pleasure that is false, life that 24
leads unto death, joy that becomes sorrow. Love that is
not the procurator of happiness, declares itself the antipode of Love; and Love divine punishes the joys of this 27
false sense of love, chastens its affection, purifies it, and
turns it into the opposite channels.

Material life is the antipode of spiritual life; it mocks 30

1 the bliss of spiritual being; it is bereft of permanence and peace.

3 When human sense is quickened to behold aright the error, — the error of regarding Life, Truth, Love as material and not spiritual, or as both material and spir-
6 itual, — it is able for the first time to discern the Science of good. But it must first see the error of its present erroneous course, to be able to behold the facts of Truth
9 outside of the error; and, *vice versa,* when it discovers the truth, this uncovers the error and quickens the true consciousness of God, good. May the human shadows of
12 thought lengthen as they approach the light, until they are lost in light and no night is there!

In Science, sickness is healed upon the same Principle
15 and by the same rule that sin is healed. To know the supposed bodily belief of the patient and what has claimed to produce it, enables the practitioner to act more under-
18 standingly in destroying this belief. Thus it is in heal-ing the moral sickness; the malicious mental operation must be understood in order to enable one to destroy
21 it and its effects. There is not sufficient spiritual power in the human thought to heal the sick or the sinful. Through the divine energies alone one must either get
24 out of himself and into God so far that his consciousness is the reflection of the divine, or he must, through argu-ment and the human consciousness of both evil and good,
27 overcome evil.

The only difference between the healing of sin and the healing of sickness is, that sin must be *uncovered* before
30 it can be destroyed, and the moral sense be aroused to reject the sense of error; while sickness must be cov-ered with the veil of harmony, and the consciousness be

allowed to rejoice in the sense that it has nothing to mourn  1
over, but something to forget.

Human concepts run in extremes; they are like the  3
action of sickness, which is either an excess of action or
not action enough; they are fallible; they are neither
standards nor models.  6

If one asks me, Is my concept of you right? I reply, The
human concept is always imperfect; relinquish your human
concept of me, or of any one, and find the divine, and you  9
have gained the right one — and never until then. People
give me too much attention of the misguided, fallible sort,
and this misrepresents one through malice or ignorance.  12

My brother was a manufacturer; and one day a work-
man in his mills, a practical joker, set a man who applied
for work, in the overseer's absence, to pour a bucket of  15
water every ten minutes on the regulator. When my
brother returned and saw it, he said to the jester, "You
must pay that man." Some people try to tend folks, as  18
if they should steer the regulator of mankind. God makes
*us* pay for tending the action that He adjusts.

The regulator is governed by the principle that makes  21
the machinery work rightly; and because it *is* thus governed, the folly of tending it is no mere jest. The divine
Principle carries on His harmony.  24

Now turn from the metaphor of the mill to the Mother's
four thousand children, most of whom, at about three
years of scientific age, set up housekeeping alone. Certain  27
students, being too much interested in themselves to think
of helping others, go their way. They do not love Mother,
but pretend to; they constantly go to her for help, interrupt  30
the home-harmony, criticise and disobey her; then "return
to their vomit," — world worship, pleasure seeking, and

1 sense indulgence, — meantime declaring they "never disobey Mother"! It exceeds my conception of human
3 nature. Sin in its very nature is marvellous! Who but a
moral idiot, sanguine of success in sin, can steal, and lie
and lie, and lead the innocent to doom? History needs it,
6 and it has the grandeur of the loyal, self-forgetful, faithful Christian Scientists to overbalance this foul stuff.

When the Mother's love can no longer promote peace
9 in the family, wisdom is not "justified of her children."
When depraved reason is preferred to revelation, error
to Truth, and evil to good, and sense seems sounder than
12 Soul, the children are tending the regulator; they are
indeed losing the knowledge of the divine Principle and
rules of Christian Science, whose fruits prove the nature
15 of their source. A little more grace, a motive made pure,
a few truths tenderly told, a heart softened, a character
subdued, a life consecrated, would restore the right action
18 of the mental mechanism, and make manifest the movement of body and soul in accord with God.

Instead of relying on the Principle of all that really
21 exists, — to govern His own creation, — self-conceit, ignorance, and pride would regulate God's action. Experience shows that humility is the first step in Christian
24 Science, wherein all is controlled, not by man or laws
material, but by wisdom, Truth, and Love.

Go gaze on the eagle, his eye on the sun,
27 Fast gathering strength for a flight well begun,
As rising he rests in a liberty higher
Than genius inflated with worldly desire.

30 No tear dims his eye, nor his pinions lose power
To gaze on the lark in her emerald bower —
Whenever he soareth to fashion his nest,
33 No vision more bright than the dream in his breast.

## THE WAY 1

The present stage of progress in Christian Science presents two opposite aspects, — a full-orbed promise, and 3 a gaunt want. The need, however, is not of the letter, but the spirit.

Less teaching and good healing is to-day the acme of 6 "well done;" a healing that is not guesswork, — chronic recovery ebbing and flowing, — but instantaneous cure. This absolute demonstration of Science must be revived. 9 To consummate this *desideratum*, mortal mind must pass through three stages of growth.

First, self-knowledge. The physician must know him- 12 self and understand the mental state of his patient. Error found out is two-thirds destroyed, and the last third pierces itself, for the remainder only stimulates and gives 15 scope to higher demonstration. To strike out right and left against the mist, never clears the vision; but to lift your head above it, is a sovereign panacea. Mental dark- 18 ness is senseless error, neither intelligence nor power, and its victim is responsible for its supposititious presence. "Cast the beam out of thine own eye." Learn what in 21 thine own mentality is unlike "the anointed," and cast it out; then thou wilt discern the error in thy patient's mind that makes his body sick, and remove it, and rest 24 like the dove from the deluge.

"Physician, heal thyself." Let no clouds of sin gather and fall in mist and showers from thine own mental 27 atmosphere. Hold thy gaze to the light, and the iris of faith, more beautiful than the rainbow seen from my window at the close of a balmy autumnal day, will span 30 thy heavens of thought.

1 A radiant sunset, beautiful as blessings when they take their flight, dilates and kindles into rest. Thus will a
3 life corrected illumine its own atmosphere with spiritual glow and understanding.

The pent-up elements of mortal mind need no terrible
6 detonation to free them. Envy, rivalry, hate need no temporary indulgence that they be destroyed through suffering; they should be stifled from lack of air and
9 freedom.

My students, with cultured intellects, chastened affections, and costly hopes, give promise of grand careers.
12 But they must remember that the seedtime is passed, the harvest hour has come; and songs should ascend from the mount of revelation, sweeter than the sound of
15 vintage bells.

The seed of Christian Science, which when sown was "the least of all seeds," has sprung up, borne fruit, and
18 the birds of the air, the uplifted desires of the human heart, have lodged in its branches. Now let my faithful students carry the fruit of this tree into the rock-ribbed
21 nests of the raven's callow brood.

The second stage of mental development is humility. This virtue triumphs over the flesh; it is the genius of
24 Christian Science. One can never go up, until one has gone down in his own esteem. Humility is lens and prism to the understanding of Mind-healing; it must be
27 had to understand our textbook; it is indispensable to personal growth, and points out the chart of its divine Principle and rule of practice.

30 Cherish humility, "watch," and "pray without ceasing," or you will miss the way of Truth and Love. Humility is no busybody: it has no moments for trafficking

in other people's business, no place for envy, no time for
idle words, vain amusements, and all the *et cetera* of the
ways and means of personal sense.

Let Christian Scientists minister to the sick; the schoolroom is the *dernier ressort.* Let them seek the lost sheep
who, having strayed from the true fold, have lost their
great Shepherd and yearn to find living pastures and
rest beside still waters. These long for the Christlikeness that is above the present status of religion and beyond the walks of common life, quite on the verge of
heaven. Without the cross and healing, Christianity has
no central emblem, no history.

The seeds of Truth fall by the wayside, on artless
listeners. They fall on stony ground and shallow soil.
The fowls of the air pick them up. Much of what has
been sown has withered away, but what remaineth has
fallen into the good and honest hearts and is bearing
fruit.

The third stage of mental growth is manifested in *love,*
the greatest of all stages and states of being; love that
is irrespective of self, rank, or following. For some time
it has been clear to my thought that those students of
Christian Science whose Christian characters and lives
recommend them, should receive full fellowship from us,
no matter who has taught them. If they have been taught
wrongly, they are not morally responsible for this, and
need special help. They are as lambs that have sought
the true fold and the great Shepherd, and strayed inno-
cently; hence we should be ready and glad to help them
and point the way.

Divine Love is the substance of Christian Science, the
basis of its demonstration, yea, its foundation and super-

1 structure. Love impels good works. Love is greatly
needed, and must be had to mark the way in divine
3 Science.

The student who heals by teaching and teaches by
healing, will graduate under divine honors, which are
6 the only appropriate seals for Christian Science. State
honors perish, and their gain is loss to the Christian
Scientist. They include for him at present naught but
9 tardy justice, hounded footsteps, false laurels. God
alone is his help, his shield and great reward. He that
seeketh aught besides God, loseth in Life, Truth, and
12 Love. All men shall be satisfied when they "awake in
His likeness," and they never should be until then. Human pride is human weakness. Self-knowledge, humility,
15 and love are divine strength. Christ's vestures are put
on only when mortals are "washed in the blood of the
Lamb;" we must walk in the way which Jesus marked
18 out, if we would reach the heaven-crowned summit of
Christian Science.

Be it understood that I do not require Christian Sci-
21 entists to stop teaching, to dissolve their organizations,
or to desist from organizing churches and associations.

The Massachusetts Metaphysical College, the first
24 and only College for teaching Christian Science Mind-
healing, after accomplishing the greatest work of the
ages, and at the pinnacle of prosperity, is closed. Let
27 Scientists who have grown to self-sacrifice do their
present work, awaiting, with staff in hand, God's
commands.

30 When students have fulfilled all the good ends of
organization, and are convinced that by leaving the
material forms thereof a higher spiritual unity is won,

then is the time to follow the example of the *Alma Mater*.  1
Material organization is requisite in the beginning; but
when it has done its work, the purely Christly method  3
of teaching and preaching must be adopted. On the same
principle, you continue the mental argument in the practice of Christian healing until you can cure without it  6
instantaneously, and through Spirit alone.

St. Paul says: "When I was a child, I spake as a
child, I understood as a child, I thought as a child: but  9
when I became a man, I put away childish things. For
now we see through a glass, darkly; but then face to
face." Growth is restricted by forcing humanity out of  12
the proper channels for development, or by holding it in
fetters.

For Jesus to walk the water was scientific, insomuch  15
as he was able to do this; but it is neither wisdom nor
Science for poor humanity to step upon the Atlantic until
we can walk on the water.    18

Peter's impetuosity was rebuked. He had to learn
from experience; so have we. The methods of our
Master were in advance of the period in which he per-  21
sonally appeared; but his example was right, and is
available at the right time. The *way* is absolute divine
Science: walk ye in it; but remember that Science is  24
demonstrated by degrees, and our demonstration rises
only as we rise in the scale of being.

## SCIENCE AND PHILOSOPHY    27

Men give counsel; but they give not the wisdom to
profit by it. To ask wisdom of God, is the beginning of
wisdom.    30

13

1 Meekness, moderating human desire, inspires wisdom
and procures divine power.   Human lives are yet un-
3 carved, — in the rough marble, encumbered with crude,
rude fragments, and awaiting the hammering, chiselling,
and transfiguration from His hand.

6 Great only as good, because fashioned divinely, were
those unpretentious yet colossal characters, Paul and
Jesus.   Theirs were modes of mind cast in the moulds
9 of Christian Science: Paul's, by the supremely natural
transforming power of Truth; and the character of
Jesus, by his original scientific sonship with God.   Phi-
12 losophy never has produced, nor can it reproduce, these
stars of the first magnitude — fixed stars in the heavens
of Soul.   When shall earth be crowned with the true
15 knowledge of Christ?

When Christian Science has melted away the cloud of
false witnesses; and the dews of divine grace, fall-
18 ing upon the blighted flowers of fleeting joys, shall
lift every thought-leaflet Spiritward; and "Israel after
the flesh," who partaketh of its own altars, shall be
21 no more, — then, "the Israel according to Spirit"
shall fill earth with the divine energies, understanding,
and ever-flowing tides of spiritual sensation and con-
24 sciousness.

When mortal mind is silenced by the "still, small voice"
of Truth that regenerates philosophy and logic; and
27 Jesus, as the true idea of Him, is heard as of yore saying
to sensitive ears and dark disciples, "I came from the
Father," "Before Abraham was, I am," coexistent and
30 coeternal with God, — and this idea is understood, —
then will the earth be filled with the true knowledge of
Christ.   No advancing modes of human mind made

Jesus; rather was it their subjugation, and the pure 1
heart that sees God.

When the belief in material origin, mortal mind, sen- 3
sual conception, dissolves through self-imposed suffering,
and its substances are found substanceless, — then its
miscalled life ends in death, and death itself is swallowed 6
up in Life, — spiritual Life, whose myriad forms are
neither material nor mortal.

When every form and mode of evil disappear to hu- 9
man thought, and mollusk and radiate are spiritual concepts testifying to one creator, — then, earth is full of
His glory, and Christian Science has overshadowed all 12
human philosophy, and being is understood in startling
contradiction of human hypotheses; and Socrates, Plato,
Kant, Locke, Berkeley, Tyndall, Darwin, and Spencer 15
sit at the feet of Jesus.

To this great end, Paul admonished, "Let us lay aside
every weight, and the sin which doth so easily beset us, 18
and let us run with patience the race that is set before
us, looking unto Jesus the author and finisher of our
faith." So shall mortals soar to final freedom, and rest 21
from the subtlety of speculative wisdom and human
woe.

God is the only Mind, and His manifestation is the 24
spiritual universe, including man and all eternal individuality. God, the only substance and divine Principle
of creation, is by no means a creative partner in the firm 27
of error, named matter, or mortal mind. He elucidates
His own idea, wherein Principle and idea, God and man,
are not one, but are inseparable as cause and effect. If 30
one, who could say which that "one" was?

His ways are not as our ways. The divine modes

1 and manifestations are not those of the material senses;
for instance, intelligent matter, or mortal mind, material
3 birth, growth, and decay: they are the forever-existing
realities of divine Science; wherein God and man are
perfect, and man's reason is at rest in God's wisdom, —
6 who comprehends and reflects all real mode, form, individuality, identity.

Scholastic dogma has made men blind.  Christ's *logos*
9 gives sight to these blind, ears to these deaf, feet to these
lame, — physically, morally, spiritually.  Theologians
make the mortal mistake of believing that God, having
12 made *all*, made evil; but the Scriptures declare that all
that He made was good.  Then, was evil part and parcel
of His creation?

15  Philosophy hypothetically regards creation as its own
creator, puts cause into effect, and out of nothing would
create something, whose noumenon is mortal mind,
18 with its phenomenon matter, — an evil mind already
doomed, whose modes are material manifestations of
evil, and that continually, until self-extinguished by
21 suffering!

Here revelation must come to the rescue of mortals,
to remove this mental millstone that is dragging them
24 downward, and refute erring reason with the spiritual
cosmos and Science of Soul.  We all must find shelter
from the storm and tempest in the tabernacle of Spirit.
27 Truth is won through Science or suffering: O vain mortals! which shall it be?  And suffering has no reward,
except when it is necessary to prevent sin or reform
30 the sinner.  And pleasure is no crime except when it
strengthens the influence of bad inclinations or lessens
the activities of virtue.  The more nearly an erring so-

called mind approaches purity, the more conscious it  1
becomes of its own unreality, and of the great reality of
divine Mind and true happiness.                          3

The "ego" that claims selfhood in error, and passes
from molecule and monkey up to man, is no ego, but is
simply the supposition that the absence of good is mind  6
and makes men, — when its greatest flatterer, identifica-
tion, is piqued by Him who compensateth vanity with
nothingness, dust with dust!                             9

The mythology of evil and mortality is but the material mode of a suppositional mind; while the immortal
modes of Mind are spiritual, and pass through none of  12
the changes of matter, or evil.   Truth said, and said from
the beginning, "Let us [Spirit] make man perfect;"  and
there is no other Maker: a perfect man would not desire 15
to make himself imperfect, and God is not chargeable
with imperfection.   His modes declare the beauty of holiness, and His manifold wisdom shines through the visible 18
world in glimpses of the eternal verities.   Even through
the mists of mortality is seen the brightness of His
coming.                                                 21

We must avoid the shoals of a sensual religion or
philosophy that misguides reason and affection, and
hold fast to the Principle of Christian Science as the 24
Word that is God, Spirit, and Truth.   This Word corrects the philosopher, confutes the astronomer, exposes
the subtle sophist, and drives diviners mad.   The Bible 27
is the learned man's masterpiece, the ignorant man's
dictionary, the wise man's directory.

I foresee and foresay that every advancing epoch of 30
Truth will be characterized by a more spiritual apprehension of the Scriptures, that will show their marked

1 consonance with the textbook of Christian Science Mind-
healing, "Science and Health with Key to the Scriptures."
3 Interpreting the Word in the "new tongue," whereby
the sick are healed, naturally evokes new paraphrase
from the world of letters. "Wait patiently on the Lord,
6 and He will renew your strength." In return for individual sacrifice, what a recompense to have healed, through
Truth, the sick and sinful, made the public your friend,
9 and posterity your familiar!

Christian Science refutes everything that is not a
postulate of the divine Principle, God. It is the soul of
12 divine philosophy, and there is no other philosophy. It
is not a search after wisdom, it *is* wisdom: it is God's
right hand grasping the universe, — all time, space,
15 immortality, thought, extension, cause, and effect; constituting and governing all identity, individuality, law,
and power. It stands on this Scriptural platform:
18 that He made all that was made, and it is good, reflects
the divine Mind, is governed by it; and that nothing
apart from this Mind, one God, is self-created or evolves
21 the universe.

Human hypotheses predicate matter of Spirit and
evil of good; hence these opposites must either cooperate
24 or quarrel throughout time and eternity, — or until
this impossible partnership is dissolved. If Spirit is the
lawgiver to matter, and good has the same power or
27 modes as evil, it has the same consciousness, and there
is no absolute good. This error, carried to its ultimate,
would either extinguish God and His modes, or give
30 reality and power to evil *ad infinitum*.

Christian Science rends this veil of the temple of gods,
and reproduces the divine philosophy of Jesus and Paul.

This philosophy alone will bear the strain of time and
bring out the glories of eternity; for "other foundation can no man lay than that is laid," which is Christ,
Truth.

Human theories weighed in the balances of God are
found wanting; and their highest endeavors are to Science
what a child's love of pictures is to art. The school whose
schoolmaster is not Christ, gets things wrong, and is ignorant thereof.

If Christian Science lacked the proof of its goodness
and utility, it would destroy itself; for it rests alone on
demonstration. Its genius is right thinking and right
acting, physical and moral harmony; and the secret of
its success lies in supplying the universal need of better
health and better men.

Good health and a more spiritual religion form the
common want, and this want has worked out a moral
result; namely, that mortal mind is calling for what immortal Mind alone can supply. If the uniform moral
and spiritual, as well as physical, effects of divine Science
were lacking, the demand would diminish; but it continues, and increases, which shows the real value of
Christian Science to the race. Even doctors agree that
infidelity, bigotry, or sham has never met the growing
wants of humanity.

As a literature, Christian metaphysics is hampered by
lack of proper terms in which to express what it means.
As a Science, it is held back by the common ignorance
of what it is and of what it does, — and more than all
else, by the impostors that come in its name. To be
appreciated, it must be conscientiously understood and
introduced.

1 If the Bible and "Science and Health with Key to the Scriptures" had in our schools the time or attention that
3 human hypotheses consume, they would advance the world. True, it requires more study to understand and demonstrate what they teach than to learn the doctrine
6 of theology, philosophy, or physics, because they contain and offer Science, with fixed Principle, given rule, and unmistakable proof.

9 The Scriptures give the keynote of Christian Science from Genesis to Revelation, and this is the prolonged tone: "For the Lord He is God, and there is
12 *none beside Him.*" And because He is All-in-all, He is in nothing unlike Himself; and nothing that worketh or maketh a lie is in Him, or can be divine con-
15 sciousness.

At this date, poor jaded humanity needs to get her eyes open to a new style of imposition in the field of
18 medicine and of religion, and to "beware of the leaven of the scribes and Pharisees," the doctrines of men, even as Jesus admonished. From first to last, evil insists on
21 the unity of good and evil as the purpose of God; and on drugs, electricity, and animal magnetism as modes of medicine. To a greater or less extent, all mortal con-
24 clusions start from this false premise, and they necessarily culminate in sickness, sin, disease, and death. Erroneous doctrines never have abated and never will
27 abate dishonesty, self-will, envy, and lust. To destroy sin and its sequence, is the office of Christ, Truth, — according to His mode of Christian Science; and this is
30 being done daily.

The false theories whose names are legion, gilded with sophistry and what Jesus had not, namely, mere book-

learning, — letter without law, gospel, or demonstration, 1
— have no place in Christian Science. This Science requires man to be honest, just, pure;  to love his neighbor 3
as himself, and to love God supremely.

Matter and evil are subjective states of error or mortal
mind.  But Mind is immortal;  and the fact of there 6
being no mortal mind, exposes the lie of suppositional
evil, showing that error is not Mind, substance, or
Life.  Thus, whatever is wrongfully-minded will dis- 9
appear in the proportion that Science is understood,
and the reality of being — goodness and harmony — is
demonstrated.                                      12

Error says that knowing all things implies the necessity of knowing evil, that it dishonors God to claim that
He is ignorant of anything;  but God says of this fruit 15
of the tree of knowledge of *both* good and evil, "In the
day that thou eatest thereof, thou shalt surely die."  If
God is infinite good, He knows nothing but good;  if He 18
did know aught else, He would not be infinite.  Infinite
Mind knows nothing beyond Himself or Herself.  To
good, evil is never present;  for evil is a different state of 21
consciousness.  It was not against evil, but against *knowing* evil, that God forewarned.  He dwelleth in light;
and in the light He sees light, and cannot see darkness. 24
The opposite conclusion, that darkness dwelleth in light,
has neither precedent nor foundation in nature, in logic,
or in the character of Christ.                     27

The senses would say that whatever saves from sin,
must know sin.  Truth replies that God is too pure
to behold iniquity;  and by virtue of His ignorance of 30
that which is not, He knoweth that which *is*, and
abideth in Himself, the only Life, Truth, and Love,

1 — and is reflected by a universe in His own image and likeness.

3 Even so, Father, let the light that shineth in darkness, and the darkness comprehendeth it not, dispel this illusion of the senses, open the eyes of the blind, and cause 6 the deaf to hear.

"Truth forever on the scaffold, Wrong forever on the throne.
Yet that scaffold sways the future, and, behind the dim unknown,
9 Standeth God within the shadow, keeping watch above His own."
LOWELL

## "TAKE HEED!"

12 We regret to be obliged to say that all are not metaphysicians, or Christian Scientists, who call themselves so. Charlatanism, fraud, and malice are getting into 15 the ranks of the good and pure, sending forth a poison more deadly than the upas-tree in the eastern archipelago. This evil obtains in the present false teaching 18 and false practice of the Science of treating disease through Mind. The silent address of a mental malpractitioner can only be portrayed in these words of the apostle, 21 "whisperers," and "the poison of asps is under their tongue."

Some of the mere puppets of the hour are playing 24 only for money, and at a fearful stake. Others, from malice and envy, are working out the destinies of the damned. But while the best, perverted, on the mortal 27 plane may become the worst, let us not forget that the Lord reigns, and that this earth shall some time rejoice in His supreme rule, — that the tired watchmen on the

walls of Zion, and the true Christian Scientist at the foot 1
of the mount of revelation, shall look up with shouts and
thanksgiving, — that God's law, as in divine Science, 3
shall be finally understood; and the gospel of glad tidings
bring "on earth peace, good will toward men."

THE CRY OF CHRISTMAS-TIDE 6

Metaphysics, not physics, enables us to stand erect
on sublime heights, surveying the immeasurable universe
of Mind, peering into the cause which governs all effects, 9
while we are strong in the unity of God and man. There
is "method" in the "madness" of this system, — since
madness it seems to many onlookers. This method sits 12
serene at the portals of the temple of thought, while
the leaders of materialistic schools indulge in mad
antics. Metaphysical healing seeks a wisdom that is 15
higher than a rhubarb tincture or an ipecacuanha pill.
This method is devout enough to trust Christ more than
it does drugs. 18

Meekly we kneel at our Master's feet, for even a crumb
that falleth from his table. We are hungry for Love,
for the white-winged charity that heals and saves; we 21
are tired of theoretic husks, — as tired as was the prodigal son of the carobs which he shared with the swine,
to whom he fed that wholesome but unattractive food. 24
Like him, we would find our Father's house again —
the perfect and eternal Principle of man. We thirst
for inspiring wine from the vine which our Father tends. 27
We crave the privilege of saying to the sick, when their

1 feebleness calls for help, "Rise and walk." We rejoice
to say, in the spirit of our Master, "Stretch forth thy
3 hand, and be whole!"

When the Pharisees saw Jesus do such deeds of mercy,
they went away and took counsel how they might remove
6 him. The antagonistic spirit of evil is still abroad; but
the greater spirit of Christ is also abroad, — risen from
the grave-clothes of tradition and the cave of ignorance.
9 Let the sentinels of Zion's watch-towers shout once
again, "Unto us a child is born, unto us a son is
given."

12 In different ages the divine idea assumes different
forms, according to humanity's needs. In this age it
assumes, more intelligently than ever before, the form
15 of Christian healing. This is the babe we are to cherish.
This is the babe that twines its loving arms about the
neck of omnipotence, and calls forth infinite care from
18 His loving heart.

### BLIND LEADERS

What figure is less favorable than a wolf in sheep's
21 clothing? The braying donkey whose ears stick out is
less troublesome. What manner of man is it that has
discovered an improvement on Christian Science, a "met-
24 aphysical healing" by which error destroys error, and
would gather all sorts into a "national convention" by
the sophistry that such is the true fold for Christian heal-
27 ers, since the good shepherd cares for all?

Yes; the *good* Shepherd does care for all, and His
first care is to separate the sheep from the goats; and

this is among the first lessons on healing taught by our 1
great Master.

If, as the gentleman aforesaid states, large flocks of 3
metaphysicians are wandering about without a leader,
what has opened his eyes to see the need of taking them
out of the care of the great Shepherd, and behold the 6
remedy, to help them by his own leadership? Is it that
he can guide Christian Scientists better than they, through
the guidance of our common Father, can guide them- 9
selves? or is it that they are incapable of helping themselves thus?

I as their teacher can say, They know far more of 12
Christian Science than he who deprecates their condition
appears to, and my heart pleads for them to possess
more and more of Truth and Love; but mixing all grades 15
of persons is not productive of the better sort, although
he who has self-interest in this mixing is apt to propose it.                                              18

Whoever desires to say, "good right, and good wrong,"
has no truth to defend. It is a wise saying that "men
are known by their enemies." To sympathize in any 21
degree with error, is not to rectify it; but error always
strives to unite, in a definition of purpose, with Truth,
to give it buoyancy. What is under the mask, but error 24
in borrowed plumes?

### "CHRIST AND CHRISTMAS"

An Illustrated Poem                                   27

This poem and its illustrations are as hopelessly original as is "Science and Health with Key to the Scrip-

1 tures." When the latter was first issued, critics declared
that it was incorrect, contradictory, unscientific, unchris-
3 tian; but those human opinions had not one feather's
weight in the scales of God. The fact remains, that
the textbook of Christian Science is transforming the
6 universe.

"Christ and Christmas" voices Christian Science
through song and object-lesson. In two weeks from the
9 date of its publication in December, 1893, letters extoll-
ing it were pouring in from artists and poets. A mother
wrote, "Looking at the pictures in your wonderful book
12 has healed my child."

Knowing that this book would produce a stir, I sought
the judgment of sound critics familiar with the works
15 of masters in France and Italy. From them came such
replies as the following: "The illustrations of your poem
are truly a work of art, and the artist seems quite familiar
18 with delineations from the old masters." I am delighted
to find "Christ and Christmas" in accord with the
ancient and most distinguished artists.

21 *The Christian Science Journal* gives no uncertain declaration concerning the spirit and mission of "Christ and
Christmas."

24 I aimed to reproduce, with reverent touch, the modest
glory of divine Science. Not by aid of foreign device
or environment could I copy art, — never having seen
27 the painter's masterpieces; but the *art* of Christian
Science, with true hue and character of the living God,
is akin to its *Science:* and Science and Health gives
30 scopes and shades to the shadows of divinity, thus imparting to humanity the true sense of meekness and
might.

One incident serves to illustrate the simple nature of 1
art.

I insisted upon placing the serpent behind the woman 3
in the picture "Seeking and Finding." My artist at the
easel objected, as he often did, to my sense of Soul's
expression through the brush; but, as usual, he finally 6
yielded. A few days afterward, the following from Roth-
erham's translation of the New Testament was handed
to me, — I had never before seen it: "And the serpent 9
cast out of his mouth, *behind* the woman, water as a
river, that he might cause her to be river-borne." Neither
material finesse, standpoint, nor perspective guides the 12
infinite Mind and spiritual vision that should, does, guide
His children.

One great master clearly delineates Christ's appear- 15
ing in the flesh, and his healing power, as clad not in
soft raiment or gorgeous apparel; and when forced out
of its proper channel, as living feebly, in kings' courts. 18
This master's thought presents a sketch of Christianity's state, in the early part of the Christian era, as
homelessness in a wilderness. But in due time Chris- 21
tianity entered into synagogues, and, as St. Mark
writes, it has rich possession here, with houses and
lands. In Genesis we read that God gave man do- 24
minion over all things; and this assurance is followed
by Jesus' declaration, "All power is given unto me
in heaven and in earth," and by his promise that the 27
Christlike shall finally sit down at the right hand of the
Father.

Christian Science is more than a prophet or a proph- 30
ecy: it presents not words alone, but works, — the daily
demonstration of Truth and Love. Its healing and sav-

1 ing power was so great a proof of Immanuel and the
realism of Christianity, that it caused even the publi-
3 cans to justify God. Although clad in panoply of power,
the Pharisees scorned the spirit of Christ in most of its
varied manifestations. To them it was cant and carica-
6 ture, — always the opposite of what it was. Keen and
alert was their indignation at whatever rebuked hypocrisy
and demanded Christianity in life and religion. In view
9 of this, Jesus said, "Wisdom is justified of all her
children."

Above the fogs of sense and storms of passion, Chris-
12 tian Science and its art will rise triumphant; ignorance,
envy, and hatred — earth's harmless thunder — pluck
not their heaven-born wings. Angels, with overtures,
15 hold charge over both, and announce their Principle and
idea.

It is most fitting that Christian Scientists memorize
18 the nativity of Jesus. To him who brought a great light
to all ages, and named his burdens light, homage is indeed due, — but is bankrupt. I never looked on my
21 ideal of the face of the Nazarite Prophet; but the one
illustrating my poem approximates it.

Extremists in every age either doggedly deny or fran-
24 tically affirm what is what: one renders not unto Cæsar
"the things that are Cæsar's;" the other sees "Helen's
beauty in a brow of Egypt."

27 Pictures are portions of one's ideal, but this ideal is
not one's personality. Looking behind the veil, he that
perceives a semblance between the thinker and his thought
30 on canvas, blames him not.

Because my ideal of an angel is a woman without
*feathers* on her wings, — is it less artistic or less natu-

ral?  Pictures which present disordered phases of ma- 1
terial conceptions and personality blind with animality,
are not my concepts of angels.  What is the material ego, 3
but the counterfeit of the spiritual?

The truest art of Christian Science is to be a Christian Scientist; and it demands more than a Raphael to 6
delineate *this* art.

The following is an extract from a letter reverting to
the illustrations of "Christ and Christmas": — 9

"In my last letter, I did not utter all I felt about the
wonderful new book you have given us.  Years ago,
while in Italy, I studied the old masters and their great 12
works of art thoroughly, and so got quite an idea of
what constitutes true art.  Then I spent two years in
Paris, devoting every moment to the study of music and 15
art.

"The first thing that impressed me in your illustrations was the conscientious application to detail, which 18
is the foundation of true art.  From that, I went on to
study each illustration thoroughly, and to my amazement
and delight I find an almost identical resemblance, in 21
many things, to the old masters!  In other words, the art
is perfect.

"The hands and feet of the figures — how many times 24
have I seen these hands and feet in Angelico's 'Jesus,'
or Botticelli's 'Madonna'!

"It gave me such a thrill of joy as no words can ex- 27
press, to see produced to-day that art — the only true
art — that we have identified with the old masters, and
mourned as belonging to them exclusively, — a thing of 30
the past, impossible of reproduction.

"All that I can say to you, as one who gives no mean

1 attention to such matters, is that the art is perfect. It
is the true art of the oldest, most revered, most authen-
3 tic Italian school, revived. I use the words *most au-
thentic* in the following sense: the face, figure, and
drapery of Jesus, very closely resemble in detail the
6 face, figure, and drapery of that Jesus portrayed by the
oldest of the old masters, and said to have been authen-
tic; the face having been taken by Fra Angelico from
9 Cæsar's Cameo, the figure and garments from a description, in *The Galaxy,* of a small sketch handed down
from the *living reality. Their* productions are expres-
12 sionless copies of an engraving cut in a stone. *Yours*
is a palpitating, living Saviour engraven on the heart.
You have given us back our Jesus, and in a much better
15 form."

<br>

SUNRISE AT PLEASANT VIEW

Who shall describe the brave splendor of a November
18 sky that this morning burst through the lattice for me,
on my bed? According to terrestrial calculations, above
the horizon, in the east, there rose one rod of rainbow
21 hues, crowned with an acre of eldritch ebony. Little
by little this topmost pall, drooping over a deeply dazzling sunlight, softened, grew gray, then gay, and glided
24 into a glory of mottled marvels. Fleecy, faint, fairy
blue and golden flecks came out on a background of
cerulean hue; while the lower lines of light kindled into
27 gold, orange, pink, crimson, violet; and diamond, topaz,
opal, garnet, turquoise, and sapphire spangled the gloom
in celestial space as with the brightness of His glory.
30 Then thought I, What are we, that He who fashions for-

ever such forms and hues of heaven, should move our 1
brush or pen to paint frail fairness or to weave a web
of words that glow with gladdening gleams of God, so 3
unapproachable, and yet so near and full of radiant relief
in clouds and darkness!

# CHAPTER X

## INKLINGS HISTORIC

1 ABOUT the year 1862, while the author of this work
was at Dr. Vail's Hydropathic Institute in New
3 Hampshire, this occurred: A patient considered incurable left that institution, and in a few weeks returned
apparently well, having been healed, as he informed
6 the patients, by one Mr. P. P. Quimby of Portland,
Maine.

After much consultation among ourselves, and a struggle
9 with pride, the author, in company with several other
patients, left the water-cure, *en route* for the aforesaid
doctor in Portland. He proved to be a magnetic practi-
12 tioner. His treatment seemed at first to relieve her, but
signally failed in healing her case.

Having practised homœopathy, it never occurred to the
15 author to learn his practice, but she did ask him how
manipulation could benefit the sick. He answered kindly
and squarely, in substance, "Because it conveys *electricity*
18 to them." That was the sum of what he taught her of
his medical profession.

The readers of my books cannot fail to see that meta-
21 physical therapeutics, as in Christian Science, are farther
removed from such thoughts than the nebulous system
is from the earth.

After treating his patients, Mr. Quimby would retire 1
to an anteroom and write at his desk. I had a curiosity
to know if he indited anything pathological relative to 3
his patients, and asked if I could see his pennings on
my case. He immediately presented them. I read the
copy in his presence, and returned it to him. The com- 6
position was commonplace, mostly descriptive of the general appearance, height, and complexion of the individual,
and the nature of the case: it was not at all metaphysi- 9
cal or scientific; and from his remarks I inferred that
his writings usually ran in the vein of thought presented
by these. He was neither a scholar nor a metaphysician. 12
I never heard him say that matter was not as real as Mind,
or that electricity was not as potential or remedial, or
allude to God as the divine Principle of all healing. He 15
certainly had advanced views of his own, but they commingled error with truth, and were not Science. On
his rare humanity and sympathy one could write a 18
sonnet.

I had already experimented in medicine beyond the
basis of *materia medica,* — up to the highest attenuation 21
in homœopathy, thence to a mental standpoint not understood, and with phenomenally good results; [1] meanwhile, assiduously pondering the solution of this great 24
question: Is it matter, or is it Mind, that heals the
sick?

It was after Mr. Quimby's death that I discovered, 27
in 1866, the momentous facts relating to Mind and its
superiority over matter, and named my discovery Christian Science. Yet, there remained the difficulty of ad- 30
justing in the scale of Science a metaphysical *practice,*

[1] See Science and Health, p. 47, revised edition of 1890, and
pp. 152, 153 in late editions. 33

1 and settling the question, What shall be the outward
sign of such a practice: if a divine Principle alone heals,
3 what is the human modus for demonstrating this, — in
short, how can sinful mortals prove that a divine Principle
heals the sick, as well as governs the universe, time,
6 space, immortality, man?

When contemplating the majesty and magnitude of
this query, it looked as if centuries of spiritual growth
9 were requisite to enable me to elucidate or to demonstrate what I had discovered: but an unlooked-for,
imperative call for help impelled me to begin this stu-
12 pendous work at once, and teach the first student in
Christian Science. Even as when an accident, called
fatal to life, had driven me to discover the Science of
15 Life, I again, in faith, turned to divine help, — and commenced teaching.

My students at first practised in slightly differing
18 forms. Although *I* could heal mentally, without a sign
save the immediate recovery of the sick, my students'
patients, and people generally, called for a sign — a ma-
21 terial evidence wherewith to satisfy the sick that something was being done for them; and I said, "Suffer it
to be so now," for thus saith our Master. Experience,
24 however, taught me the impossibility of demonstrating
the Science of metaphysical healing by any outward form
of practice.

27 In April, 1883, a bill in equity was filed in the United
States Circuit Court in Boston, to restrain, by decree and
order of the Court, the unlawful publishing and use of an
30 infringing pamphlet printed and issued by a student of
Christian Science.

Answer was filed by the defendant, alleging that the

copyrighted works of Mrs. Eddy were not original with
her, but had been copied by her, or by her direction,
from manuscripts originally composed by Dr. P. P.
Quimby.

Testimony was taken on the part of Mrs. Eddy, the
defendant being present personally and by counsel. The
time for taking testimony on the part of the defendant
having nearly expired, he gave notice through his counsel that he should not put in testimony. Later, Mrs.
Eddy requested her lawyer to inquire of defendant's
counsel why he did not present evidence to support his
claim that Dr. Quimby was the author of her writings!
Accordingly, her counsel asked the defendant's counsel
this question, and he replied, in substance, "There is
no evidence to present."

The stipulation for a judgment and a decree in favor
of Mrs. Eddy was drawn up and signed by counsel.
It was ordered that the complainant (Mrs. Eddy)
recover of the defendant her cost of suit, taxed at
($113.09) one hundred thirteen and $\frac{9}{100}$ dollars.

A writ of injunction was issued under the seal of the
said Court, restraining the defendant from directly or
indirectly printing, publishing, selling, giving away,
distributing, or in any way or manner disposing of,
the enjoined pamphlet, on penalty of ten thousand
dollars.

The infringing books, to the number of thirty-eight
hundred or thereabouts, were put under the edge of
the knife, and their unlawful existence destroyed, in
Boston, Massachusetts.

It has been written that "nobody can be both founder
and discoverer of the same thing." If this declaration

1 were either a truism or a rule, my experience would contradict it and prove an exception.

3     No works on the subject of Christian Science existed, prior to my discovery of this Science. Before the publication of my first work on this doctrine, a few manu-
6 scripts of mine were in circulation. The discovery and founding of Christian Science has cost more than thirty years of unremitting toil and unrest; but, comparing those
9 with the joy of knowing that the sinner and the sick are helped thereby, that time and eternity bear witness to this gift of God to the race, I am the debtor.

12     In the latter half of the nineteenth century I discovered the Science of Christianity, and restored the first patient healed in this age by Christian Science. I taught
15 the first student in Christian Science Mind-healing; was author and publisher of the first books on this subject; obtained the first charter for the first Christian Science
18 church, originated its form of government, and was its first pastor. I donated to this church the land on which in 1894 was erected the first church edifice of this de-
21 nomination in Boston; obtained the first and only charter for a metaphysical medical college, — was its first and only president; was editor and proprietor of the first
24 Christian Science periodical; organized the first Christian Scientist Association, wrote its constitution and by-laws, — as also the constitution and by-laws of the
27 National Christian Science Association; and gave it *The Christian Science Journal;* inaugurated our denominational form of Sunday services, Sunday School, and
30 the entire system of teaching and practising Christian Science.

    In 1895 I ordained that the Bible, and "Science and

Health with Key to the Scriptures," the Christian Science 1
textbook, be the pastor, on this planet, of all the churches
of the Christian Science denomination. This ordinance 3
took effect the same year, and met with the universal approval and support of Christian Scientists. Whenever
and wherever a church of Christian Science is established, 6
its pastor is the Bible and my book.

In 1896 it goes without saying, preeminent over ignorance or envy, that Christian Science *is founded by its* 9
*discoverer,* and built upon the rock of Christ. The elements of earth beat in vain against the immortal parapets
of this Science. Erect and eternal, it will go on with the 12
ages, go down the dim posterns of time unharmed, and
on every battle-field rise higher in the estimation of
thinkers and in the hearts of Christians. 15

# CHAPTER XI

## POEMS

### COME THOU

1

C OME, in the minstrel's lay;
3  When two hearts meet,
And true hearts greet,
And all is morn and May.

6 Come Thou! and now, anew,
To thought and deed
Give sober speed,
9 Thy will to know, and do.

Stay! till the storms are o'er —
The cold blasts done,
12  The reign of heaven begun,
And Love, the evermore.

Be patient, waiting heart:
15  Light, Love divine
Is here, and thine;
You therefore cannot part.

18 "The seasons come and go:
Love, like the sea,
Rolls on with thee, —
21 But knows no ebb and flow.

"Faith, hope, and tears, triune,  1
   Above the sod
   Find peace in God,  3
And one eternal noon."

Oh, Thou hast heard my prayer;
   And I am blest!  6
   This is Thy high behest:
Thou, here and *everywhere*.


MEETING OF MY DEPARTED MOTHER AND HUSBAND  9

"Joy for thee, happy friend! thy bark is past
The dangerous sea, and safely moored at last —
      Beyond rough foam.  12
Soft gales celestial, in sweet music bore —
Spirit emancipate for this far shore —
      Thee to thy home.  15

"You've travelled long, and far from mortal joys,
To Soul's diviner sense, that spurns such toys,
      Brave wrestler, lone.  18
Now see thy ever-self; Life never fled;
Man is not mortal, never of the dead:
      The dark unknown.  21

"When hope soared high, and joy was eagle-plumed,
Thy pinions drooped; the flesh was weak, and doomed
      To pass away.  24
But faith triumphant round thy death-couch shed
Majestic forms; and radiant glory sped
      The dawning day.  27

1 "Intensely grand and glorious life's sphere, —
Beyond the shadow, infinite appear
3      Life, Love divine, —
Where mortal yearnings come not, sighs are stilled,
And home and peace and hearts are found and filled,
6      Thine, ever thine.

"Bearest thou no tidings from our loved on earth,
The toiler tireless for Truth's new birth
9      All-unbeguiled?
Our joy is gathered from her parting sigh:
This hour looks on her heart with pitying eye, —
12      What of my child?"

"When, severed by death's dream, I woke to Life,
She deemed I died, and could not know the strife
15      At first to fill
That waking with a love that steady turns
To God; a hope that ever upward yearns,
18      Bowed to His will.

"Years had passed o'er thy broken household band,
When angels beckoned me to this bright land,
21      With thee to meet.
She that has wept o'er thee, kissed my cold brow,
Rears the sad marble to our memory now,
24      In lone retreat.

"By the remembrance of her loyal life,
And parting prayer, I only know my wife,
27      Thy child, shall come —
Where farewells cloud not o'er our ransomed rest —
Hither to reap, with all the crowned and blest,
30      Of bliss the sum.

"When Love's rapt sense the heart-strings gently sweep, 1
With joy divinely fair, the high and deep,
                    To call her home, 3
She shall mount upward unto purer skies;
We shall be waiting, in what glad surprise,
                    Our spirits' own!" 6

## LOVE

Brood o'er us with Thy shelt'ring wing,
   'Neath which our spirits blend 9
Like brother birds, that soar and sing,
   And on the same branch bend.
The arrow that doth wound the dove 12
Darts not from those who watch and love.

If thou the bending reed wouldst break
   By thought or word unkind, 15
Pray that his spirit you partake,
   Who loved and healed mankind:
Seek holy thoughts and heavenly strain, 18
That make men one in love remain.

Learn, too, that wisdom's rod is given
   For faith to kiss, and know; 21
That greetings glorious from high heaven,
   Whence joys supernal flow,
Come from that Love, divinely near, 24
Which chastens pride and earth-born fear,

1  Through God, who gave that word of might
   Which swelled creation's lay:
3  "Let there be light, and there was light."
   What chased the clouds away?
   'T was Love whose finger traced aloud
6  A bow of promise on the cloud.

   Thou to whose power our hope we give,
     Free us from human strife.
9  Fed by Thy love divine we live,
     For Love alone is Life;
   And life most sweet, as heart to heart
12  Speaks kindly when we meet and part.

## WOMAN'S RIGHTS

   Grave on her monumental pile:
15  She won from vice, by virtue's smile,
   Her dazzling crown, her sceptred throne,
   Affection's wreath, a happy home;

18  The right to worship deep and pure,
   To bless the orphan, feed the poor;
   Last at the cross to mourn her Lord,
21  First at the tomb to hear his word:

   To fold an angel's wings below;
   And hover o'er the couch of woe;
24  To nurse the Bethlehem babe so sweet,
   The right to sit at Jesus' feet;

To form the bud for bursting bloom, 1
The hoary head with joy to crown;
In short, the right to work and pray, 3
"To point to heaven and lead the way."

## THE MOTHER'S EVENING PRAYER

O gentle presence, peace and joy and power; 6
  O Life divine, that owns each waiting hour,
Thou Love that guards the nestling's faltering flight!
  Keep Thou my child on upward wing to-night. 9

Love is our refuge; only with mine eye
  Can I behold the snare, the pit, the fall:
His habitation high is here, and nigh, 12
  His arm encircles me, and mine, and all.

O make me glad for every scalding tear,
  For hope deferred, ingratitude, disdain! 15
Wait, and love more for every hate, and fear
  No ill, — since God is good, and loss is gain.

Beneath the shadow of His mighty wing; 18
  In that sweet secret of the narrow way,
Seeking and finding, with the angels sing:
  "Lo, I am with you alway," — watch and pray. 21

No snare, no fowler, pestilence or pain;
  No night drops down upon the troubled breast,
When heaven's aftersmile earth's tear-drops gain, 24
  And mother finds her home and heavenly rest.

1                    JUNE

Whence are thy wooings, gentle June?
3        Thou hast a Naiad's charm;
Thy breezes scent the rose's breath;
    Old Time gives thee her palm.
6    The lark's shrill song doth wake the dawn:
    The eve-bird's forest flute
Gives back some maiden melody,
9        Too pure for aught so mute.


The fairy-peopled world of flowers,
    Enraptured by thy spell,
12    Looks love unto the laughing hours,
    Through woodland, grove, and dell;
And soft thy footstep falls upon
15        The verdant grass it weaves;
To melting murmurs ye have stirred
    The timid, trembling leaves.


18    When sunshine beautifies the shower,
    As smiles through teardrops seen,
Ask of its June, the long-hushed heart,
21        What hath the record been?
And thou wilt find that harmonies,
    In which the Soul hath part,
24    Ne'er perish young, like things of earth,
    In records of the heart.

## WISH AND ITEM

Written to the Editor of the *Item*, Lynn, Mass.

I hope the heart that's hungry          3
    For things above the floor,
Will find within its portals
    An item rich in store;          6

That melancholy mortals
    Will count their mercies o'er,
And learn that Truth and wisdom          9
    Have many items more;

That when a wrong is done us,
    It stirs no thought of strife;          12
And Love becomes the substance,
    As item, of our life;

That every ragged urchin,          15
    With bare feet soiled or sore,
Share God's most tender mercies, —
    Find items at our door.          18

Then if we've done to others
    Some good ne'er told before,
When angels shall repeat it,          21
    'T will be an item more.

1    THE OAK ON THE MOUNTAIN'S SUMMIT

Oh, mountain monarch, at whose feet I stand, —
3 Clouds to adorn thy brow, skies clasp thy hand, —
Nature divine, in harmony profound,
With peaceful presence hath begirt thee round.

6 And thou, majestic oak, from yon high place
Guard'st thou the earth, asleep in night's embrace, —
And from thy lofty summit, pouring down
9 Thy sheltering shade, her noonday glories crown?

Whate'er thy mission, mountain sentinel,
To my lone heart thou art a power and spell;
12 A lesson grave, of life, that teacheth me
To love the Hebrew figure of a tree.

Faithful and patient be my life as thine;
15 As strong to wrestle with the storms of time;
As deeply rooted in a soil of love;
As grandly rising to the heavens above.


18           ISLE OF WIGHT

Written on receiving a painting of the Isle

Isle of beauty, thou art singing
21         To my sense a sweet refrain;
To my busy mem'ry bringing
        Scenes that I would see again.

Chief, the charm of thy reflecting, 1
  Is the moral that it brings;
Nature, with the mind connecting, 3
  Gives the artist's fancy wings.

Soul, sublime 'mid human *débris*,
  Paints the limner's work, I ween, 6
Art and Science, all unweary,
  Lighting up this mortal dream.

Work ill-done within the misty 9
  Mine of human thoughts, we see
Soon abandoned when the Master
  Crowns life's Cliff for such as we. 12

Students wise, he maketh now thus
  Those who fish in waters deep,
When the buried Master hails us 15
  From the shores afar, complete.

Art hath bathed this isthmus-lordling
  In a beauty strong and meek 18
As the rock, whose upward tending
  Points the plane of power to seek.

Isle of beauty, thou art teaching 21
  Lessons long and grand, to-night,
To my heart that would be bleaching
  To thy whiteness, Cliff of Wight. 24

1                    HOPE

'T is borne on the zephyr at eventide's hour;
3 It falls on the heart like the dew on the flower, —
An infinite essence from tropic to pole,
The promise, the home, and the heaven of Soul.

6 Hope happifies life, at the altar or bower,
And loosens the fetters of pride and of power;
It comes through our tears, as the soft summer rain,
9 To beautify, bless, and make joyful again.

The harp of the minstrel, the treasure of time;
A rainbow of rapture, o'erarching, divine;
12 The God-given mandate that speaks from above, —
No place for earth's idols, but hope thou, and love.


                    RONDELET

15              "The flowers of June
        The gates of memory unbar:
            The flowers of June
18      Such old-time harmonies *re*tune,
        I fain would keep the gates ajar, —
        So full of sweet enchantment are
21              The flowers of June."
                        JAMES T. WHITE

### TO MR. JAMES T. WHITE

Who loves not June
Is out of tune
With love and God;
The rose his rival reigns,
The stars reject his pains,
His home the clod!

And yet I trow,
When sweet *rondeau*
Doth play a part,
The curtain drops on June;
Veiled is the modest moon —
Hushed is the heart.

### AUTUMN

*Written in childhood, in a maple grove*

Quickly earth's jewels disappear;
    The turf, whereon I tread,
Ere autumn blanch another year,
    May rest above my head.

Touched by the finger of decay
    Is every earthly love;
For joy, to shun my weary way,
    Is registered above.

The languid brooklets yield their sighs,
    A requiem o'er the tomb
Of sunny days and cloudless skies,
    Enhancing autumn's gloom.

1   The wild winds mutter, howl, and moan,
     To scare my woodland walk,
3   And frightened fancy flees, to roam
     Where ghosts and goblins stalk.

     The cricket's sharp, discordant scream
6     Fills mortal sense with dread;
     More sorrowful it scarce could seem;
     It voices beauty fled.

9   Yet here, upon this faded sod, —
     O happy hours and fleet, —
     When songsters' matin hymns to God
12    Are poured in strains so sweet,

     My heart unbidden joins rehearse;
     I hope it 's better made,
15   When mingling with the universe,
     Beneath the maple's shade.

### CHRIST MY REFUGE

18   O'er waiting harpstrings of the mind
     There sweeps a strain,
     Low, sad, and sweet, whose measures bind
21    The power of pain,

     And wake a white-winged angel throng
     Of thoughts, illumed
24   By faith, and breathed in raptured song,
     With love perfumed.

Then His unveiled, sweet mercies show 1
    Life's burdens light.
I kiss the cross, and wake to know 3
    A world more bright.

And o'er earth's troubled, angry sea
    I see Christ walk, 6
And come to me, and tenderly,
    Divinely talk.

Thus Truth engrounds me on the rock, 9
    Upon Life's shore,
'Gainst which the winds and waves can shock,
    Oh, nevermore! 12

From tired joy and grief afar,
    And nearer Thee, —
Father, where Thine own children are, 15
    I love to be.

My prayer, some daily good to do
    To Thine, for Thee; 18
An offering pure of Love, whereto
    God leadeth me.


## "FEED MY SHEEP" 21

    Shepherd, show me how to go
        O'er the hillside steep,
    How to gather, how to sow, — 24
        How to feed Thy sheep;

1    I will listen for Thy voice,
       Lest my footsteps stray;
3    I will follow and rejoice
       All the rugged way.

     Thou wilt bind the stubborn will,
6      Wound the callous breast,
     Make self-righteousness be still,
       Break earth's stupid rest.
9    Strangers on a barren shore,
       Lab'ring long and lone,
     We would enter by the door,
12       And Thou know'st Thine own;

     So, when day grows dark and cold,
       Tear or triumph harms,
15   Lead Thy lambkins to the fold,
       Take them in Thine arms;
     Feed the hungry, heal the heart,
18       Till the morning's beam;
     White as wool, ere they depart,
       Shepherd, wash them clean.


21              COMMUNION HYMN

     Saw ye my Saviour?   Heard ye the glad sound?
     Felt ye the power of the Word?
24   'T was the Truth that made us free,
     And was found by you and me
     In the life and the love of our Lord.

Mourner, it calls you, — "Come to my bosom,   1
Love wipes your tears all away,
And will lift the shade of gloom,   3
And for you make radiant room
Midst the glories of one endless day."

Sinner, it calls you, — "Come to this fountain,   6
Cleanse the foul senses within;
'T is the Spirit that makes pure,
That exalts thee, and will cure   9
All thy sorrow and sickness and sin."

Strongest deliverer, friend of the friendless,
Life of all being divine:   12
Thou the Christ, and not the creed;
Thou the Truth in thought and deed;
Thou the water, the bread, and the wine.   15

### LAUS DEO!

Written on laying the corner-stone of The Mother Church

*Laus Deo,* it is done!   18
Rolled away from loving heart
    Is a stone.
Lifted higher, we depart,   21
    Having one.

*Laus Deo,* — on this rock
(Heaven chiselled squarely good)   24
    Stands His church, —
God is Love, and understood
    By His flock.   27

*Laus Deo*, night star-lit
Slumbers not in God's embrace;
       Be awake;
Like this stone, be in thy place:
       Stand, not sit.

Grave, silent, steadfast stone,
Dirge and song and shoutings low
       In thy heart
Dwell serene, — and sorrow?  No,
       It has none,
       *Laus Deo!*

## A VERSE

### MOTHER'S NEW YEAR GIFT TO THE LITTLE CHILDREN

Father-Mother God,
       Loving me, —
Guard me when I sleep;
Guide my little feet
       Up to Thee.

### TO THE BIG CHILDREN

Father-Mother good, lovingly
       Thee I seek, —
       Patient, meek,
In the way Thou hast, —
Be it slow or fast,
       Up to Thee.

# CHAPTER XII

## TESTIMONIALS

### LETTERS FROM THOSE HEALED BY READING "SCIENCE AND HEALTH WITH KEY TO THE SCRIPTURES"

The Editor of *The Christian Science Journal* (Falmouth and St. Paul Streets, Boston, Mass.) holds the original of most of the letters that authenticate these.

IT is something more than a year and a half since I was cured of a complication of diseases through reading "Science and Health with Key to the Scriptures."

Becoming at an early age disgusted with drugs, I learned hygiene, and practised it faithfully for over twenty years; then I began to lose all faith in its efficacy, became greatly discouraged, and, as I had never been cured of a single ailment, I rapidly grew worse in health. Hearing of this, a dear sister brought me Science and Health. Her admonition was, "Now read it, E——; I have heard that just the reading of that book has been known to heal the sick."

I had read to, and through, the chapter on Healing and Teaching,[1] and was so deeply interested that I began reading that blessed chapter over again, — when I found I was cured of my dyspepsia, that I could use my strength in lifting without feeling the old distressing pain in my side, and also that the pain in the kidneys only came on

---

[1] Page 292 of the revised edition of 1890.

at night, waking me out of sleep. Then I began my first conscious treatments: of course I followed no formula, and I needed none. A cry for help, knowing it would be answered; precious texts from the Bible, which had already become like a new book to me; sweet assurance of faith by the witnessing Spirit; strong logical conclusions, learned from Science and Health: what a wealth of material! Before finishing the book, all tendency to my old aches and pains had left me, and I have been a strong, healthy woman ever since.

My first demonstration with another than myself was also before I had finished my first reading. My husband was cured of the belief of bilious fever by not over ten minutes' treatment; the fever and pain in head and limbs disappearing in that instantaneous way as soon as I could summon sufficient courage to offer my services in this, to us, new but glorious work. He slept soundly that night (the treatment was given about 10 A. M.), and ate and worked as usual the next day, with no symptoms of a relapse then or afterward. That was in March, 1888; in the following August I met in one of our Rocky Mountain berry patches a lady who complained so bitterly that I felt compelled to offer her treatment. Her words, when I visited her at her home during Christmas week, will give some idea of the result: —

"Yes, I am doing three women's work, — attending to my own and my son's housework, and caring for his wife and new-born babe; but I am equal to it, when I think of all the Lord has done for me! Why, Mrs. S., I was cured with that first treatment you gave me, I know; because I went out to gather berries that day and was caught in a drenching shower, — and for ten years before

I could not bear the least exposure without suffering from those dreadful headaches I told you about, and from dysentery, — but that day I had neither. I had once been laid out for dead, — lying there perfectly conscious, hearing my friends grieving over me, — but I did not want to come to, I suffered so. No, I never have any of those ailments. I am a well, hearty woman, — and that is not all. I had been seeking religion for more than twenty years, but I never knew how Christians felt till I told you I was cured that day on the camp-ground."

On the first of this year I was so blessed as to receive a course of lessons from one of our teacher's students. Now I am only trusting that the time will come when I may be enabled to teach others the way of Truth, as well as to add to the many demonstrations God has given me. — E. D. S.

A student of Christian Science was employed in the Massachusetts State Prison at Charlestown, to teach the prisoners to make shoes. He carried his copy of "Science and Health with Key to the Scriptures" and the *Journal* with him, and as he had the opportunity would tell the men what this wonderful truth could do for them, setting them free in a larger and higher sense than they had dreamed of.

We make extracts from a number of letters that one of the prisoners has written to those who are interesting themselves in this work.

"*Editor of The Christian Science Journal:* — At the prison, once a week, there are Christian papers given to the inmates. But none of those papers point out so clearly the fallibility of the mortal or carnal mind, and the infallibility of the divine Mind, as does the teaching of Christian Science.

"I was strangely blind and stupid. I loved sin, and it seemed as though I never would be able to forsake it. I did everything that would be expected of one entirely ignorant of God.

"I also had a complication of diseases. I could not begin to describe the medicines I have taken.

"I no longer look for material treatment, but humbly seek for the divine assistance of Jesus, through the way Christian Science has taught me. I am, indeed, an altered man. I now have no more doubt of the way of salvation than I have of the way to the prison workshop.

"I am very grateful to the students of Christian Science, for the interest they have taken in me and my fellow-prisoners. Their letters and books have been of great profit, and in accordance with their wish I have done what I could for the others.

"I gave the *Journal* to every man who would accept it, and related my experience to those who would listen. I told them they need go no farther than myself to see what the demonstration was; for not only have my eyes been healed, but many other ailments have disappeared.

"Some of the fellows told me I was becoming religiously insane, but acting upon your advice, I did not stop to argue with those opposed; and I am glad to be able to tell you that those who expressed interest were more than those who opposed.

"The chaplain told me I could keep Science and Health until I got through with it. I never should get through with that book, but, as others were waiting for it, I did not like to keep it too long.  God bless the author!

"I need have no fear after leaving here; I feel that I can make an honest living.  I can honestly add, that my bad reputation is largely due to my lack of education.  What little I do know, I learned here and in the House of Correction.  I tell you this, for I feel that I must be honest with the kind friends who have done so much for me.

"Providing I should not be paroled, I shall remain here until the 24th of next December.  God bless you all. — J. C."

I am glad to tell how I was healed.  Beliefs of consumption, dyspepsia, neuralgia, piles, tobacco, and bad language held me in bondage for many years.  Doctors that were consulted did nothing to relieve me, and I constantly grew worse.  Nearly two years ago a lady told me that if I would read a book called "Science and Health with Key to the Scriptures" I would be healed.  I told her I would "go into it for all it is worth," and I have found that it is worth all.  I got the book, and read day and night.  I saw that it must be true, and believed that what I could not then understand would be made clear later.

After some days' reading I was affected with drowsiness, followed by vomiting.  This lasted several hours; when I fell into a sleep, and awoke healed.  The good I have received, and that I have been able to do in healing others, has all come from Science and Health.  I received some instructions from teachers; but they did me more

harm than good: I asked for bread, but they gave me a
stone. I held to what I could understand of Science and
Health; and the truth does not forsake me, but enables
me to heal others.

Last February, I was called to treat a child that the
M. D.'s said was dying from lung fever; after the third
treatment the child got up and ran about, completely
healed. Another child was brought to me, with rupture;
after the second treatment the truss was thrown away.
An aged lady was healed of heart disease and chills, in
one treatment. These cases brought me many more, that
were also healed.

The husband of a lady in the State Lunatic Asylum
asked me to treat her; she had been for two years and
a half in the asylum, and though taken home in this time
once or twice, she had had to be taken back. After two
weeks of absent treatment, the husband visited her, and
the doctor reported great improvement during the pre-
ceding two weeks. At the end of another two weeks I
went with the husband to the asylum, and the doctor told
us that she was well enough to go home. The husband
asked the doctor how it was that she had improved so
rapidly, and he said that he could not account for it. We
said nothing about the Christian Science treatment, and
took the lady home. This was about a year ago, and she
has remained perfectly well.

Many cases as striking as this can be referred to in
this town, as evidence that Truth is the healer of sickness
as well as of sin. — J. B. H.

No. 1. A lady friend, who was found to have a severe
attack of dysentery, was assured that such attacks could

be cured without medicine, and advised to take no more. She was more than astonished at the result; for in less than an hour all pain and other symptoms of the trouble ceased, and she felt perfectly well the next day.

No. 2.   While she was visiting relatives in the country, an infant of theirs was attacked severely with croup, and appeared to be on the verge of suffocation, giving its parents much alarm.   The infant was taken in the arms of the lady, in thirty minutes was completely relieved, went to sleep, and awoke in good health the next morning.

No. 3.   The mother of this child was subsequently attacked with a scrofulous swelling on the neck, just under the ear, which was very painful and disfiguring; the side of the face, also, being badly swollen.   It was feared that this would develop into and undergo the usual phenomenon of abscess, as other similar swellings had done previously.   She had great faith in the metaphysical treatment, because of the experience which she had had with her baby, and wrote a letter describing her case.   This was immediately answered, and absent treatment was begun.   In twenty-four hours after receipt of the letter, to the astonishment of herself and family, the tumor had entirely disappeared: there was not a trace of it left; although the day before it was fully as large as a hen's egg; red, and tender to the touch.

These instances are only a few of the many cures which have been performed in this way, and they are mentioned simply to show what good work may be done by any earnest, conscientious person who has gained by reading my works the proper understanding of the Principle of Christian Science.

What a wonderful field for enlightenment and profit lies open to those who seek after Truth. Alas, that the feet of so few enter it!

*Rev. M. B. G. Eddy:* — Will you kindly spare me a few moments for the perusal of these lines from a stranger, — one who feels under a debt of gratitude to you, — for, through the divine Science brought to light by you, I have been "made whole." I have been cured of a malignant cancer since I began to study Christian Science, and have *demonstrated the truth* of it in a number of cases. I have only studied your good books, having been *unable* to take the lectures for want of means. I dare not think of these, for there is no prospect that I shall be in a position to take the course at all. I do not allow myself to complain, but cheerfully take up my books and study, and feel thankful for this light.

M. E. W., Cañon City, Col.

*Dear Madam:* — May I thank you for your book, "Science and Health with Key to the Scriptures," and say how much I owe to it — almost my very life — at a most critical time. . . .

If it were not for the heat of your American summers (I had nine attacks of dysentery in the last one), and the expense, I should dearly like to learn from you personally; but I must forego this, — at any rate, for the present. If you would write me what the cost would be for a course on divine metaphysics, I would try to manage it later on.

Meanwhile, I should be grateful if you would refer me to any one in this country who is interested similarly, for I get more kicks than halfpence in discussing it.

Your obliged friend,   (REV.) I. G. W. BISHOP,

Bovington Vicarage, Hemel Hempstead,
Herts, England

Extract from a letter to Rev. M. B. G. Eddy

A gentleman here had hired all the most skilled doctors in the United States — nothing helped him.   He was a ghost to look upon.   I told him just to read my copies of your books.   I talked to him, told him what he could do for himself if he but tried.   He laughed at me.   I was willing he should laugh, for it was very unusual for him to do this.   He had your books two months, and last Sunday he returned them.   I wish you could see him: *he is well*.   He is happy, and told me he was going to write to you for the books for himself this week. — E. E. B.

*Dear Madam:* — I have been a sickly person all my life, until a few months ago, and was confined to my bed every little while.   It was during one of many attacks that your book, "Science and Health with Key to the Scriptures," was handed me.   I read it only a very short time, when I arose, well, went out into the kitchen, prepared a large dinner, and ate heartily of it.

I have been up and well ever since, — a marvel to my friends and family, and sometimes they can hardly believe it is I;  and feeling so grateful, I must tell you of it. I wish everybody in the world would read your book, for all would be benefited by it.

Gratefully yours,      ANNA M. SMITH

*Dear Madam:* — About seven years ago I was compelled to go to an oculist and have an operation performed upon my eyes. He fitted me with glasses, which I wore for a considerable time, and then removed; but the pain and difficulty returned, and I was obliged to go again to the oculist, who advised me never to take my glasses off again.

I continued wearing them for fully five years longer, until some time in last January, when, upon reading your book, "Science and Health with Key to the Scriptures," I again took them off. Since that time, though I have been in the courts reporting, and reading fine notes frequently, I have experienced no difficulty with my eyes.

Very respectfully,

WILLIAM A. SMITH, Wilmington, Del.

*Dear Mrs. Eddy:* — We have been studying "Science and Health with Key to the Scriptures" for a year, and I cannot tell you how much it has done for us; giving us health instead of sickness, and giving us such an understanding of God as we never had before. Christian Science was our only help two weeks ago, when our baby was born. My husband and myself were alone. I dressed myself the next day; commenced doing my work the third day, and am well and strong. It must be pleasing to you to know how much good your work is doing.

KITTIE BECK, Elmwood, Cass Co., Neb.

I was a helpless sufferer in August, 1883, and had been so for many years. The physicians said I had cancer of the uterus. I heard of your book, "Science and Health with Key to the Scriptures," bought a copy, began reading it, and a great light seemed to break through the darkness. I cried aloud in joy, "This is what I have been hungering for, these many years!" I studied it closely, and healed myself and several of my friends before I had taken instruction of any teacher.

Mrs. S. A. McMahon, Wyandotte, Kans.

I was healed thoroughly of the belief of chronic hepatitis and kidney disease, by reading "Science and Health with Key to the Scriptures." I have never, to this day, had the slightest return of it.

J. P. Filbert, Council Bluffs, Iowa

You, dear Mrs. Eddy, have saved my life, through Science and Health; and I feel that the patients healed through me should give the first thanks to God and to you. — Mrs. D. S. Harriman, Kansas City, Mo.

How grand your book, "Science and Health with Key to the Scriptures," is! It is a translation of Truth. No amount of money could buy the book of me, if I could not get another. No matter what suffering comes, physical or mental, I have only to take Science and Health, and almost invariably the first sentence brings relief. It seems to steady the thought. I do not think any student old enough to neglect reading it. When we think we are advanced far enough to let that book alone, then are we in danger.

MRS. ELLEN P. CLARK, Dorchester, Mass.

Many thanks for the good received from your books. When I commenced reading them, I was carrying about a very sick body. Your books have healed me. I am now in perfect health. People look at me with surprise, and say they do not understand it; but when they see the sick ones made well, they are not always willing to believe it.

MRS. JOSEPH TILLSON, South Hanson, Mass.

*Rev. M. B. G. Eddy:* — I add one more testimony of a cure from reading your book, "Science and Health with Key to the Scriptures." Five years ago I lay prostrate with piles and inflammation of the bowels. All the coating came off, apparently. A stricture was formed, beyond medical reach. I then lived in Chicago; one of the best physicians, who made a specialty of treating piles, attended me. The pain was relieved, but my bowels were inactive, and remained so until New Year's eve.

I determined to trust all to God, or die before I would take any more medicine, as I never had an action unless I took a free dose of some laxative. If I forgot to take the medicine one night, or allowed myself to be without it, I had a terrible sick headache for two or three days, and terrible backache. I never had backache at any other time, and the piles would be so much inflamed, in two days' time, that I could hardly tell where I suffered the worst.

Since I have learned to trust all to God, I have not had the least trouble with the piles, nor one twinge of the backache. I have an easy action of the bowels each morning. It was five days after I resolved to leave medicine alone, before a natural movement took place; and ever since I have been perfectly regular. It was a great effort for me to take that step, for I knew I was running the risk of throwing myself back into all misery, and perhaps into a worse state than before. By reading Science and Health, I learned that God was able to save the body as well as the soul, and I believed His promises were for me.

MATTIE E. MAYFIELD, Des Moines, Iowa

For the Cause of Truth, I submit the following testimonial for publication; may it bring *one* more, at least, into the fold of divine Science! The truth, as it is stated in "Science and Health with Key to the Scriptures," has done much towards making our home the abiding-place of peace and harmony. I now write of the wonderful demonstration of Truth over the birth of my baby boy, two weeks ago. Sunday, September 23, we went for a long drive of three hours; at night I retired at the usual hour; toward morning I was given a little warning; when I awoke at seven o'clock, the birth took place. Not more than ten minutes after, I ate a hearty breakfast, and then had a refreshing sleep; at ten o'clock walked across the room while my bed was dressed; at twelve took a substantial dinner; most of the afternoon sat up in bed, without any support but Truth; at six in the evening dressed myself and walked to the dining-room, and remained up for two hours. Next morning I arose at the usual hour, and have kept it up ever since, — was not confined to my bed one whole day. The second day was out walking in the yard, and the third day went for a drive in the morning and received callers in the afternoon. If it had not been for the presence of my young hopeful, it would have been hard to believe that there had so recently been a belief of a birth in the house; but then, I was sustained by Love, and had no belief of suffering to take my strength away. Before baby was two weeks old, I cooked, swept, ran the sewing machine, etc., assisting with the housework generally. How grateful I am for the obstetrics of this grand Science! Mothers need no longer listen to the whispering lies of the old serpent, for the law of mortal mind is broken by Truth.

Mrs. Dora Hossick, Carrolton, Mo.

My wife and I have been healed by reading your book, "Science and Health with Key to the Scriptures." We both feel very grateful to you.

Five months ago my wife gave birth to a child, without pain or inconvenience, has done all the housework since, and has been every minute perfectly well. Neither she nor the child have been ill, — as was constantly the case with former children, — so we have thought it right to name the child Glover Eddy.

We have been reading Science and Health nearly

two years, and have sold several copies to others. We are reading the *Journal* also this year.

Yours respectfully, JOHN B. HOUSEL, Lincoln, Neb.

*Dear Mother:* — The most blessed of women! Oh, how I long to sit within range of your voice and hear the truth that comes to you from on high! for none could speak such wondrous thoughts as have come from your pen, except it be the Spirit that speaketh in you.

Two years ago last October, while laboring under a great strain of care and anxiety in regard to financial affairs, I heard of Christian Science. I borrowed "Science and Health with Key to the Scriptures," and began to read. I bless God that I was driven to it by such an extremity. After reading some one hundred and fifty pages, I was convinced that it was the truth for which I had searched during twenty years. While I was reading the chapter on Imposition and Demonstration,[1] I was healed of endometritis and prolapsus uteri of over twenty years' standing, pronounced incurable by eminent physicians. Professor Ludlam, the dean of Hahnemann Medical College, of Chicago, Ill., was one of my doctors.

Before I was healed, to walk seven or eight blocks would so fatigue me that it would take me a week to recover. I now started out and walked, and was on my feet all day and for several succeeding days, but felt no weariness from my labors.

I felt, after being healed, I must have a Science and Health of my own. I had no money to buy it, so earned

---

[1] Page 234, revised edition of 1890.

it by getting subscribers for the *Journal*. It has gone with me everywhere I have been. I have been well ever since.

I had suffered from bodily ailments, but they were nothing compared to my mental trials. Grief, hatred, jealousy, and revenge had well-nigh bereft me of reason. I had lost a home of plenty, been reduced to almost abject poverty, and had become a cheerless woman, — could not smile without feeling I had sinned.

All my griefs and sorrows are now turned to joy, and my hatred is changed to love. "Glory to God in the highest, and on earth peace, good will toward men." I read Science and Health, and all your other books, together with the New Testament, every minute I can get. — E. B. C., Omaha, Neb.

I must add one more to your great pile of letters, to tell you what your book, "Science and Health with Key to the Scriptures," has done for me and my family. More than a year ago, my husband was suffering from an injury received about a year previous, and he went to Mrs. B. for treatment. His shoulder had been fractured, his collar-bone broken, and he had sustained internal injuries. Several M. D.'s had attended him, but had given him very little relief. Mrs. B. treated him a short time, and he received much benefit. He bought Science and Health. From reading it, I was cured of a belief of chronic liver complaint. I suffered so much from headaches and constipation, and other beliefs, that I seldom ever saw a well day; but, thanks to you and divine Principle, I now seldom ever have a belief of feeling badly.

November 4th, last, I was confined. I was alone, because I knew no one whose thought was in harmony with Science. I thought I could get along without help, and I did. My little girl was sleeping in the same room with me, and after the birth she called a woman who was asleep upstairs, to take care of the baby. This woman was much frightened; but, on seeing how composed I was, she got over her fright. I was sitting up in bed, holding the child, and feeling as well as I ever did in my life. I never had seen a Scientist nor been treated, but got all my ideas from Science and Health. My baby was born on Sunday morning, and I got up Monday at noon, and stayed up. I never got along so well with a baby as I did with this one.

I am very thankful for the knowledge of Science I have gained through your book. I want so much to be a Scientist; but we are very poor. My husband is a brakeman on the railroad; and I have very little education. There is comfort in the thought that, if I can't be a Scientist, my children may be.

Yours with much love, C. A. W., Lexington, Mo.

In the February *Journal* it appears there is some one who says that "Science and Health with Key to the Scriptures" is hard to understand, and who thinks she can explain it. Perhaps my experience with Science and Health may help some one who might otherwise take up this thought, and so be led away from the truth. After reading and studying it for some time, and talking to the Scientists I met in my travels, the thought came to me, "Why not try these truths on yourself?" I did so, and to my surprise and great joy I found immediate relief. Dyspepsia (the trouble of most commercial travellers), catarrh, and many lesser beliefs, left me, so that in a short time I was a *well man,* and by no other means than trusting to the Saviour's promises as explained in Science and Health. This took place while I was travelling about the country.

On my return home, I gave my wife treatments. In many instances the blessing came before the treatment was finished, and often we proved that only a thought of the power of Truth was sufficient to give relief.

One Sunday morning, soon after my return, a friend called and asked if I could give him anything to relieve his wife, who, he said, had been suffering for some days with rheumatism in her shoulder, so severely that she could neither dress alone nor comb her hair. I told him that the only medicine we had in the house was Christian Science. He laughed at the idea; but before he left, he asked if I would give his wife a treatment. I told him I was very young in Science, but if she wished it, I would. He went home, but returned immediately, saying she wished me to come. Then I asked help from the fountain of Truth, and started for my first treatment to be given away from home. When I left their room fifteen minutes later, she was shaking her hand high above her head, and exclaiming, "I am all right; I am well!" That was in November, 1887, and she has had no return of the belief since.

A friend told me that his son, twelve years old, had catarrh so badly that his breath was very offensive, his throat troubled him all the time, and that he had been deaf since he had the measles. In less than three weeks both beliefs vanished. This was a case of absent treatment. I could give you other cases, but I think I have said enough to prove that Science and Health *is not hard to understand,* for my work has all been done without my ever attending class.

                              H. H. B., New York City

A lady, with no other instructor than "Science and Health with Key to the Scriptures," has demonstrated beyond many who have taken numerous lessons. Persuaded, through her reading, of the allness of God, — and the perfectness of idea, — she would know nothing else. A daughter, so badly affected by poison oak (ivy) that for weeks death was feared from blood-poisoning, had recovered with a terrible dread of that plant. As the next season's picnic time drew near, she was regretting that she dared not go again. The mother, with her new-born faith in the Science of being, said, "Certainly you can go, for nothing can harm you." Assured by these words, the daughter went, and in her rambles fell into a mass of the dreaded plant; but trusting to the word of Truth, she thought nothing of it till one who knew of her previous trouble said, in her mother's presence, "See, her face is showing red already." But the mother was prompt in denial and assurance. Next morning, old symptoms were out in force, but they yielded at once and finally to the positive and uncompromising hold on Truth. Another daughter, that was thought too delicate to raise, from bronchial and nervous troubles, always dosed with medicine and wrapped in flannels, now runs free and well without either of these, winter and summer. The mother was recently attacked by mesmerism from the church that believed she was influencing her daughter to leave. She overcame by the same unwavering trust in God, seeing Truth clearer than ever before. Her demonstrations come through no form of treatment, but by letting the Spirit bear witness, — by the positive recognition and realization of no reality but ever-present good.

The other night her husband was attacked with an old belief, similar to one that some time before had ended in a congestive chill which the doctor thought very serious, and from which he had been a long time in recovering. The wife simply recognized no reality in the belief, and, seeing only perfect being, felt no fear. She did nothing, — no "treating" in the usual sense. There is nothing to do but to understand that all is harmony, always. He felt the presence that destroys the sense of evil, and next morning — there was nothing left to recover from.

A lady, while doing some starching, thoughtlessly put her hand into the scalding starch to wring out a collar. Recalled to mortal sense by the stinging pain, she immediately realized the all-power of God. At once the pain began to subside; and as she brushed off the scalding starch, she could see the blister-swelling go down till there was but a little redness to show for the accident; absorbed in her thankfulness, she mechanically wrung out the collar with the same hand, and with no sense of pain, thus verifying the demonstration. This woman (not reading English) only knows Science as she has received it from her practitioner during the treatments received within the last month. So much has come to her from Spirit through her loyalty to Christ, in so far as she could understand.

A case of ulcerated tooth and neuralgic belief would only partially yield after repeated treatments, till it was discovered that the patient was antagonizing Truth by holding the thought that her old remedy, laudanum, would give relief; treated from this standpoint, relief was immediate and final.

One morning after Rev. —— had been preaching to thousands for several days, he told them that he had never felt such a sense of depression nor had so little showing of results. Some Scientists hearing this, at once saw his trouble. He had been fearlessly exposing and denouncing evil; and it had turned on him, till the mesmerism was likely to overcome him entirely, for he did not understand the seeming power. The effect of the silent word to uplift and sustain, was very manifest that evening in his preaching, and was a beautiful demonstration of Science. He probably only felt Spirit-inspiration as he had not before, without a thought as to what had broken the evil spell; but we never know the what, or when, or where, of the harvest we can sow — "God giveth the increase." — E. H. B., Sacramento

I had two German patients who were anxious to have you publish "Science and Health with Key to the Scriptures" in their language. I advised them to buy it and try to read it. They commenced reading, and now can read all of Science and Health, but do not read well any other book or paper, and they do not need to.  With great love. — M. H. P.

I sold three copies of "Science and Health with Key to the Scriptures" to friends, not long ago.  One of them, fifty years of age, said to me, "I never had one day's sickness in my life;  but after reading Science and Health I found that I was bruised and mangled, from the crown of my head to the soles of my feet.  I have been reaching after something that, before reading Science and Health, seemed to me unattainable;"  and with tears in her eyes, she rejoiced in the God of her salvation. Did not Jesus say, "If these should hold their peace, the stones would immediately cry out"?

P. L., Lexington, Ky.

For eight years I suffered terribly with my eyes;  I could not read fifteen minutes without the most agonizing sick headache.  Oculists called it a case of double vision, and said that the only chance for a cure lay in cutting the muscles of the eyes.  This was done, but the pain was worse than before.  One of the most famous oculists of New York said I would simply have to endure it for life, as it was a case of severe astigmatism.

I suffered so that my health gave way.  A friend spoke to me of Christian Science, but I scoffed at the idea. Later on, in desperation, I asked her to lend me "Science and Health with Key to the Scriptures," thinking I might be able to read five minutes a day in it.  I opened the book at the chapter on Physiology, and began. Time passed unnoticed: every page seemed illuminated. I said, "This is everything or nothing; if everything, then you need no glasses." I took off the heavy ground glasses, and went on. What a terrible headache I had the next morning! but I fought it with the truth laid down in the book. I said again, "This is everything or nothing," and the truth triumphed. The headache ceased, but I felt miserably. I recalled what was said about chemicalization, and persevered.

In four days my eyes were well; I read as many hours a day as I pleased; my strength returned. I conquered one belief after another, until now, strong and well, I meet every belief with confidence. "I will fear *no* evil: for *Thou* art with me." For two years I have realized the peace and confidence which the knowledge that God is all-powerful and always present alone can give. Feeling a great desire to spread Christian Science, that it may do the good to others that it has to me, not only physically but spiritually, I ask if you have any missionaries in the work. Being a member of the Episcopal Church, I have always sent what I could to help foreign missions through that church. Will it do the most good to continue so doing, as our foreign missionaries are devoted men, or have you Christian Science missionaries who devote their lives to the work?

An answer addressed to me, or published in the *Journal*, would help one who is seeking to do right.

Yours sincerely,          K. L. T.

I do wish to add my testimony of being healed by reading "Science and Health with Key to the Scrip-

15

tures." I had been an invalid for over twenty years, and had given up all hope of ever being well again. I had read the book about six weeks, when it seemed I was made all over new, and I could "run, and not be weary; and . . . walk, and not faint." I did not understand it, but it was the savior from death unto life with me; I have remained well ever since I was healed, — more than five years ago. I commenced to treat others as soon as I was born anew into the kingdom of Truth. My patients were healed right along, before I had taken lessons in a class, and they have remained well to this day.

Christian Science has made me as young as a girl of sixteen. If this should meet the eye of any sufferers who may be led to go and do as I did, they will be healed. — N. A. E.

Language is inadequate when bearing grateful testimony to the book "Science and Health with Key to the Scriptures." By its simple reading, I was healed of ills which baffled the skill of specialists and all curatives that love and money could command. After eighteen years of invalidism, and eight years of scepticism, without hope, with no God, — except a First Cause, — I was given up to die.

A loving friend told me of this book, which was soon brought; and thirty-five pages of the first chapter were read to me that evening. The next morning I got up, walked, and read the book for myself.

I mention the chapter, for the reason that nearly two years have passed since those wonderful words of Life were first read to me, and *still* their sacred sweetness is ever the same. Now I exclaim, *God is* All!

MRS. MARY A. R.

It is impossible for me to keep still any longer. In 1885, when I had not known a well day in five years, "Science and Health with Key to the Scriptures" was placed in my hands by a dear lady who insisted upon my reading it, saying she believed it would heal me. Like many, I was afraid of it, — until I learned what it really was. The friend's words were verified. I *was* healed by the reading of the book, and for one year continued to read nothing whatever but the Bible and Science and Health. They were my constant study. Through the understanding gained, that *God is All,* I came to demonstrate with great success, and with but one thought, — for I knew nothing about giving a "treatment;" I wish I knew as little now, for I believe that healing in Christian Science is to be done in a moment. I became anxious to learn more, to study with the teacher, but funds would not allow, — and I thought to substitute a course in Chicago, perhaps. Every time I would speak of it, however, my dear mother would say, "You have Science and Health and the Bible, and God for your teacher — what more do you need? If I could not go to the teacher, I would not go to any one."

If I had only heeded the blessed counsel of Truth!

I went to Chicago, however, so full of confidence in Christian Science that I supposed every one who had studied with Mrs. Eddy must be right. Unfortunately, I took my course with a spiritualist who had been through two of her classes; discovered my mistake, and went to a mind-cure, — only to find the mistake repeated. Being an earnest seeker for Truth, I tried again to go to the Massachusetts Metaphysical College; but it was uncertain when there would be a class, so I took a course with one of Mrs. Eddy's students in Boston. The darkness now rolled away. Science and Health once more revealed the light to me as of old.

All this time, the mind-curers had me in view, and were sending me reading-matter; but, *praise the Lord!* Truth is victorious.

My dear brothers and sisters, let us be safely guided by the counsels of our Mother, in Science and Health! I, for one, am astounded that I was so led astray; but I did it all through ignorance, — and the *sincere* desire to know the truth and to *do* it, saved me.

Your sister in truth,          R. D.

I have been reading Science and Health for one year and a half, and have had some wonderful demonstrations. People here are antagonistic to the Science, and tell me that I am a "fit subject for the asylum." Physicians threaten me with arrest, also, but I walk straight on, knowing *well in whom I trust.*

E. I. R., Wauseon, Ohio

A little over two years ago, while living in Pittsburgh, my wife and I had Christian Science brought to our attention. We were at once interested, and bought a copy of "Science and Health with Key to the Scriptures."

At the time, Mrs. A—— was suffering with severe belief of astigmatism of the eyes. She had been treated by a number of specialists, during seven years, the last being the late Dr. Agnew of New York, who prescribed two sets of glasses. He said that he could do nothing more for her, as the trouble was organic; that she must wear glasses constantly; that if she attempted to go without, she would become either blind or insane. The glasses were in operation, and still life had become a burden from constant pain, when Christian Science came to our relief. Mrs. A—— had not in years read for two consecutive minutes, and could not use her eyes in sewing at all. The lady that told us of the Science, insisted that she *could* read Science and Health, which she actually did, — reading it through twice, and studying it carefully each time. After the second reading, there came the thought that she did not need the glasses, and she at once abandoned them, and went about her usual duties. In about two weeks from that day the eyes were perfectly healed, and are well and strong to-day.

E. G. A., New York City

*My Dear Teacher:* — Yours without date is at hand. Could you know out of what depths of material *débris* the first reading of the first volume of Science and Health, six years ago last December, lifted me, you would believe it had always been "all I could ask." It was *only* words from the pen of *uninspired* writers that gave me pain. As the revelation of the All-good appeared to me, all other books, all forms of religion, all methods of healing, to my sense became void. Chronic beliefs of disease of twenty years' standing, dimness of sight from the belief of age, all disappeared *instantly;* indeed, material life seemed a blank. The *why?* I could not explain, but this I did know, in this realm of the real I found joy, peace, rest, love to all, unbounded, unspeakable. Human language had lost its power of expression, for no words came to me; and in all this six years of bliss I still have found no words to tell my new-found life in God. The most chronic forms of disease have sometimes been healed instantly and without argument. With great love and gratitude. — M. H. P.

I take great comfort in reading "Science and Health with Key to the Scriptures," and will cling firmly to the light I have, knowing that more will be given me. While in Salt Lake City, I met at the hotel a lady who had been an invalid all her life. I talked with her about Christian Science, and loaned her Science and Health, together with the *Journals* I had with me. She had become very much discouraged, having lost all faith in doctors and medicine, and did not know where to turn next. She became very much absorbed in the book, feeling she had found salvation. She at once laid aside the glasses she was wearing, and now reads readily without them. She and her husband have accepted this truth beautifully. — Mrs. G. A. G., Ogden, Utah

On a trip through Mexico I met a woman who told me that, although she did not believe in Christian Science, on her way from Wisconsin, her home, she had bought a copy of Science and Health. When she reached M——, she met a minister from the North, whom the M. D.'s had sent there because of consumption, — they had given him two months to live. She gave him Science and Health, and while doing so, felt it was all absurd. The minister read it, and was healed *immediately*. Was not this a beautiful demonstration of the power of Truth, and good evidence that Science and Health is the word of God?

I had while in Mexico a glorious conquest over the fear of smallpox. There were hundreds of cases in some small towns where we were. After the fear was cast out, never a thought of it as real came to me or my husband, or troubled us in any way. On the street I met three men who were being taken to the pest-house with that loathsome disease. — F. W. C.

A lady to whom I sold "Science and Health with Key to the Scriptures," writes me: "My longing to know God has been answered in this book; and with the answer has come the healing." She is an intimate friend of Will Carleton, the poet. This is doing much good in the social circles. He has for a long time been interested, but his wife has declared it could not heal, and was not Christian. She will now be obliged to acknowledge this healing, for the lady above referred to has been, to sense, a great sufferer. — P. J. L.

Some of the experiences given in the *Journal* have been so helpful to me, I have been moved to give to its readers a little experience of my own, which occurred when I first began the study of "Science and Health with Key to the Scriptures."

I had already been healed of sick headache, almost instantly, by declaring that I was God's child, and, as God is perfect, His child must be perfect also. This had given me great happiness, and a quiet, peaceful state of mind I never had known before. My family did not seem to see anything good in Christian Science, but to me it was sacred.

One Monday morning, I awoke feeling very ill indeed. The morning was warm and sultry. I thought I certainly could not wash that day; but when I went downstairs, I found my daughter had made preparations for such work. I thought, "Well, if she feels like washing, I will not say anything; perhaps I shall get over this." After breakfast I went about my work, thinking I could lean against the tub and wash with more ease than I could do up the morning work. I tried to treat myself as I had done before, — tried to realize that "all is Mind, there is no matter;" that "God is All, there is nothing beside Him," but all to no purpose. I seemed to grow worse all the time. I did not want my family to know how badly I was feeling, and it was very humiliating to think that I must give up and go to bed.

All at once these questions came to me, as though spoken by some one, taking me away from my line of thought entirely: How is God an ever-present help? How does He know our earnest desires? Then, without waiting for me to think how, the answer came in the same way, God is conscious Mind. Instantly the thoughts came: Is God conscious of me? Can I be conscious of Him? I was healed instantly: every bad feeling was destroyed. I could see that the morning had not changed a particle, but I was oblivious of the weather. It did not seem that I had anything more to do with that washing. It was finished in good season, while I was "absent from the body, and present with the Lord."

That was the beginning of the battle with sin and self, but at the same time it was the dawning of the resurrection. Since then (over four years) I have had many experiences, some of which seem too sacred to give to the world. False literature has caused me much suffering; sorrow has visited my home; but, through all this, the light that came to me on that Monday morning — that new and precious sense of omnipresent Life, Truth, and Love — has never left me one moment. It was the light that cannot be hid.

MRS. H. B. J., Cambridge, Ill.

### HEALING

Four years ago I learned for the first time that there was a way to be healed through Christ. I had always been sick, but found no relief in drugs; still, I thought that if the Bible was true, God could heal me. So, when my attention was called to Christian Science, I at once bought "Science and Health with Key to the Scriptures," studied it, and began to improve in health. I seemed to see God so near and so dear, — so different from the God I had been taught to fear. I studied alone night and day, until I found I was healed, both physically and mentally.

Then came a desire to tell every one of this wonderful truth. I expected all to feel just as pleased as I did; but to my sorrow none would believe. Some, it is true, took treatment and were helped, but went on in the old way, without a word of thanks. But still I could not give up. I seemed to know that this was the way, and I had rather live it alone than to follow the crowd the other way. But as time passed, I had some good demonstrations of this Love that is our Life.

I am the only Scientist in Le Roy, as yet, but the good seed has been sown, and where the people once scoffed at this "silly new idea," they are becoming interested, and many have been healed, and some are asking about it. One dear old lady and I study the Bible Lessons every Tuesday afternoon. She came to call, and as we talked, she told me of her sickness of years' standing; and was healed during our talk, so that she has never felt a touch of the old trouble since.

One lady, whom I had never seen, was healed of consumption in six weeks' treatment. She had not left her bed in four months, and had been given up by many physicians.

MRS. FLORENCE WILLIAMS, Le Roy, Mich.

I like the *Journal* and *Quarterly*, and have many of Rev. Mary B. G. Eddy's works, which make my little world. I have a great desire to learn more of this Love that casts out all fear, and to work in this Science. It is the greatest pleasure I have, to talk this truth, as far as I understand it, to any who will listen; and am waiting for others to learn of this blessed Science.

I give my experience in reading "Science and Health with Key to the Scriptures" aloud to a little child. A letter published in the *Journal*, written by a lady who had relieved a two-year-old child by reading to her, first suggested this course to me. At the time, my little one was a trifle over a year old. I was trying to overcome for him a claim which, though not one of serious illness, was no small trial to me, because of its frequent occurrence and its seeming ability to baffle my efforts. One day as I sat near and treated him, it occurred to me to read aloud. I took up one of the older editions of Science and Health lying near, began at the words, "Brains can give no idea of God's man," and read on for two or three paragraphs, endeavoring — as the writer suggested — to understand it myself; yet thinking, perchance, the purer thought of the babe might grasp the underlying meaning sooner than I. So it proved. Before the disturbance felt by me had been calmed, the weary expression on the face of the child was replaced by one of evident relief.

When putting him to sleep, I had often repeated the spiritual interpretation of the Lord's Prayer. One night he was very restless, fretful, and cried a great deal, while I seemed unable to soothe him. At last I perceived that he was asking for something, and it dawned upon me that the Prayer might be his desire. I began repeating it aloud, endeavoring to *mean* it also. He turned over quietly, and in a few minutes was sweetly sleeping.

The last time my attention was specially called to this subject, was about a year after the first experience. Various hindrances had been allowed to keep me from

Science and Health all day; and it was toward evening when I recognized that material sense had been given predominance, and must be put down. I soon felt drawn to read the book. The little boy had seemed restless and somewhat disturbed all day; but without thinking specially of him, rather to assist in holding my own thought, I began to read aloud, "Consciousness constructs a better body, when it has conquered our fear of matter." In a minute or two a little hand had touched mine, and I looked down into a sweet face fairly radiant with smiles. I read it over. The child was evidently delighted, and was restful and happy all the rest of the day. — A. H. W., Deland, Florida

A week ago a friend wrote to me on business, and in the letter stated that his wife had been very ill for six weeks. At once the thought came, "Tell her to read the chapter on Healing, in Science and Health." In my answer to his letter I obeyed the thought. A few days after, I had occasion to call; found her much better, and *reading* Science and Health. They had done as directed, and had received the promise. — R., New York

The first allusion to Christian Science reached me in an article I read on that subject. Later, a friend came to visit me, bringing a copy of "Science and Health with Key to the Scriptures." For two weeks I read it eagerly; then I sent for a copy for myself. When it came, I began to study it. The Bible, of which I had had but a dim understanding, began to grow clearer. The light grew brighter each day. Finally, I began to treat my-self against ills that had bound me for twenty-eight years. At the end of six weeks I was *healed,* much to the amazement of all who knew me. From that time, my desire was to help others out of their suffering, and to talk this wonderful truth. After a while I took the class lectures, and am doing what I can to spread this healing gospel. — A. M. G.


Rev. Mary B. G. Eddy

*My Dear Leader:* — I will try to tell you how I was led to Christian Science. Heretofore I have not tried to lead a Christian life, but have always firmly believed that if one truly desired and needed help, he would get it from God by asking for it. I suffered, as I think but very few have, for fourteen years; yet I did not think it sufficient to warrant me in asking God to help me, until I gave up all hope elsewhere, — and this occurred in the spring of 1891. I then thought that the time had come to commit myself to God. Being at home alone, after going to bed I prayed God to deliver me from my tor-ments, this sentence being the substance of my prayer, "What shall I do to be saved?"

I repeated that sentence, I suppose, until I fell asleep. About twelve o'clock at night, I saw a vision in the form of a man with wings, standing at the foot of my bed, — wings partly spread, — one arm hanging loosely at his side, and one extended above his head. At the same time there was a bright light shining in my room, which made all objects shine like fire. I knew where I was, and was not afraid. The vision (for such it was), after looking directly at me for some time, spoke this one sentence, and then disappeared: "Do right, and thou shalt be saved."

I immediately tried to live according to that precept, and found relief in proportion to my understanding. I soon after learned of Christian Science. One of my brothers in Kansas, having been healed by it, persuaded me to buy "Science and Health with Key to the Scriptures," wherein I learned that the above precept was the key to Christian Science; that it is Christian Science to do right, and that nothing short of right living has any claim to the name.

I have been learning my way in Christian Science about one year, and have been successful in healing. I have all of your books, and am a subscriber for the *Journal* and *Quarterly Bible Lessons*. Some of the cases I have treated have yielded almost instantly. I am a stranger to you, but I have told you the truth, just as it occurred. Yours in truth,

SAM SCHROYER, Oklahoma City, Okla.


I desire to make known the great good I have received by reading the blessed book "Science and Health with Key to the Scriptures." Four years have now passed since I began to read it. It has been my only healer and teacher, as I never have had an opportunity to go through a class; but I find that the "Spirit of truth" will teach us all things if we will but practise well what we know. After two years and a half of study, I thought, as many beginners think, that I had travelled over the worst part of this narrow path.

Soon after, it came about that I was separated from every one who had ever heard of Christian Science; and, as I lived in the country, no one came to visit me for about eight months. At first, I thought the Lord had wrought a great evil. I had no one to talk to, but would take my Science and Health every morning, before going about my work, and read; yet mortal mind would say, "You can do no good, with no one to talk with." At last, one morning after listening to the serpent's voice, I looked out at the little wild flowers as they waved to and fro; they seemed to be a living voice, and this is what they said: "On earth peace, good will toward men." There was also a mocking-bird that would sit on the house and sing. For the first time, I realized that divine Love was the only friend I needed. Soon after, I sent the *Journal* to my nearest neighbor, by her little son who came to play with my children. Afterward she told me that when she began to read it she said to the family, "God has sent this book to me." Calling to see her one evening, I found her suffering from heart disease. I began talking to her about Christian Science, and in less than an hour she declared herself healed. She is to-day a happy woman. I would say to all suffering ones, that if you will buy a copy of this wonderful book, "Science and Health with Key to the Scriptures," by the Rev. Mary Baker G. Eddy, and study it, and practise its teachings, you will find it a pearl of great price.

MRS. FANNIE MEEKS, Bells, Grayson Co., Texas

On my arrival in New York, last July, my brother spoke to me of "Science and Health with Key to the

Scriptures;" and, coming in contact with a number of Scientists, all wishing me to procure the book, I did so. I read it through in the same manner in which I would read any other book, to find out the contents.

Before I got to the end, having partly understood its meaning, I began to demonstrate over old physical troubles, and they disappeared. A belt that I had worn for over twelve years, I took off, and threw overboard (being a seafaring man).

Up to that time I had been a constant smoker, and chewed tobacco; but I gradually lost all pleasure in it, and now look upon it with disgust.

I was brought up in the Lutheran doctrine, and when a boy received a good knowledge of Scripture; but I never understood it until explained to me in Science and Health.                      H. F. WITKOV,
27 Needham Road, Liverpool, England


In a letter received a few days ago from one of my absent patients, there was such a glorious testimonial for Science and Health that I feel as if I ought to send it in for the pages of our *Journal,* trusting it may be the means of helping many others to turn for help and comfort, in every emergency, to this book.

In her letter, this lady says: "A few days since, I had quite a serious claim attack me. I left my mending, took Science and Health and read all the afternoon and evening; when all trace of the claim was gone, and I have felt nothing of it since."

When this dear woman applied to Truth, she was a great sufferer. Her gratitude knows no bounds. Many chronic ailments, which have bound her with heavy chains for many years, are being removed one by one. It is such a sweet privilege to lead her out of this bondage of flesh, for she turns with such childlike trust and obedience to the book, and looks to that for aid in every trial and affliction. It is beautiful to see, and is a rebuke to some of us older in the thought, who depend so much on personality.

She is far away, in a little country town where Science has hardly been heard of; but she is so happy with her book that she has no desire for other reading.

I have always tried to show her that God was with her there as well as with us here; that in Him she possesses all; and that with her Bible and Science and Health no harm can befall her, for the remedy for every ill she has at hand. — Mrs. C. H. S., Woburn, Mass.

I have been an interested reader of the *Journal* for some time, and thought I would contribute my mite by giving one of my latest demonstrations in Christian Science.

An accident occurred as follows: Officers, while hunting for a criminal in thick underbrush, fired upon each other through mistake, and it was found that one was shot six times; two of the bullets passing through the abdomen, and one through the hips.

Two physicians who examined him had no hope. He asked me to help him. I took the case. Relief came almost instantly. I treated him for eight days; the fifth, I heard one of three physicians, who held a private consultation over my patient, ask him this question:

"Mr. F——, have you not got one bit of pain?" I was rewarded by hearing him answer, "No, sir; not the least bit." No one else seemed to have any hope for him; but I held firmly to the thought that God is an ever-present help, never doubting, and Christian Science has again won a victory. Many people call it a miracle, and it has set them to thinking.

The harvest is now ripe and ready for the reaper. I wish some good Christian Science teacher would come and help us. I can help in my own way, but am not advanced enough to lead and teach others. I have only studied Science and Health a little over a year, and have not been through a class yet.

S. G. SCHROYER, Oklahoma City, Oklahoma

I became interested in Christian Science through being healed. I had no faith in doctors, therefore would not consult any; but felt that something must be done, or I would soon follow a brother and sister who had passed on with the same claim. In my extremity I thought of the "great Physician," and took my case to Him, and realized that He alone could help me.

A relative, finding I would not consult a doctor or take any drug, gave me "Science and Health with Key to the Scriptures" to read; saying that, although a dear friend thought she was greatly helped by a Christian Scientist, he himself had no faith in that kind of treatment, and had no use for the book.

I had heard of the people called Christian Scientists, and of their textbook, Science and Health, but knew nothing about either; yet I wanted to know, and took the book gladly, and was soon deeply interested in it. It was a revelation to me. Although I could only understand it in part, I knew it was the truth, and the truth was making me free. I felt that I had been bound and in prison; and that now, one after another, the bonds were being broken, and I was lifted into the pure air and light of heaven. I was healed before I had read half-way through the precious volume; for I was obliged to read slowly, and some passages over and over again. When I came to page 304, line 10 (47th edition), I then and there felt that I must add my testimony, though already there were "heaps upon heaps;" but since then, I have tried to put the thought of those dark days away from me, and only refer to them now in the hope that some one who is bound may be released and brought into the light of divine Love, which alone can heal, and make us "every whit whole."

L. M. C., Brooklyn, N. Y.

I have been thinking for a long time that I would give my experience in coming out of sickness into the knowledge of health by reading "Science and Health with Key to the Scriptures."

I was sixty years old (as we mortals count time) before I ever read one word of Christian Science. On July 2, 1890, I met a Scientist who gave me a pamphlet called "Christian Healing," by the Rev. Mary B. G. Eddy. At that time I was almost helpless. This lady advised me to buy Science and Health. I did so, and tried to read it; but my hands were so lame I could not hold it, and I let it fall to the floor so often that it became unbound, and I laid it away and resumed my medicine.

The following May, the Scientist visited in this city again. She advised me to burn all my medicines and to lean unreservedly on the promises of God. I took her advice; had my book rebound in three volumes, so I could hold it more easily, and now read it constantly, reading nothing else. Sometimes I would suffer intensely, then I would get a little better; then more suffering, and so on, until August, 1891, when all pain left me. I have had no return of it, and no disagreeable sensations of any kind, and am perfectly well in all respects.

Surely, if we will but trust our heavenly Father, He is sufficient for us. I hope some one of, or near, my age, who is afflicted, may read this and take courage; for I have *demonstrated* the fact that, by reading Science and Health, in connection with the Bible, and trying to follow the teaching therein, one in the autumn of life may be made over new. I am so thankful to God for my great recovery!

That remark of Sojourner Truth helps me to a better understanding of Life in God: "God is the great house that holds all His children; we dwell in Him as the fishes dwell in the seas." — P. T. P.


Until about one year ago, I had no thought of investigating Christian Science. Previous to that time it had been presented to me in such a way that I condemned it as unreasonable and absurd. At that time it was presented to me in a more reasonable light. I determined to divest myself of prejudice (as far as was possible) and investigate it, thinking that if there was anything in it, it was for me as well as others; that I surely needed it, and if I found no good in it, I could then with some show of reason condemn it.

I had been reading Science and Health about two weeks, when one morning I wanted my cane. It had been misplaced; and while looking for it the thought came to me, If all is Mind, I need no cane. I went out without it, have not used it at all since, and do not need it as a support; but for a time I did miss it from my hand. I had used it for years as a support to a very lame back.

I before went much stooped, because it pained me to straighten up; but from the time I laid my cane aside I straightened up, free from pain. Occasionally I have a slight pain in my back, but it is nothing to compare with what it had been.

In a short time after laying my cane aside, my pipe and tobacco went out into the street and have not returned. I had smoked for sixty-five years, and chewed for fifty. I have no desire for either of them; in fact, the smoke is offensive to me.

Many times before I had tried to quit, but the desire for it was so strong that I would go back to it; and when I tried to "taper off," I would make the taper end the longest.

Many other physical claims have disappeared, and it is a common thing for acquaintances to say when they meet me, "You look better than I have seen you for years; what have you been doing?" My reply is, I not only look better, but feel better, and am better; and Christian Science has done it.

With all this, I seem to have very little spiritual understanding of the truth; am endeavoring to get more, but

it seems slow.   If there is a shorter road to it than I have
found, I should like to be directed to it.

                                   J. S. M., Joplin, Mo.


Four years ago I was healed by reading "Science and
Health with Key to the Scriptures."   The third day,
one of my worst claims gave way.   The book was full of
light, and disease vanished as naturally as darkness gives
place to light, although it was about six months before
I was entirely healed.

Seeing this truth in its purity, showed me where to
take my stand;  and in defending it I have the prince of
this world to meet.   Mortal mind has even called me
crazy;  but what a blessing to know the nothingness of
that mind, and that divine Principle governs all its ideas,
and will place each where it belongs!

If our Master was persecuted, can his servants hope to
escape?   I know in some degree what Paul meant when
he said he rejoiced in tribulations, "for when I am weak,
then am I strong."

Many claims that have baffled the skill of the physi-
cians have disappeared through my understanding of
Truth.   What a blessing that we can break the bread of
Life to others, and so add to our crown of rejoicing!

                                   S. E. R., Kansas City, Mo.


A dear little six-year old boy of my acquaintance was
invited by his teacher, with the rest of his class in kinder-
garten school, to attend a picnic one afternoon.   He did
not feel that he wanted to go;  seemed dumpish, and

according to mortal belief was not well; at noon, he said he wanted to go to sleep.

His mother took him in her lap and began to read to him from "Science and Health with Key to the Scriptures." Very soon he expressed a wish to go to the picnic, and did go. His father, happening to pass the place where the little ones were spending the afternoon, and somewhat surprised to see him playing, as happy and active as any there, called to him and asked, "How long did you sleep?" The little fellow replied, "I did not sleep at all; mamma read to me from Science and Health, and I was well in a minute." — K. L. H.

One evening I was calling on a neighbor, and somehow the subject of Christian Science came up. I asked her what it was, and what they believed.

She then told me of a friend of hers who had become a Christian Scientist. This friend had passed through great sorrow and disappointment; her health had failed her, and her cheerful disposition had entirely changed; she could talk of nothing but her troubles, and was a most unhappy woman. A few years ago she visited my neighbor, who, greatly surprised at her changed appearance, — for she was happy and well, — asked where her troubles were. The reply was, "I have no troubles. I have found true happiness; for I have become a Christian Scientist."

I became deeply interested, and asked if the students in Clinton had public meetings on Sundays. She replied that they had, and told me where they were.

The next Sunday, I went. All was quiet when I entered, for they were engaged in silent prayer. Soon they repeated the spiritual interpretation of the Lord's Prayer. I shall never forget the impression that made on me; all the next week I heard the leader's voice repeating the first sentence.

I was invited to come again, and did so. One of the ladies loaned me "Science and Health with Key to the Scriptures," and offered to get me one; which she did the next week. I have studied it in connection with the Bible. I have greatly improved in health, having had only one attack of a physical trouble which caused great suffering, since that time, and that was a year ago.

At first, I did not think anything about being healed, or of my physical infirmity. I only loved the sacred teaching. How true, that God's word does not return unto Him void! The words of truth that my neighbor's friend spoke to her, were what first awakened me. If the one who first hears it does not receive it, it goes to some one who is ready, and it takes root and bears fruit.

Mrs. G. H. I., Clinton, N. Y.


About three years ago I was near death's door with various troubles; also, was seventy years old. I had a desire to know something of Christian Science.

I procured the textbook, and studied it with a desire to know the truth. At first all was dark; but light began slowly to come, and at the end of three months I found my physical claims all gone and my eyesight restored. At the end of three months more, I had gained thirty-five pounds in weight.

I had been an infidel, and the change from that came more slowly; but now I know that my Redeemer lives, and I am able by divine grace to make very convincing demonstrations. — J. S., Rudd, Iowa

For a long time I have felt that I must in some way express my great debt of gratitude for Christian Science. I know no better way to do so than to give an account, through the *Journal,* of some of the many blessings I have received as a result of our Leader's untiring toil and self-sacrificing love for suffering mortals, in giving to us the wonderful book, "Science and Health with Key to the Scriptures."

When I first heard of Christian Science, about six years ago, I was satisfied that it was the religion of Christ Jesus, because Jesus had so plainly said, "And these signs shall follow them that believe; In my name shall they cast out devils; . . . they shall lay hands on the sick, and they shall recover."

I had been a church-member since my girlhood, but was not satisfied that my belief would take me to heaven, as I did not have these "signs following" — and this had always troubled me; so, when I heard that an old acquaintance living at a distance had not only been raised from a dying condition to health, but her life had been changed and purified through Christian Science, I could hardly wait to know more of this Christlike religion which was casting out evils and healing the sick. I searched every bookstore in the city for Science and Health, at last found a copy, and was delighted to get hold of it, but little realized what a treasure it was to be to me and my household.

At first it was like Greek to me, and I could not understand much of it, but gleaned enough to keep on reading, and longed for some one to talk to me of it.

After I had been reading it about a year's time, I suddenly became almost blind. I knew no Scientist to go to, so went to physicians; they told me that my case was hopeless, that it was certain my sight never could be restored, and the probabilities were that I would soon be totally blind.

I felt sure that Christian Science would help me if I could only fully understand it; but there was no one from whom I could ask help, that I knew of. I gave all the time that I could use my eyes to studying Science and Health, — which at first was not more than five minutes two, and sometimes three, times a day; gradually my sight returned, until it was fully restored.

During this time God and the "little book" were my only help. My understanding was very limited; but like the prodigal son, I had turned away from the husks, towards my Father's house, and while I "was yet a great way off" my Father came to meet me. When this great cloud of darkness was banished by the light of Truth, could I doubt that Christian Science was indeed the "Comforter" that would lead us "into all truth"?

Again I lay at the point of death; but holding steadfastly to the truth, knowing, from the teaching of this precious book, that God is Life and there is no death, I was raised up to health, — restored to my husband and little children, all of whom I am thankful to say are now with me in Science.

I had no one to talk with on this subject, knew no one of whose understanding I felt sure enough to ask for help; but I was careful from the first not to read or inquire into anything except genuine Christian Science, and how thankful I am for it! Since then, I have been through a class.

I cannot express in words what Christian Science has done for my children, or my gratitude that the light of Truth has come to them in their innocent childhood, — healing all claims of sickness, and showing us how to overcome the more stubborn claims of sin. — L. F. B.

It is a little over one year since a very esteemed friend, of this city, invited me to partake of the heavenly manna contained in the revelation of "Science and Health with Key to the Scriptures." I had, up to that time, been for fifteen years a victim of hip-joint disease; this eventually confining me to my bed, where I had been ten months when the "book of prophecy" was opened for me. I was not long in finding the light I needed, — that gave "feet to the lame," enabling me now to go, move, and walk, where I will, without crutch or support of any description, save the staff of divine Science.

In proportion as my thoughts are occupied with the work in Science, does the peace and joy come inwardly that transforms the blight of error externally.

T. G. K., Tacoma, Wash.

I wish to acknowledge the blessings which Christian Science has brought to me through reading "Science and Health with Key to the Scriptures." My first demonstration was over the tobacco habit; I had smoked for at least fifteen years: I have now no desire for tobacco.

I was then healed of two claims which had bound me for ten years. My prayer is that I may be so filled with the truth that I can carry the message to my brother man.

F. W. K., Angelica, N. Y.

I take advantage of the great privilege granted us, to give my testimony for Christian Science through the pages of our much loved *Journal*. The blessing has been so bountiful that words can but poorly express my gratitude.

A little over six years ago, a relative came from Denver, Colorado, to visit us. She was a Christian Scientist, having herself been healed of a severe claim that M. D.'s, drugs, and climate could not relieve; and her husband having been in the drug business, she had had a chance to give them a fair trial.

My sister-in-law did not talk much on the subject, as I remember; but what was better, lived the truth before us as she realized it.

One day (a blessed day to me), I ventured to open Science and Health, and read the first sentence in the Preface. I closed the book, wondering what more it could contain, this seeming to cover the whole ground. When my sister-in-law returned to the room, I asked her if I might read it. Her reply was, "Yes; but begin at the first."

That night, after all had retired, I began to read; within forty-eight hours I destroyed all drugs, applications, etc., notwithstanding the fact that my husband had just paid fifty dollars to a travelling specialist for part of a treatment. With the drugs disappeared ailments of nine years' standing, which M. D.'s had failed to relieve.

I now understand that my sudden healing was due to my turning completely away from material methods; for I was convinced I should never use them again. I realized that God was my health, my strength, my Life, therefore All. As I read Science and Health, I wondered why others had not discerned this truth, — physicians, ministers, and others who had devoted their lives to benefit mankind. Yes! why? Because they had been seeking in the opposite direction to Truth, namely, for cause and effect in matter, when all cause and effect are mental.

I mention physicians and ministers, because one class claims to heal disease, the other claims to heal sin; but Christian Science heals physically and morally, — it contains all; "its leaves are for the healing of the nations."

L. B. A., Memphis, Tenn.

I was for years a great sufferer. I called doctor after doctor, getting no help. The last one, after treating me for one year, told me he would give me one year more to live.

One evening a near neighbor came in and asked me to go home with her; and as it was only a few steps, I did so.

She took up a new book, Science and Health, read me a few chapters, and then gave me some Christian Science tracts, which I read, and one of them I almost committed to memory.

I bought a copy of "Science and Health with Key to

the Scriptures," and studied it carefully. I am healed
of all those claims which troubled me so long. I was
lifted out of darkness into light.

M. J. P., Burns, Oregon

Chicago, March 19, 1894

*Rev. Mary B. G. Eddy, Boston, Mass.:* — I wish to
thank you for the true light that was revealed to me by
reading your book, "Science and Health with Key to the
Scriptures," and at once adopting its teaching. It was
one year ago to-day that I put on the armor, determined
never to surrender to the enemy; and you may know I
have looked forward to this day with a great deal of
pleasure, to show my friends that the Lord is constantly
with me to help overcome all evil.

Some said, when I first started in this new path, "Wait
until you get one of your stomach attacks, and you will
change your mind." For months they have waited, and
are beginning to see the truth in my actions, that speak
for themselves, and show that all is *Mind.*

For nearly thirty years I had been a sufferer from
throat and stomach troubles; bronchitis, dyspepsia, gas-
tralgia, and gastritis, etc., were the terms applied by
my physicians. About eighteen years of that time I was
engaged in the drug business, had constant opportunities
for consulting the best physicians, and took such medicine
as I felt assured would cure me; but only to be disappointed each time.

The last few years I had been living on oatmeal crackers
and hot water; suffering more or less all the time, and
could not eat anything else without suffering intense

pain. I felt as though I could not live many months more, and was getting ready to give up the fight when a dear friend and neighbor, Mrs. Corning, left a copy of Science and Health at our home. At first I did not care to read it; having been educated, for many years, in the belief that medicine can cure all diseases, I could not conceive of anything else to cure the sick.

One Sunday I had the curiosity to know something about this Christian Science, and read Science and Health. The more I read, the more interested I became, and finally said to myself, "I will try it." I took a large porous plaster and four thicknesses of flannel off my stomach, and threw them in the corner, saying, "Now it shall be Mind over matter; no more matter over Mind." I filled a large basket full of bottles containing medicine, and put it in the shed (where all medicine should be). From that day I have eaten of everything on the table, and all I wished. Coffee was my worst enemy, and I had not tasted it for years without suffering untold agony. Several days passed before I cared to drink it; then, one morning, I told my family I would commence to use it; I did, and have used it every day since, and don't know that I have a stomach, as it never has caused me any trouble since that morning.

I am happy to say I have not used a drop of any kind of medicine, internally or externally, from that day, and *I know that all is Mind.* I read the Bible and Science and Health nearly every day, thanking the Lord for the years of suffering which have led me to the truth as taught by our Saviour; for I feel it was only through its victory over the suffering that the truth could have been revealed in my case.

I have had some demonstrations to make over error, but each time it becomes easier.  God is ever present and ready to help me, and I trust in Him;  my faith is planted on a rock that is immovable.

Yours truly,     FRANK S. EBERHART

P. S.  If you think this letter, or any part of it, will help some one out of darkness into the light of Truth, you are at liberty to have it published.

Having so many occupations and interruptions, I have not found time to read "Science and Health with Key to the Scriptures" sufficiently, but will not on that account delay thanking you for its excellence.

HENRY W. LONGFELLOW, Cambridge, Mass.

I am an old-school practitioner;  have served as surgeon in two European wars;  practised medicine for about ten years in New York city and Brooklyn, until my health compelled me to relinquish my profession.  I became a victim of the morphia habit, taking daily thirty grains of that drug.  My physicians declared me consumptive, and abandoned all hopes of recovery.  Shortly after this I made the acquaintance of a student of the author of "Science and Health with Key to the Scriptures," who presented me with her works;  and as drugs did me no good, I stopped taking any whatever, save morphia, without which I thought it impossible to get along, and to my astonishment began to gain in flesh, and my ambition returning in proportion.  I finally felt that I would stop my loathsome habit of morphia-eating, and did so in one week, without any discomfort worth mentioning. For a test I administered one fourth of a grain of morphia to the aforesaid Scientist, hypodermically, without the slightest physiological effect, clearly proving the existence of metaphysical laws. I have read Science and Health carefully, and consider my present improved health solely due to mental influence.

OTTO ANDERSON, M. D., Cincinnati, Ohio

The profound truths which you announce, sustained by facts of the immortal life, give to your work the seal of inspiration — reaffirm in modern phrase the Christian revelations. In times like these, so sunk in sensualism, I hail with joy your voice, speaking an assured word for God and immortality, and my joy is heightened that these words are of woman's divinings.

A. BRONSON ALCOTT, Concord, Mass.

I was sick six years; tried many physicians and remedies, but received no lasting benefit from any of them, and concluded I must remain sick the rest of my life. In this condition, I purchased the book "Science and Health with Key to the Scriptures," read it, was deeply interested, and noticed that my health began to improve; and the more I read the book, the better I became in health. This I can say truly: it did more for my health than all the physicians and remedies that I had ever tried. — DR. S. G. TODD, 11 School St., Newburyport

I had been a nervous sufferer for nine years; had a belief of incurable disease of the heart, and was subject
16

to severe nervous prostration if I became the least weary. I was told that if I should read your books they would cure me. I commenced reading them: in ten days I was surprised to find myself overcoming my nervous spasms without the aid of medicine; and ever since then I have been improving, and I now can walk twenty miles without fatigue, and have been able to rise above all ailments.

MRS. JULIA A. B. DAVIS,
Central Village, Westport, Mass.

I would inform my friends and the public, that after twelve years of sickness I am restored to health; and, with renewed vigor and keen enjoyment, take up the pleasures and duties of life once more; all labor now seems less arduous, and all happiness more perfect. To Christian Science, as taught in "Science and Health with Key to the Scriptures," I am indebted for my restoration. I can cordially recommend this book to all.

ROSE A. WIGGLESWORTH, Lowell, Mass.

When I commenced reading "Science and Health with Key to the Scriptures," I could sit up but a very short time, and could not eat the most simple food without great distress. In a few days there was a great change, and I have been growing better ever since.

E. D. RICHARDSON, Merrimac, Mass.

I have not been as well for years as I have been since reading "Science and Health with Key to the Scriptures," all of which I impute to its teaching.

(MRS.) MARY A. WILLIAMS, Freeport, Ill.

Had been in ill-health for several years; had been confined to my bed three months, when I got your book and read it.  At first I was unable to read it myself, and others read it to me, and the truth revealed in your book restored me to health.

(COL.) E. J. SMITH, Washington, D. C.


I have been perusing with great interest your work on metaphysical Science, for the last four months, and to great advantage; you make the path to health so plain, that a wayfaring man, though a fool, cannot err therein.

R. I. BARKER, Bethel, Me.


"Science and Health with Key to the Scriptures" "is a lamp unto my feet, and a light unto my path;" your missiles of Mind have battered down the illusions of sense, allowing Life to appear an eternal monument, whose spirited hieroglyphics, Truth and Love, unlike those cut in marble, shall grow more luminous to consciousness as sickness, sin and death fade out of belief.

ARTHUR T. BUSWELL,
*Office of Associated Charities,* Cincinnati, O.


"Science and Health with Key to the Scriptures" is beautiful in its form of thought and expression.  I have perused it with interest.  Your book tends to lead us to new thoughts and practices in the healing art, and for many maladies I have no doubt the treatment your excellent work introduces will be the only remedy.

(COL.) ROB'T B. CAVERLY, Centralville, Mass.

Undoubtedly "Science and Health with Key to the Scriptures" is the greatest and grandest book ever published; and that by pulpit and press it will be so acknowledged, is only a question of time. Yours has, indeed, been a pioneer work, and will be; and I believe that you, of all the millions, are selected and chosen because of your peculiar fitness for this great work — this grand work of opening the gates and leading the way, that fallen humanity may follow step by step; reach up to Christ, and be made whole! That all this should be systematized and proven with mathematical precision, — that there can be no guesswork or quackery, — is simply astounding. Science and Health has given me a new impetus heavenward.

           M. A. HINKLEY, Williamsport, Pa.

The book "Science and Health with Key to the Scriptures" is the most wonderful work that has been written in the past five thousand years. I wish you could get ten dollars per copy. I am of the opinion that I can heal the sick on its basis, from reading the work.

           H. D. DEXTER, M. D., Dundee, N. Y.

Rev. Mary B. G. Eddy's book, "Science and Health with Key to the Scriptures," has been duly catalogued and placed on our shelves for use. In behalf of the trustees, let me convey cordial thanks to the earnest-minded author for this interesting contribution. My own idea is, that the power of Mind or Spirit is supreme in character, and destined to supremacy over all that is adverse to divine order.     WILLIAM H. KIMBALL,

      *Librarian New Hampshire State Library*

I am reading the work, "Science and Health with Key to the Scriptures," for the third time; and I am convinced of the truth of the Science of which it treats, — instructing us how to attain holiness of heart, purity of life, and the sublime ascendency of soul over body.

C. CLEMENT, McMinnville, Warren Co., Tenn.

I was sick for a number of years with what some of the most skilful physicians pronounced an incurable disease. The more I tried to get help, the worse I became, until a life of pain and helplessness seemed unavoidable. Two years ago I heard of "Science and Health with Key to the Scriptures," began reading it and trying to live up to its teachings. At first, my beliefs were so strong I made but little progress; but gradually my disease gave way, and finally disappeared, and to-day I am a well woman. I cannot express the gratitude I feel for what the light shining through the teachings of that book did for me.

(MRS.) EMILY T. HOWE, Norway, Me.

I have been reading "Science and Health with Key to the Scriptures," and feasting — like a starving, shipwrecked mariner, on the food that was to sustain him — on truths which ages to come will appreciate, understand, and accept. Many of the theories which at first appear abstruse and obscure, at length become clear and lucid. The candle of intellect requires occasional snuffing to throw the clear light of penetration on the page.

(MRS.) S. A. ORNE, Malden, Mass.

The mother of a little girl about eight years old told me her child was having a severe attack of cold, and was delicate and easy to take cold. I told her the little girl would be all right; not to give her any medicine, but read Science and Health to her. When I next saw the mother, she told me the little girl was entirely well; that the cold had all disappeared, and with it a claim of night-sweats that the child had been under for more than a year. The little girl had been out sliding down-hill in the snow a number of times; had her feet very wet, but it did not affect her at all. They were all pleased, — especially the child; her face was beaming with happiness and smiles. This is just one little instance of the good that comes from reading Science and Health.

T. W. H.

### OPINIONS OF THE PRESS

This is, perhaps, the most remarkable book on health, in some respects, which has appeared in this country. The author evidently discards physiology, hygiene, mesmerism, magnetism, and every form of medication, bathing, dieting, etc., — all go by the board; no medicine, manipulation, or external applications are permitted; everything is done through the mind. Applied to certain conditions, this method has great value: even the reading of the author's book has cured hopeless cases. The author claims that her methods are those used by Christ and his apostles, and she has established a church and school to propagate them. — *Herald of Health,* N. Y. (M. L. HOLBROOK, *Publisher*)

The Christian Scientists claim that the power of healing is not lost, and have supported that claim by inducing cures astonishingly like those quoted from the New Testament.  And even more good they hope to achieve, as this power which they possess is better understood and the new light gains strength in the world.  Experience has taught us that the nearer we approach to the source of a report of miraculous power, the smaller does the wonder grow.  In the instance of the Christian Scientists, the result has been rather the reverse; if third parties have related a remarkable circumstance, the person of whom the fact was alleged has been found to make the assertion still stronger. — *Boston Sunday Globe*

"Science and Health with Key to the Scriptures," by Mary Baker G. Eddy, President of the Massachusetts Metaphysical College, is a remarkable publication, claiming to elucidate the influence of mentality over matter.  Mrs. Eddy announces herself as the discoverer of this metaphysical Science, and receives students, to whom she imparts so much of her metaphysics as their minds are capable of receiving.  The volumes are a vigorous protest against the materialism of our modern scientists, Darwin, Huxley, Tyndall, etc.  Her Science of Mind was first self-applied: having been ill and treated by doctors of the various schools without benefit, she discovered the grand Principle of all healing to be God, or Mind.  Relying on this Principle alone, she regained her health, and for the last sixteen years has taught this theory to others, and has healed the sick in all cases where the patient's mentality was sufficiently strong to understand her teachings and act upon them. — *Brooklyn Eagle*

The book "Science and Health with Key to the Scriptures" is certainly original, and contains much that will do good. The reader will find this work not influenced by superstition or pride, but striking out boldly, — full of self-sacrifice and love towards God and man. — *Christian Advocate,* Buffalo, N. Y.

The doctrines of "Science and Health with Key to the Scriptures" are high and pure, wholly free from those vile theories about love and marriage which have been so prevalent among the spiritualists. This new sect devotes itself to a study of the Bible, and a practice of curing disease without mesmerism or spiritualism. It treats Darwin and materialists with a lofty scorn. — *Springfield Republican*

"Science and Health with Key to the Scriptures" is indisputably a wonderful work. It has no equal. No one can read the book and not be benefited by it in mind and body. The work is endorsed by some of the best men of the age. — *Star-Spangled Banner*

We shall watch with keen interest the promised results of "Science and Health with Key to the Scriptures." The work shows how the body can be cured, and how a better state of Christianity can be introduced (which is certainly very desirable). It likewise has a hard thrust at spiritualism; and, taken altogether, it is a very rare book. — *Boston Investigator*

The author of "Science and Health with Key to the Scriptures," which is attracting much attention, shows her ability to defend her cause with vigor. —*Boston Weekly Journal*

(*By permission*)

HOW TO UNDERSTAND SCIENCE AND HEALTH

*My Dear Friend H.:* — Your good letter of the 26th ult. came duly to hand several days ago, and I am not greatly surprised at its contents. You say, in substance, that you procured the book, "Science and Health with Key to the Scriptures," which I recommended, and that to your surprise and disgust you found it to be a work on faith-cure, and ask by what process of reasoning I could possibly bring myself to adopt or accept such visionary theories. In answer to your very natural question, I will try, in my own way, to give you what appears to me to be a reason for the hope that is in me.

My religious views of fifteen years ago are too familiar to you to need any exposition at my hands at this time. Suffice it to say that the religion of the Bible, as taught by the churches, to my mind appeared to be

self-contradictory and confusing, and their explanations
failed to explain. During the next eleven years my
convictions underwent little change. I read everything
that came in my way that had any bearing upon, or
pretended in any degree to explain, the problem of life;
and while I gained some knowledge of a general nature,
I was no nearer the solution of life's problem than when
I began my investigations years ago, and I had given
up all hope of ever being able to come to a knowledge
of the truth, or a satisfactory explanation of the enigma
of life.

In all my intellectual wanderings I had never lost my
belief in a great First Cause, which I was as well satisfied to call God as anything else; but the orthodox explanations of His or its nature and power were to my
mind such a mixture of truth and error, that I could not
tell where fact left off and fancy began. The whole effort of the pulpit being put forth, seemed directed to the impossible task of harmonizing the teachings of Jesus Christ
with the wisdom of the world; and the whole tendency
of our religious education was to befog the intellect and
produce scepticism in a mind that presumed to think
for itself and to inquire into the why and the wherefore.
I fully believe that the agnosticism of yourself and myself was produced by the futile attempt to mix and har-
monize the wisdom of the world with the philosophy of
the Christ.

In my investigations into the researches of the savants
and philosophers I found neither any satisfactory explanation of things as they seemed to exist, nor any solution of the great and all-absorbing question, "What is
Truth?" Their premises appeared to be sound, and

their reasonings faultless; but in the nature of things, no final conclusion of the whole matter could be reached from premises based wholly on material knowledge. They could explain "matter" and its properties to their own satisfaction, but the intelligence that lay behind or beyond it, and which was manifested in and through it, was to them as much of a mystery as it was to the humblest of God's creatures. They could prove pretty conclusively that many of the generally accepted theories had no basis in fact; but they left us as much in the dark regarding Life and its governing Principle as had the divines before them.

About four years ago, while still in the mental condition above indicated, my attention was called to what at that time appeared to me to be a new phase of spiritism, and which was called by those who professed to believe in it, *Christian Science.* I thought that I had given some attention to about all the *isms* that ever existed, and that this was only another phantasm of some religionist lost in the labyrinths of mental hallucination.

In my reflections at that time it seemed to me that life was an incomprehensible enigma; that the creator had placed us on this earth, and left us entirely in the dark as to His purpose in so doing. We seemed to be cast upon the ocean of time, and left to drift aimlessly about, with no exact knowledge of what was required of us or how to attain unto the truth, which must certainly have an existence somewhere. It seemed to me that in the very nature of things there must be a great error somewhere in our understanding, or that the creator Himself had slipped a cog when He fitted all things into their proper spheres. That there had been a grand mistake somewhere I had no doubt; but I still had doubt enough of my own capabilities and understanding to believe that the mistake, whatever it was, was in me and not in the creator. I knew that, in a fair measure at least, I had an honest desire to live aright, as it was given me to see the right, and to strive to some extent to do the will of God, if I could only know certainly just what it was.

While in this frame of mind, I inwardly appealed to the great unseen power to enlighten my understanding, and to lead me into a knowledge of the truth, promising mentally to follow wherever it might lead, if I could only do so understandingly.

My wife had been investigating Christian Science to some extent, but knowing my natural antipathy to such vagaries, as I then thought them, had said very little to me about it; but one day, while discussing the mysteries of life with a judge of one of our courts, he asked me whether I had ever looked into the teachings of the Christian Scientists. I told him that I had not, and he urged me very strongly to do so. He claimed to have investigated their teachings, and said that he had become a thorough believer in them. This aroused my curiosity, and I procured the book called "Science and Health with Key to the Scriptures," and read it. Before reading very far in it, I became pretty thoroughly nauseated with what I thought the chimerical ideas of the author, but kept on reading, — more because I had promised to read the book than because of interest in its teachings; but before I had gotten through with it, I did become interested in the Principle that I thought I discovered the author was striving to elucidate; and when I got through it, I began again and reread it very carefully. When I had finished reading this book the second time, I had become thoroughly convinced that her explanation of the religion taught by Jesus Christ, and what he did teach, afforded the only explanation which, to my mind, came anywhere near harmonizing and making cohesive what had always seemed contradictory and inexplicable in the Bible. I became satisfied that I had found the truth for which I had long been seeking, and I arose from the reading of the book a changed man; doubt and uncertainty had fled, and my mind has never been troubled with a serious doubt upon the subject from that day to this.

I do not pretend to have acquired the power it is claimed we may attain to; but I am satisfied that the fault is in me, and not in the Principle. I think I can almost hear you ask, What! do you believe in miracles? I answer unhesitatingly, Yes; I believe in the manifestations of the power of Mind which the world calls miraculous; but which those who claim to understand the Principle through which the works are done, seem to think not unnatural, but only the logical result of the application of a known Principle.

It always did seem to me that Truth should be self-evident, or at least susceptible of unmistakable proof, — which all religions seemed to lack, at least in so far as I had known them. I now remember that Jesus furnished unmistakable proofs of the truth of his teachings, by his manifestations of the power of Mind, or, as some might call it, Spirit; which power he plainly taught would be acquired by those who believed in the Principle which he taught, and which manifestations would follow as signs that an understanding of his philosophy had been reached. It does seem to me, that where the signs do not follow professing Christians which Christ said should follow them, there must be something wrong, either in his teachings or their understanding of them; and to say the least, the foundations of their faith require a careful re-examination, with a view to harmonizing them with the plain teachings of the Christ in whose footsteps they profess to follow.

I never could understand how God could be ever-present as a personal Being, but I think I can and do understand how divine Principle can pervade every thing and place.

I never could understand how heaven could be a place with gorgeous fittings, but I think I can and do understand how it might be a spiritual (or if you please;mental) condition. Jesus said, "The kingdom of God cometh not with observation: neither shall they say, Lo here! or, lo there! for, behold, the kingdom of God is within you."

"Knowledge (or understanding) is power." Since adopting the views of life as set forth in "Science and Health with Key to the Scriptures," I have seen proofs of what can be accomplished through a knowledge of the truth, which to my mind amount to demonstrations, and which no longer seem incredible, but which I do not ask another to accept upon my statements. Every one must see or feel for himself in order to be convinced; but I am satisfied that any who will lay aside their preconceived notions, and deal honestly with themselves and the light they have, will come to a knowledge of the truth as illustrated in the teachings and life of Jesus Christ; that is, that Mind, or Soul, or whatever you may be pleased to call it, is the real Ego, or self, and that mortal mind with its body is the unreal and vanishing, and eventually goes back to its native nothingness.

Truth is, and ever has been, simple; and because of its utter simplicity, we in our pride and selfishness have been looking right over it. We have been keeping our eyes turned toward the sky, scanning the heavens with a far-off gaze in search of light, expecting to see the truth blaze forth like some great comet, or in some extraordinary manner; and when, instead of coming in great pomp and splendor, it appears in the simpleness of demonstration, we are staggered at it, and refuse to accept it; our intellectual pride is shocked, and we are sure that there has been some mistake. Human nature is ever the same. The Jews were looking for something transcendently wonderful, and the absence of it made the Christ, Truth, to them a stumbling-block. It was foolishness to the Greeks, who excelled in the worldly wisdom of that day; but in all ages of the world it has ever been the power of God to them that believe, not blindly, but because of an enlightened understanding.

I always did think that there was something beautiful in the philosophy of life as taught by Jesus Christ, but that it was impracticable and not susceptible of application to the affairs of life in a world constituted as this appeared to be. As I now view it, that belief was the result of ignorance of the real power that "moves the universe," — too much faith in matter or effect, and not enough in Mind or cause, which is God.

To one who can accept the truth that all causation is in Mind, and who therefore begins to look away from matter and into Mind, or Spirit, for all that is real and eternal, and for all that produces anything that is lasting, the doubts and petty annoyances of life become dissolved in the light of a better understanding, which has been refined in the crucible of charity and love; and they fade away into the nothingness from whence they came, never having had any existence in fact, being only the inventions of erring human belief.

Read the teachings of the Christ from a Christian Science standpoint, and they no longer appear vague and mystical, but become luminous and powerful, — and, let me say, intelligible.

It is true, as you intimate, that this theory of life is much more generally accepted by women than by men, and it may be true that as a rule their reasoning is much less rigid in its nature than that of the sterner sex, and that they may be liable to scan their premises less keenly; but may it not also be true, that they are of finer texture and more spiritual in their natures, and that they may be just as likely to arrive at the truth through their intuitions, in connection with their logic, as we are through the more rugged courses?  If it be true that man is the more logical, the fallibility of our own reasonings very frequently becomes painfully apparent even to ourselves, and they are therefore not the safest gauge by which to judge others.

I believe, myself, that when it comes to standing up for Truth in the face of the world, and possibly at the sacrifice of position and popularity, women possess the necessary courage in a much greater degree than do men.

I had not intended to weary you with such a long

letter, but after getting into the subject, I hardly knew where to stop. As an old and loved friend, I have given you a glimpse of my inner life, because I hardly knew how to explain my mental condition to you in any other way. . . .

## WOULD YOU LIKE TO KNOW MORE
## ABOUT CHRISTIAN SCIENCE?

There exists today a vast treasury of writings on Christian Science that is virtually unknown to the world. These writings have been accumulating since 1866, when Christian Science was discovered by Mary Baker Eddy.

The Bookmark was established in 1980 to offer outstanding books and papers on Christian Science from the early days of the movement up through the present time. This literature includes works by Mrs. Eddy, the Discoverer and Founder of Christian Science, and those of her students. It also offers writings by contemporary Christian Scientists who are advancing scientifically in the same line of light. These writings adhere strictly to the teachings of Mrs. Eddy.

To learn more about Christian Science, send for a free Bookmark Catalogue which offers a large selection of excellent papers and books on this Science -- many of them available only through The Bookmark.

You will find in these timeless writings spiritual enlightenment, inspiration and healing. They explain how to heal through prayer alone, how to understand God, and how this closeness to Him meets every human need.

For your free Bookmark Catalogue write:

### THE BOOKMARK
Post Office Box 801143A
Santa Clarita, California 91380
United States of America

We look forward to hearing from you.